ADVANCED
FIXED-INCOME
VALUATION TOOLS

WILEY FRONTIERS IN FINANCE

Series Editor: Edward I. Altman, New York University

ADVANCED FIXED-INCOME VALUATION TOOLS

Narasimhan Jegadeesh
Bruce Tuckman

JOHN WILEY & SONS, INC.
New York • Chichester • Weinheim • Brisbane • Singapore • Toronto

Library of Congress Cataloging-in-Publication Data:

Jegadeesh, Narasimhan.

    Advanced fixed-income valuation tools / Narasimhan Jegadeesh & Bruce Tuckman.
        p.   cm. — (Wiley frontiers in finance)
    ISBN 0-471-25419-3 (cl. : alk. paper)
    1. Fixed-income securities—Valuation—Mathematical models.
  2. Bonds—Valuation—Mathematical models I. Tuckman, Bruce.
  II. Title. III. Series.
  HG465.J44   2000
  332.63' 2044—dc21   99-30540

Printed in the United States of America.

10 9 8 7 6 5 4 3 2 1

Contributors

Leif Andersen
General Re Financial Products
New York, New York

David Backus
Department of Finance
Stern School of Business
New York University
New York, New York

Gurdip Bakshi
Department of Finance
Smith School of Business
University of Maryland
College Park, Maryland

Pierluigi Balduzzi
Department of Finance
Carroll Graduate School of
    Management
Boston College
Chestnut Hills, Massachusetts

Jacob Boudoukh
Department of Finance
Stern School of Business
New York University
New York, New York

Phelim P. Boyle
Center for Advanced Studies in
    Finance
University of Waterloo
Waterloo, Ontario, Canada

John M.R. Chalmers
Department of Finance
Lundquist College of Business
University of Oregon
Eugene, Oregon

Zhiwu Chen
Department of Finance
School of Management
Yale University
New Haven, Connecticut

Sanjiv Ranjan Das
Department of Finance
Harvard Business School
Harvard University
Boston, Massachusetts

Silverio Foresi
Goldmann Sachs
New York, New York

Mark Grinblatt
Department of Finance
Anderson School of
    Management
UCLA
Los Angeles, California

Lakhbir Hayre
Salomon Smith Barney
New York, New York

Steve Heston
Goldmann Sachs
New York, New York

Antti Ilmanen
Salomon Smith Barney
London, UK

Narasimhan Jegadeesh
Department of Finance
College of Commerce and
    Business Administration
University of Illinois at
    Urbana-Champaign
Champaign, Illinois

David Lando
Department of Operations
    Research
University of Copenhagen
Copenhagen, Denmark

Neil D. Pearson
Department of Finance
College of Commerce and
    Business Administration
University of Illinois at
    Urbana-Champaign
Champaign, Illinois

Arvind Rajan
Salomon Smith Barney
New York, New York

Matthew Richardson
Department of Finance
Stern School of Business
New York University
New York, New York

Richard Stanton
Department of Finance
Haas School of Business
University of California at
    Berkeley
Berkeley, California

Rangarajan K. Sundaram
Department of Finance
Stern School of Business
New York University
New York, New York

Chris Telmer
Department of Finance
Graduate School of Industrial
    Administration
Carnegie-Mellon University
Pittsburgh, Pennsylvania

Robert F. Whitelaw
Department of Finance
Stern School of Business
New York University
New York, New York

Guofu Zhou
Department of Finance
Olin School of Business
Washington University
St. Louis, Missouri

Preface

The use of mathematical models to price and hedge fixed-income securities is becoming more and more widespread. Whereas one-factor models used to be state-of-the-art, multifactor models are now common. Whereas default used to be handled in a heuristic way, mathematical models of default are spreading. As a result, practitioners have to expand their understanding of these tools to maintain their edge in this very competitive industry.

Over the past ten years, several text books have been written in the area of fixed-income portfolio management. These books typically deal with basic concepts such as duration and convexity, and in some cases introduce simple binomial models of interest rate dynamics. Our goal for this book is to take the reader to the next level of understanding and knowledge that is critical for success in this highly competitive and rapidly evolving field.

This book presents cutting edge theory and application from a user's perspective. To do so, we have invited academics and practitioners, who develop models and apply them in their research, consulting, and work environments, to share their insights into their various areas of expertise. The result is this collection of 13 chapters from 24 authors affiliated with leading universities and investment banks.

The book is organized into four parts.

PART I: ADVANCED FIXED-INCOME MATHEMATICS

The first three chapters explain convexity and the market price of interest rate risk. Without a complete understanding of these fundamental concepts, one cannot fully understand the pricing and return behavior of fixed-income securities. The chapters in Part I explore these concepts from three different angles. Chapter 1 shows how one can go very much astray by ignoring convexity and risk premia when pricing long-term bonds. Chapter 2 examines the connection between convexity and bond returns. Chapter 3 illustrates how the difference between futures and forward rates follows from the convexity of bond prices.

PART II: TERM STRUCTURE MODELING

In a relatively short time, practitioners have moved from a situation in which they could not easily access any term structure model to a situation in which they can access many different term structure models, each furnishing different pricing and hedging implications. Chapter 4 critically surveys existing models and provides insights into the suitability of various models for various applications. Chapters 5 and 6 introduce recent innovations in term structure modeling. Unlike many existing models, the model described in Chapter 5 assumes that the target interest rate (perhaps set by the Federal Reserve) is itself stochastic. For readers not familiar with multifactor models, this chapter can also serve as an introduction to the advantages of models with more than one factor. Chapter 6 develops a model in which interest rates can jump from one level to another: in most existing models interest rates are assumed to change only in small increments.

PART III: OTHER RISK FACTORS

Many fixed-income securities are exposed to sources of risk in addition to interest rate risk. The risk factors covered in Part III are default risk, prepayment risk, exchange rate risk, and implied tax rate risk. Chapter 7 presents a model of credit risk, an empirical calibration of the model, and an application to credit derivatives. Chapter 8 discusses prepayment risk and methods of modeling prepayments. Chapter 9 provides an introduction to nonparametric methods in the context of mortgage-backed securities. Chapter 10 discusses the pricing of municipal bonds and the fact that they are often quite advantageous for the taxable investor. Finally, Chapter 11 introduces a model of exchange rate dynamics and applies it to the valuation of exchange rate derivatives.

PART IV: NUMERICAL VALUATION TECHNIQUES

When academics and practitioners first began to use mathematical models to price securities, there was a strong preference for models that resulted in closed-form solutions for prices and hedge ratios. These solutions allowed one to understand easily how the parameters of the models affected the solutions. Now, however, that the properties of these models are relatively well understood, there is a premium on models that most accurately capture interest rate dynamics even at the expense of closed-form solutions. Therefore, numerical techniques to solve for prices and hedge ratios have become increasingly important. Chapter 12 discusses building "trees" and methods for solving the partial differential equations that arise in security pricing. Chapter 13 surveys Monte Carlo simulation techniques with an emphasis on efficiently obtaining accurate results.

We would like to thank the authors who contributed the chapters to this book. It was a pleasure to work with these leaders in their fields who shared our desire to bring current research to end users in an easily accessible form. We are also indebted to John Willig of Literary Services for his editorial assistance.

Narasimhan Jegadeesh
Bruce Tuckman

Champaign, Illinois
New York, New York
December 1999

Contents

ADVANCED FIXED-INCOME VALUATION TOOLS

Advanced Fixed-Income Mathematics

Part I of this book is about convexity and interest rate risk premia. Familiarity with these concepts is crucial to a deep understanding of fixed income mathematics and fixed income markets.

Prices of bonds without embedded options are convex functions of interest rates. In other words, the fall in a bond's price due to a 1 basis point increase in rates is less than the increase in price due to a 1 basis point decline in rates. Given this property, consider what would happen if there were a 50% chance that rates instantaneously increase by 1 basis point and a 50% chance that they drop by 1 basis point. Since the price rise due to the rate decrease exceeds the price fall due to the rate increase, the expected price change is positive even though the expected rate change is zero. Hence, investors should be willing to pay for convexity.

Now assume that rates are expected to fluctuate by only 0.1 basis points. It is still true that the increase in a bond's price due to a 0.1 basis point fall exceeds the decrease in a bond's price due to a 0.1 basis point rise. However, the difference between these price changes is small compared to the differences resulting from a 1 basis point fluctuation. Therefore, the expected bond price change for a 0.1 basis point fluctuation is positive, but small. Conversely, if rate volatility is 10 basis points, the difference between the price increase due to a rate fall and the price decrease due to a rate rise is larger than in the original example and, consequently, the expected price change is larger than in that example. In short, the return advantages from a bond's convexity increase with interest rate volatility.

Turning to risk premia, it is generally accepted that investors are risk averse. In particular, investors would prefer a short-term bond offering a risk-free return of 5% to the return on a long-term bond of 10% or 0% with equal probability. Alternatively, investors will be attracted to the long-term bond only if its expected return is greater than 5%. The difference between the expected return required by investors from the long-term bond and the risk-free return of 5% is the risk premium of that bond. If a second long-term bond exhibited greater interest rate risk,[1] it would presumably command a greater risk premium. At the same time, if a third bond exhibited less interest rate risk, it would presumably command a smaller risk premium. In fact, it can be shown that a security's risk premium will be proportional to its interest rate risk (e.g., Ingersoll (1987), p. 381). Therefore, any security's risk premium, normalized by that security's interest rate risk, will equal some common interest rate risk premium.

To explore convexity and risk premia in a simple mathematical setting, assume a 1-factor model of interest rates. It then follows that the price of a bond, P, may be written as a function of its yield, y, and time, t: $P(y,t)$. Using Taylor's approximation, the change in the price of the bond, ΔP, over some small time interval, Δt, is given by the following equation:

$$\Delta P = \frac{\partial P}{\partial y} \Delta y + \frac{\partial P}{\partial t} \Delta t + \frac{1}{2} \frac{\partial^2 P}{\partial y^2} (\Delta y)^2$$

Dividing both sides by P,

$$\frac{\Delta P}{P} = \frac{1}{P} \frac{\partial P}{\partial y} \Delta y + \frac{1}{P} \frac{\partial P}{\partial t} \Delta t + \frac{1}{2} \frac{1}{P} \frac{\partial^2 P}{\partial y^2} (\Delta y)^2$$

---

[1] This discussion implicitly assumes a 1-factor model of interest rates. In a multifactor model there will be a risk premium due to each risk factor.

Now, by definition, the modified duration of a bond, D, equals

$$-\frac{1}{P}\frac{\partial P}{\partial y}$$

while the convexity of a bond, C, equals

$$\frac{1}{P}\frac{\partial^2 P}{\partial y^2}$$

Furthermore, the return on a bond from the passage of time alone, plus its continuously paid coupon rate, c, is equal to its yield. Mathematically,

$$\frac{1}{P}\frac{\partial P}{\partial t}+c=y$$

Hence,

$$\frac{\Delta P}{P}+c\Delta t=-D\Delta y+y\Delta t+\frac{1}{2}C(\Delta y)^2$$

The left-hand side of this equation is the total return from the bond. The right-hand side breaks this return down into three components. First, the contribution of changing yields to the total return is minus the duration times the change in yield. Second, the contribution of the passage of time is the yield times how much time has passed. Third, the contribution of convexity is one-half of the convexity times the change in yield squared.

Taking the expectation of both sides of the equation gives the expected total return of the bond. Note that, over small time intervals, $E[(\Delta y)^2]$ is the variance of yields over time interval Δt, denoted $\sigma^2\,\Delta t$:

$$E\left[\frac{\Delta P}{P}\right]+c\Delta t=-DE[\Delta y]+y\Delta t+\frac{1}{2}C\sigma^2\Delta t$$

If there are no arbitrage opportunities in bond markets, then the expected return from any bond must equal the short-term rate, r, plus a risk premium that is proportional to the interest rate risk of that particular bond. Denoting that risk premium by λ,[2] the no-arbitrage condition states that

$$E\left[\frac{\Delta P}{P}\right] + c\Delta t = r\Delta t + \frac{1}{P}\frac{\partial P}{\partial y}\lambda\Delta t$$

Or,

$$E\left[\frac{\Delta P}{P}\right] + c\Delta t = r\Delta t - D\lambda\Delta t$$

Note that, for the risk premium to increase the returns of bonds with higher durations (i.e., with more interest rate risk, λ must be negative).

Substituting this no-arbitrage condition into the expected total return equation and rearranging terms gives this final result:

$$y = r + D\{E[\Delta y] - \lambda\} - \frac{1}{2}C\sigma^2$$

So, the yield on a bond can be broken down into the following components: the short-term rate, representing the reward for holding the bond over time; the duration times the expected change in yields, representing the reward or penalty for expected interest rate changes; minus the duration times λ, representing the risk premium for bearing interest rate risk; and a subtraction from yield to offset the convexity benefits of holding that bond. Note that, as discussed above, this convexity benefit increases with the volatility of rates.

Chapter 1 shows how convexity, interest rate risk premia, and other subtleties of fixed income mathematics impact the pricing of very long-term bonds. This application is pedagogically useful because many effects that are "subtle" for shorter term securities become economically significant for longer term securities. Furthermore, there had recently been a spate of issuance in 50- and 100-year bonds. Many market participants believed that these were

[2] While λ is written here without arguments, it may depend on interest rates or calendar time.

not issued at prices consistent with the principles described in Chapter 1, and, therefore, they offered relatively attractive investment opportunities.

Chapter 2 describes the effects of convexity on the shape of the yield curve and on expected returns across maturities. The chapter also presents a great deal of empirical evidence on the magnitude of these effects.

Another extremely important manifestation of convexity in fixed income markets is the difference between futures and forward rates. Chapter 3 explains the reason for this difference in the context of Eurodollar futures rates. The chapter then uses a particular term structure model to illustrate the theoretical magnitude of the futures-forward effect and compares the results with historical evidence on empirical futures-forward effects.

1

Fixed-Income Subtleties and the Pricing of Long Bonds

Neil D. Pearson

Suppose that a 40-year noncallable bond is offered at par and has a coupon (and therefore a yield) of 8% per year. A 100-year noncallable bond from the same issuer is also offered at par and has a coupon (and yield) of 8¼% per year. Which should an investor buy? At first glance, the answer might seem ambiguous. After all, it is common for the yield on the 30-year U.S. Treasury bond to be ¼% higher than the yield on the 10-year note. A difference of ¼% might not seem like a very large term premium for extending the maturity from 40 to 100 years.

Contrary to this first impression, however, the answer is clear. This chapter follows that of Dybvig and Marshall (1996) in arguing that, unless an investor has extreme views about future interest rates or the market risk premium, he should prefer the 100-year bond yielding 8¼%.

You can reach this conclusion in four steps. First, because long-term forward rates have a very small impact on bond prices and yields, forward rates from years 40 to 100 must be very large to generate a ¼% difference in yield between 40- and 100-year bonds. In fact, that seemingly small yield difference requires that annual forward rates at specific terms exceed 31%.

Second, because interest rates are volatile and because bond prices are convex in interest rates, forward rates (as well as spot rates and yields) will be below expected future rates under the risk-neutral probability measure. Furthermore, since convexity increases with maturity, long-term forward rates will be very much below these expected future rates. Therefore, for forward rates to exceed 31%, expected future rates must be much larger than 31%.

Third, expected future rates under the risk-neutral measure are a combination of investors' expectations of future rates and of the market premium for interest rate risk. So, generating the extremely large risk-neutral expectations necessary to produce a term premium of ¼% between 40 and 100 years requires unrealistically high expectations about future rates or an unrealistically high risk premium.

Fourth, uncertainty that investors have with respect to their interest rate models or model parameters also pushes forward rates below expected future rates. Hence, model uncertainty also leads one to question a large-term premium on yields between 40 and 100 years.

As you will see next, the existence of significant term premia in the yields of very long-term bonds implies that distant forward rates are very high. This conclusion depends only on arbitrage arguments and is therefore very robust. We then show how the convexity of bond prices in interest rates lowers forward rates (as well as spot rates and yields) below risk-neutral expected rates and does so in a way that increases with maturity. We then turn to the relationships among expected rates under the risk-neutral probability measure, investors' expectations of forward rates, and the market's interest rate risk premium. Finally, we consider the effect on prices of uncertainty about the parameters of a term structure model.

FORWARD RATES IMPLICIT IN THE YIELDS OF LONG BONDS

To illustrate the effect of long-term forward rates on bond prices and yields, it is useful to derive the price of a coupon bond as a function of spot and forward rates. For ease of exposition, it is assumed that coupons are paid continuously and interest rates are continuously compounded, but the conclusions would be the same without this assumption.

If continuously compounded spot interest rates are flat at r, the value of $1 to be received at time s is given by

$$e^{-rs}$$

So the value of a coupon payment of c at time s is given by

$$ce^{-rs}$$

If the coupon is paid continuously from time 0 to time T, the value of the stream of coupon payments is

$$\int_0^T ce^{-rs}ds$$

Finally, then, the value of a coupon bond paying a continuous coupon at a rate of c on a face value of 100 until time T and paying that face value at time T is

$$\int_0^T 100ce^{-rs}ds + 100e^{-rT}$$

Evaluating this expression gives the value of

$$\frac{100c}{r}(1 - e^{-rT}) + 100e^{-rT}$$

Now assume that spot interest rates are flat at r until time t and then forward rates are flat at f. The value of $1 to be received at time $s > t$ is

$$e^{-rt - f(s - t)}$$

The value of a coupon bond maturing at time T is

$$\int_0^t 100ce^{-rs}ds + \int_t^T 100ce^{-rt-f(s-t)}ds + 100e^{-rt-(T-t)f}$$

Performing the integrations gives a value of

$$\frac{100c}{r}(1-e^{-rt})+\frac{100c}{f}e^{-rt}(1-e^{-f(T-t)})+100e^{-rt-f(T-t)}$$

Apply these equations to a specific example: Suppose that spot rates are flat at 8% for 40 years and that forward rates are flat at f thereafter. Then, the price of a 40-year bond that has a face value of $100 and pays a continuous coupon at the rate of 8% per year is equal to its face value, that is,

$$100 = \frac{8}{0.08}(1-e^{-0.08\times40})+e^{-0.08\times40}100$$

while the price of a 100-year 8¼% bond is

$$P = \frac{8.25}{0.08}(1-e^{-0.08\times40})+e^{-0.08\times40}\left(\frac{8.25}{f}\right)(1-e^{-60f})+e^{-0.08\times40}e^{-f\times60}100 \qquad (1.1)$$

If $P = 100$, then the yield to maturity of the 100-year bond is 8¼% and the forward rate f must be greater than 8¼%. In fact, in order for Equation (1.1) to hold, it must be the case that $f = 31.175\%$. The forward rate must be so high because long-dated forward rates have little impact on the price of a coupon bond. In the expression above, this fact appears in the form of the coefficient $e^{-0.08\times40} = 0.0476$ that multiplies the terms involving the forward rate. The small size of this coefficient implies that changes in the forward rate f have a small impact on the bond price.

Figure 1.1 shows how the forward rate varies with the term premium h. It shows the pairs (h, f) that satisfy the equation

$$100 = \frac{8+100h}{0.08}(1-e^{-0.08\times40})+e^{-0.08\times40}\left(\frac{8+100h}{f}\right)(1-e^{-60f}) \qquad (1.2)$$

Strikingly, a term premium of only 12.5 basis points implies that the implied forward rate f is 12.85%, and a term premium of 37.5 basis points is impossible because when $100h = .375$ there is no forward

FIGURE 1.1. Forward Rate from Year 40 to Year 100 as a Function of the Term Premium

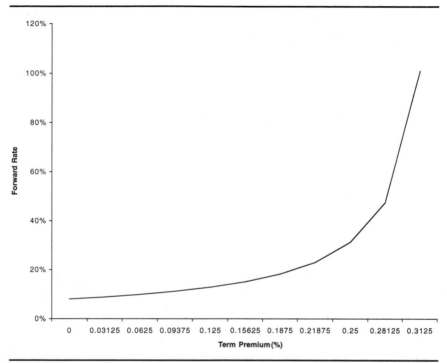

rate that satisfies Equation (1.2).[1] The figure indicates that, when the interest rate for the first 40 years is about 8%, beyond 40 years the par yield curve must be virtually flat.

FORWARDS, YIELDS, AND RISK-NEUTRAL EXPECTATIONS

The instantaneous forward rate at some time T is less than the expected instantaneous spot rate at time T where expectations are computed using "risk-neutral" probabilities. Also, the yield on a zero coupon bond maturing at time T is less than the average

---

[1] This follows since, when $100h = .375$, the first term $\left(\dfrac{8 + 100h}{0.08} \right)(1 - e^{-0.08 \times 40}) > 100.$

expected instantaneous spot rate from now to time T where, again, expectations are computed using risk-neutral probabilities. (The next section will connect true expectations and the price of interest rate risk with these risk-neutral expectations.)

Let $B(t,T)$ denote the price at time t of a zero-coupon bond paying \$1 at time T, and define the instantaneous forward rates through the relation

$$B(t,T) = \exp\left[-\int_t^T f(t,s)ds\right]$$

From the definition, $f(t,T)$, the forward rate applying to time T as observed at time t, is

$$f(t,T) = -\frac{\partial \ln B(t,T)}{\partial T}$$

Forward rates are related to the expected, instantaneous spot interest rates because the price of the zero-coupon bond can also be characterized as

$$B(t,T) = E_Q\left[\exp\left(-\int_t^T r(s)ds\right)\right] \tag{1.3}$$

where E_Q denotes expectation under the risk-neutral probability, conditional on the information available at time t. Performing the differentiation on the right-hand side,

$$f(t,T) = -\frac{\partial \ln B(t,T)}{\partial T}$$

$$= -\frac{1}{B(t,T)}\frac{\partial B(t,T)}{\partial T}$$

$$= \frac{E_Q\left[r(T)\exp\left(-\int_t^T r(s)ds\right)\right]}{E_Q\left[\exp\left(-\int_t^T r(s)ds\right)\right]}$$

where the last equality follows from Equation (1.3).

This result says that the forward rate is a weighted average of the spot rates $r(T)$ that might be observed at time T, where the weights

$$\frac{\exp\left(-\int_t^T r(s)ds\right)}{E_Q\left[\exp\left(-\int_t^T r(s)ds\right)\right]}$$

depend on the interest rates between t and T. For sample paths for which

$$\int_t^T r(s)ds$$

is large, the interest rate $r(T)$ receives little weight, while when

$$\int_t^T r(s)ds$$

is small, $r(T)$ receives more weight. An economic interpretation is that the right to receive a cash flow is less valuable when interest rates are high, and more valuable when they are low. Since interest rates tend to move together so that $r(T)$ is large when

$$\exp\{-\int_t^T r(s)ds\}$$

is small and $r(T)$ is small when

$$\exp\{-\int_t^T r(s)ds\}$$

is large, the forward rate will be less than the expected spot rate.[2]

---

[2] The precise condition sufficient for the result is that $E_Q\left[r(T)\mid\int_t^T r(s)ds\right]$ is increasing in $\int_t^T r(s)ds$.

Thus,

$$f(t,T) \le E_Q[r(T)] \tag{1.4}$$

where the inequality is strict if interest rates are not deterministic.

Since forward rates are less than expected spot rates under risk-neutral probabilities, a forward rate larger than 31%, as required in the 100-year bond example, would imply an expected spot rate even greater than that. Without any intuition about how risk-neutral expectations relate to actual expectations, however, one cannot conclude that 31% is too high a number to be reasonable. The next section relates those two expectations and shows that a risk-neutral expectation of 31% is indeed too high.

Focusing on forward rates makes it very clear that pricing the 100-year bond at a yield of 8¼% raises some serious questions. But similar issues arise by focusing on yields. This is not surprising since the yields on zero-coupon bonds are averages of forward rates. An investor may assume that an 8¼% yield implies that risk-neutral expected rates are, on average over the life of the bond, 8¼%. But, this would be a mistake: Just as forward rates are below risk-neutral expected rates, so are yields below average risk-neutral expected rates. In other words, for the 100-year bond to be priced at a yield of 8¼%, the average of future expected risk-neutral rates over the life of the bond would have to exceed 8¼%.

To illustrate this point, consider the case of a zero-coupon bond. The yield at time t on a zero-coupon bond maturing at time T, $R(t,T)$, is defined such that

$$B(t,T) = e^{-R(t,T)(T-t)}$$

Therefore,

$$R(t,T) = -\frac{\ln B(t,T)}{T-t}$$

$$= -\frac{\ln E_Q\left[\exp\left(-\int_t^T r(s)ds\right)\right]}{(T-t)}$$

$$\leq \frac{E_Q\left[-\ln\left(\exp\left(-\int_t^T r(s)ds\right)\right)\right]}{(T-t)}$$

$$= \frac{E_Q\left(\int_t^T r(s)ds\right)}{(T-t)}$$

where the inequality follows from Jensen's inequality. It is strict unless

$$\int_t^T r(s)ds$$

is known at time t, i.e. unless there is no interest rate volatility.

ACTUAL AND RISK-NEUTRAL EXPECTATIONS

The local expectations hypothesis asserts that all fixed-income securities have the same short-term expected return. Since the universe of fixed-income securities includes very short-term instruments, the hypothesis implies that the expected rate of return on all fixed-income securities is equal to the short-term interest rate.

A justification for the local expectations hypothesis would be along the following lines. If the expected return from holding security A were greater than that from holding security B, investors would sell their holdings of security B to buy security A. In the process they would push down the price of security B and push up the price of security A, i.e. push up the expected return of security B and push down the expected return of security A. These portfolio adjustments would continue until the expected returns of the two securities were equal.

While the local expectations hypothesis is logically possible, it seems unreasonable as a description of bond market equilibrium because it implies that investors do not require compensation for bearing interest rate risk in the form of extra expected return. In other words, it seems more reasonable to assume that if security A is riskier than security B, its expected return would be commensurately higher. Any expected return above (or below) the short-term rate is, therefore, called a risk premium.

In some markets, it is easy to argue that bearing certain risks should earn positive risk premia. For example, the stock market is often thought to be a good proxy for aggregate wealth. Since aggregate wealth fluctuates up and down, some set of individuals must, in equilibrium, bear stock market risk. But, risk averse as they are, individuals would not expose themselves to this risk unless they were paid to do so in the form of excess expected returns. The standard conclusion, therefore, is that stocks with exposure to the risks of aggregate wealth, namely positive beta stocks, earn an expected return above the short-term interest rate or a positive risk premium. Similarly, negative beta stocks (to the extent they exist) would earn an expected return below the short-term interest rate or a negative risk premium.

The theory of risk premia in the fixed-income markets is not as straightforward. Does aggregate wealth increase or decrease with interest rates? In other words, do investors need to earn positive risk premia in order to hold assets that increase in value with the level of interest rates or in order to hold assets that decrease in value with the level of rates? While this point can be debated, the historical evidence is quite clear. Securities that fall in value when interest rates rise, like coupon bonds, earn a positive risk premium. Furthermore, the more sensitive a bond is to interest rate changes, the greater its risk premium.[3]

Given the existence of risk premia in fixed-income markets, bonds can be priced in one of two ways. First, one could compute the expected present value of a bond's cash flows using the actual probabilities of future rates and then penalize that value in accordance with the interest rate risk of that particular bond. Or, second, one could construct risk neutral probabilities that account for risk premia and compute the expected present value of a bond's cash flows using those probabilities. A standard result (see, e.g., Duffie (1996), Chapter 6) is that, in the absence of arbitrage opportunities, there is a risk-neutral probability such that the expected rate of return on each asset is equal to the short-term rate of interest. Or, equivalently,

---

[3] For a recent study of this phenomenon, see Dhillon and Lasser (1998).

there is a risk-neutral probability such that the prices of fixed-income securities are given by their expected discounted values.

To illustrate the risk-neutral pricing procedure and the relationship between actual and risk-neutral probabilities, consider a simple model that has reasonable qualitative properties (e.g., Vasicek, 1978). In this model, under the actual probability, the short rate follows the process

$$dr(t) = \kappa(\theta - r(t))dt + \sigma dW(t)$$

and the expected value of the interest rate at time s, given its value at time t, is

$$E[r(s) \mid r(t)] = r(t)e^{-\kappa(s - t)} + \theta(1 - e^{-\kappa(s - t)}) \tag{1.5}$$

Letting s get large it can be easily seen that θ is the *long-run* or *steady-state* mean of the interest rate.

The risk-neutral process for the short-term rate in this model is

$$dr(t) = [\kappa(\theta - r(t)) - \lambda\sigma]dt + \sigma dW(t)$$

where λ is the risk premium for bearing interest rate risk per unit of interest rate volatility. Under this probability,

$$E_Q[r(s) \mid r(t)] = r(t)e^{-\kappa(s - t)} + (\theta - \lambda\sigma/\kappa)(1 - e^{-\kappa(s - t)}) \tag{1.6}$$

Here, the long-run mean of the interest rate is $\theta - \lambda\sigma/\kappa$ instead of θ.

Bond prices in this model can be computed using Equation (1.3). Note that the risk-neutral process has to be used in computing the relevant expectation. The resulting price is

$$B(t,T) = e^{a(T - t) + b(T - t)r(t)}$$

where

$$a(T - t) = \left(\theta - \frac{\lambda\sigma}{\kappa} - \frac{\sigma^2}{2\kappa^2}\right)\left[\frac{1 - e^{-\kappa(T-t)}}{\kappa} - (T - t)\right] - \frac{\sigma^2}{4\kappa^3}[1 - e^{-\kappa(T-t)}]^2$$

$$b(T - t) = -\frac{1 - e^{-\kappa(T-t)}}{\kappa}$$

Finally, the instantaneous forward rates can be obtained through the relation

$$f(t,T) = -\frac{\partial \ln B(t,T)}{\partial T}$$

To understand the role of the risk-neutral process, verify by Ito's Lemma that

$$E_Q\left(\frac{dB}{B}\right) = rdt$$

while

$$E\left(\frac{dB}{B}\right) = rdt + \lambda\sigma\frac{B_r}{B}$$

where B_r is the partial derivative of the bond price with respect to the short rate. The first of these expectations is true by construction: The risk-neutral process is determined such that the expected return of each bond, under the risk-neutral process, equals the short-term rate. However, the actual expected return of each bond (i.e., that computed using the actual probabilities) equals the short-term rate plus a risk premium. The interest rate risk of a bond, per dollar invested, is B_r/B. The market risk premium per unit of interest rate risk is $\lambda\sigma$, which may be further divided into the price of interest rate risk per unit of interest rate volatility, λ, and the amount of interest rate volatility, σ. In total, the expected return of a bond above the short-term rate is $\lambda\sigma(B_r/B)$. Note that since $B_r < 0$, λ must be negative for the risk premium to be positive.

The above discussion reveals that the risk-neutral process transforms the risk premium into probabilities so that the expected return on any bond equals the short-term rate. To see how this is done, compare the expected rates under the risk-neutral process to those under the actual process. From the Equations (1.5) and (1.6),

$$E_Q[r(s)\,|\,r(t)] - E[r(s)\,|\,r(t)] = -\frac{\lambda\sigma}{\kappa}(1 - e^{-\kappa(s-t)})$$

So, if $\lambda < 0$, as the empirical evidence suggests, the expectation of rates under the risk-neutral measure is above the expectation under the actual probabilities.

For this model, plausible parameter values are $r(0) = .06$, $\theta = 0.06$, $\kappa = 0.2$, and $\sigma = 0.02$. These parameter choices imply that the long-run mean of the short rate is 6%, the first-order autocorrelation of monthly interest rates is $\exp(-\kappa/12) = 0.983$, and the standard deviation of the steady-state distribution of the short-rate is $\sqrt{\sigma^2/(2\kappa)} = 0.0316$. While these choices of parameters are only "ballpark" estimates, they have little impact on the conclusions. The choice of λ is more important.

In constructing Figure 1.2, λ is set to -0.125, corresponding to a risk premium for holding a 30-year zero-coupon bond over the next

FIGURE 1.2. Comparison of Expected Short Rates under the Original and Risk-Neutral Probabilities to the Implied Forward Rates

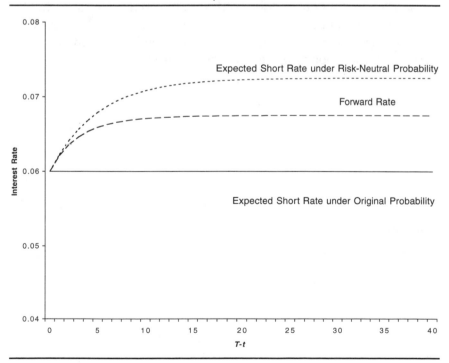

instant of 1.247 or 124.7 basis points per year. This value is consistent with recent empirical work, e.g. Dhillon and Lasser (1998).

Figure 1.2 shows the expected short rate under both the original and risk-neutral probabilities and the forward rate for maturities of up to 40 years. Because $r(0) = \theta$, the expected interest rate under the original probability is simply equal to θ, regardless of maturity. The expected interest rate under the risk-neutral probability increases with maturity because $r(t)$ is less than the long-run mean $\theta - \lambda\sigma/\kappa$. Consistent with Equation (1.4), the forward rate is less than $E_Q[r(T)]$, the expected spot rate under the risk-neutral probability. However, the forward rate is greater than $E[r(T)]$.

To the extent that the model and parameters used to construct Figure 1.2 are reasonable, investors who use the traditional form of the expectations hypothesis will tend to overvalue long-term bonds. Put another way, an investor who prices bonds by discounting at expected interest rates will arrive at prices that are too high. Similarly, although it is almost certainly a rare error, investors who correctly account for the risk premium but ignore the convexity effects discussed in the previous section will tend to discount at rates that are too high and, hence, undervalue long-term bonds.

This argument could also have been made in terms of yield. Since

$$B(t,T) = \exp\left[-\int_t^T f(t,s)ds \right]$$

and

$$B(t,T) = e^{-R(t,T)(T-t)}$$

it follows that

$$R(t,T) = \frac{1}{T-t}\int_t^T f(t,s)ds$$

The zero-coupon yield curve is an average of the forward curve. This fact, in combination with the finding that, for reasonable estimates of the risk premium, forward rates exceed expected spot rates under the actual probabilities, implies that yields also exceed these expected spot rates. Hence, an investor who sets yields equal to average expected spot rates will tend to overvalue long-term bonds. Similarly, an investor who sets yields equal to average expected spot rates under risk-neutral probabilities, thus ignoring the lessons of the previous section, will tend to undervalue long-term bonds.

Figure 1.3 illustrates the relationship between actual expectations, risk-neutral expectations, and yields in this example. In Figure 1.4 the interest rate volatility has been set to $\sigma = 0.06$, which implies that the standard deviation of the steady-state distribution of the short-rate is 0.0949. While this is an unreasonably large value, the figure shows that even with a risk premium the forward rate may fall below the expected short rate at the longer maturities.

FIGURE 1.3. Comparison of Expected Short Rates under the Original and Risk-Neutral Probabilities to the Yields to Maturity for Various Maturities

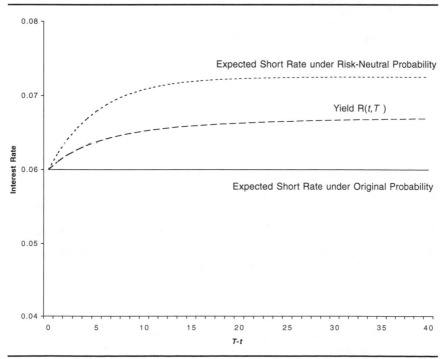

FIGURE 1.4. Comparison of Expected Short Rates under the Original and Risk-Neutral Probabilities to the Implied Forward Rates

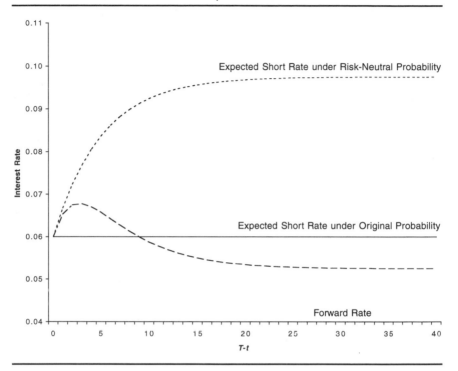

PARAMETER UNCERTAINTY

In the results and figures we assumed perfect knowledge of the model and the parameters. Of course, actual market participants don't know the model and parameters. What implications does this have for the yields on long bonds? Could this justify high yields on long bonds? In particular, could this indicate that yields on long bonds should be greater than expected future interest rates?

Strikingly, Dybvig, and Marshall (1996) prove a result which suggests that uncertainty about the model and/or its parameters implies that yields on long bonds should be *less* than the expected future long-run average interest rate. The argument is based on the fact that the price of a long-term zero-coupon bond is dominated by

interest rate paths with the lowest average interest rate. To understand the intuition behind this result, consider the following simple
example.

Suppose that all uncertainty about future values of the short
rate will be resolved in the next instant. Specifically, assume that in
the next instant the short interest rate will become either x or y,
where $y > x$, and remain at that value forever. Also assume for simplicity that investors demand no risk premium for this interest rate
risk. Then, the value of a zero-coupon bond paying one dollar at
time T is

$$B(T) = p \exp[-xT] + (1-p) \exp[-yT]$$

where p is the probability that the interest rate turns out to be x. Because $y > x$, as T becomes large, the first term becomes dominant. In
particular, the limiting ratio of the first to the second term is

$$\lim_{T \to \infty} \frac{p \exp[-xT]}{(1-p) \exp[-yT]} = \frac{p}{1-p} \exp[(x-y)T] = \infty$$

From this, it follows that the long bond yield

$$\lim R(T) = -\lim \frac{\ln B(T)}{T}$$

$$= -\lim \frac{\ln p(\exp[-xT])}{T}$$

$$= x$$

So, since $y > x$, the yield on a long bond, x, is less than the expected rate, $px + (1 - p)y$. Thus, uncertainty about the model and its
parameters cannot explain high yields on long-term bonds. See
Dybvig and Marshall (1996) for a more general proof.

CONCLUSION

This chapter showed why, if a 40-year bond has a yield of 8%, it is extremely unlikely that a 100-year bond should sell at a yield of 8¼%.

This seemingly small term premium would require that forward rates be remarkably high. But, it is unreasonable to assume that expected rates are anywhere near as high as these forward rates. Also, any reasonable value of the interest rate risk premium would not generate forward rates of the required magnitude. Furthermore, interest rate volatility and the convexity of bond prices tend to lower the yield of the 100-year bond relative to the yield of the 40-year bond. Finally, model uncertainty also tends to lower the yields of long bonds. In short, term premia of very long bonds cannot be as high as some investors, at first glance, might believe.

REFERENCES

Dhillon, U.S. and D.J. Lasser. (1998). "Term Premium Estimates from Zero Coupon Bonds: New Evidence on the Expectations Hypothesis," *The Journal of Fixed Income* (June), 52–58.

Duffie, D. (1996). *Dynamic Asset Pricing Theory*, Princeton, NJ: Princeton University Press.

Dybvig, P.H. and W.J. Marshall. (1996). "Pricing Long Bonds: Pitfalls and Opportunities," *Financial Analysts Journal* (January–February), 32–39.

Vasicek, O. (1978). "An Equilibrium Characterization of the Term Structure," *Journal of Financial Economics*, 5, 177–188.

2

Convexity Bias and the Yield Curve

Antti Ilmanen

Few fixed-income assets' values are linearly related to interest rate levels; most bonds' price-yield curves exhibit positive convexity or negative convexity (concavity). Market participants have long known that positive convexity can enhance a bond portfolio's performance. Therefore, convexity differentials across bonds have a significant effect on the yield curve's shape and on bond returns. This chapter describes these effects and presents empirical evidence of their importance in the U.S. Treasury market.

For a given level of expected returns, many investors are willing to accept lower yields for more convex bond positions. Long-term bonds are much more convex than short-term bonds because convexity increases very quickly as a function of duration. Because of the

This chapter was written for Salomon Smith Barney as a research report in September 1995. The author would like to thank Larry Bader, Eduardo Canabarro, Francis Glenister, Robin Grieves, Bill Hoskins, Ray Iwanowski, Cal Johnson, Tom Klaffky, Stan Kogelman, Veli-Antti Koura, Marty Leibowitz, Y.Y. Ma, Trifon Natsis, Richard Noble, Janet Showers, and Charlie Ye for their helpful comments.

value of convexity, long-term bonds can have lower yields than short-term bonds and yet, offer the same near-term expected return. Thus, the *convexity differentials* across bonds tend to make the Treasury yield curve *inverted or humped.* We refer to the impact of such convexity differentials on the yield curve shape as the *convexity bias.* Our historical analysis shows that the bias is small at the front end of the curve, but it can be quite large at the long end.

Convexity bias can also be viewed from another perspective—the value of convexity as a part of the expected bond return. Widely used relative value tools in the Treasury market, such as yield to maturity and rolling yield, assign no value to convexity. We show how yield-based expected return measures can be *adjusted to include the value of convexity.* The value of convexity depends crucially on the yield volatility level; the larger the yield shift, the more beneficial positive convexity is. In contrast, the rolling yield is a bond's expected holding-period return given *one* scenario, an unchanged yield curve. Thus, the rolling yield implicitly assumes zero volatility and ignores the value of convexity, making it a downward-biased measure of near-term expected bond return. To counteract this problem, we can simply add up the two sources of expected return. *A bond's convexity-adjusted expected return is approximately equal to the sum of its rolling yield and the value of convexity.* Figure 2.1 shows that, at long durations, the convexity-adjusted expected returns can be substantially different from the yield-based expected returns. (We describe the construction of this figure further in the chapter.)

We define convexity, describe how it varies across bonds, and discuss the relation between volatility and the value of convexity. We then examine convexity's impact on the yield curve shape and on expected returns and explain why we advocate the use of convexity-adjusted expected returns in the evaluation of duration-neutral barbell-bullet trades. Finally, we present historical evidence about convexity's impact on realized long-term bond returns and on the performance of a barbell-bullet trade.

While this chapter focuses on convexity's impact on the yield curve (and on bond returns), we stress that the convexity bias is not the only determinant of the yield curve shape. Positive bond risk premia tend to offset the negative impact of convexity, making the yield curve slope upward, at least at short durations. Moreover, the market's expectations about future rate changes can make the yield

FIGURE 2.1. Three Alternative Expected Return Curves, as of September 1, 1995

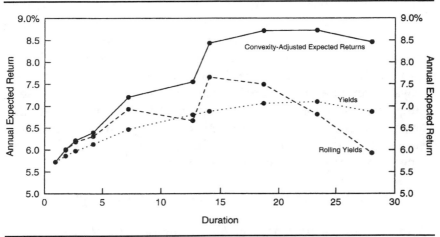

Note: Each curve is constructed by connecting ten individual bonds' yields, rolling yields or convexity-adjusted expected returns. The first six points on each curve represent par bonds of 1- to 30-year maturities and the last four points represent zero-coupon bonds of 15- to 30-year maturities, estimated from the Salomon Brothers Treasury Model curve.

curve take any shape. (See Chapter 1 for a discussion of these effects.)

BASICS OF CONVEXITY

This section provides a brief overview of convexity. Readers who are not familiar with this concept may want to read first a text with a more extensive discussion, such as Klotz (1985) or Tuckman (1995), Chapters 11 and 12.

What Is Convexity and How Does It Vary across Treasury Bonds?

Convexity refers to the curvature (nonlinearity) in a bond's price-yield curve. All noncallable bonds exhibit varying degrees of positive convexity. When a price-yield curve is positively convex, a bond's price rises more for a given yield decline than it falls for a similar yield increase. It is often stated that positive convexity can only improve a bond portfolio's performance. Figure 2.2, which shows the price-yield curve of a 30-year zero, illustrates in what sense this statement is true: A linear approximation of a positively convex curve always lies below the curve. That is, a duration-based approximation of a bond's price change for a given yield change will always understate the bond price. The error is small for small yield changes but large for large yield changes. We can approximate the true price-yield curve much better by adding a quadratic (convexity) term to the linear approximation. Thus, a bond's percentage price change ($100 \times \Delta P/P$) for a given yield change is:

$$100 \times \Delta P/P \approx -\text{Duration} \times \Delta y + 0.5 \times \text{Convexity} \times (\Delta y)^2 \qquad (2.1)$$

where duration = $-(100/P) \times (dP/dy)$, convexity = $(100/P) \times (d^2P/dy^2)$, Δy is the yield change, and yields are expressed in percentage terms. Equation (2.1) is based on a two-term Taylor series expansion of a bond's price as a function of its yield, divided by the price. The Taylor series can be used to approximate the bond price with any desired level of accuracy. A duration-based approximation is based

FIGURE 2.2. Price-Yield Curve of a 30-Year Zero-Coupon Bond

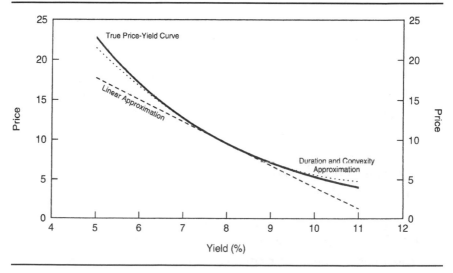

on a one-term Taylor series expansion; it only uses the first derivative of the price function (dP/dy). The two-term Taylor series expansion also uses the second derivative (d^2P/dy^2) but ignores higher-order terms. In Equation (2.1), the word convexity is used narrowly for the difference between the two-term approximation and the linear approximation, but the word is sometimes used more broadly for the whole difference between the true price-yield curve and the linear approximation. Given the price-yield curves of Treasury bonds and typical yield volatilities in the Treasury market, the two-term approximation in Equation (2.1) is quite accurate. As an "eyeball test," Figure 2.2 shows the most nonlinear price-yield curve among noncallable Treasury bonds and yet, the two-term approximation is visually indistinguishable from the true price-yield curve within a 300-basis-point yield range.

In general, the most important determinants of bond convexity are *option features* attached to bonds. Bonds with embedded short options often exhibit negative convexity. The negative convexity arises because the borrower's call or prepayment option effectively caps the bond's price appreciation potential when yields decline. However, this chapter does not analyze bonds with option features. For a discussion of how option features affect convexity, see, for example, Tuckman (1995), Chapter 17. For noncallable bonds, convexity depends on *duration* and on the *dispersion* of cash flows (see Appendix 2.1 for details).

Figure 2.3 shows the convexity of zero-coupon bonds as a function of (modified) duration. Convexity not only increases with duration, but it increases at a rising speed. For zeros, a good rule-of-thumb is that convexity equals the square of duration (divided by 100).[1] Convexity also increases with the dispersion of cash flows. A

---

[1] The convexity of a given security can be quoted in many ways, depending, in part, on the way that yields are quoted. If yields are *expressed in percent* (200 basis points = 2%), as in Equation (2.1), the convexity of a long zero with a duration of 15 is quoted as roughly 2.25 (= $15^2/100$). However, if yields are *expressed in decimals* (200 basis points = 0.02), the same bond's convexity is quoted as 225 (= 15^2). We decided to use the former method of expressing yields and quoting convexity because it is more common in practice. Fortunately, the quotation method does not influence convexity's impact on bond returns. The convexity impact of a 200-basis-point yield change on the long zero's return is approximately $0.5 \times \text{convexity} \times (\Delta y_{\text{percent}})^2 = 0.5 \times 2.25 \times 2^2 = 4.5\%$. We get the same result if the yield change is expressed in percent and convexity is scaled correctly: $0.5 \times (100 \times \text{Convexity}) \times (\Delta y_{\text{decimal}})^2 = 0.5 \times 225 \times 0.02^2 = 0.045$ or 4.5%.

FIGURE 2.3. Convexity of Zeros as a Function of Duration

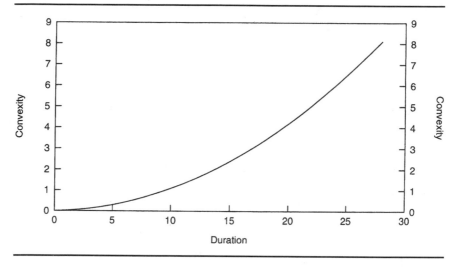

barbell portfolio of a short-term zero and a long-term zero has more dispersed cash flows than a duration-matched bullet intermediate-term zero. Of all bonds with the same duration, a zero has the smallest convexity because it has no cash flow dispersion. As discussed in Appendix 2.1, a coupon bond's or a portfolio's convexity can be viewed as the sum of a duration-matched zero's convexity and the additional convexity caused by cash flow dispersion.

Volatility and the Value of Convexity

Convexity is valuable because of a basic characteristic of positively convex price-yield curves that we alluded to earlier: A given yield decline raises the bond price more than a yield increase of equal magnitude reduces it. Even if investors know nothing about the direction of rates, they can expect gains to be larger than losses because of the nonlinearity of the price-yield curve. Figure 2.2 illustrated that convexity has little impact on the bond price if the yield shift is small, but a big impact if the yield shift is large. The more convex the bond and the larger the absolute magnitude of the yield shift, the greater the realized value of convexity is. We do not know

FIGURE 2.4. Value of Convexity in the Price-Yield Curve of a 30-Year Zero (bp Basis Points)

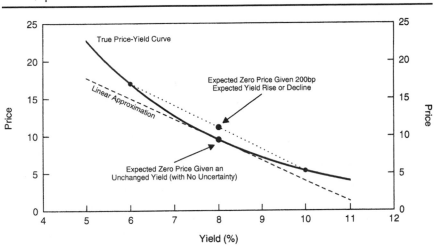

in advance how large the realized yield shift will be, but we can measure its expected magnitude with a volatility forecast.[2] If we expect high near-term yield volatility, we expect a high value of convexity.

The value of convexity is a nebulous concept; it may be hard for investors to see how higher volatility can increase expected returns. We try to make the concept more concrete and intuitive with the following example. Figure 2.4 compares the expected value of a 30-year zero in a world of certainty and in a world of uncertainty. In a world of certainty, investors know that a bond's yield will remain unchanged at 8%; thus, there is no volatility and convexity has no value. In the second case, we introduce uncertainty in the simplest possible way: The bond's yield either moves to 10% or to 6% immediately, with equal probability. That is, investors do not know in which direction the rates are moving (on average, they expect no change), but they do know that the rates will shift up or down by

---

[2] Equation (2.1) shows that the impact of convexity on percentage price changes can be approximated by $0.5 \times \text{Convexity} \times (\Delta y)^2$. The expected value of convexity is, therefore, $0.5 \times \text{Convexity} \times E(\Delta y)^2$. Appendix 2.2 shows that $E(\Delta y)^2$ is roughly equal to the squared volatility of basis-point yield changes, $[\text{Vol}(\Delta y)]^2$.

200 basis points. Note that the two possible final bond prices ($y =$ 10%, $P = \$5.40$ and $y = 6\%$, $P = \$17.00$) are higher than those implied by a linear approximation. The expected bond price is an average of the two possible final prices: $E(P) = 0.5 \times \$5.40 + 0.5 \times \$17.00 =$ \$11.20. This expected price is higher than the price given no yield change ($y = 8\%$, $P = \$9.50$). The \$1.70 price difference reflects the expected value of convexity; the bond's expected price is \$1.70 higher if volatility is 200 basis points than if volatility is 0 basis points. Thus, higher volatility enhances the (expected) performance of positively convex positions.[3]

The impact of volatility is very clear in the spread behavior between positively and negatively convex bonds (noncallable government bonds versus callable bonds or mortgage-backed securities). It is more subtle in the spread behavior within the government bond market where all bonds exhibit positive convexity. When volatility is high, the yield curve tends to be more humped and is more likely to be inverted at the long end, widening the spreads between duration-matched barbells and bullets and between duration-matched coupon bonds and zeros.

CONVEXITY, YIELD CURVE AND EXPECTED RETURNS

Convexity Bias: The Impact of Convexity on the Curve Shape

We have demonstrated that positive convexity is a valuable property for a fixed-income asset and that different-maturity bonds exhibit large convexity differences. Now we will show that these convexity differences give rise to offsetting yield differences across maturities. Investors tend to demand less yield for more convex positions because they have the prospect of enhancing their returns as a result of convexity. In particular, Figure 2.3 showed that long-term bonds

---

[3] This example suggests that scenario analysis is one way to incorporate the value of convexity to expected returns. If we compare the average expected bond price from two rate scenarios (+/−2%) to the expected price given one scenario, the difference will be positive for positively convex bonds (if the scenarios are not biased). In reality, more than two possible rate scenarios exist, but the same intuition holds. The expected value of convexity depends on volatility or the expected absolute value of yield change (also if this is computed by a probability-weighted average absolute yield change from 500 scenarios instead of two).

exhibit very high convexity. Because of their high convexity, these bonds can offer lower yields than a short-term bond and still offer the same near-term expected returns.

We isolate the impact of convexity on the yield curve shape, or the convexity bias, by presenting a hypothetical situation where the other influences on the curve shape are neutral. Specifically, we assume that all bonds have the same expected return (8%) and that the market expects the short-term rates to remain at the current (8%) level, and we examine the behavior of the spot curve and the curve of 1-year forward rates. With no bond risk premia and no expected rate changes, one might expect these curves to be horizontal at 8%. Instead, Figure 2.5 shows that they slope down at an increasing pace because lower yields are needed to offset the convexity advantage of long-duration bonds (and thus to the equate near-term expected returns across bonds). Note the symmetry between the curve shapes in Figures 2.3 and 2.5.

FIGURE 2.5. Pure Impact of Convexity on the Yield Curve Shape

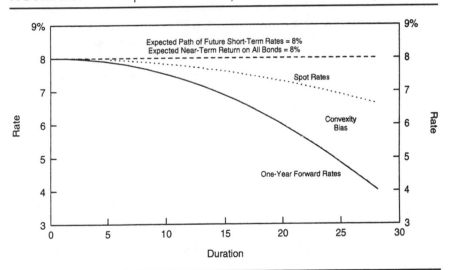

Note: Convexity bias is the difference between the curve of one-year forward rates and the expected return curve. Formally, Convexity bias $\approx -0.5 \times$ Convexity $\times [\text{Vol}(\Delta y)]^2$, adjusted for the fact that the bond price changes do not occur instantaneously but at the end of a one-year horizon. The assumed yield volatility is 100 basis points per annum for all bonds, that is, $\text{Vol}(\Delta y) = 1\%$.

Where did the numbers in Figure 2.5 come from? Unlike the real world, where the spot rates are the easiest to observe, in this example, we take the expected returns as given and work our way back to forward rates and then to spot rates. Given our assumption that the market has no directional views about the yield curve, each zero earns near-term expected return from rolling yield[4] and from convexity:[5]

$$\begin{array}{c}\text{Convexity-adjusted} \\ \text{expected return}\end{array} = \text{Rolling yield} + \text{Value of convexity} \qquad (2.2)$$

where value of convexity $\approx 0.5 \times \text{Convexity} \times [\text{Vol}(\Delta y)]^2$. Using our assumption that all bonds have convexity-adjusted expected return of 8% and using some volatility assumption (which determines the value of convexity), we can back out the rolling yields for various-maturity zeros from Equation (2.2). Our volatility assumption of 100 basis points means roughly that we expect all rates to move 100 basis points (up or down) from their current level over the next year. For example, if the convexity of a long zero is 2.25, the value of convexity is approximately $0.5 \times 2.25 \times 1^2 = 1.125\%$. The zero's rolling yield is 6.875% but its annualized near-term expected return is 8%, by assumption. For coupon bonds, which have smaller convexities, the value of convexity is much smaller. The final step in constructing Figure 2.5 is to compute the spot curve from the curve of 1-year forward rates (the rolling yield curve).

Convexity bias is simply the inverse of the value of convexity, or $-0.5 \times \text{Convexity} \times [\text{Vol}(\Delta y)]^2$. Figure 2.5 shows that the convexity

[4] The rolling yield is a bond's holding-period return given an unchanged yield curve. If a downward-sloping yield curve remains unchanged, long-term bonds earn their initial yields and negative rolldown returns (because they "roll up the curve" as their maturities shorten). An n-year zero-coupon bond's rolling yield over the next year is equal to the one-year forward rate between $n-1$ and n. For details, see Ilmanen (1996a) or Tuckman (1995), Chapter 2.

[5] Here is an intuitive proof: A bond's expected holding-period return can be split into *a part that reflects an unchanged yield curve* (the rolling yield) and *a part that reflects expected changes in the yield curve*. The second part can be approximated by taking expectations of Equation (2.1). If we expect the yield curve to remain unchanged, as a base case, but allow for positive volatility, the duration impact will be zero, leaving only the value of convexity. (Some modifications are needed because Equation (2.1) holds instantaneously for constant-maturity rates, while the actual bond price changes occur over a horizon.)

bias, by itself, tends to make the yield curve inverted, especially at long durations. However, actual yield curves rarely invert as they do in this hypothetical example, in which we assumed, in particular, that all bonds across the curve have the same near-term expected return and the same basis-point yield volatility. We now relax each of these two assumptions, one at a time. First, convexity is not the only influence on the curve shape. The typical historical yield curve shape is upward sloping, probably reflecting positive bond risk premia (the fact that investors require higher expected returns for long-term bonds than for short-term bonds). At the front end of the curve, the convexity bias is so small that it does not offset the impact of positive bond risk premia. At the long end, the convexity bias can be so large that the yield curve becomes inverted in spite of positive risk premia. Figure 2.6 shows that in the presence of positive risk

FIGURE 2.6. Impact of Convexity with Positive Bond Risk Premia

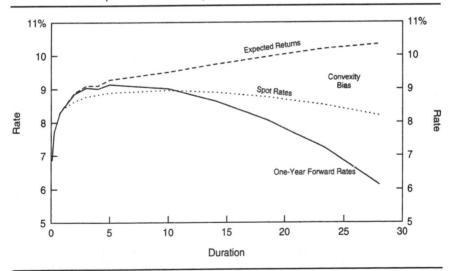

Note: The figure is constructed in the same way as Figure 2.5 except that the bonds' expected returns are not 8% but are based on the (arithmetic) mean realized returns of Treasury bond maturity subsectors between 1970 and 1994. The curve is extrapolated between 10- and 30-year durations because of a lack of data. The curve of one-year forward rates is computed by adding the convexity bias from Figure 2.5 to the expected return curve. The spot curve is computed from the curve of one-year forward rates.

premia, convexity bias tends to make the yield curve humped rather than inverted. In this figure, we use historical average returns of various maturity subsectors to proxy for expected returns.

As explained earlier, the value of convexity increases with yield volatility. Thus far we have assumed that yield volatility is equally high across the curve. Figure 2.7 shows that historically, the term structure of volatility has often been inverted—long-term rates have been less volatile than short-term rates. Therefore, the value of convexity does not increase quite as a square of duration even though convexity itself does. However, the value of convexity does increase quite quickly with duration even when the volatility term structure is taken into account; its inversion only dampens the rate of increase (see Figure 2.8).

FIGURE 2.7. Historical Term Structure of (Basis-Point) Yield Volatility

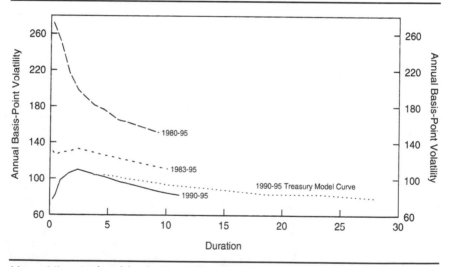

Note: Historical yield volatility is the annualized standard deviation of weekly basis-point yield changes. Yield volatilities are computed for several on-the-run Treasury bill and bond series (and plotted on their average durations) over three sample periods. In addition, yield volatilities are computed for the 5-, 10-, 15-, 20-, 25-, and 30-year points on the Salomon Brothers Treasury Model spot curve over the January 1990–August 1995 period. Yields are compounded annually and the yield volatilities are expressed in basis points.

FIGURE 2.8. Value of Convexity Given Various Volatility Structures (bp Basis Points)

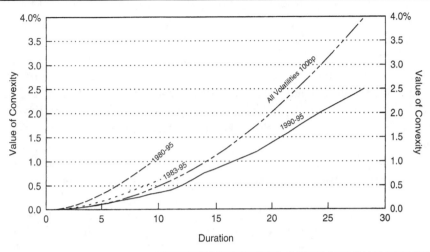

Note: Value of Convexity = $0.5 \times \text{Convexity} \times [\text{Vol}(\Delta y)]^2$, expressed in percent per annum, adjusted for the fact that the bond price changes do not occur instantaneously but at the end of a one-year horizon. Yield volatilities are based on Figure 2.7. Because we only have spot rate data for the 1990s, we cannot compute long zeros' value of convexity for the two longer samples.

The levels and shapes of the volatility term structures are very different in Figure 2.7, depending on the sample period. In the 1980s—and especially at the beginning of the decade—yield volatilities were very high and the term structure of volatility was inverted. In the 1990s, volatilities have been lower and the term structure of volatility has been flat or humped. It is difficult to choose the appropriate sample period for computing the yield volatility and Figure 2.8 shows that this choice will have a significant impact on the estimated value of convexity. Our view is that the relevant choice is between the 1983–1995 and the 1990–1995 sample periods because we do not expect to see again the volatility levels experienced in 1979–1982—at least not without clear warning signs. This period coincided with a different monetary policy regime in which the Federal Reserve targeted the money supply and tolerated much higher yield volatility than after October 1982.[6]

Instead of sample-specific historical volatilities, we could use implied volatilities from current option prices (based on the cap-curve swaptions, options on various futures contracts, on OTC options on individual on-the-run bonds) to compute the (expected) value of convexity. The main reason that we have not done this is that such implied volatilities are not available for all maturities. In addition, it is not clear from empirical evidence that implied volatilities predict future yield volatilities any better than historical volatilities do.

In Appendix 2.2, we describe the various volatility measures used in this chapter and discuss the relations between them. In particular, we emphasize that the option prices are typically quoted in relative yield volatilities [Vol($\Delta y / y$)] rather than in the basis-point volatilities [Vol(Δy)] that we use. For example, a 13% implied volatility quote has to be multiplied by the yield level, say 7%, to get the basis-point volatility (91 basis points = 0.91% = 13% × 7%).

The Impact of Convexity on Expected Bond Returns

Figure 2.8 shows that positive convexity can be quite valuable, especially in a high-volatility environment. However, yield-based measures of expected bond return assign no value to convexity. For

[6] Whenever the period 1979–1982 is included in a historical sample, the estimated volatilities will be much higher, the term structures of volatility will be more inverted and basis-point yield volatilities will appear to be more "level-dependent" than if the sample period begins after 1982. In many countries outside the United States, the inversion and the level-dependency also have been apparent features of the volatility structure recently. These features seem to become stronger if the central bank subordinates the short-term rates to be tools for some other monetary policy goal, such as money supply (United States 1979–1982) or currency stability (for example, countries in the European Monetary System). Figure 2.7 also illustrates interesting findings about the term structure of volatility in the 1990s. The shape is humped, not inverted, because the intermediate-term yields have been more volatile than either the short-term or the long-term yields. Moreover, yield volatility is not just a function of duration; it also depends on the bond's cash flow distribution. For a given duration, zeros have exhibited greater yield volatility than coupon bonds. This pattern probably reflects the coupon bonds' diversification benefits (unlike zeros, these bonds have cash flows in many parts of the yield curve that are imperfectly correlated) as well as the humped shape of the volatility structure.

example, the rolling yield is a bond's holding-period return given *one* scenario (an unchanged yield curve), essentially assuming no rate uncertainty. *Because volatility can only be positive, the rolling yield is a downward-biased measure of expected return* for bonds with positive convexity.[7] Fortunately, it is possible to add the impact of rate uncertainty (the expected value of convexity) to rolling yields. Equation (2.2) shows that if the base case expectation is an unchanged yield curve, a bond's near-term expected return is simply the sum of the rolling yield and the value of convexity. This relation holds approximately for coupon bonds as well as for zeros.

In Table 2.1, we calculate three expected return measures (yield, rolling yield, convexity-adjusted expected return) and the value of convexity on September 1, 1995, for six Treasury par bonds and four long-duration zeros (estimated from the Salomon Brothers Treasury Model curve which represents off-the-run bonds). In addition, we describe two barbell positions that can be compared with duration-matched bullets. Figure 2.1 showed graphically the three alternative expected return curves as a function of duration.

We use maturity-specific historical volatilities from the 1990–1995 period to proxy for expected volatility, and we use a one-year horizon. These choices give one illustration of the ideas developed in this report; we stress that it is possible to use other volatility measures or other horizon. In particular, Figure 2.7 shows that the volatility estimates would be much higher if we extended our sample period to the 1980s. (The par bonds' yield volatilities are similar to those of the on-the-run bonds in Figure 2.7.) For a given yield curve, these higher volatility estimates could more than double the estimated value of convexity and, thus, increase the convexity-adjusted expected returns. Using a one-year horizon makes the notation easier because the value of convexity is expressed in annualized terms as are yields and volatilities. If we used a three-month horizon, all three expected return measures and the value of convexity would be roughly one fourth of the numbers in Table 2.1. For example, if a 30-year par bond's convexity is 2.57 and the annual volatility is 82 basis points, the quarterly volatility is approximately

---

[7] This point is most easily seen by considering a horizontal yield curve. All bonds have same yields and rolling yields, but their expected returns are not the same. Long-term bonds are more convex than short-term bonds; thus, they have higher near-term expected returns.

TABLE 2.1. Expected One-Year Returns on Various Bonds as of September 1, 1995

	(Modified) Duration	Convexity	Historical Vol(Δy)	(Annual) Yield	Rolling Yield	Value of Convexity	Conv.-Adjusted Expected Return
Par Bonds							
1 Year	0.95	0.02	0.98%	5.73%	5.73%	0.00%	5.73%
2 Year	1.84	0.05	1.06	5.87	6.00	0.01	6.01
3 Year	2.67	0.10	1.10	5.98	6.18	0.03	6.21
5 Year	4.20	0.23	1.04	6.13	6.31	0.09	6.40
10 Year	7.20	0.67	0.95	6.47	6.94	0.27	7.21
30 Year	12.66	2.57	0.82	6.81	6.67	0.88	7.55
Long Zeros							
15 Year	14.03	2.10	0.89%	6.88%	7.66%	0.78%	8.44%
20 Year	18.68	3.66	0.83	7.07	7.49	1.22	8.71
25 Year	23.34	5.67	0.83	7.11	6.81	1.91	8.72
30 Year	28.07	8.14	0.79	6.88	5.93	2.53	8.46
Par Barbells							
1 Year and 10 Year	4.19	0.36	0.95%	6.11%	6.35%	0.14%	6.50%
1 Year and 30 Year	7.18	1.38	0.82	6.30	6.23	0.47	6.70

Note: Convexity-adjusted expected return = Rolling yield + Value of convexity, where Rolling yield = Yield + Rolldown return and where value of convexity = $0.5 \times$ Convexity $\times [\text{Vol}(\Delta y)]^2$, adjusted for the fact that the bond price changes do not occur instantaneously but at the end of the one-year horizon. Historical volatilities are the annualized standard deviations of weekly basis-point yield changes between January 1990 and August 1995. All measures use annually compounded yields and are expressed in percentage terms. The first (second) barbell is a combination of the one-year par bond and the 10-year (30-year) par bond, duration-matched to the end-of-horizon duration of the 5-year (10-year) par bond; thus, the current durations are not exactly matched. All other measures for the barbells are market value-weighted averages, but the barbell's yield volatility is (Market value × Duration) weighted.

41 basis points ($82/\sqrt{4}$), and the quarterly value of convexity is $0.5 \times 2.57 \times 0.41^2 = 0.22\%$ ($\approx 0.88\%/4$), or 22 basis points.

Figure 2.1 and Table 2.1 show that the convexity adjustment has little impact at short durations because short-term bonds exhibit little convexity. Even for the longest coupon bond, the annual impact is 88 basis points. In contrast, for the longest zeros, the value of convexity is very large both as an absolute number (253 basis points) and as a proportion of their expected return (30% = 2.53/8.46). More generally, the value of convexity can partly explain the rolling yield curve's typical concave (humped) shape, but even the convexity-adjusted expected return curve inverts after 25 years. The longest maturity zeros appear to have genuinely low expected returns, perhaps reflecting their liquidity and financing advantage.

One advantage of this analysis is that it gives an improved view of the overall reward-risk trade-off in the government bond market. Until the 1970s, fixed-income investors evaluated this reward-risk tradeoff by plotting bond yields on their maturities. Eventually investors learned that the rolling yield measures near-term expected return better than yield and that duration measures risk better than maturity. In the mid-1980s investors became familiar with the concept of convexity, although few have incorporated it formally into their expected return measures. However, convexity-adjusted expected returns are even better expected return measures than rolling yields—and the adjustment is reasonably simple. To move all the way to mean-variance analysis, as advocated by the modern portfolio theory, we should adjust bond durations by their yield volatilities; then, Figure 2.1 would plot bonds' expected returns on their return volatilities. Of course, convexity-adjusted expected returns are not perfect; for example, if investors can predict yield curve reshapings consistently, they can construct even better expected return measures.

In addition, our analysis helps investors to interpret varying yield curve shapes, and more directly, it gives them tools to evaluate relative value trades between duration-matched barbells and bullets and between duration-matched coupon bonds and zeros. This is discussed next.

Applications to Barbell-Bullet Analysis

A barbell-bullet trade involves the sale of an intermediate bullet bond and the purchase of a barbell portfolio of a short-term bond and a long-term bond. Often the trade is weighted so that it is cash-neutral and duration-neutral; that is, one unit of the intermediate bond is sold, a duration-weighted amount of the long bond is bought and the remaining proceeds from the sale are put into cash (a short-term bond that matures at the end of horizon). For simplicity, we will only study such barbells in this report. In Appendix 2.1, we explain that a barbell portfolio has a convexity advantage over a duration-matched bullet because the barbell's duration varies more (inversely) with the yield level. Figure 2.3 provides another illustration of the convexity difference between barbells and bullets. If we draw a straight line between any two points on the zeros' convexity-duration curve, each point on this line corresponds to a barbell portfolio (with varying weights of the long-term and the short-term zero). The convexity of this barbell is the market-value-weighted average of the component bonds' convexities. Because the connecting straight line always lies above the zeros' convexity-duration curve, the barbell's convexity is always higher than that of a duration-matched bullet. Furthermore, the maximum convexity pick-up for any duration occurs when we connect the shortest and longest zeros.

In a similar way, we can connect any two points in Figure 2.5 and find that the rolling yield of any barbell is below the rolling yield of a duration-matched bullet. More generally, the rolling yield curve (as well as the yield curve) almost always has a concave shape as a function of duration; that is, the curve increases at a decreasing rate. Therefore, a rolling yield disadvantage tends to offset the convexity advantage of a barbell-bullet trade. If an investor wants to evaluate the relative cheapness of a barbell-bullet trade, he needs to compare two numbers, the rolling yield give-up and the convexity pick-up. The advantage of the convexity-adjusted expected return is that it provides a single number to measure the attractiveness of these trades. For example, the 1s to 30s barbell in Table 2.1 has a 71-basis-point rolling yield give-up relative to the 10-year bullet (= 6.23% − 6.94%), but how does this give-up compare with the convexity pick-up (1.38 versus 0.67)? The numbers in the last column show that measured in terms of convexity-adjusted expected returns, the barbell still has a 51-basis-point give-up (= 6.70% − 7.21%). Incidentally, the shorter barbell in Table 2.1 even picks up rolling yield over the duration-matched five-year bullet; this exceptional situation reflects the convex shape in parts of the rolling yield curve in Figure 2.1.

The performance of a duration-neutral barbell-bullet trade depends on curve reshaping, on parallel curve shifts and on the initial yields: (1) The trade profits from curve flattening and loses from curve steepening (between the two longer bonds); (2) the trade is constructed to be neutral to small parallel curve shifts, but the barbell profits from large shifts in either direction because of its convexity advantage; and (3) the initial rolling yield give-up is greater the more curved (concave) the yield curve is. Such a shape may be caused by the market's expectations of curve flattening or of high volatility, either of which would generate capital gains for the trade in the future.

Typical barbell-bullet trades are more curve flattening trades than convexity trades. The following break-even analysis illustrates this point. Consider the long barbell-bullet trade in Table 2.1. It consists of selling a 10-year par bond (rolling yield 6.94%) and buying a barbell of the 30-year par bond (rolling yield 6.67%) and the one-year bond (rolling yield 5.73%), with a one-year investment horizon. Thus, at the end of horizon, the components will be a nine-year bond, a 29-year bond and cash. The constraints that the trade is duration-neutral and cash-neutral require weights 0.53 and 0.47 for the long bond and the short bond. Given the duration-neutral weighting of the barbell, the rolling yield give-up is 71 basis points (= 0.53 × 6.67% + 0.47 × 5.73% − 5.73%). We isolate the flattening and convexity effects in the trade by asking two questions:

1. How much would the yield spread between 10s and 30s (or more exactly, between 9s and 29s at the end of horizon) have to narrow to offset this give-up, if no parallel shifts occur?

2. How large must the parallel shifts be to make the convexity advantage offset this give-up, if no curve reshaping occurs?

A little math shows that the necessary break-even changes are an 11-basis-point spread narrowing (curve flattening) and a 138-basis-point parallel shift. Historical experience suggests that the former event is more plausible than the latter: Over the past 15 years, the 10s to 30s spread narrowed by at least 11 basis points in a year 30% of the time, while the 10-year yield level shifted by more than 138 basis points in a year only 17% of the time. Thus, it is more likely that a given rolling yield disadvantage is offset via curve flattening than via the barbell's convexity advantage. However, the relative roles of curve-reshaping and convexity vary across different barbell-bullet trades. The reshaping effects are clearly more important at shorter durations (between most coupon bonds), while convexity can be more important at longer durations (between very long zeros). It follows that the time-variation in the rolling yield spread between barbell and bullet coupon bonds—or in the yield curve curvature below the ten-year duration—depends more on the

FIGURE 2.9. Payoff Profile of a Barbell-Bullet Trade, Assuming Parallel Yield Curve Shifts

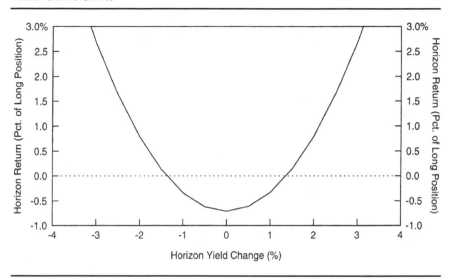

market's changing expectations about future curve flattening/ steepening than on its changing volatility expectations.

The convexity aspect of the previous example illustrates the similarity between a barbell-bullet trade and a purchase of a long option straddle (a purchase of a call and a put with the same strike price and exercise date). Figure 2.9 shows the almost U-shaped pattern that is familiar from option analysis. The rolling-yield disadvantage corresponds to the long call and put positions' initial cost (premium), which large market movements in either direction would offset. The trade would only be profitable if the yield level increased or declined by at least 138 basis points, assuming parallel yield shifts. If the yield curve does not move at all from the initial level, the maximum loss (71 basis points) occurs. Of course, Figure 2.9 ignores the substantial curve-reshaping risk in this trade.[8]

---

[8] The barbell-bullet trade that we analyze over a static one-year horizon is comparable to a strategy of buying and holding a straddle. Readers familiar with options know that the profitability of this strategy depends solely on the starting and ending yield levels and not on the yield path during the horizon. Option traders may use this strategy if

Another way to measure the cheapness of the barbell-bullet trade is to compute its implied yield volatility and compare it with the implied volatility in option markets. We can back out an implied volatility number for each barbell-bullet trade based on the observable rolling yield spread and convexity difference, if we assume that the duration-matched barbell and bullet earn the same expected returns and that the rolling yield spread reflects only the value of convexity—and no curve-flattening expectations.[9] High curvature (concavity) in the yield curve and high bullet-barbell rolling yield spreads indicate high implied volatility. In contrast, if the yield curve is a convex function of duration, barbells pick up yield *and* convexity and the implied volatility is negative—typically an indication of the market's strong expectations about near-term curve steepening.

---

they expect yields to end up far away from the current levels. It is useful to contrast this option strategy with another option strategy: buying a delta-hedged straddle and rebalancing the position dynamically throughout the horizon. The profitability of this strategy depends on the level of volatility (yield path) during the horizon and not on the ending yield level. Option traders initiate this strategy (and "go long volatility") when they think that the current implied volatility is too low. If the realized volatility turns out to be higher than the initial implied volatility, the trade makes money from profitable rebalancing trades—even if the ending yield is the same as the starting yield. These two option positions are analogous to two types of barbell-bullet strategies. In the first type (our example), the barbell and the bullet are duration-matched to horizon and no rebalancing occurs. In the second type, the trade is duration-matched instantaneously and the match is rebalanced frequently. The appropriate strategy in a given situation depends on several factors, including the following: (1) whether the investor has a particular view about the likely horizon yields (for example, "far away from the current level") or about the implied volatility during the horizon; (2) whether the investor tolerates some duration drift (because in the first case, the duration would drift during the year) or has a strict duration target; and (3) whether the investor expects rates to be mean-reverting (in which case he may want to rebalance and lock in the convexity gains after significant rate movements).

[9] The assumption of no curve-flattening expectations is realistic when describing the long-run average behavior of the yield curve, but may be unrealistic at times, especially if the Fed has recently begun easing or tightening. Because the performance of the barbell-bullet trade depends more on the curve reshaping than on convexity effects, curvature (the rolling yield spread between a barbell and a bullet) provides very noisy implied volatility estimates. Thus, it might be more useful to try to extract the market's curve-flattening expectations from the curvature by subtracting the value of convexity (based on, say, the implied volatility from option prices) from the rolling yield spread.

HISTORICAL EVIDENCE ABOUT CONVEXITY
AND BOND RETURNS

The intuition behind convexity-adjusted expected returns is that if investors care about expected return rather than yield, they will rationally accept lower yields and rolling yields from more convex bonds. In this sense, convexity is priced: It influences *bond yields*. However, a more subtle question is whether convexity also influences *expected returns* that are not directly observable. It is possible that the rolling yield disadvantage exactly offsets convexity advantage so that two bond positions with the same duration but different convexities have the same near-term expected return. It is also possible that convexity is such a desirable characteristic—because of the insurance-type payoff pattern—that the market (investors in the aggregate) accepts lower expected returns for more convex bonds. Finally, it is possible that current-income seekers dominate the marketplace, leading to a price premium (lower expected returns) for higher-yielding, less convex bonds. The jury is still out on this question. The evidence from historical bond returns that we present below suggests that more convex positions earn somewhat lower returns in the long run than less convex positions.

In this final section, we examine the historical performance of a long-term bond position and of a wide barbell-bullet position between January 1980 and December 1994, focusing on the impact of convexity on realized returns. The first strategy involves always investing in the on-the-run 30-year Treasury bond; this strategy is long convexity by holding a long-duration bond. The second strategy involves rolling over a fives-thirties flattening trade each month. Specifically, we sell short the on-the-run 5-year Treasury bond each month and buy a barbell of the 30-year bond and one-month bill. The trade is duration-matched to horizon; that is, the weight of the 30-year bond in the barbell is such that the barbell and the bullet have the same expected duration at the end of the month. A little algebra shows that the weight is the ratio of the five-year bond's duration to the 30-year bond's duration (at horizon). Although the trade is cash-neutral and duration-neutral, it is long convexity because a barbell is more convex than a bullet.

We first show some summary statistics of various bond positions in Table 2.2 but focus on the last two columns. The bullet has

TABLE 2.2. Description of Various On-the-Run Bond Positions, 1980–1994

	1-Month	30-Year	5-Year "Bullet"	"Barbell"
Average Return	7.21%	10.34%	9.75%	8.69%
Volatility of Return	0.91	12.84	7.02	5.43
Average Yield	7.34	9.61	9.20	8.22
Volatility of Yield Change	3.46	1.44	1.88	1.44
Average Duration	0.08	9.87	3.91	3.91
Average Convexity	0.00	1.79	0.19	0.69

Note: Average returns are simply annualized by $\times 12$ and volatilities by $\times\sqrt{12}$. The barbell is a combination of the one-month bill and the 30-year bond, duration-matched each month to the end-of-month duration of the five-year bond. All other measures for the barbell are market value-weighted averages, but the barbell's yield volatility is (Market value $\times$ Duration) weighted.

roughly a 100-basis-point higher average return and average yield than the duration-matched barbell.[10] Thus, the barbell's convexity pick-up (0.69 versus 0.19) and the impact of yield curve reshaping do not offset its initial yield give-up. However, the barbell does have clearly lower return volatility than the bullet, reflecting the lower yield volatility of the 30-year bond than the 5-year bond.

We can decompose any bond's holding-period return into four parts: the yield impact, the duration impact, the convexity impact, and a residual term. Recall from Equation (2.1) that duration and convexity effects can approximate a bond's instantaneous return well. Over time, a bond also earns some income from coupons or from price accrual; we estimate this income from a bond's yield. Thus, we approximate a bond's holding-period return by Equation (2.3).[11] The difference between the actual return and its three-term

---

[10] The bullet's outperformance is consistent with the finding in Ilmanen (1996b) that historical average returns do not increase linearly with duration. Instead, the average return curve is concave, indicating that the intermediate-term bonds earn higher average returns than duration-matched pairs of short-term bonds and long-term bonds.

[11] Why is the first term on the right-hand side of Equation (2.3) yield and not rolling yield? Equation (2.3) is the correct way to approximate a bond's holding-period return when we study actual bond-specific yield changes (which can be viewed as the sum of the rolldown yield changes and the changes in constant-maturity rates). In this case, the rolldown return is a part of the duration and convexity impact. Alternatively, if we studied in Equation (2.3) the changes in constant-maturity rates (which do not include the rolldown yield change), we should include the rolldown return into the first term on the right-hand side; it would be rolling yield instead of yield.

TABLE 2.3. Decomposing Returns to Yield, Duration, and Convexity Effects

1980-94	Total Return	Yield Impact	Duration Impact	Convexity Impact	Residual
30-Year Bond's Monthly Returns					
Average Return	10.34%	9.41%	-0.49%	1.48%	-0.06%
Volatility of Return	12.84	0.61	12.66	0.61	0.11
Pct. of Average Return	100	91	-5	14	-1
Pct. of Volatility of Return	100	5	99	5	1
Subperiod Average Returns					
1980-82	11.19%	12.21%	-3.70%	2.83%	-0.15%
1983-85	14.83	11.22	2.24	1.44	-0.07
1986-88	8.16	8.27	-1.73	1.65	-0.03
1989-91	13.57	8.26	4.56	0.80	-0.04
1992-94	3.94	7.10	-3.81	0.67	-0.02
Barbell-Bullet Trade's Monthly Returns					
Average Return	-1.05%	-0.95%	-0.36%	0.30%	-0.04%
Volatility of Return	2.96	0.19	2.93	0.18	0.09
Pct. of Average Return	100	90	34	-28	4
Pct. of Volatility of Return	100	6	99	6	3
Subperiod Average Returns					
1980-82	-1.44%	-0.66%	-1.10%	0.42%	-0.09%
1983-85	-1.86	-1.21	-0.94	0.39	-0.10
1986-88	0.58	-0.97	1.12	0.42	0.01
1989-91	-2.39	-0.65	-1.90	0.17	-0.01
1992-94	-0.14	-1.25	1.02	0.10	0.00

Note: For the bond, the returns and their components are raw returns. For the barbell-bullet, these figures are return differences between the barbell and the duration-matched five-year bullet. Averages of total returns and their components are annualized by × 12 and expressed in percent; volatilities are annualized by ×√12. Yield impact is the return from yield (where the barbell's yield is market value-weighted). Duration impact is −Duration-at-horizon × Δy, where the yield change for the barbell is Market value × Duration-weighted. Convexity impact is $0.5 \times$ Convexity-at-horizon × $(\Delta y)^2$. Residual is the difference between the total return and the three components (yield impact, duration impact, and convexity impact).

approximation is the residual term; if the approximation is good, the residual should be relatively small. We split the 30-year bond's monthly returns to four components and describe the average behavior and volatility of each component in the top panel of Table 2.3.[12]

$$\text{Return} \approx \text{Yield impact} - \text{Duration} \times \Delta y + 0.5 \times \text{Convexity} \times (\Delta y)^2 \qquad (2.3)$$

[12] The percentage contributions of average returns in Table 2.3 may not add up to 100% because we use an approximate method of annualizing monthly returns (multiplying by 12). In contrast, the percentage contributions of volatilities do not add up to 100% because volatilities are not additive (whether annualized or not).

The return volatility numbers in the top panel of Table 2.3 show that in any given month, the duration impact largely drives the long bond's return—it is the source behind 99% of the monthly return fluctuations. However, yield increases and decreases tend to offset each other over time, having little impact on long-term average returns.[13] Over our 15-year sample period, the long bond's average return reflects more the average yield (91%) and less the convexity (14%) and duration (−5%) effects. The residual term has a small mean and volatility, indicating that the approximation in Equation (2.3) works well. Subperiod analysis shows that over three-year horizons, the duration effect can still have a significant positive or negative impact—the 1983–1985 and 1989–1991 subperiods were clearly bull markets and the three other subperiods were bear markets. In contrast, the yield and convexity effects are always positive (by construction). The convexity impact was largest in the early 1980s when yield volatility was very high. During the whole sample, the annualized convexity impact was 148 basis points. In the 1990s, it was about half of that.

Similarly, we can split the 5-year bullet's and the duration-matched barbell's monthly returns into four components based on Equation (2.3). The lower panel of Table 2.3 describes the average behavior and volatility of their difference, which can be viewed as a duration-matched and cash-neutral barbell-bullet trade. Again, the volatility numbers show that most of the monthly fluctuations (99%) come from the duration impact. The trade is duration-neutral;

---

[13] A careful reader may find it puzzling that the average duration impact on bond returns is negative over a sample period when the bond yields declined, on average. There are two explanations. First, the duration impact is a product of duration and yield changes, and it turns out that yield declines (from high yield levels) tended to coincide with relatively short durations, while yield increases (from low yield levels) tended to coincide with long durations. Thus, yield increases are "weighted" more heavily than yield declines. Second, historical yield changes that are based on a time series of on-the-run yield levels can be misleading because they ignore the impact of changing on-the-run bonds. For example, if a new bond is issued on August 15, the on-the-run yield change from July 31 to August 31 compares the yields of different bonds, the old one and the new one. Typically, the old bond loses some of its liquidity premium; thus, its end-of-month yield tends to be higher than that of the new bond—a pattern hidden in the on-the-run yield level series. For the analysis in Table 2.3, we create a clean series of yield changes that always compares the beginning- and end-of-month yields of one bond. The average monthly yield change in the clean series is one basis point higher than in the unadjusted series.

thus, the duration impact refers to the capital gains or losses caused by curve reshaping. That is, although $\text{Dur}_{\text{Barbell}} = \text{Dur}_{\text{Bullet}}$, the duration impacts of the barbell and the bullet differ unless the yield changes are parallel ($-\text{Dur}_{\text{Barbell}} \times \Delta y_{\text{Barbell}} \neq -\text{Dur}_{\text{Bullet}} \times \Delta y_{\text{Bullet}}$). Over the whole sample, these effects tend to cancel out, and the average return depends largely (90%) on initial yields. The barbell has a 105-basis-point lower average annual return than the bullet, mainly because of its yield disadvantage (–95 basis points) and partly due to losses caused by the curve steepening (–36 basis points); these are only partly offset by the barbell's convexity advantage (30 basis points). In four out of five subperiods, the bullet outperformed the barbell, suggesting that a barbell's convexity advantage is rarely sufficient to offset the negative carry over a multiyear period.[14] In addition, the impact of curve-reshaping is larger, in absolute magnitude, than the convexity impact in each subperiod. Again, the residual has a small mean and volatility; thus, the approximation in Equation (2.3) appears to work well.

Table 2.3 describes the impact of convexity, and two other effects, on realized bond returns. While characterization of past returns is sometimes useful, most investors are more interested in the future impact of convexity. If volatility and convexity were constant, we could use the historical average convexity impact to proxy for the expected value of convexity. However, volatility and convexity vary over time. Figure 2.10 shows the behavior of convexity, the rolling 20-day historical volatility and the (expected) value of convexity of the 30-year bond between 1980 and 1994. (Recent historical volatility is often used as an estimate for near-term future volatility.) Convexity has increased as yields declined, but the volatility level has declined even more except for spikes after the 1987 stock market crash and after the Fed's tightening in spring 1994. In the early 1980s, convexity was worth several hundred basis points for the 30-year bond—while more recently, the value of convexity has rarely exceeded 100 basis points. Such variation implies that any estimates of the value of convexity are as good as the underlying estimates of

---

[14] One should not generalize these findings about wide barbells to narrower barbells. The yield curve exhibits less curvature in the intermediate sector than between the extreme front end and long end. For example, a barbell-bullet trade from fives to twos and tens tends to have a much smaller yield give-up than the trade from fives to cash and thirties—and a smaller convexity advantage.

FIGURE 2.10. Convexity and Volatility of the 30-Year Bond over Time

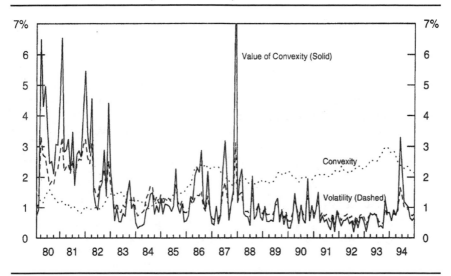

Note: Volatility [Vol(Δy)] is the annualized 20-day historical volatility of the 30-year on-the-run bond's basis-point yield changes. Convexity is the same bond's convexity. Value of convexity $\approx 0.5 \times$ Convexity $\times$ [Vol(Δy)]^2.

future volatility. Therefore, when computing convexity-adjusted expected returns, investors should use the information in the current yield curve combined with their best forecasts of the near-term yield volatility.

APPENDIX 2.1

HOW DOES CONVEXITY VARY ACROSS
NONCALLABLE TREASURY BONDS?

For bonds with known cash flows, convexity depends on the bond's duration and on the dispersion of the bond's cash flows. The longer the duration, the higher the convexity (for a given cash flow dispersion), and the more dispersed the cash flows, the higher the convexity (for a given duration). In this subsection, we discuss the algebra and the intuition behind these relations. We begin by analyzing zero-coupon bonds.

The price of an n-year zero is

$$P = \frac{100}{(1 + y / 100)^n} \qquad (2.4)$$

where P is the bond's price, y is its annually compounded yield, expressed in percent, and n is its maturity. Taking the derivative of price with respect to yield reveals that

$$\frac{dP}{dy} = \frac{-n}{(1 + y / 100)^{n+1}} = \frac{-n \times (P / 100)}{1 + y / 100} \qquad (2.5)$$

The second equality holds because $1/(1 + y/100)^n = P/100$, based on Equation (2.4). Multiplying both sides of Equation (2.5) by $(-100/P)$ gives the definition of (modified) duration:

$$\text{Dur} \equiv -\frac{100}{P} \times \frac{dP}{dy} = \frac{n}{1 + y / 100} \qquad (2.6)$$

For zeros, maturity (n) equals Macaulay duration (T). Thus, Equation (2.6) confirms the familiar relation between modified duration and Macaulay duration: $\text{Dur} = T/(1 + y/100)$, given annual compounding.

Taking the second derivative of price with respect to yield reveals that

$$\frac{d^2 P}{dy^2} = \frac{-n \times (-n-1)}{100 \times (1 + y / 100)^{n+2}} = \frac{(n^2 + n) \times (P / 100)}{100 \times (1 + y / 100)^2} \qquad (2.7)$$

Multiplying both sides by $(100/P)$ gives the definition of convexity (Cx):

$$\text{Cx} \equiv \frac{100}{P} \times \frac{d^2 P}{dy^2} = \frac{n^2 + n}{100 \times (1 + y / 100)^2} \qquad (2.8)$$

Expressed in terms of Macaulay duration or modified duration, a zero's convexity is $(T^2 + T)/[100 \times (1 + y/100)^2] = [\text{Dur}^2 + \text{Dur}/(1 + y/100)]/100$. For long-term bonds, the square of duration is much larger than duration. Thus, the rule of thumb that the convexity of zeros increases as a square of duration divided by 100. For example, for a zero with modified duration of 20 and yield of 8%, convexity is approximately $4.0 (= 20^2/100 \approx (20^2 + 20/1.08)/100 = 4.18)$.

The relation between the convexity and duration of zeros, illustrated in Figure 2.3, is simply a mathematical fact. With Figure 2.11 we try to offer some intuition as to *why* long-term bonds have much *more nonlinear* (convex) price-yield curves than short-term bonds. This figure shows price as a function of yield for various-maturity zeros. All curves are downward sloping but not linear. However large the discounting term $(1 + y/100)^n$ is, prices cannot become negative as long as $y > 0$. Intuitively, high convexity (that is, a large change in the slope of the price-yield curve) is needed to keep bond prices positive if the price-yield curve is initially very steep. Otherwise the linear approximation of the long bond's price-yield curve would hit zero very fast (at a yield of 11% for a 30-year zero in Figure 2.11 versus at a yield of 43% for a three-year zero).

For a given duration, convexity increases with the dispersion of cash flows. A barbell portfolio of a short-term zero and a long-term zero has more dispersed cash flows than a duration-matched bullet intermediate-term zero. The bullet, in fact, has no cash flow dispersion. The barbell exhibits more convexity because of the inverse relation between yield level and portfolio duration. A given yield rise

FIGURE 2.11. Price-Yield Curves of Zeros with Various Maturities and Their Linear Approximations

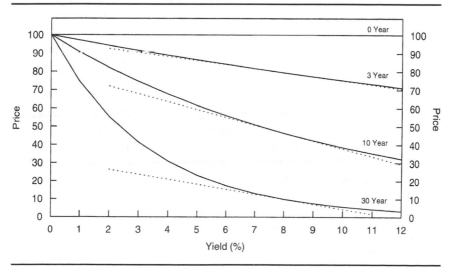

reduces the present value of the longer cash flow more than it lowers that of the shorter cash flow, and the decline in the longer cash flow's relative weight shortens the barbell's duration, limiting losses if yields rise further. (Recall that the Macaulay duration of a portfolio is the *present-value-weighted* average duration of its constituent cash flows.) Of all bonds with the same duration, a zero has the smallest convexity because it has no cash flow dispersion. Thus, its Macaulay duration does not vary with the yield level.

In fact, a coupon bond's or a portfolio's convexity can be viewed as a sum of a duration-matched zero's convexity and additional convexity caused by cash flow dispersion. That is, the convexity of a bond portfolio with a Macaulay duration T is:

$$Cx = \frac{T^2 + T}{100 \times (1 + y / 100)^2} + \frac{\text{Dispersion}}{100 \times (1 + y / 100)^2} \qquad (2.9)$$

where the first term on the right-hand side equals a duration-matched zero's convexity (see Equation (2.8)) and "dispersion" is the standard deviation of the maturities of the portfolio's cash flows about their present-value-weighted average (the Macaulay duration).[15]

Figure 2.12 illustrates the convexity difference between a bullet (a 30-year zero) and a duration-matched barbell portfolio of ten-year and 50-year zeros. We use such an extreme example and a hypothetical 50-year bond only to make the difference in the two price-yield curve shapes visually discernible. If the yield curve is flat at 8% and can undergo only parallel yield shifts, the barbell will, at worst, match the bullet's performance (if yields stay at 8%) and, at best, outperform the bullet substantially (if yields shift up or down by a large amount). Clearly, high positive convexity is a valuable characteristic. In fact, because it is valuable, the situation in Figure 2.12 is unrealistic. If the flat curve/parallel shifts assumption were literally true, investors could earn riskless arbitrage profits by being long the barbell and short the bullet. In reality, market prices adjust so that the yield curve is typically concave rather than flat (that is, the barbell has a lower yield than the bullet), and nonparallel shifts such as curve steepening can make the bullet outperform the barbell.

---

[15] Stan Kogelman derived Equation (2.9) in "Dispersion: An Important Component of Convexity and Performance," an unpublished research piece, Salomon Brothers Inc., 1986.

FIGURE 2.12. Price-Yield Curves of a Barbell and a Bullet with the Same Duration (30 Years)

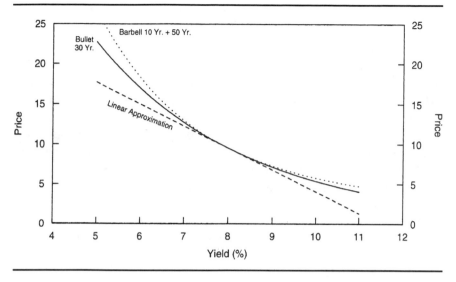

APPENDIX 2.2

RELATIONS BETWEEN VARIOUS VOLATILITY MEASURES

Equation (2.1) shows that $0.5 \times Cx \times (\Delta y)^2$ approximates the impact of convexity on a bond's percentage price changes. Thus, the expected value of convexity $\approx 0.5 \times Cx \times E(\Delta y)^2$. Now we discuss relations between $E(\Delta y)^2$ and some volatility measures. The variance of basis-point yield changes is defined as

$$\text{Var}(\Delta y) = E(\Delta y - E(\Delta y))^2 \qquad (2.10)$$

Because yield changes are mostly unpredictable, it is reasonable to assume that $E(\Delta y) \approx 0$. Therefore, $\text{Var}(\Delta y) = E(\Delta y - 0)^2 \approx E(\Delta y)^2$. The volatility of yield changes [$\text{Vol}(\Delta y)$] is often measured by standard deviation—the square root of variance. Thus,

$$\text{Value of convexity} \approx 0.5 \times Cx \times \text{Var}(\Delta y) \approx 0.5 \times Cx \times [\text{Vol}(\Delta y)]^2 \quad (2.11)$$

As long as $E(\Delta y) \approx 0$, volatility is roughly equal to the expected absolute magnitude of the yield change, $E(|\Delta y|)$. Note that it makes sense to assume that $E(|\Delta y|)$ is positive even when $E(\Delta y) = 0$. Even if an investor thinks that the current yield curve is the best forecast for next year's yield curve, he can think that the curve is likely to move up or down by, say, 100 basis points from the current level over the next year. In fact, it would be extreme to assume that $E(|\Delta y|) = 0$; this assumption would imply zero volatility (no rate uncertainty).

Next we show that for zero-coupon bonds the value of convexity is proportional to the variance of returns. Both yields and returns are expressed in percent. Short-term fluctuations in bonds' holding-period returns (h) mostly reflect the duration effect ($-\mathrm{Dur} \times \Delta y$) because the yield and convexity effects are either so stable or so small that they contribute little to the return variance (see Equation (2.3) and Table 2.3). Therefore,

$$\mathrm{Var}(h) \approx \mathrm{Var}(-\mathrm{Dur} \times \Delta y) \approx \mathrm{Dur}^2 \times \mathrm{Var}(\Delta y) \approx 100 \times \mathrm{Cx} \times \mathrm{Var}(\Delta y) \quad (2.12)$$

The relation $\mathrm{Cx} \approx \mathrm{Dur}^2/100$ is explained below Equation (2.8). A comparison of Equations (2.11) and (2.12) shows that the value of convexity for zeros is approximately equal to the variance of returns divided by 200. Interestingly, also the difference between an arithmetic mean and a geometric mean is approximately equal to the variance of returns divided by 200.[16] It appears that a duration extension enhances convexity and increases the (arithmetic) expected return, but the ensuing increase in volatility drags down the geometric mean and offsets the convexity advantage.

Equation (2.12) illustrates the relation between a bond's return volatility and yield volatility. We finish by stressing the distinction between the volatility of basis-point yield changes $\mathrm{Vol}(\Delta y)$ and the volatility of relative yield changes $\mathrm{Vol}(\Delta y/y)$. The volatility quotes in option

---

[16] The arithmetic mean (AM) and geometric mean (GM) are computed using the following equations:

$\mathrm{AM} = (h_1 + h_2 + \ldots + h_K) / K$ and $\mathrm{GM} = ([(1 + h_1 / 100) \times (1 + h_2 / 100) \times \ldots \times (1 + h_K / 100)]^{1/K} - 1) \times 100$, where h_k is the one-period holding-period return at time k, and K is the sample size. It can be shown that $\mathrm{GM} \approx \mathrm{AM} - \mathrm{Var}(h) / 200$.

markets and in Bloomberg or Yield Book typically refer to $\text{Vol}(\Delta y / y)$, while our analysis focuses on $\text{Vol}(\Delta y)$.

$$\text{Vol}(h) \approx \text{Dur} \times \text{Vol}(\Delta y) \approx \text{Dur} \times \text{Vol}(\Delta y / y) \times y \qquad (2.13)$$

In Figure 2.7, we use the historical basis-point yield volatility to proxy for the expected basis-point yield volatility. Alternatively, we could compute the historical relative yield volatility and multiply it by the current yield level. The latter approach would be appropriate if the relative yield volatility is believed to be constant over time, making the basis-point yield volatility vary one-for-one with the yield level. Empirically, this has not been the case in the United States since 1982 (see footnote 6).

REFERENCES

Ilmanen, A. (1996a). "Market Rate Expectations and Forward Rates," *Journal of Fixed Income* (September), 8–22.

Ilmanen, A. (1996b). "Does Duration Extension Enhance Long-Term Expected Returns?" *Journal of Fixed Income* (September), 23–36.

Klotz, R. (1985). *Convexity of Fixed-Income Securities,* Salomon Brothers Inc, October.

Kogelman, S. (1986). "Dispersion: An Important Component of Convexity and Performance," unpublished manuscript, Salomon Brothers, Inc.

Tuckman, B. (1995). *Fixed-Income Securities,* John Wiley & Sons.

3

Futures vs. Forward Prices: Implications for Swap Pricing and Derivatives Valuation

Mark Grinblatt and *Narasimhan Jegadeesh*

The Chicago Mercantile Exchange (CME) introduced Eurodollar futures contracts in 1982. Due to their popularity with investors, the CME progressively introduced Eurodollar contracts of longer maturities. Today, contracts with up to 10-year maturities are traded. Eurodollar futures contracts are among the most actively traded futures contracts in the world. Because of the large trading volume in this market and price transparency, market participants tend to use futures market prices to determine prices of interest rate swaps and other derivative securities.

In many of the pricing applications, investors have to infer forward rates from these futures rates. It is important to understand the distinction between these two rates. Exchanges that trade futures contracts require market participants to settle their losses and gains at the close of each trading day—a *mark-to-market* feature designed to minimize the risk of investors' defaulting when futures prices move against their positions. Forward contracts by contrast, lacking the requirement that counterparties settle on a daily basis, do not entail any cash flow between the time a contract is opened and the final settlement date at maturity. The difference in the timing of loss settlement due to the mark-to-market feature drives a wedge between futures and forward rates.

This chapter presents analytic formulas for pricing Eurodollar futures and forward contracts under the Cox-Ingersoll-Ross (CIR) model (1985) for interest rate dynamics. It then presents the theoretical differences between futures and forward rates and examines the factors that determine the magnitude of these differences. Two factors that affect the theoretical futures-forward rate difference are interest rate volatility and contract maturity. The futures-forward rate difference increases almost directly in proportion to interest rate variance (i.e., a 50% increase in interest rate variance leads to a 50% increase in the futures-forward rate difference).

The futures-forward rate difference is increasing in the maturity of the contract. For instance, this difference for a contract with three months to maturity is only .2 basis points while that for a contract with 10 years to maturity is about 30 basis points. As a result, long maturity interest rate swap contracts can be significantly mispriced if one fails to properly distinguish futures from forward rates in swap yield calculations.

Previous research has recognized that futures prices should differ from forward prices. Cox, Ingersoll, and Ross (1981), for example, show that futures prices will differ from forward prices when futures prices and interest rates are correlated (e.g., see French, 1983; Park & Chen, 1985). For most futures contracts, this correlation is small and one can comfortably treat futures and forward prices as if they were identical. However, this is generally not the case with interest rate futures such as Eurodollar contracts. The analytic results presented here enable us to calibrate the magnitude of these differences for Eurodollar futures and examine their effects on the valuation of other derivatives. Much of the analysis in this chapter relates closely to Grinblatt and Jegadeesh (1996).

The first part of the chapter uses a simple binomial example to illustrate the distinction between futures and forward rates. This is followed by a general analysis of futures and forward contracts. The theoretical formula for futures prices using the interest rates generated by the CIR model is derived and the differences between futures and forward rates for contracts with different maturities are calibrated. Some historical data on Eurodollar futures and forward rates are presented followed by an examination of the implications of futures and forward rate differences for determining swap yields.

FUTURES-FORWARD RATE DIFFERENCE IN A SIMPLE BINOMIAL MODEL

Consider the following binomial model of interest rates:

Interest Rate Path

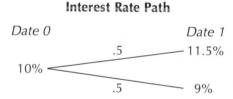

In this model, the interest rate today (Date 0) is 10% and one period from now (Date 1) it can either increase to 11.5% (at the Date 1 *up* node) or decrease to 9% (at the Date 1 *down* node). Let the risk-neutral probability of the interest rate rising (the *up* node) be .5.[1] The standard deviation of the proportional change in interest rates implied by the parameters of this model is 12.25%.

Consider a futures contract on the Date 1 interest rate. Let the settlement price of this futures contract at maturity (Date 1) be $100 - r$ where r is the one-period rate at maturity. In this model,

---

[1] Risk-neutral probabilities adjust the "true" probabilities so that prices can be computed by discounting expected cash flows at risk-free interest rates. See Chapter 1, Grinblatt and Titman (1998), or Chapter 6 in Tuckman (1995) for discussions of the relation between true probabilities and equivalent risk neutral probabilities.

the settlement price for this contract at Date 1 will be 88.5 (100 − 11.5) in the *up* node and 91 (100 − 9) in the *down* node.

By convention, futures prices are set such that futures contracts are traded without any exchange of cash. In other words, the value of a contract at the time it is bought or sold is zero. At the end of a trading day in which the futures price has risen or fallen, holders of contracts mark-to-market their positions (i.e., settle their gains or losses). Their positions are then automatically rolled into a new futures positions at the new futures price. Hence, after a futures position has been marked-to-market, it is again worth zero.

Since the contract is worth zero, the discounted expected value of the payoff from the futures contract, under risk neutral probabilities, must be zero. Furthermore, since the contract is worth zero after the mark-to-market settlement, its payoff over a single trading period is exactly that mark-to-market settlement. Returning to the numerical example, let the price of the futures contract at Date 0 be $P_F(0)$. Then, the payoff of a long position in the contract is 88.5 − $P_F(0)$ in the *up* node and 91 − $P_F(0)$ in the *down* node. Setting the expected discounted value of these payoffs to zero, under the risk neutral probabilities, implies that

$$P_F(0) = .5 \times 88.5 + .5 \times 91 = 89.75$$

It follows that the futures rate, F, at Date 0 is 10.25% (100 − 89.75). More generally, the futures price or rate equals the expected future price or rate under the risk neutral probabilities. (See Chapter 14 in Tuckman [1995] for a more detailed discussion of the features and pricing of interest rate futures contracts.)

Consider now the forward rate computed from the prices of zero-coupon bonds maturing one period and two periods from now. The price of a one-period zero-coupon bond $P(1)$ in this model is:

$$P(1) = \frac{100}{(1+.1)} = 90.91$$

It is also straightforward to determine the price of a two-period zero-coupon bond in this model. The computation of the price of this bond may be shown as:

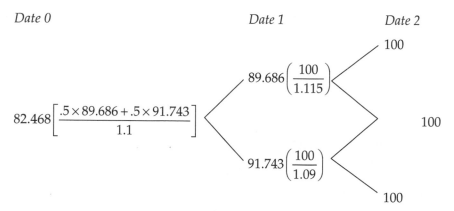

To determine the price of a two-year zero-coupon bond (hereafter called zero), we start with the contractual feature that this bond pays $100 at maturity (Date 2) regardless of the interest rate at that time. At Date 1, the bond price will be $89.686 at the *up* node, which is $100 discounted at 11.5%, and $91.743 at the *down* node, which is $100 discounted at 9%. Working back to Date 0, the bond price is $82.468, which is the expected value of the Date 1 price discounted at 10%, the current one-period interest rate.

The forward rate from Date 1 to Date 2 (denoted $f_0(1,2)$) is the interest rate for this period that one can lock in at Date 0. The forward rate can be locked in by buying the two-year zero and short-selling a face amount of the one-year zero that costs the same as the two-year zero. Given the prices of one- and two-year zero-coupon bonds in this example the forward rate is:

$$f_0(1,2) = \frac{P(1)}{P(2)-1} = \frac{90.91}{82.468-1} = 0.10236$$

The forward rate of 10.236% is 1.4 basis points smaller than the futures rate of 10.25%. As we shall see later, the forward rate will in general be lower than the futures rate because of the mark-to-market feature.

FUTURES AND FORWARD CONTRACTS: A GENERAL ANALYSIS

This section considers the difference between futures and forward prices more generally in order to highlight the source of the difference.

Consider a futures contract that matures at T. This futures contract can be on any index, asset, or commodity, although we will refer to the underlying instrument as a commodity for ease of exposition. Let S_T be the spot price of this commodity at T (which is not known at Date 0). As discussed in the previous section, the futures price at Date 0 is the expectation of S_T,

$$F_0(T) = E_0(S_T)$$

where $E_0(\ )$ is the expectation operator under the risk neutral measure.

Let there also be a T-period forward contract on this commodity. The forward contract calls for settlement of any gains or losses at maturity T and no cash exchange takes place until that time. Using arbitrage arguments it is easy to show that the forward price is simply the future value of the commodity price to the delivery date T (Tuckman, 1995, Chapter 14). Since the price of a zero-coupon bond maturing at date T is

$$E_0\left[\exp\left(-\int_0^T r_t dt\right)\right]$$

the forward price is given by

$$f_0(T) = \frac{S_0}{E_0}\left[\exp\left(-\int_0^T r_t dt\right)\right] \tag{3.1}$$

Also, since the commodity price today is the expectation of its Date T value, under the risk neutral probabilities,

$$S_0 = E_0\left[S_T \exp\left(-\int_0^T r_t dt\right)\right]$$

Using the definition of covariance,

$$S_0 = COV_0\left[S_T, \exp\left(-\int_0^T r_t dt\right)\right] + E_0[S_T]E_0\left[\exp\left(-\int_0^T r_t dt\right)\right]$$

Dividing by the zero price will, according to (1), give the forward price. Hence,

$$
f_0(T) = \frac{E_0[S_T] + COV_0\left[S_T, \exp\left(-\int_0^T r_t dt\right)\right]}{E_0\left[\exp\left(-\int_0^T r_t dt\right)\right]}
$$

Finally, using the definition of the futures price,

$$
f_0(T) = \frac{F_0(T) + COV_0\left[S_T, \exp\left(-\int_0^T r_t dt\right)\right]}{E_0\left[\exp\left(-\int_0^T r_t dt\right)\right]}
$$

Thus, the sign of the difference between the forward price and the futures price depends on the covariance between the stochastic discount factor from dates 0 to T,

$$
\exp\left(-\int_0^T r_t dt\right)
$$

and the terminal spot price, S_T. If the spot price tends to be high when interest rates are high (and zero prices low), then this covariance will be negative and the forward price is less than the futures price. Similarly, if the spot price tends to be high when interest rates are low, then this covariance will be positive and the forward price is greater than the futures price. In the case of Eurodollar futures, the settlement price is negatively related to interest rates so the forward price will be greater than the futures price. And, the futures rate (100 less this price) will be *larger* than the forward rate. As an aside, this relation between futures and forward rates also holds for other interest rate futures such as T-Bill futures rates.

The intuition behind the above result is as follows: In contrast to a forward contract, the mark-to-market feature calls for the long side in a futures contract to pay the short side whenever the futures price declines from the previous day's settlement price and vice versa. In the case of Eurodollar futures contracts, the price declines when the interest rate rises, implying that the long position pays the short side at times of high interest rates and receives payments when interest rates fall. But, paying out a loss over time instead of paying it on the delivery date is particularly bad when investment opportunities are good, that is, when rates are high. Furthermore, receiving a gain over time instead of at the delivery date is least valuable when investment opportunities are bad, that is, when rates are low. To compensate the long position for these disadvantages, the futures price must be set *lower* than what it would have been in the absence of the mark-to-market feature. Since the futures rate is 100 minus the futures price, the futures rate will be *larger* than the corresponding forward rate.

THEORETICAL PRICING DIFFERENCES BETWEEN EURODOLLAR FUTURES AND FORWARDS

To calibrate the futures-forward price difference for interest rate contracts, it is necessary to build a term structure model and go beyond the level of generality of the discussions in the last section. We base our calibration on the one-factor Cox, Ingersoll, and Ross (1985) interest rate model. Grinblatt and Jegadeesh (1996) and Jegadeesh (1996) show that other specifications for interest rates, such as the Vasicek model or the extended Vasicek model, yield differences between futures and forward rates close to what we obtain here under the CIR process. The Cox, Ingersoll, and Ross model specifies that the short-term interest rate $r(t)$ follows the square root process below,

$$dr = \kappa(\mu - r)dt + \sigma\sqrt{r}dz \tag{3.2}$$

where dr = the change in the instantaneous interest rate r
μ = the unconditional mean of this "short rate"
κ = the parameter that governs the speed of mean-reversion
σ = the instantaneous volatility parameter
and dz denotes the standard Weiner process.

Under this specification, interest rate drift is negative when the rate is larger than μ and positive when it is smaller than μ. As a result $r(t)$ is pulled toward its long-term mean at a rate κ. The speed at which the interest rate reverts to its mean is proportional to its distance from the mean. The volatility of interest rates is proportional to the square root of its level which, of course, implies that the volatility is higher when rates are higher.

Cox, Ingersoll, and Ross (1985) show that under this process the time t_1 prices of a zero-coupon bond that pays one dollar at time t_2 is given by:

$$P(t_1, t_2) = A(t_2 - t_1) \exp[-B(t_2 - t_1)r(t_1)]$$

where
$$A(x) = \left[\frac{2\gamma \exp[(\kappa^* + \gamma)x/2]}{(\kappa^* + \gamma)(\exp(\gamma x) - 1) + 2\gamma} \right]^{2\kappa^*\mu^*/\sigma^2}$$

$$B(x) = \left[\frac{2(\exp(\gamma x) - 1)}{(\kappa^* + \gamma)(\exp(\gamma x) - 1) + 2\gamma} \right]$$

$$\gamma = [(\kappa^*)^2 + 2\sigma^2]^{1/2}$$

$$\kappa^* = \kappa + \lambda$$

$$\mu^* = \frac{\kappa}{(\kappa + \lambda)}$$

λ = the market price of interest rate risk

Denote

$L_s(y) = y$ – year LIBOR rate prevailing at time s[2]

$d(s, \tau)$ = LIBOR conversion factor; defined as $360/$(number of days between s and τ), $\tau > s$

$P(s, \tau) = 1/[1 + L_s(\tau - s)/d(s, \tau)]$. The time s price of $1 paid at τ in the Eurodollar market, $\tau > s$

$f(s, \tau)$ = Annualized Eurodollar forward rate at time 0 for the interval s to τ

$F(s, \tau)$ = Annualized Eurodollar futures rate at 0 for the interval s to τ

$r(t)$ = Annualized instantaneous interest rate at time t (i.e., the short rate)

[2] LIBOR is conventionally quoted on a 360-day simple interest basis.

Given this solution for discount bond prices, the forward rates in the CIR model are given by:

$$f(s,\tau) = d(s,\tau)\frac{P(0,s)}{P(0,\tau)-1}$$

$$= d(s,\tau)\left\{\frac{A(s)}{A(\tau)}\exp[(B(\tau)-B(s))r(0)]-1\right\}$$

(3.3)

Consider the futures contract next. Since there is no cash outlay at the time a futures contract is opened, the expected change in the futures rate at any instant equals the premium for bearing the interest rate risk of that position.[3] Grinblatt and Jegadeesh (1996) show that under the CIR interest rate process the equilibrium Eurodollar futures rate, which equals the risk neutral expected value of the terminal 3-month interest rate, is given by

$$F(s,\tau) = d(s,\tau)\left\{\left[\frac{1}{A(\tau-s)}\right]E[\exp(B(\tau-s)r(s))]-1\right\}$$

where the *Date* 0 expectation

$$E[\exp(B(\tau-s)r(s))] = \frac{\dfrac{\exp[B(\tau-s)\exp(-\kappa^*s)r(0)}{(1-B(\tau-s)\sigma^2b_c(s)/2)]}}{\left[1-B(\tau-s)\sigma^2b_c(s)/2\right]^{2\kappa^*\mu^*/\sigma^2}}$$

(3.4)

and where

$$b_c(s) = \left(\frac{1}{\kappa^*}\right)[1-\exp(-\kappa^*s)]$$

Comparing Equations (3.3) and (3.4) we see that the differences between the futures and forward rates depend on the interest rate process parameters κ, μ, and σ, the market price of interest rate risk λ, and the short-term rate r. Grinblatt and Jegadeesh use a Kalman

---

[3] If the interest rate process (3.2) is expressed in its risk-neutral form then the premium for bearing interest rate risk is zero.

filtering technique and obtain the following estimates for the process parameters: $\kappa = .167$, $\mu = .074$, and $\sigma = .06$. Table 3.1 presents the theoretical 3-month Eurodollar futures-forward yield spreads using these process parameters and setting the market price of interest rate risk equal to zero. The short rate is set equal to 6% in the table which is roughly the historical average rate.

The results in Table 3.1 indicate that for these process parameters, the futures rate exceeds the forward rate by a trivial amount for short maturing forwards and futures. However, for maturities of 2 years or more, the futures forward differences is more substantial,

TABLE 3.1. Theoretical Differences between Eurodollar Futures and Forward Rates

Contract Maturity	Difference between Futures and Forward Rate (Basis Points)		
	$\sigma = .04$	$\sigma = .06$	$\sigma = .08$
3 months	0.00	0.00	0.00
6 months	0.08	0.19	0.33
9 months	0.22	0.48	0.86
1 year	0.39	0.87	1.55
2 year	1.41	3.18	5.63
3 year	3.16	6.24	11.03
4 year	4.71	9.65	17.00
5 year	6.29	13.14	23.05
7 year	8.92	19.73	34.29
10 year	12.65	27.72	47.53

Note: This table presents the differences between futures and forward rates at various maturities. The following interest rate process is assumed for the short rate:

$$dr = \kappa(\mu - r)dt + \sigma r^{1/2}dz$$

The parameters used in this table are $\kappa = .167$, $\mu = .074$, $r = 6\%$ and the market price of risk is assumed to be zero. The differences between futures and forward rates are tabulated above for different levels of volatility σ and for contracts of various maturities.

with the futures interest rate exceeding the forward rate. For 10-year futures contract, the futures rate exceeds the corresponding forward rate by 27.72 basis points.

Table 3.1 also presents the theoretical yield differences for σ = .04 and σ = .08. When σ = .04, the yield difference for the 10-year futures contract is 12.75 basis points while it is 47.53 basis points when σ = .08. The results here indicate that interest rate volatility has a significant effect on futures-forward yield differences and that the yield difference increases roughly in proportion to the variance of interest rates. Therefore, investors need to obtain good estimates of interest rate volatility before using information in futures prices to infer forward rates.

HISTORICAL DIFFERENCES BETWEEN FUTURES AND FORWARDS INTEREST RATES

This section empirically compares Eurodollar futures rates with forward rates. Eurodollar futures prices are obtained from the CME. Spot LIBOR quotations are obtained from Data Resources International. We use 1-, 3-, 6-, 9-, and 12-month spot rate quotations in our analysis. The futures contracts mature in quarterly cycles at fixed calendar dates while the spot rate quotations, used to compute forward rates, are available only for fixed terms. The futures rate intervals therefore do not coincide with forward rate intervals.

Two interpolation methods are used to align the intervals. With the "futures interpolation method," we fit a cubic spline to the futures rates of the four nearest maturing contracts to construct an interpolated "term structure of futures rates." From this curve, we pick interpolated futures rates for intervals that coincide with the forward rate intervals. The interpolated futures rates, $F(.25, .5)$, $F(.5, .75)$, and $F(.75, 1)$, are then compared with the implied forward rates, $f(.25, .5)$, $f(.5, .75)$, and $f(.75, 1)$. The second interpolation method, "the spot LIBOR interpolation method," applies a cubic spline to the spot LIBOR curve to obtain the entire term-structure of spot rates. Each of the three nearest maturing futures contracts, with futures rate $F(s, s + .25)$, is then compared with an implied forward rate, $f(s, s + .25)$, computed from these zero-coupon bond prices using Equation 3.1.

TABLE 3.2. Historical Differences between Eurodollar Futures and Forward Rates

Panel A

Sample Period	DIFF.25_.5		DIFF.5_.75		DIFF.75_1	
	Mean	Median	Mean	Median	Mean	Median
8204-9212	3.64	2.62	17.81	8.32	35.03	23.1
	(5.25)		(12.06)		(1.26)	
8204-8706	7.84	6.43	36.16	26.64	60.26	56.06
	(6.57)		(14.93)		(24.46)	
8707-9212	−0.35	−0.81	0.40	0.30	11.11	11.57
	(−0.53)		(0.43)		(12.71)	

Panel B

Sample Period	Contract 1		Contract 2		Contract 3	
	Mean	Median	Mean	Median	Mean	Median
8204-9212	−2.75	−2.71	11.69	6.21	26.60	15.25
	(−4.18)		(11.01)		(16.60)	
8204-8706	−2.08	−2.93	23.84	17.00	48.82	42.78
	(−1.87)		(13.77)		(19.00)	
8707-9212	−3.05	−2.63	0.18	−0.28	5.53	5.54
	(−5.28)		(0.22)		(6.87)	

Note: This table presents differences between Eurodollar futures rates and corresponding forward rates.

Panel A computes implied forward rates from the LIBOR term structure and compares it with futures rates of corresponding maturity, obtained by interpolating the futures term structure. DIFF.25_.5 is the difference between the interpolated futures rate over the period three to six months in the future and the corresponding forward rate, DIFF.5_.75 is difference between the interpolated futures rate over the period six to nine months in the future and the corresponding forward rate, and DIFF.75_.1 is difference between the interpolated futures rate over the period 9 to 12 months in the future and the corresponding forward rate.

Panel B presents futures-forward rate differences for the three nearest maturity Eurodollar futures contracts and their corresponding implied forward contracts. The column Contract 1 reports the futures-forward rate differences for the nearest maturity futures contract, Contract 2 for the next to nearest maturity contract, and Contract 3 for third nearest maturity.

The rate differences are reported in basis points. The numbers in parentheses are the t-statistics. The sample period is from 1982 to 1992.

Table 3.2 (Panel A) presents Eurodollar futures-forward yield differences. We denote DIFF.25_.5, DIFF.5_.75, and DIFF.75_1 to be the difference between the 3-month futures and forward rates when the futures interpolation method is used. For example, DIFF.25_.5 is the difference between the interpolated futures rate, $F(.25, .5)$, and the corresponding forward rate, $f(.25, .5)$, which is computed from spot LIBOR. Table 3.2 (Panel B) presents the difference for the nearest, second nearest, and third nearest maturing futures contract when the forwards are computed from interpolated spot rates.[4] The mean value of DIFF.25_.5 over the entire sample period is 3.64 basis points. The average yield difference becomes large as we increase maturity. For DIFF.5_.75, the sample mean is 17.81 basis points and for DIFF.75_1, the sample mean is 35.03. Thus, the futures rates are typically significantly larger than the corresponding forward rates.

Table 3.2 also presents the results for April 1982 to June 1987 and July 1987 to December 1992 subperiods. While the average difference between forward and future rates appears to be fairly large in the earlier sample period, it is significantly smaller in the latter period. For example, in the first subperiod, average DIFF.5_.75 and DIFF.75_1 are 36.16 and 60.26 basis points respectively, while the corresponding differences in the second subperiod are .40 and 11.11 basis points.

Figure 3.1 plots the 12-week moving average of DIFF.25_.5, DIFF.5_.75, and DIFF.75_1 along with their 95% confidence intervals. The confidence intervals, computed from moving average data, are distanced two sample standard deviations on either side of each moving average, and are computed using the 52 weeks that are nearest to the data point (which means they are centered around the data point, except for the first 26 and last 26 observations). As Figure 3.1 illustrates, the differences between the futures and forward rates for the longer maturities are remarkably large in the early years. For example, the moving averages of DIFF.5_.75 and DIFF.75_1 in Panels B and C are over 100 basis points at the beginning of the sample period and they gradually decline to close to zero over time.

The interesting aspect of Figure 3.1 is not the occasional erratic behavior of the moving averages, but their general trend. After mid-1982, both series trend downward at a rapid rate until early 1985 for DIFF.5_.75 and early 1987 for DIFF.75_1. At these points in

---

[4] Note that the maturity of the contracts associated with the spot LIBOR interpolation method varies over time and they are on average of shorter maturity than fixed maturity futures contracts used for computing DIFF.25_.5, DIFF.5_.75, and DIFF.75_1.

FIGURE 3.1. Three 13-Week Moving Average Charts

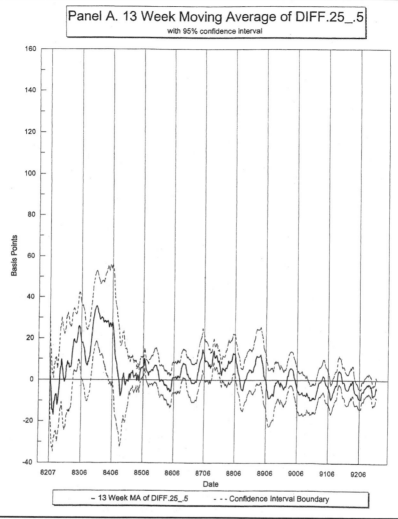

Note: This figure plots a 13-week moving average of DIFF.25_.5 (Panel A), DIFF.5_.75 (Panel B), and DIFF.75_1 (Panel C) using Thursday weekly closing data. See DIFF.25_.5 is the futures-forward rate difference for rates over the period three to six months in the future, DIFF.5_.75 is the futures-forward rate difference for rates over the period six to nine months in the future and DIFF.75_.1 is difference between interpolated futures rates over the period nine to 12 months in the future and the corresponding forward rate. Also plotted are 95% confidence intervals. The confidence intervals, computed from the moving average data, are distanced two standard deviations on either side of each moving average data point, and are computed using the 52 weeks that are nearest to the data point. The data for computing the moving average begin on April 7, 1982 and end December 30, 1992.

FIGURE 3.1. (Continued)

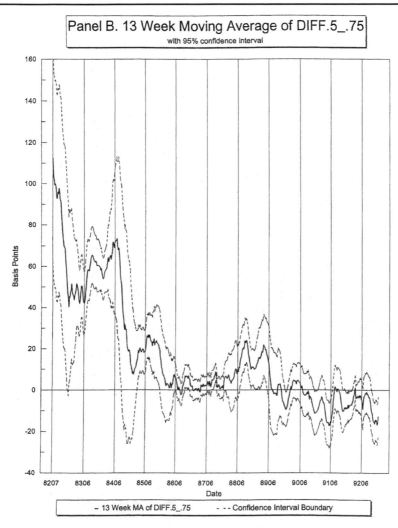

(Continued)

FIGURE 3.1. (Continued)

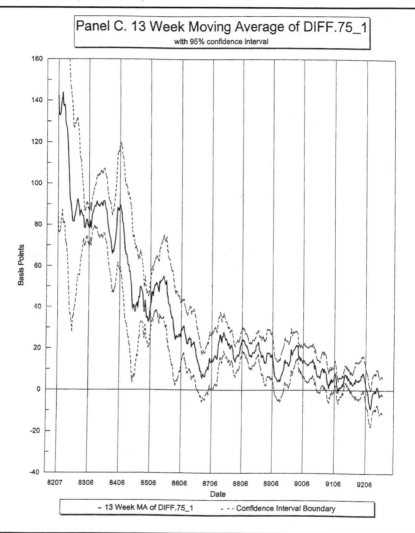

time, the yield differences are fairly close to zero and there is no noticeable trend later on.

The results in this section indicate that when Eurodollar futures contracts were first introduced, the market did not correctly understand how to price these contracts relative to the spot rates. The futures rates were too high (or futures prices were too low) relative to the spot term structure. The futures-forward rate differences were too large and not consistent with our theoretical results here. It appears that there were significant profit opportunities available to traders who recognized the relative mispricing between the spot term structure and the futures term structure at that point in time and set up arbitrage trades. But the market seems to have realized these mistakes and the differences between forward and futures rates in recent times have generally been close to zero for short maturity contracts, consistent with our theoretical results.

IMPLICATIONS FOR THE SWAP CURVE

A plain vanilla swap is a contract between two parties where one side agrees to pay a floating rate, typically equal to LIBOR, in exchange for the other party paying a predetermined fixed rate. The floating rate, LIBOR, is typically of the same maturity as the rate reset frequency. For instance, in a typical swap contract the reset frequency is six months and the floating payment is tied to 6-month LIBOR. The differences between the futures and forward rates have important implications for both determining correct swap rates and for valuing open swap positions.

The equation below gives the value of a $100 notional principal fixed for LIBOR floating swap contract to the fixed-rate payer:

$$\text{Swap value} = \sum_i (C - f_i) \times \frac{D_i}{360} \times P(T_i) \tag{3.5}$$

where C = Fixed-rate payer coupon payment

f_i = LIBOR forward rate for the ith strip

D_i = Number of days in period i

$P(T_i)$ = Zero-coupon discount factor for T_i, the time of the ith strip payment

The discount factor for the strip at T_i can be computed using a series of forward rates as in the expression below:

$$P(T_i) = \frac{1}{\left[1 + r\left(\frac{D_0}{360}\right)\right] \times \left[1 + f_1\left(\frac{D_1}{360}\right)\right] \times \dots \times \left[1 + f_i\left(\frac{D_i}{360}\right)\right]} \quad (3.6)$$

where r is spot LIBOR to the first strip payment date.

When a swap contract is opened, the terms of the fixed rate are typically set so that the value of the contract is zero. The coupon C paid by the fixed side will therefore be set so that the expression on the right-hand side of (3.5), given the forward rates, equals zero. When the first payment of the floating side is set equal to the prevailing spot rate the present value of the floating payments equals par and hence the coupon paid by the fixed side will equal the par yield on a fixed-rate bond with the same maturity as the swap.

Spot LIBOR and forward LIBOR are not widely available for maturities beyond one year. Participants in this market therefore rely on futures prices to determine swap rates when these contracts are opened and for valuing open swap positions. Naive use of futures rates in the place of forward rates in Equations (3.5) and (3.6) to determine swap value, however, could generate significant valuation errors. Given the results derived earlier, we can compute the error that will arise if one mistakenly ignores the differences between futures and forward rates.

Table 3.3 presents the error in the swap curve if one were to use futures rates in place of forward rates in Equation (3.5) to determine the swap rate C by setting the swap value to zero. When $\sigma = .06$, the average volatility over the last 15 years, the error for a one-year swap is only .39 basis points. For very short maturity swaps, therefore, mistaken use of futures rates in place of forward rates does not lead to very costly errors. On the other hand, for a 10-year swap the swap rate will be set at 9.86 basis points above the correct swap rate. This could be quite an expensive error. For example, for a 10-year swap contract with $100 million notional principal, the present value of the 9.86 basis point difference in the fixed rate payment is about $680,000. The error will be much larger in a high volatility environment. When $\sigma = .08$, for example, the error in the swap rate is 16.77 basis points.

TABLE 3.3. Theoretical Errors in Swap Rates Computed with Futures Rates in Place of Forward Rates

Swap Maturity (Years)	Swap Rate Error (Basis Points)		
	σ = .04	σ = .06	σ = .08
1	0.17	0.39	0.70
2	0.57	1.29	2.28
3	1.08	2.43	4.30
4	1.64	3.68	6.52
5	2.20	4.93	8.71
7	3.25	7.25	12.73
10	4.44	9.86	17.21

Note: This table presents the magnitude of errors in computed swap rates when differences between Eurodollar futures and forward rates are ignored and futures rates are used in place of forward rates. The swap rate errors are presented for different values of the volatility parameter (σ) in the CIR model of the term structure of interest rates.

TABLE 3.4. Swap Rates Quotes and Errors in Swap Rates Computed with Unadjusted Futures Rates in Place of Forward Rates

Maturity	Swap Rate Quote (%)	Swap Rates Computed with Future Rates (%)	Error (Basis Points)
1	5.81	5.80	−1
2	5.84	5.85	1
3	5.88	5.91	3
4	5.91	5.95	4
5	5.93	5.99	6
7	5.99	6.08	9
10	6.06	6.20	14

Note: This table presents the actual swap rate quotes on March 19, 1998 and the swap rates computed using futures settlement prices on that date, ignoring differences between Eurodollar futures and forward rates.

Does the market recognize the difference between futures and forward rates in setting swap rates? To address this question, we examine the futures rates and swap rates on March 19, 1998. The futures rate on this date ranged from 5.64% to the nearest maturity contract to 6.63% for the longest maturity contract. Table 3.4 presents the swap rates on this date. Table 3.4 also presents the swap rates calculated from (3.5) using suitably interpolated futures rates in place of forward rates. The difference between the actual swap rate and that calculated from futures prices is close to zero for a one-year swap. For 10-year swaps the difference is 14 basis points which is in the range of what we would expect from Table 3.3 at historical volatility levels. The market now, therefore, does seem to recognize the differences between futures and forward rates in pricing swaps.

CONCLUSION

This chapter presents an analytic formula for computing Eurodollar futures prices. We then compare forward rates with futures rates and show that for short maturity contracts these two rates will be nearly identical. For contracts with longer maturities, however, the differences between futures and forward rates are quite significant and at historical levels of interest rate volatility the difference will be around 30 basis points for 10-year futures contracts.

Our empirical analysis shows that the market did not recognize the correct relation between futures prices and the spot term structure until the 1990s. The futures rates in recent times are close to the forward rates for short maturity contracts consistent with our theoretical results.

The swap industry uses information in futures prices to determine the swap curve. Pricing services also use futures prices to compute values of open swap positions. Naive use of futures rates in place of forward rates for valuation will significantly overvalue swap positions for fixed-rate payers, particularly for long-term swap contracts. We show that such pricing errors will be about $680,000 for a 10-year $100 million notional principal swap contract. Simple adjustments to futures rates based on the results here will enable the user to determine correct forward rates and avoid potentially costly errors.

REFERENCES AND BIBLIOGRAPHY

Cox, J., J. Ingersoll, and S. Ross. (1981). "The Relation between Forward Prices and Futures Prices," *Journal of Financial Economics, 9,* 321–346.

Cox, J., J. Ingersoll, and S. Ross. (1985). "A Theory of the Term Structure of Interest Rates," *Econometrica, 53,* 385–407.

French, K. (1983). "A Comparison of Futures and Forward Prices," *Journal of Financial Economics, 12,* 311–342.

Grinblatt, M. (1995). "An Analytic Solution for Interest Rate Swap Spreads," working paper, University of California at Los Angeles.

Grinblatt, M. and N. Jegadeesh. (1996). "The Relative Pricing of Eurodollar Futures and Forward Contracts," *Journal of Finance, 51,* 1499–1522.

Grinblatt, M. and S. Titman. (1998). *Financial Markets and Corporate Strategy,* Burr Ridge, IL: Irwin/McGraw-Hill.

Jegadeesh, N. (1996). "An Empirical Analysis of Pricing of Interest Rate Caps," working paper, University of Illinois at Urbana-Champaign.

Park, H.Y. and A. Chen. (1985). "Differences between Futures and Forward Prices: A Further Investigation of the Marking-to-Market Effect," *Journal of Futures Markets, 5,* 77–88.

Vasicek, O. (1977). "An Equilibrium Characterization of the Term Structure," *Journal of Financial Economics, 5,* 177–188.

PART II

Term Structure Modeling

The second part of this book is about modeling the evolution of interest rate movements. But before providing an overview of model building and model selection, this introduction will discuss the purposes and uses of term structure models.

Imagine a trader who makes markets in a particular Treasury bond. If he keeps his position flat, he doesn't need quantitative tools at all. If he decides, for some reason, to go long or short a particular bond and wants to quantify the return characteristics of his position, he would need, at the very least, to estimate the bond's expected return and the volatility of that return. Assuming his expected return estimate comes from his trading experience, he might estimate the return volatility from historical data series or he might estimate the volatility of the bond's yield and multiply by the bond's duration. In any case, he would not need a term structure model in the sense that he wouldn't need to think about what his expected return estimate, his volatility estimate, or the assumptions implicit in the duration calculation imply about the return characteristics of any other bond or fixed-income security.

Now imagine that this trader makes markets in two different Treasury bonds. If he so chooses, the trader could treat his activities in each bond as a separate business. In that case, he is essentially in the same position as described in the previous paragraph and, once again, does not need a term structure model. However, this decision would not, in most cases, be optimal. First, in situations where the trader is called upon to sell one bond and purchase the other, it would be cheaper, with respect to transaction costs, to view that position as at least partially hedged rather than as one that requires fully offsetting purchases and sales in each bond issue. Second, if the trader ever has a view about the relative value of the two bond issues, due, for example, to temporary supply and demand imbalances, he would particularly wish to purchase the relatively cheap bond and sell the relatively dear bond in proportions that protect him from any changes in the level of rates. For these two reasons, then, the trader would like to be able to integrate his books in these two bond issues.

The difficulty with integrating the two books is that risk and expected return estimation becomes more complicated. The most common approach to being "flat" in this simple situation would be to adjust the position until the net DV01 were 0. But that procedure, in effect, makes use of a term structure model. The underlying assumption there is that all yields move up and down in parallel; if net DV01 were 0 but the yield of one bond changed by more or less than the yield of the other bond, there would be profits or losses. There are more sophisticated term structure models than that associated with DV01, but, if a trader wants an integrated book of two or more distinct securities, there is no way around the need to make assumptions about the relative changes in yields across the term structure. Similarly, if a trader wanted to estimate the expected return of an integrated book, he would have to make assumptions about relative returns across the term structure.

In choosing among term structure models, one must choose the number of factors assumed to generate yield curve movements. One-factor models imply that one random quantity is sufficient to determine changes in yields of all maturities. Two-factor models imply that two random quantities are sufficient to determine changes in yields of all maturities, and so on. A number of considerations enter into choosing how many factors to employ in a term structure model. First, empirical analysis repeatedly reveals that three factors account for nearly all of the volatility of yield changes across the term structure. These factors are loosely described as a parallel shift factor, a slope factor, and a curvature factor. Parallel shifts tend to explain well over 90% of yield changes while slope changes explain most of the remaining yield changes. Second, the greater the number of factors, the greater the complexity of the resulting model. This is an important consideration because increasing complexity implies increasing difficulty in understanding predictions of the model, increasing costs of implementing the model, increasing computer time to run the model, and increasing transaction costs in hedging using the model. Third, valuation and hedging of certain securities are more sensitive to the number of factors than other securities.

Consider, for example, the case of an asset manager who must choose to purchase some subset of long-term, high quality bonds that may contain embedded call provisions. Since the slope and curvature factors tend to impact the shorter end of the curve, longer term yields are described almost exclusively by parallel shifts. Furthermore, typical embedded call options on long-term, high quality bonds are not exercisable for many years. Hence, for this application, a one-factor model should suffice.

Now consider an arbitrage trader who attempts to profit by buying bonds of certain maturities and shorting bonds of different maturities. Say, for example, that the trader feels that 5-year bonds are too expensive relative to 2- and 10-year bonds, but doesn't have an opinion about any other yield curve move or reshaping. In this context, the trader would want to use at least a two-factor model so as to immunize his position against most yield curve changes. In other words, he doesn't want his position to change value if all yields move up or down by 5 basis points nor if the 2-, 5-, and 10-year yields move together in a typical slope change. He only wants to profit (or lose) if the 5-year yield rises (or falls) an unusual amount relative to changes in the 2- and 10-year yields.

After settling on the number of factors to be included, decisions about the structure of the model have to be made. Should the factors be mean reverting? Should some factors exhibit jumps? How should the volatility of rates be related to the model's factors? The chapters in Part II will describe the specific consequences of these and other model choices. This introduction will simply emphasize that, as in the case of choosing the number of factors, the particular application under question must be considered along with the statistical facts about interest rates when choosing a model's structure.

Consider, for example, the choice of whether or not to incorporate jumps into a term structure model. Ignoring the possibility of jumps, a standard assumption is that the short-term interest rate follows a diffusion so that the standard deviation of changes in the rate over a time interval Δt is equal to $\sigma\sqrt{\Delta t}$ for some quantity σ. If the change in the short rate over that time period were $10\sigma\sqrt{\Delta t}$, that is, a move of 10 standard deviations, it would be wiser to conclude that the short rate "jumped" than to accept the fact that a 10 standard deviation event occurred. For values of σ that adequately describe changes in interest rates most of the time, these jump events do seem to occur. But this does not necessarily mean that jumps should be incorporated into every model. The treasury trader making markets in several bond issues will find that suitably calibrated models with and without jumps will give similar relative values. Furthermore, since many bonds exhibit relatively low convexities, hedge ratios from a model without jumps may prove adequate in the presence of jumps. On the other hand, option prices are quite sensitive to the presence of jumps due to the effect of jumps on the skewness and kurtosis of the distribution of interest rates. Also, because option prices tend to have relatively large convexities, hedge ratios derived from a model without jumps may not be adequate when jumps do occur.

After choosing the structure of a model, one must quantify all the effects captured in the model by selecting a set of parameters. These parameters express views about the volatility of rates, the frequency at which jumps occur, the speed at which rates revert to their long-run values, and so on. There are three ways to go about parameter selection: personal views, historical values, and implied market values. If, for example, one needed a parameter to describe the volatility of the short-term interest rate, one could poll traders about what they thought this volatility would be over the next few years. The advantages of this approach are that it is forward-looking and that the rule for changing parameters is simple: change whenever the traders' best estimate changes. Following the historical approach, one could collect data on the short-term rate, calculate its volatility over the past few years, and assume that future volatility will be close to past volatility. There are several disadvantages to this approach. First, the assumption that the future will resemble the past cannot be taken for granted. Second, there is a surprising amount of arbitrariness in the approach. In the volatility example, the selection of a particular rate to serve as the short-term rate and the selection of a time horizon over which to compute the volatility can substantially affect the final result. Finally, in the implied approach, one could find the volatility parameter such that the model generates the market price of some security that traders believe is fairly priced. If the model structure is close to the truth, that is, the assumed interest rate process is close to the laws governing the actual interest rate process, then the implied approach is equivalent to saying that the implied volatility is one's best guess about future volatility. If the model structure is not close to the truth, however, the implied approach will have to bias parameter estimates in order to offset that model's weaknesses. Unfortunately, the combination of a badly specified model and biased parameters on hedge ratios and on the pricing of securities not used in calibration are, to say the least, unpredictable.

The best procedure is to use a combination of the three approaches. For example, an historical analysis might be the starting point for discussion about the past and about how traders expect the future to be similar or different. If the parameters resulting from these discussions are not very far from implied quantities, the process might be viewed as complete. If, however, they are very far from implied quantities, a discussion about the reasons for these disparities would be warranted.

Many market participants rely on the implied approach exclusively in the belief that by doing so they are not expressing an opinion, that is, that they are objectively adopting the market's beliefs. This viewpoint is naive in the following three ways.

First, it is not always desirable for a model to fit all market prices. Consider the extreme example of two U.S. Treasury zero-coupon bonds, one derived from the interest payments of a treasury issue and one from the principal payments. These two securities provide identical cash flows (both before and after taxes) and yet, for liquidity reasons, sell at different prices. Since term structure models do not yet take account of liquidity, no term structure model can possibly match the market prices of both these securities. For a less extreme case, consider the entire treasury curve. Because some bonds are much more liquid than others it would be a mistake to force the model to match all bond prices. Doing so would distort the interest rate process assumed in the model and, consequently, distort hedge ratios. In less liquid markets, prices of individual securities are often pushed away from fair values due to the presence of a particularly large market participant who, for whatever reason, needs to do a trade. In these situations as well, matching all market prices is not desirable.

Second, even when desirable, it may not be possible, with a reasonable model, to match a given set of market prices. For example, there have been times when many market participants believed that reasonable models could not match both cap and swaption prices. Moving to an unreasonable model, that is, one whose assumptions are deemed unacceptable, is hardly an option. Therefore, one can take the schizophrenic approach of using one model for caps and another for swaptions or one can conclude that one set of securities is rich or cheap relative to the other.

Other examples of how implied approaches may not be reasonable arise in the context of models in which the drift or volatility of the short rate is assumed to follow some deterministic path such that the model matches the market's term structure of rates or term structure of volatility, respectively. Because market prices contain some noise or unexplained factors, and because models are not perfectly specified, these deterministic paths can look quite odd. One is then forced to decide whether to proceed on the assumption of these unreasonable paths, whether to assume that some market prices are rich or cheap relative to others, or whether to develop a richer model.

Third, while one might try to argue that calibrating to market prices is an objective or neutral approach, the choice of a term structure model is certainly not. In other words, one cannot choose to use a 1-factor, mean reverting model of the short-term rate calibrated to a subset of market prices and claim to have no view: a 1-factor model without mean reversion or a multifactor model of any sort would give different hedge ratios and different relative values for securities not used in the calibration, In other words, calibrating to the market does not rescue a trader from the necessity of choosing the best term structure model for the occasion.

Attention now turns to the term structure models themselves. Chapter 4 surveys the landscape of existing term structure models. Chapter 5 presents an example of how to construct a new model, argues for and develops and approach in which the long-run value of the short rate is itself stochastic. Chapter 6 shows how to construct models that incorporate jumps and discusses the advantages of their inclusion.

4

Discrete-Time Models of Bond Pricing

David Backus, Silverio Foresi, and *Chris Telmer*

A newcomer to the theory of bond pricing would be struck by the enormous variety of models in use and by the variety of methods used to study them. We provide a selective review and synthesis of this diverse body of work, with the goal of clarifying differences in models and approaches. Our focus is less on theory for theory's sake and more on the properties of bond yields implied by a model's structure and parameter values. We think of this as engineering, in contrast to the physics of more theoretical papers. We are guided in this effort by four principles:

1. *Common Theoretical Language.* In the literature on bond pricing, models are variously described as arbitrage-free, equilibrium, and so on. They are developed using state prices, risk-neutral probabilities, or pricing kernels. In fact, all of these approaches share a common intellectual foundation and can be expressed in a common way. We express each in terms of a pricing kernel, but explain differences in language and approach along the way.

2. *Discrete Time.* Although occasionally less elegant than continuous time, discrete time makes fewer technical demands on users. As a result, we can focus our attention on the properties of a model rather than the technical issues raised by the method used to apply it.

3. *Continuous State Variables.* We think it's important to let interest rates assume a continuous range of real values, and not the discrete set of possibilities familiar to users of binomial models. We regard this combination of discrete time and continuous states as a convenient middle ground between the stochastic calculus of high theory and the binomial models of classroom fame.

4. *Parameter Values as Important as Models.* Duffie (1992, pp. xiii–xiv) writes: "The decade spanning roughly 1969–1979 seems like a golden age of dynamic asset pricing theory. . . . The decade or so since 1979 has, with relatively minor exceptions, been a mopping-up operation." While this may be true of theory, we think finance professionals continue to make significant progress in understanding the ability of models to explain the prices we observe in markets. In practice, the choice of parameters is critical to a model's performance and deserves as serious study as the model itself. In this respect, we think we can add something to theoretical books like Duffie's, and thus help to bridge the gap between theorists and practitioners.

With these principles in mind, we review the basic theory of asset pricing and its application to bonds. We express various models and approaches in a common theoretical framework in which time is discrete and state variables are (for the most part) continuous. The emphasis is on the use of these models by practitioners: which model to use, how to solve it, and how to choose its parameter values. With one exception, we do not explore the application of these models to the pricing of derivatives. Although this is clearly the major use of fixed-income models, both the theory and related data issues would make this a much longer chapter. Nevertheless, the foundations laid here are a necessary first step in that direction.

After summarizing the salient features of U.S. bond yields, we review the theory underlying the modern approach to asset pricing. We then describe the popular Vasicek and Cox-Ingersoll-Ross models and explain how their parameters might be chosen to approximate some of the observed properties of bond yields. Discrepancies between these models and observed bond yields motivate more complex models. Next, we discuss arbitrage-free models, in which time-dependent parameters are introduced to allow models to reproduce current market conditions, including the current yield or forward rate curve. Examples include a Ho-and-Lee-inspired version of the Vasicek model, which can be calibrated to the current yield or forward rate curve, and a linear application of the approach of Heath, Jarrow, and Morton. We then consider the popular binomial framework and derive its implicit pricing kernel. We describe Das's jump model, which allows innovations to interest rates to follow non-Gaussian distributions. The next section is devoted to multifactor affine models, including two-factor versions of Vasicek and Cox-Ingersoll-Ross, the Longstaff-Schwartz model, and models with stochastic volatility and central tendency factors. We end with a short discussion of options on zeros, emphasizing the term structure of volatility in log-normal environments in which the Black-Scholes formula holds exactly.

NOTATION AND EVIDENCE

The obvious starting point for any modeling exercise is a description of what the models are intended to explain. The models we examine are designed to explain prices of fixed-income securities of all kinds. In principle, this includes not only the prices of bonds, but of interest-rate derivatives: swaps and swaptions, interest rate futures, caps and floors, and the like. We limit ourselves, however, to U.S. Treasury bonds, whose properties are described next.

We summarize bond prices in terms of yields. One of the (small) issues that arises when we do this in discrete time is that the time interval of the model need not correspond to the time interval over which yields are reported. By convention, we report yields and other interest rates as annual percentages. Our modeling time interval, however, is one month: that is, from here on we take one period to be one month. As a result, we must at times include translation factors of 12 or 1200, converting monthly yields to annual yields or annual percentages, respectively.

With this detail out of the way, we denote the continuously-compounded *yield* or *spot rate* on an n-period discount bond at date t by y_t^n, defined by

$$y_t^n = -n^{-1} \log b_t^n \tag{4.1}$$

where b_t^n is the dollar *price* at date t of a claim to one dollar at $t + n$. One-period *forward rates* are defined by

$$f_t^n = \log\left(\frac{b_t^n}{b_t^{n+1}}\right) \tag{4.2}$$

so that yields are averages of forward rates:

$$y_t^n = n^{-1} \sum_{i=0}^{n-1} f_t^i \tag{4.3}$$

The *short rate* is $r_t = y_t^1 = f_t^0$.

In practice, yields and forward rates are estimated rather than observed. From prices of bonds for a variety of maturities, the *discount function* b_t^n (viewed as a function of n at each date t) is interpolated between missing maturities n and smoothed to reduce the impact of noise (nonsynchronous price quotes, bid/ask spreads, and so on). We use data constructed by McCulloch and Kwon (1993) from quoted prices of U.S. Treasury securities.

The properties of U.S. Treasury yields between January 1952 and February 1991 are summarized in Tables 4.1 and 4.2. We will return to these tables later, when we use them to choose values for model parameters, but for now it's worth noting their basic features. One is the shape of the average yield curve: Average yields rise with maturity between one month and 10 years, but the rate of increase falls with maturity. This concave shape is familiar to observers of bond markets, but masks a great deal of variety in the shape of the yield curve at specific times. Another feature is persistence: Autocorrelations of yields are well above 0.9 (monthly) for all maturities. Short-long spreads exhibit substantially less persistence, suggesting that some of the persistence in yields stems from something that is common to both short and long rates. A third feature is volatility, which

TABLE 4.1. Properties of U.S. Government Bond Yields

Maturity	Mean	St. Dev.	Skewness	Kurtosis	Auto
1 month	5.314	3.064	0.886	0.789	0.976
3 months	5.640	3.143	0.858	0.691	0.981
6 months	5.884	3.178	0.809	0.574	0.982
9 months	6.003	3.182	0.776	0.480	0.982
12 months	6.079	3.168	0.730	0.315	0.983
24 months	6.272	3.124	0.660	0.086	0.986
36 months	6.386	3.087	0.621	−0.066	0.988
48 months	6.467	3.069	0.612	−0.125	0.989
60 months	6.531	3.056	0.599	−0.200	0.990
84 months	6.624	3.043	0.570	−0.349	0.991
120 months	6.683	3.013	0.532	−0.477	0.992

Note: The data are monthly estimates of annualized continuously-compounded zero-coupon U.S. government bond yields computed by McCulloch and Kwon (1993), January 1952 to February 1991 (470 observations). Mean is the sample mean, St. Dev. the sample standard deviation, Skewness an estimate of the skewness measure γ_1, Kurtosis an estimate of the (excess) kurtosis measure γ_2, and Auto an estimate of the first autocorrelation. The skewness and kurtosis measures are defined, specifically, in terms of central moments μ_j: $\gamma_1 = \mu_3 / \mu_2^{3/2}$ and $\gamma_2 = \mu_4 / \mu_2^2 - 3$. Both are zero for normal random variables. Our estimates replace population moments with sample moments.

is apparent in all three variables: yields, spreads, and monthly changes in yields. Note that the maturity patterns of these variables differ substantially. A final feature is kurtosis: both yield spreads and yield changes exhibit substantial excess kurtosis, particularly at short maturities.

ARBITRAGE AND PRICING KERNELS

Although the form varies, modern asset pricing theory is based on a single theoretical result: In any arbitrage-free environment, there exists a positive random variable m that satisfies

$$1 = E_t(m_{t+1}R_{t+1}) \qquad (4.4)$$

TABLE 4.2. Properties of Yield Spreads and Monthly Changes in Yields

Maturity	Mean	St. Dev.	Skewness	Kurtosis	Auto
		(A) Spreads over Short Rate			
3 months	0.326	0.303	2.036	7.079	0.353
6 months	0.570	0.437	1.457	5.350	0.556
9 months	0.689	0.521	1.362	5.032	0.630
12 months	0.765	0.593	1.271	4.964	0.686
24 months	0.959	0.796	0.531	2.606	0.793
36 months	1.073	0.927	0.275	1.988	0.831
48 months	1.154	1.011	0.098	1.554	0.851
60 months	1.217	1.078	0.032	1.333	0.864
84 months	1.305	1.178	−0.001	1.092	0.879
120 months	1.369	1.237	−0.087	0.815	0.885
		(B) Monthly Changes in Yields			
1 month	0.008	0.644	−1.172	10.224	0.023
3 months	0.009	0.575	−1.751	14.008	0.110
6 months	0.009	0.570	−1.619	15.618	0.150
9 months	0.009	0.571	−1.240	14.680	0.148
12 months	0.010	0.547	−0.783	12.824	0.152
24 months	0.011	0.487	−0.398	11.474	0.132
36 months	0.011	0.441	−0.032	8.128	0.100
48 months	0.011	0.409	0.052	6.359	0.087
60 months	0.011	0.382	0.077	5.142	0.077
84 months	0.012	0.340	0.040	3.548	0.069
120 months	0.012	0.309	−0.205	3.288	0.068

See Table 4.1 for notes.

for (one-period) returns R on all traded assets at all dates t. We refer to m as a *pricing kernel*, since prices of assets grow from it. A model consists, then, of a description of m. The same content is sometimes expressed in terms of *state prices* or *risk-neutral probabilities*, which we discuss later.

One of the many nice things about the pricing relation (4.4) is that it applies to everything: Once we have a model that values bonds, we can (in principle) use it to value bond-related derivatives of all kinds. The catch is the qualifier, "in principle." The theory works fine; the challenge in practice is to approximate the m that theory says must exist.

Bond pricing is an elegant, if straightforward, application of (4.4). If an arbitrary claim to next-period cash flows c_{t+1} costs p_t now, then the return is $R_{t+1} = c_{t+1}/p_t$ and (4.4) implies

$$p_t = E_t(m_{t+1}c_{t+1}) \tag{4.5}$$

This takes a particularly simple and useful form with bonds. The one-period return on an $n+1$-period bond is $R_{t+1} = b_{t+1}^n / b_t^{n+1}$, so the prices satisfy

$$b_t^{n+1} = E_t(m_{t+1}b_{t+1}^n) \tag{4.6}$$

From this we can compute bond prices recursively, starting with the initial condition $b_t^0 = 1$ (a dollar today costs one dollar).

ONE-FACTOR MODELS

Two of the most popular bond pricing models are those constructed by Vasicek (1977) and Cox, Ingersoll, and Ross (1985). We describe both in this section and explain how their parameter values might be chosen to correspond to properties of bond yields. Each of these models has a single factor, by which we mean that prices depend on a single state variable z (say), typically associated with the short rate r. The models are similar, too, in having four parameters: Three governing the dynamic behavior of the state variable and one controlling the market's valuation of risk. With these ingredients, theory then tells us how long rates are connected to the short rate.

Vasicek

The archetype of bond pricing models is Vasicek (1977). In discrete time, the single state variable z follows a first-order autoregression (meaning we regress z on its own lag):

$$z_{t+1} = \varphi z_t + (1-\varphi)\theta + \sigma\varepsilon_{t+1}$$
$$= z_t + (1-\varphi)(\theta - z_t) + \sigma\varepsilon_{t+1} \tag{4.7}$$

with $\{\varepsilon_{t+1}\}$ distributed normally and independently with mean zero and variance one. The mean of z is θ. The conditional variance is σ^2 and the unconditional variance $\sigma^2/(1 - \varphi^2)$, formulas that should be familiar to those acquainted with linear time series methods (for example, Harvey, 1993). The parameter φ controls mean reversion: If $\varphi = 1$, z is a random walk and shows no tendency to return to any specific value—hence the term *random walk*. But if $0 < \varphi < 1$, z is expected to return to its mean value of θ at rate $1 - \varphi$, as in the second line of Equation (4.7). We complete the model with the pricing kernel m, which satisfies

$$-\log m_{t+1} = \delta + z_t + \lambda\varepsilon_{t+1} \tag{4.8}$$

We refer to λ as the *price of risk*, since it determines the covariance between shocks to m and z, and thus the risk characteristics of bonds and related assets. We set $\delta = \lambda^2/2$ for reasons that will be apparent momentarily.

We compute bond prices recursively using the theory outlined earlier. The pricing relation (4.6) and initial condition $b_t^0 = 1$ tell us that the price of a one-period bond is the conditional mean of the pricing kernel: $b_t^1 = E_t m_{t+1}$. Since the kernel is conditionally log-normal, we need the following property of log-normal random variables: If $\log x$ is normal with mean μ and variance σ^2, then $\log E(x) = \mu + \sigma^2/2$. From Equation (4.8) we see that $\log m_{t+1}$ has conditional mean $-(\delta + z_t)$ and conditional variance λ^2, so the one-period bond price satisfies

$$\log b_t^1 = \frac{-\delta - z_t + \lambda^2}{2}$$
$$= -z_t$$

The short rate is therefore

$$r_t = -\log b_t^1$$
$$= z_t$$

as claimed earlier. Since z is the short rate, we can base the value of the parameters of (4.7) on the properties of the short rate, such as those reported in Table 4.1.

Prices of long bonds follow by induction. Let us guess that the price of an n-period bond can be expressed

$$-\log b_t^n = A_n + B_n z_t \qquad (4.9)$$

for some choice of coefficients $\{A_n, B_n\}$. Since $b_t^0 = 1$ we know $A_0 = B_0 = 0$, so we can certainly start this process up. The expression for a one-period bond implies $A_1 = 0$ and $B_1 = 1$. Given the coefficients for maturity n, we use (4.6) to evaluate the price of an $n + 1$-period bond. The right side involves

$$\log m_{t+1} + \log b_{t+1}^n = -\delta - z_t - \lambda \varepsilon_{t+1} - A_n - B_n z_{t+1}$$
$$= -[A_n + \delta + B_n(1-\varphi)\theta] - (1 + B_n\varphi)z_t - (\lambda + B_n\sigma)\varepsilon_{t+1}$$

which has conditional moments

$$E_t(\log m_{t+1} + \log b_{t+1}^n) = -[A_n + \delta + B_n(1-\varphi)\theta] - (1 + B_n\varphi)z_t$$

and

$$Var_t(\log m_{t+1} + \log b_t^n) = (\lambda + B_n\sigma)^2$$

The implied bond price is therefore

$$-\log b_t^{n+1} = \frac{A_n + \delta + B_n(1-\varphi)\theta - (\lambda + B_n\sigma)^2}{2 + (1 + B_n\varphi)z_t}$$

Lining up coefficients with (4.9) gives us the recursions

$$A_{n+1} = \frac{A_n + \delta + B_n(1-\varphi)\theta - (\lambda + B_n\sigma)^2}{2} \qquad (4.10)$$

$$B_{n+1} = 1 + B_n\varphi \qquad (4.11)$$

These equations look complicated, but given values for $(\theta, \varphi, \sigma, \lambda)$, we can easily evaluate them on a spreadsheet. They provide a closed-form solution to the model, in the sense of being computable with a finite number of elementary operations.

Forward rates in this model take a particularly simple form, which we note for future reference:

$$f_t^n = (1 - \varphi^n)\theta + \frac{1}{2}\left[\lambda^2 - \left(\lambda + \frac{1 - \varphi^n}{1 - \varphi}\sigma\right)^2\right] + \varphi^n z_t \tag{4.12}$$

Equation 4.12 illustrates the impact of the short rate on long forwards (the impact declines with n) and the form of the risk premium (ugly, but governed by λ). This expression gives us insight into the relation between forward rates and expected future short rates. If $\lambda = \sigma = 0, f_t^n = E_t r_{t+n}$, a common version of the expectations hypothesis. When $\lambda = 0$ and $\sigma \neq 0$, the nonlinearity of the pricing relation results in a downward sloping average forward rate curve (often referred to as the effects of "Jensen's inequality"). If λ is sufficiently positive, this effect is reversed and average forward rates (hence yields) increase with maturity.

The recursions tell us how to compute bond prices given values for the parameters. In practice, however, we are often interested in the reverse question: What parameter values are indicated by observed bond prices? We choose parameters to approximate some of the salient features of bond yields reported in Table 4.1. θ is the unconditional mean of the short rate, so we set it equal to the sample mean of the one-month yield in Table 4.1:

$$\theta = \frac{5.314}{1200} = 0.004428$$

(Dividing by 1200 converts an annual percentage rate to a monthly rate.) The mean reversion parameter φ is the first autocorrelation of the short rate. In Table 4.1, the autocorrelation of y^1 is 0.976, so we set φ equal to this value. The volatility parameter σ is the standard deviation of innovations to the short rate. We choose it to equate the unconditional variance of the short rate equal to its value in the data:

$$\frac{\sigma^2}{1-\varphi^2} = \left(\frac{3.064}{1200}\right)^2$$

With $\varphi = 0.976$, the implied value is $\sigma = 0.0005560$. Thus the values of $(\theta, \sigma, \varphi)$ are chosen to match the mean, standard deviation, and autocorrelation of the short rate.

We choose the final parameter, the price of risk λ, to approximate the slope of the yield curve. A little experimentation tells us that λ governs the average slope of the yield curve, with negative values required to reproduce the upward slope we see in the data. Mean bond yields in the model are

$$E(y^n) = n^{-1}(A_n + B_n\theta) \tag{4.13}$$

The value $\lambda = -0.0824$ reproduces the mean 10-year bond yield, as we see in Figure 4.1. With more negative values the mean yield curve is steeper, and with less negative (or positive) values the yield curve is flatter (or downward sloping).

We see in Figure 4.1 that the model generates a mean yield curve with much less curvature than we see in the data. The problem is φ: The time series of the short rate indicates a value of φ close to one, but we need a smaller value to generate the required concavity of the yield curve. There is no choice of this parameter (or the others) that does both. We will see shortly that the Cox-Ingersoll-Ross model suffers from the same deficiency.

Cox-Ingersoll-Ross

The Cox-Ingersoll-Ross (CIR) model has a similar structure. The difference lies in the behavior of the state variable z: In the Vasicek model, the conditional variance is constant, while in CIR it varies with the state. Our version follows Sun (1992, Eq. 6): z obeys the "square root process"

$$z_{t+1} = (1-\varphi)\theta + \varphi z_t + \sigma z_t^{1/2}\varepsilon_{t+1} \tag{4.14}$$

FIGURE 4.1. Mean Yields in the Vasicek Model

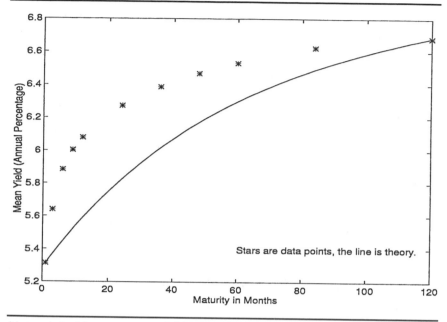

Note: Asterisks are mean yields on U.S. treasury securities, as reported in Table 4.1. The line represents mean yields in the Vasicek model using parameter values reported in the text.

with $0 < \varphi < 1$, $\theta > 0$, and $\{\varepsilon_t\}$ is distributed normally and independently with mean zero and variance one. Despite the unusual form of the innovation, (4.14) is a first-order autoregression. The unconditional mean of z is θ. (To show this, it's useful to compute the conditional expectation first, then the unconditional expectation.) The first autocorrelation is φ and higher-order autocorrelations are powers of φ. The conditional variance is

$$Var_t(z_{t+1}) = z_t \sigma^2$$

which has a mean of $\theta \sigma^2$. The unconditional variance is $Var(z) = \theta \sigma^2 / (1 - \varphi^2)$.

The most interesting feature of (4.14) is that it guarantees non-negative z if the time interval is small: With the square-root process the conditional variance gets smaller as z approaches zero, which reduces the chance of getting a negative value. If ε is assumed to be normally distributed, then there is still a positive probability that z_{t+1} is negative, but the probability falls to zero as the time interval shrinks. In continuous time, z is strictly positive under the stated conditions. This is a useful feature in a bond pricing model, since the existence of currency places a lower bound of zero on nominal interest rates.

The pricing kernel for a discrete time version of CIR is

$$-\log m_{t+1} = \left(\frac{1+\lambda^2}{2}\right)z_t + \lambda z_t^{1/2}\varepsilon_{t+1} \tag{4.15}$$

so again the kernel is conditionally log-normal. We will see shortly that the coefficient of z is a fortuitous choice, intended to make z the short rate.

Bond pricing in this setting is similar to Vasicek: We apply the pricing relation (4.6) to the pricing kernel (4.15) and compute bond prices recursively. The key to making this work is that both the conditional mean and the conditional variance are linear functions of z. As a result, bond prices are log-linear functions of z as in Equation (4.9). Using the same methods we applied to the Vasicek model, we find that the coefficients of the log-linear bond price formulas satisfy the recursions,

$$A_{n+1} = A_n + B_n(1-\varphi)\theta$$

$$B_{n+1} = \frac{1+\lambda^2}{2} + B_n\varphi - \frac{(\lambda + B_n\sigma)^2}{2}$$

starting with $A_0 = B_0 = 0$. Since $A_1 = 0$ and $B_1 = 1$, z is the short rate.

We choose values for parameters much as we did for the Vasicek model. We set the autocorrelation parameter φ equal to the autocorrelation of the short rate: $\varphi = 0.976$. We set θ equal to the mean short rate, which again implies $\theta = 0.004428$. We choose σ to reproduce the variance of the short rate:

$$\frac{\theta\sigma^2}{1-\varphi^2} = \left(\frac{3.064}{1200}\right)^2$$

which implies $\sigma = 0.008356$. Average yields follow (4.13). The average 10-year bond yield implies $\lambda = -1.07$. The results of this exercise are pictured in Figure 4.2, which is virtually identical to Figure 4.1.

Technical Issues

With the understanding that many readers may choose to skip this section, we review a number of technical issues.

1. *Unit Roots.* Some have suggested that the short rate process should have a unit root: that φ should be one. The evidence from short rates isn't wildly at odds with this idea, perhaps not at odds at all given the low power of unit root tests against nearby alternatives. What is left out, however, is the implication of a unit root for the spread between long and short rates: The mean spread gets increasingly negative at

FIGURE 4.2. Mean Yields in the Cox-Ingersoll-Ross Model

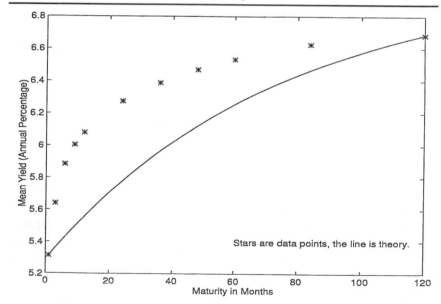

Note: Asterisks are mean yields on U.S. treasury securities, as reported in Table 4.1. The line represents mean yields in the Cox-Ingersoll-Ross model using parameter values reported in the text.

long enough maturities, approaching minus infinity in the limit. In practice, this might become apparent only at maturities beyond the interest of any practitioner. Another issue is the lower bound of zero imposed on the short rate by the CIR model. This is inconsistent, in this setting, with a unit value for φ.

2. *Normalizations.* In the pricing kernels, we chose coefficients of z equal to 1 (Vasicek) and $1 + \lambda^2/2$ (CIR), both with the purpose of equating z to the short rate. There's nothing sacred about this. We could have chosen normalizations that equated z to the 5-year forward rate, the 10-year yield, minus the short rate, or the spread between the 10-year yield and the short rate. Since all are linear in z, they result in linear transformations of the model. In the Vasicek model, all such versions are observationally equivalent. In the CIR model, such versions are equivalent for all rates or spreads that are increasing in the state variable. (The square root means that z has a sign as well as a magnitude.)

3. *Intercepts in Pricing Kernels.* If we allow δ in (4.8) to be an additional free parameter in the pricing kernel of the Vasicek model (earlier we set it equal to $\lambda^2/2$), we find that bond prices depend only on the sum $\delta + \theta$. Neither parameter can be identified separately. We chose (effectively) to drop δ from the model. An equivalent choice is to drop θ by setting it equal to zero. The two versions of the model imply identical asset prices. In the CIR model, this isn't the case; see Pearson and Sun (1994).

ASSESSMENT

These one-factor models are a good place to start, but they are not a good place to stop: There are simply too many discrepancies between them and the world around us. These discrepancies make greater demands on modelers and make this a longer chapter.

One discrepancy in the Vasicek and CIR models is the shape of the mean yield curve: If φ is chosen to reproduce the autocorrelation of the short rate, the mean yield curve is substantially less concave in the models than it is in the data. This anomaly was pointed out by Gibbons and Ramaswamy (1993) and remains, in our view, one of the obvious signs that one-factor models are inadequate.

Another discrepancy is the pattern of autocorrelations. Both of these models are linear: yields of all maturities, yield spreads, and, indeed, all linear combinations of yields are linear functions of z. As a consequence, they share with z its autocorrelation. In the data, however, long yields and yield spreads exhibit, respectively, higher and lower autocorrelations than the short rate. A related issue is the decline in volatility with maturity, such as the standard deviations of one-month changes reported in Table 4.2b. These models imply less variability of long rates than short rates, but the rate of decline is greater in both models than we see in the data.

Yet another discrepancy is that innovations in z are conditionally normal. The evidence suggests, to the contrary, that interest-rate innovations have substantial excess kurtosis. Note, for example, the kurtosis of one-month changes in the short rate (Table 4.2b).

All of these discrepancies point toward the more complex models to come.

ARBITRAGE-FREE MODELS

Ho and Lee (1986) started a revolution in industry practice that has been carried on by Black, Derman, and Toy (1990); Heath, Jarrow, and Morton (1992); Hull and White (1990, 1993); and many others. The logic of most academic work is to choose parameter values that approximate average behavior of bond yields. For practical use, this kind of approximation is inadequate. The four parameters of the Vasicek and CIR models can be chosen to match five points on the yield curve (four parameters plus the short rate), but cannot approximate the complete yield curve to the degree of accuracy required by market participants. Ho and Lee suggested that such models might include additional time-dependent adjustment factors that could be used to "tune" them to observed asset prices. In the most common applications, adjustment factors are used to allow the model to match the current yield curve exactly. Such models are generally referred to (with some violence to the language) as *arbitrage-free*.

The Approach of Ho and Lee

Although Ho and Lee (1986) used a binomial model, we can illustrate their insight in the Vasicek model. The result bears more than a passing resemblance to Hull and White's (1990, 1993) "extended Vasicek model."

Consider a variant of the Vasicek model with state equation

$$z_{t+1} = \varphi z_t + \sigma \varepsilon_{t+1} \tag{4.16}$$

and pricing kernel

$$-\log m_{t+1} = \frac{\lambda^2}{2} + \delta_t + z_t + \lambda \varepsilon_{t+1}$$

One change from the model in the first section is the elimination of θ. This comes without loss of generality, for reasons outlined previously (θ and δ perform the same function). The critical change is the presence of the time-dependent intercept δ in the pricing kernel. We will see shortly that we can choose (δ_t, δ_{t+1}, ...) to reproduce any observed yield curve.

Once again prices are log-linear functions of z, but the functions depend on time:

$$-\log b_t^n = A_{nt} + B_{nt} z_t$$

The pricing relation implies

$$A_{n+1,t} = \frac{A_{n,t+1} + \lambda^2}{2} + \frac{\delta_t - (\lambda + B_{nt}\sigma)^2}{2}$$

$$B_{n+1,t} = 1 + B_{n,t+1}\varphi$$

The boundary conditions, $B_{0t} = 0$ for all t, imply

$$B_{nt} = 1 + \varphi + \ldots + \varphi^{n-1} = \frac{1 - \varphi^n}{1 - \varphi}$$

for all t. Forward rates are therefore

$$f_t^n = A_{n+1,t} - A_{nt} + (B_{n+1,t} - B_{nt})z_t$$

$$= \delta_{t+n} + \frac{1}{2}\left[\lambda^2 - \left(\lambda + \frac{1 - \varphi^n}{1 - \varphi}\sigma\right)^2\right] + \varphi^n z_t \tag{4.17}$$

It's immediately apparent that we can choose the δs to make forward rates—and hence yields—anything we like.

Ho and Lee developed this approach in a binomial model, but the idea is more general: to add time-dependent parameters that allow users to match observed bond yields. Since then, others have noted that other parameters might also be allowed to vary with time. The most important of these is the volatility parameter σ, which Black, Derman, and Toy (1990) showed could be chosen to reproduce the volatility of different parts of the yield curve. This extension was critical to the pricing of interest-rate related options, for which volatility is a key parameter. Moreover, there is overwhelming evidence in these markets that volatility varies with maturity as well as time. Hull and White (1990, 1993) further refined the approach by allowing analogs of θ and φ to vary with time.

These additional parameters are clearly needed in applied work, where a model that fails to reproduce the current yield curve can hardly be trusted to price more complex securities. At the same time, they are no panacea: even a bad model can be tuned to reproduce the current yield curve with enough extra parameters. What's needed is a balance between the fundamental parameters of the model (φ, σ, λ) and the time-dependent adjustment factors (δ_t in our example). The modeling efforts in this paper contribute primarily to constructing a model that is good on average. Once this is done, practical application will almost certainly call for adjustment factors along the lines described here.

The Approach of Heath, Jarrow, and Morton

Heath, Jarrow, and Morton (1992) owe a debt to Ho and Lee in using time-dependent parameters, but they approach them from a novel and interesting direction: They focus on forward rates and the movement of the entire forward rate curve from one date to the next. Their approach exploits simplifications that stem from modeling forward rates directly and sheds new light on the role of volatility parameters in pricing models. We describe the implications of their approach for the pricing kernel, and describe how it can be used to calibrate models to both the forward rate curve and the term structure of volatility.

We illustrate the Heath, Jarrow, and Morton (HJM) approach with a linear one-factor example. Suppose the forward rate curve evolves according to

$$f_{t+1}^{n-1} = f_t^n + \alpha_{nt} + \sigma_{nt}\varepsilon_{t+1} \qquad (4.18)$$

for all $n \geq 0$, where $\{\varepsilon_t\}$ is (as usual) iid normal with mean zero and variance one. HJM pose the question: What restrictions are placed on the parameters $\{\alpha_{nt}, \sigma_{nt}\}$ by the assumption that movements in forward rates are free from arbitrage opportunities? They attack this question by focusing directly on forward rates. If forward rates follow (4.18), the return on an $n+1$-period bond can be expressed

$$\log R_{t+1} = r_t \sum_{j=1}^{n} (f_{t+1}^{j-1} - f_t^j)$$

$$= r_t - \sum_{j=1}^{n} \alpha_{jt} - \sum_{j=1}^{n} \sigma_{jt}\varepsilon_{t+1} \qquad (4.19)$$

$$= r_t - A_{nt} - S_{nt}\varepsilon_{t+1}$$

with the obvious definitions of the partial sums A_{nt} and S_{nt}.

At this point we take two different paths, one followed by HJM, the other more in keeping with our focus on the pricing kernel. HJM's path starts with the moments of the bond return, which include

$$Var_t(\log R_{t+1}) = S_{nt}^2,$$

$$\log E_t R_{t+1} = \frac{r_t - A_{nt} + S_{nt}^2}{2}$$

(This trickery with logs is less troublesome in continuous time.) HJM assume that for some specific maturity τ, the expected excess return is proportional to its standard deviation:

$$\frac{-A_{\tau t} + S_{\tau t}^2}{2} = -\gamma_t S_{\tau t} \qquad (4.20)$$

They refer to the proportionality factor γ_t as the market price of risk. Absence of arbitrage opportunities then places restrictions on the parameters.

A second path is based on a pricing kernel. We replace HJM's price of risk relation (4.20) with a pricing kernel of the form

$$-\log m_{t+1} = \delta_t + \lambda_t \varepsilon_{t+1} \tag{4.21}$$

Applying the pricing relation (4.4) to the return (4.19) gives us

$$r_t = \frac{\delta_t + A_{nt} - (\lambda_t + S_{nt})^2}{2}$$

for all $n \geq 0$, with the convention $A_{0t} = S_{0t} = 0$. The difference between this equation for $n = 0$ and $n = \tau$ implies the restrictions

$$\frac{A_{\tau t} - \lambda_t S_{\tau t} - S_{\tau t}^2}{2} = 0 \tag{4.22}$$

for all $\tau \geq 0$.

The two solution paths are readily shown to lead to the same destination. Equation (4.20) implies

$$\frac{A_{\tau t} - \gamma_t S_{\tau t} - S_{\tau t}^2}{2} = 0$$

which is equivalent to (4.22) if $\gamma_t = \lambda_t$. This equivalence should come as no surprise. We know that absence of arbitrage opportunities implies the existence of a pricing kernel satisfying (4.4). Given the linearity of the forward rate Equations (4.18), it should be no surprise either that the pricing kernel takes the log-linear form of (4.21).

The benefits of working directly with forward rates are apparent if we compare the HJM characterization of the solution, Equations (4.18) and (4.22), to that implied by our treatment previously. Our time-dependent version of Vasicek, summarized by Equations (4.16 and 4.17), implies

$$f_{t+1}^{n-1} = f_t^n + \frac{1}{2}\left[\left(\lambda + \frac{1-\varphi^n}{1-\varphi}\sigma\right)^2 - \left(\lambda + \frac{1-\varphi^{n-1}}{1-\varphi}\sigma\right)^2\right] + \varphi^{n-1}\sigma\varepsilon_{t+1}$$

This is a special case of our HJM example with

$$\sigma_{jt} = \varphi^{j-1}\sigma$$

$$\alpha_{jt} = \frac{1}{2}\left[\left(\lambda + \frac{1-\varphi^j}{1-\varphi}\sigma\right)^2 - \left(\lambda + \frac{1-\varphi^{j-1}}{1-\varphi}\sigma\right)^2\right]$$

These choices satisfy (4.22), but the computations are substantially more complex than (4.22), even in this linear setting.

One of the most useful features of the HJM approach is the ability to specify arbitrary volatilities. As we just saw, the Vasicek model implies geometrically declining volatility, the direct result of mean reversion in the state variable. With HJM, we can choose any volatilities we like, including those implied by option prices. This suggests a sequential choice of parameter values. First, we choose volatilities σ_{jt} to match the term structure of volatilities implied by (say) options on interest rate futures. Given these choices (and a value for λ_t), we choose "drift" parameters α_{jt} to satisfy Equation (4.22). The resulting prices are arbitrage-free by construction.

BINOMIAL MODELS

Binomial models are easily explained and implemented, which undoubtedly accounts for their widespread use in teaching and industry. They are based on a discrete state variable: The short rate either rises or falls each period by a preset amount. They are also invariably described using state prices or risk-neutral probabilities, rather than a pricing kernel. Our purpose here is to explain the connections between the various languages used to describe models.

Alternatives to the Pricing Kernel

In binomial models, the state can either go "up" or "down" over any unit of time. These movements have been described in a variety of ways, but the Ho and Lee model serves as a prototype for fixed income. In this model, as in the Vasicek and Cox-Ingersoll-Ross models, the state variable is generally taken to be the short rate. Between any two consecutive dates t and $t + 1$, changes in the short rate follow

$$r_{t+1} = r_t + \alpha_t + \sigma\varepsilon_{t+1} \tag{4.23}$$

with

$$\varepsilon_{t+1} = \begin{cases} +2(1-\pi) & \text{with probability } \pi \\ -2\pi & \text{with probability } 1-\pi \end{cases}$$

This differs from Equation (4.7) of the Vasicek model in two respects: there is no mean reversion and (this is the key) the innovation takes on only two values. The parameter α governs the expected change or "drift" in the short rate and σ governs its conditional variance. The spread between the up and down states is 2σ. The variance is

$$Var_t(r_{t+1}) = 4\sigma^2\pi(1-\pi)$$

so the standard deviation is σ when $\pi = 0.5$, less than σ for other values. We refer to π and $1 - \pi$ as the true probabilities to distinguish them from their risk-neutral counterparts.

Our approach to pricing has been to use a pricing kernel. Suppose the cash flows c_{t+1} are either c_u in the up state or c_d in the down state. Equation (4.5) tells us that they are worth

$$p_t = E_t(m_{t+1}c_{t+1}) = \pi m_u c_u + (1-\pi)m_d c_d \tag{4.24}$$

where m_u and m_d represent the values of the kernel in the two states. Despite the discreteness, the principle is the same one we outlined earlier.

The pricing kernel highlights the interaction of probabilities and risk. Given a choice of m, a lower probability reduces the value of a payment in that state. Given probabilities, m summarizes the market's attitude toward risk. To see this, suppose m is constant. Since the probabilities sum to one (they're probabilities, after all), this constant value is just the price of a one-period bond: $m_u = m_d = b_t^1 = \exp(-r_t)$. The pricing relation (4.24) then becomes

$$p_t = e^{-r_t}[\pi c_u + (1-\pi)c_d] = e^{-r_t}E_t(c_{t+1})$$

The price, in other words, is the discounted value of expected cash flows. Since only the expected cash flow affects the price, we might regard pricing as risk neutral, this being the way a person who didn't care about risk would value it. In general, of course, m is not the same in all states, and we can think of variations in m across states as reflecting attitudes toward risk of market participants.

A second theoretical language to describe pricing is based on *state prices*. Let q_u be the value now of one dollar next period in the up state and q_d the analogous value in the down state. We define these state prices by

$$q_u = \pi m_u$$

$$q_d = (1-\pi)m_d$$

Then Equation (4.24) can be rewritten as

$$p_t = q_u c_u + q_d c_d \tag{4.25}$$

State prices, then, are an equivalent approach to valuation.

The most common language for describing binomial models is based on *risk-neutral probabilities*. We denote them by $(\pi^*, 1 - \pi^*)$ and define them by

$$\pi^* = \frac{q_u}{(q_u + q_d)} = e^{r_t}\pi m_u$$

$$1 - \pi^* = \frac{q_d}{(q_u + q_d)} = e^{r_t}(1-\pi)m_d$$

the second equality following from $q_u + q_d = b_t^1 = \exp(-r_t)$. The pricing relation becomes

$$p_t = \exp(-r_t)[\pi^* c_u + (1-\pi^*)c_d] = \exp(-r_t)E_t^*(c_{t+1}) \tag{4.26}$$

where $E_t^*(c_{t+1})$ means the conditional expectation of c_{t+1} computed from the risk-neutral probabilities.

The terminology deserves some explanation. People refer to (π^*, $1 - \pi^*$) as *probabilities* for one obvious reason: they are positive and they sum to one. But unless m is constant, they are not the true probabilities. The modifier *risk neutral* is added to distinguish them from the true probabilities, and because the form of (4.26) is the same as our risk-neutral pricing with constant m. This is a little misleading: the effects of risk aversion are built in.

Pricing Risk

We now have three equivalent ways of describing models: a pricing kernel, state prices, and risk-neutral probabilities. The choice among them is a matter of convenience. Given the relations between them we can address a more substantive question: In a binomial model, what is the analog to the pricing kernel? The missing ingredient here is λ. Analogs to the other parameters are apparent from (4.23): θ has been replaced by α_t, φ has been set equal to one, and σ plays similar roles in both binomial and continuous-state models. λ, however, remains a mystery.

Suppose we start, as commonly done in binomial models, with the risk neutral probability π^*. Given such a choice (one-half comes to mind), we apply (4.26) to value cash flows at each date. With a little effort, we can use the definitions of risk-neutral probabilities to compute the pricing kernel. The result is

$$-\log m_{t+1} = \delta^* + \tau_t + \lambda \varepsilon_{t+1}$$

where $\delta^* = \pi \log\left(\dfrac{\pi}{\pi^*}\right) + (1 - \pi) \log\left[\dfrac{(1 - \pi)}{(1 - \pi^*)}\right]$ and

$$2\lambda = \log\left(\dfrac{\pi}{\pi^*}\right) - \log\left[\dfrac{(1 - \pi)}{(1 - \pi^*)}\right]$$

In other words, the risk parameter λ is implicit in the difference between true and risk-neutral probabilities. This relation, moreover, is independent of the short rate process, whose only role here is to define the true probabilities used in (4.24).

DAS'S JUMP MODEL

The original Vasicek and CIR models are based on continuous-time "diffusions" which means, essentially, that the innovations ε are normal. In fact, innovations in interest rates appear markedly non-normal, typically with fat tails indicative of kurtosis. Table 4.2b is suggestive: one-month changes in the short rate exhibit excess kurtosis of about 10. Since departures from normality can have a significant impact on prices of options and related derivatives, we discuss them at some length.

In continuous time, departures from normality over short time intervals are modeled with "point processes" or "jumps." In discrete time, we simply choose a non-normal distribution for the innovation ε. We illustrate this idea by modifying the Vasicek model described by Equations (4.7) and (4.8). The approach is adapted from Das (1994) and Das and Foresi (1996). One of the simplest "abnormal" distributions is a mixture of normals:

$$\varepsilon_{t+1} = \begin{cases} \varepsilon_{1t+1} \text{ with probability } 1 - \pi \\ \varepsilon_{2t+1} \text{ with probability } \pi \end{cases}$$

with each ε_{it} an independent draw from a normal distribution with mean zero and variance τ_i. The mean of ε is therefore zero and the variance is $(1 - \pi)\tau_1 + \pi\tau_2 = 1$ (the latter a continuation of our unit-variance convention).

Despite the modification, bond prices remain log-linear functions of the state variable z:

$$-\log b_t^n = A_n + B_n z_t$$

We compute coefficients the usual way, starting with $A_0 = B_0 = 0$ and applying (4.6) to relate (A_n, B_n) to (A_{n+1}, B_{n+1}). The only difficulty involves terms of the form

$$E_t(\varepsilon^{c\varepsilon_{t+1}}) = (1 - \pi)e^{c^2\tau_1/2} + \pi e^{c^2\tau_2/2}$$

for an arbitrary constant c. The recursions are

$$A_{n+1} = A_n + \delta + B_n(1-\varphi)\theta + \log\left[(1-\pi)e^{(\lambda+B_n\sigma)^2\tau_1/2} + \pi e^{(\lambda+B_n\sigma)^2\tau_2/2}\right]$$

$$B_{n+1} = 1 + B_n\varphi$$

The choice

$$\delta = \log\left[(1-\pi)e^{\lambda^2\tau_1/2} + \pi e^{\lambda^2\tau_2/2}\right]$$

delivers $A_1 = 0$ and $B_1 = 1$, and thus sets the short rate r equal to z.

This model introduces some new parameters to the model: those governing the behavior of the mixture. Otherwise, our approach to choosing parameters is identical to our earlier treatment of the Vasicek model. We set the mixing probability $\pi = 0.05$ in the interest of simplicity. This is not an easy parameter to estimate precisely, although maximum likelihood or other methods can be applied. Our interest, however, is in reproducing the kurtosis of short rate innovations, which we label γ_2^ε. We estimate this to be 9.302, a slightly smaller value than we report in Table 4.2b for short rate changes. This value is computed from the residuals of a first-order autoregression for the short rate. The kurtosis of the model's innovation is

$$\gamma_2^\varepsilon = 3\frac{(1-\pi)+\pi\tau^2}{[(1-\pi)+\pi\tau]^2} - 3$$

where $\tau = \tau_2/\tau_1$. With $\pi = 0.05$, our estimated value of γ_2^ε implies $\tau = 14.56 = 3.815^2$. This means that there is a five percent chance of drawing an interest rate innovation from a distribution whose standard deviation is almost 4 times its usual value. Given τ, the variances τ_1 and τ_2 are chosen to produce an overall variance of one:

$$1 = (1-\pi)\tau_1 + \pi\tau_2 = \tau_1(1-\pi+\pi\tau)$$

The result is $\tau_1 = 0.7720^2$ and $\tau_2 = 2.945^2$.

We proceed to identify the remaining parameters. As in the Vasicek model, the autocorrelation, mean, and standard deviation of the short rate determine $\varphi = 0.976$, $\theta = 0.004428$, and $\sigma = 0.0005560$.

We again choose λ to reproduce the average 10-year bond yield, setting $\lambda = -0.0817$. The resulting mean yield curve is indistinguishable from that of the Vasicek model (Figure 4.1).

We see, then, that Das's jump model provides a good approximation to the kurtosis in the short-term rate of interest and its innovations. What it cannot do is account for differences in kurtosis of yields and yield changes for different maturities: Since bond yields are linear functions of the same state variable z, their levels and changes have identical excess kurtosis for all maturities. Still, it provides a useful starting point for thinking about the role of jumps in pricing fixed-income derivatives. In related work on currencies, we have found a Gram-Charlier expansion to be a more tractable nonnormal distribution for pricing options; see Backus, Foresi, Li, and Wu (1998). Most of that work can be translated directly to fixed income.

MULTIFACTOR MODELS

We turn now to multifactor models, in which bond yields are governed by the movements in two or more state variables. The motivation for such models should be clear from the earlier discussion: Single-factor models cannot account for the average shape of the yield curve, the dynamics of interest rate spreads, or the pattern of interest-rate volatilities across maturities. For these reasons and others, practitioners often use models with multiple factors.

The Vasicek model is again the archetype. Its simple structure makes it relatively easy to understand and to assign parameter values. We develop the two-factor version at some length. We follow with a more cursory study of other multifactor "affine" or linear models, including two-factor CIR and Longstaff and Schwartz (1992) models. Our goal is the resolution of two discrepancies between the one-factor Vasicek and CIR models and observed bond yields. One is the average shape of the yield curve. As we saw in Figures 4.1 and 4.2, these one-factor models cannot simultaneously reproduce the observed curvature of the yield curve and persistence in the short rate. The second is the dynamics of yield spreads. In linear one-factor models, yield spreads have the same persistence as the short rate. In the data (Table 4.2), they are substantially less persistent. A two-factor model allows improvement along both dimensions.

Multifactor Vasicek Model

We base a multifactor generalization of Vasicek model on independent state variables or factors z_i following

$$z_{it+1} = \varphi_i z_{it} + \sigma_i \varepsilon_{it+1} \tag{4.27}$$

with innovations ε_{it} normally distributed with mean zero and variance one and independent across i and t. The pricing kernel is

$$-\log m_{t+1} = \delta + \sum_i \left(\frac{\lambda_i^2}{2} + z_{it} + \lambda_i \varepsilon_{it+1} \right) \tag{4.28}$$

The kernel implies that the short rate is

$$r_t = \delta + \sum_i z_{it} \tag{4.29}$$

Note that we have set the means of z_i equal to zero. In their place, we use δ to reproduce the mean of the short rate. This choice is dictated by the data: There is only one mean and it can determine only one parameter.

As in the one-factor model, each parameter has a clear role and interpretation. δ is the mean short rate. The variance and autocorrelation of the short rate—and other rates, as well—are controlled by $\{\sigma_i\}$ and $\{\varphi_i\}$. Finally, the λs govern the correlation between innovations in the state variables and the pricing kernel: risk, in other words.

We construct bond prices from these components by the usual method. Bond prices remain log-linear functions of the state variables:

$$-\log b_t^n = A_n + \sum_i B_{in} z_{it} \tag{4.30}$$

for some choice of coefficients $\{A_n, B_{in}\}$. The pricing relation (4.6) implies that the coefficients satisfy the recursions

$$A_{n+1} = A_n + \delta + \frac{1}{2}\sum_i \left[\lambda_i^2 - (\lambda_i + B_{in}\sigma_i)^2\right]$$

$$B_{in+1} = 1 + B_{in}\varphi_i$$

starting with $A_0 = B_{i0} = 0$. The solution implies forward rates of

$$f_t^n = \delta + \frac{1}{2}\sum_i \left[\lambda_i^2 - \left(\lambda_i + \frac{1-\varphi_i^n}{1-\varphi_i}\sigma_i\right)^2\right] + \sum_i \varphi_i^n z_{it} \qquad (4.31)$$

Note that more persistent factors (those with larger φs) have relatively greater influence on long forward rates and yields. If a particular φ_i is close to one, then its effect is similar across maturities and state variable i has little effect on a yield or forward rate spread. In the two-factor case, we can estimate (roughly speaking) the parameters of the more persistent factor from long rates and those of the less persistent factor from yield spreads.

We consider parameter values in the two-factor version, a close relative of Brennan and Schwartz's (1979) two-factor model. The choice of parameters follows familiar logic, but the greater complexity of the model makes some of the steps a little more difficult. We now have seven parameters: δ and two choices of the triplet (φ_i, σ_i, λ_i). We compute them from the moments in Tables 4.1 and 4.2 as follows:

- We estimate δ from the mean short rate: $\delta = 0.004428$.
- We compute $\{\sigma_i, \varphi_i\}$ to reproduce the variances and autocorrelations of the short rate and the spread between the short rate and the 5-year yield. The difficulty is that volatility (σ_i) and persistence (φ_i) parameters are now intertwined. Theory implies that an arbitrary yield or yield spread s is a linear function of the state variables:

$$s_t = c_0 + c_1 z_{1t} + c_2 z_{2t}$$

with coefficients $\{c_i\}$ related to $\{A_n, B_{in}\}$ as indicated by (4.1, 4.30). Each spread has variance

$$Var(s) = c_1^2 Var(z_1) + c_2^2 Var(z_2) \qquad (4.32)$$

and autocorrelation

$$Auto(s) = \frac{c_1^2 Var(z_1)}{c_1^2 Var(z_1) + c_2^2 Var(z_2)} \varphi_1 + \frac{c_2^2 Var(z_2)}{c_1^2 Var(z_1) + c_2^2 Var(z_2)} \varphi_2 \quad (4.33)$$

Observations of variances and autocorrelations for two spreads allow us, in principle, to compute two σs and two φs. The difficulty is that the parameters must be computed simultaneously. Since B_{ni} in this model depends only on φ_i, each c_i is a function of φ_i alone. We can then compute the moments of spreads in this order. Given the φs, we compute c_1 and c_2 and, from (4.32), the variances of the state variables. From them, we compute the volatility parameters σ_i. Given variances of the state variables, we can compute the autoregressive parameters $\{\varphi_i\}$ from (4.33). We are done when this circular path returns to the same values of $\{\varphi_i\}$ with which we started.

The results of these computations, using "spreads" $s_t = r_t$ and $s_t = y^{60} - r_t$, are $\varphi_1 = 0.997$, $\sigma_1 = 0.000177$, $\varphi_2 = 0.858$, and $\sigma_2 = 0.000511$. Note that the first factor is the more persistent one.

- We estimate the λ's from the mean yields for maturities of 60 and 120 months. The intermediate 60-month rate captures the curvature that the one-factor model failed to reproduce. The implied values are $\lambda_1 = -0.0240$ and $\lambda_2 = -0.2884$.

These parameters go some ways toward resolving two of the problems with the one-factor model. We come much closer to the curvature of the average yield curve by using a small λ on the more persistent factor (the first one) and a larger one (in absolute value) on the second factor. This comes considerably closer to mean yields than the one-factor model (see Figure 4.3). We also reproduce the difference in autocorrelations of the short rate and the 5-year spread. The short rate is dominated by the more persistent factor and therefore inherits its persistence. The 5-year spread, on the

FIGURE 4.3. Mean Yields in One- and Two-Factor Vasicek Models

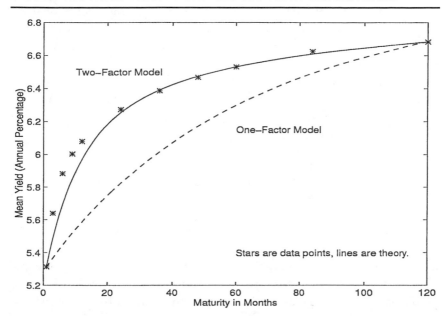

Note: Asterisks are mean yields on U.S. treasury securities, as reported in Table 4.1. The lines represent mean yields in the one-factor (dashed line) and two-factor (solid line) Vasicek models using parameter values reported in the text.

other hand, emphasizes the less persistent factor and is therefore less highly autocorrelated.

This model isn't the last word in bond pricing, but it illustrates clearly how multiple factors can help to account for the unusual shifts and twists of the yield curve. Using the forward rate as a guide, Equation (4.31) shows us that an increase in z_i is almost a parallel shift in the forward rates, since φ_1^n declines very slowly with n. The second factor is much less persistent, however, so an upward shift in z_2 has greater impact at short maturities (a "twist").

Affine Models

The multifactor Vasicek model is an example of a larger class of "affine" models, in which bond prices are log-linear functions of a vector of state variables. The underlying theory was developed by Duffie and Kan (1996). At the risk of increasing the level of abstraction, we summarize this class now to spare ourselves the effort of solving special cases separately. Casual readers should turn immediately to the next section.

Expressed in discrete time, Duffie and Kan's affine models are based on a k-dimensional vector of state variables z that follow

$$z_{t+1} = (I - \Phi)\theta + \Phi z_t + V(z_t)^{1/2}\varepsilon_{t+1} \tag{4.34}$$

where $\{\varepsilon_t\} \sim \text{NID}(0,I)$, $V(z)$ is a diagonal matrix with typical element

$$\upsilon_i(z) = \alpha_i + \beta_i^T z$$

β_i has nonnegative elements, and ϕ is stable with positive diagonal elements. The process for z requires that the volatility functions υ_i be positive, which places restrictions on the parameters. The pricing kernel takes the form

$$-\log m_{t+1} = \delta + \gamma^T z_t + \lambda^T V(z_t)^{1/2}\varepsilon_{t+1} \tag{4.35}$$

Details are given in Duffie and Kan (1996) and translated into discrete time by Backus, Foresi, and Telmer (1996).

The multifactor Vasicek model is a special case. The parameters are related by

Affine Model	Vasicek Model
θ_i	0
Φ	$diag(\varphi_1, \ldots, \varphi_\kappa)$
α_i	σ_i^2
β_i	0
δ	$\dfrac{\sum_i \lambda_i^2}{2}$
γ_i	1
$\lambda_i \alpha_i^{1/2}$	λ_i

With these choices, the affine structure reduces to the multifactor Vasicek model in the last subsection.

The primary benefit here of reviewing the general affine model is that we can characterize its solution once and be done with it. Bond prices are again log-linear functions of the state:

$$-\log b_t^n = A_n + B_n^T z_t$$

Applying the pricing relation (4.6) generates the recursions:

$$A(n+1) = A(n) + \delta + B(n)^T(I - \Phi)\theta - \frac{1}{2}\sum_{j=1}^{k}(\lambda_j + B(n)_j)^2 \alpha_j \qquad (4.36)$$

$$B(n+1)^T = (\gamma^T + B(n)^T\Phi) - \frac{1}{2}\sum_{j=1}^{k}(\lambda_j + B(n)_j)^2 \beta_j^T \qquad (4.37)$$

starting with $A(0) = 0$ and $B(0) = 0$. Moments of bond yields follow directly from those of the state variables. The state vector z has mean θ, so mean yields are

$$E(y^n) = n^{-1}(A_n + B_n^T\theta)$$

The covariance matrix for z is Γ_0, which can be computed as

$$vec(\Gamma_0) = (I - \Phi \otimes \Phi)^{-1} vec[V(\theta)]$$

where $vec(A)$ is the vector formed from the columns of the matrix A. Autocovariance matrices obey

$$\Gamma_{j+1} = \Phi\Gamma_j$$

for $j \geq 0$. Thus the first autocorrelation of an arbitrary linear combination $x = c^T z$ can be calculated as

$$Corr(x_t, x_{t-1}) = \frac{c^T\Gamma_1 c}{c^T\Gamma_0 c}$$

These relations allow us to compute means, variances, and autocorrelations of bond yields and yield spreads, as needed. The details will be familiar to readers with previous exposure to vector time series methods, mysterious to most others. The relevant material is described in Harvey (1989, Chapter 8).

None of this holds much interest for us in the abstract, but it can be applied directly to the special cases to which we now turn.

Other Affine Examples

Two-Factor CIR.   The two-factor CIR model is a special case of the affine model in which z is two-dimensional, Φ is diagonal with elements φ_i, $\alpha = 0$, β_i has a single nonzero element σ_i^2 in its ith position, $\delta = 0$, $\gamma_i = 1 + \lambda_i^2 / 2$, and λ_i corresponds to $\lambda_i \beta_{ii}^{1/2}$. The short rate is then $r_t = z_{1t} + z_{2t}$. We compute bond prices using Equations (4.36, 4.37).

This model has eight parameters, one more than the two-factor Vasicek model, and therefore requires one more feature of the data to estimate. The extra parameter is one of θ_1 and θ_2, which was replaced by the single parameter δ in the Vasicek model. θ_1 and θ_2 are, however, notoriously hard to pin down. In the two-factor Vasicek model, θ_1 and θ_2 are not separately identified. In the CIR model, we have found no features of the data that lead to clear and precise estimates of their values. We could use, for example, estimates of the conditional variance or unconditional higher moments of the short rate. None of the alternatives are easy, and none work very well. Interested readers might consult Chen and Scott (1993); Duffie and Singleton (1997); or Backus, Foresi, Mozumdar, and Wu (1998).

The following models can be viewed as attempts to restrict the two-factor affine model further, thereby simplifying the estimation process.

Longstaff and Schwartz.   The Longstaff and Schwartz (1992) model is a special case of the two-factor CIR model in which one of the risk parameters has been set equal to zero. The model consists of the equations

$$z_{1t+1} = (1 - \varphi_1)\theta_1 + \varphi_1 z_{1t} + \sigma_1 z_{1t}^{1/2}\varepsilon_{1t+1}$$

$$z_{2t+1} = (1 - \varphi_2)\theta_2 + \varphi_2 z_{2t} + \sigma_2 z_{2t}^{1/2}\varepsilon_{2t+1}$$

$$-\log m_{t+1} = \left(\frac{1 + \lambda_1^2}{2}\right)z_{1t} + z_{2t} + \lambda_1 z_{1t}^{1/2}\varepsilon_{1t+1}$$

The model implies $r_t = z_{1t} + z_{2t}$. Note the absence of λ_2 in the last equation.

Central Tendency.   A model that addresses directly the difficulty of estimating the means of the two-factor CIR model is the Balduzzi-Das-Foresi (1998) model of central tendency. Our version consists of

$$z_{1t+1} = (1 - \varphi_1)z_{2t} + \varphi_1 z_{1t} + \sigma_1 z_{1t}^{1/2}\varepsilon_{1t+1}$$

$$z_{2t+1} = (1 - \varphi_2)\theta_2 + \varphi_2 z_{2t} + \sigma_2 z_{2t}^{1/2}\varepsilon_{2t+1}$$

$$-\log m_{t+1} = \left(\frac{1 - \lambda_1^2}{2}\right)z_{1t} + \left(\frac{\lambda_2^2}{2}\right)z_{2t} + \lambda_1 z_{1t}^{1/2}\varepsilon_{1t+1} + \lambda_2 z_{2t}^{1/2}\varepsilon_{2t+1}$$

The short rate is $r_t = z_{1t}$. Balduzzi, Das, and Foresi refer to z_2 as the "central tendency," since the short rate adjusts toward it. As a result, there is no θ_1 in the model. That leaves us with seven parameters: θ_2, φ_1, φ_2, σ_1, σ_2, λ_1, and λ_2. We could estimate them using the same features of bond yields we used to estimate the seven parameters of the two-factor Vasicek model.

Stochastic Volatility.   Another interesting feature of the CIR model and its affine generalizations is that they exhibit stochastic volatility. In the one-factor CIR model, the conditional variance of the short rate is proportional to the short rate:

$$Var_t(r_{t+1}) = \sigma^2 r_t$$

In the two-factor CIR and Longstaff and Schwartz models, the conditional variance depends on both state variables:

$$Var_t(r_{t+1}) = \sigma_1^2 z_{1t} + \sigma_2^2 z_{2t}$$

Here we consider a third stochastic volatility model in which the conditional variance is a state variable in its own right:

$$z_{1t+1} = (1 - \varphi_1)\theta_1 + \varphi_1 z_{1t} + z_{2t}^{1/2}\varepsilon_{1t+1}$$

$$z_{2t+1} = (1 - \varphi_2)\theta_2 + \varphi_2 z_{2t} + \sigma_2 z_{2t}^{1/2}\varepsilon_{2t+1}$$

$$-\log m_{t+1} = z_{1t} + \left(\frac{\lambda_2^2}{2} + \frac{\lambda_2^2}{2}\right)z_{2t} + \lambda_1 z_{1t}^{1/2}\varepsilon_{1t+1} + \lambda_2 z_{2t}^{1/2}\varepsilon_{2t+1}$$

With this structure, z_1 is the short rate and z_2 its conditional variance. This model, too, has seven parameters.

Three-Factor Models.   Additional affine models can be constructed by combining elements of those listed above or heading off in new directions. Interested readers should consult Balduzzi, Das, Foresi, and Sundaram (1996); Chen and Scott (1993); and Dai and Singleton (1997).

INTRODUCTION TO OPTIONS

Thus far, we have focused our efforts on bonds, ignoring entirely the use of these models to value fixed-income derivatives. We now provide a brief overview of European options on zero-coupon bonds with two goals in mind. The first is to illustrate the principles involved: we apply the same pricing relation we used for bonds. As we noted earlier, options and other derivatives are simply more complex applications of Equation (4.4) and its successors. The second is to describe, in a log-normal environment, the behavior of implied volatility across maturities of options and bonds. We note, in particular, the role of mean reversion in determining the volatility of long options and options on long bonds.

Suppose, for the sake of concreteness, that interest rate derivatives are governed by the Vasicek model. The convenient implication in this context is that call prices obey the Black-Scholes formula. A call option on a zero must specify three terms: the strike price k, the maturity τ of the option, and the maturity n at expiration of the bond on which the option is written. The price of such a call option is

$$c_t^{\tau,n} = E_t\left[M_{t,t+\tau}(b_{t+\tau}^n - k)^+\right]$$

a direct application of (4.6) with $\log M_{t,t+n} = \sum_{i=1}^{n} \log m_{t+i}$. The expression x^+ means the positive part of x, that is, $\max(0,x)$. The result is

$$c_t^{\tau,n} = b_t^{\tau+n}N(d) - kb_t^{\tau}N(d - \upsilon_{\tau,n}) \tag{4.38}$$

where N is the cumulative normal distribution function and

$$d = \frac{\log\left[\dfrac{b_t^{\tau+n}}{b_t^{\tau}k}\right] + \dfrac{\upsilon_{\tau,n}^2}{2}}{\upsilon_{\tau,n}} \tag{4.39}$$

$$\upsilon_{\tau,n}^2 = Var_t(\log b_{t+\tau}^n) = \left(\frac{1-\varphi^{2\tau}}{1-\varphi^2}\right)\left(\frac{1-\varphi^n}{1-\varphi}\right)^2 \sigma^2$$

The tedious details of this calculation have been worked out in a number of places, including Backus, Foresi, and Zin (1998, Appendix A.4).

Equation (4.39) reminds us that volatility $\upsilon_{\tau,n}$ is a two-dimensional array. Practitioners treat it as such, most commonly in a matrix of swaption volatilities. To us, the most interesting feature of (4.39) is the role of the mean reversion parameter. If φ were one, volatility would be

$$\upsilon_{\tau,n}^2 = \tau(n\sigma)^2$$

As in the original version of the Black-Scholes formula, volatility squared is proportional to the maturity τ of the option. The more complex form of (4.39) stems from two distinct roles played by the mean reversion parameter φ in determining prices of long bonds in the Vasicek model. Mean reversion appears, first, in the impact of short rate innovations on future short rates:

$$Var_t(z_{t+\tau}) = \sigma^2(1 + \varphi^2 + \varphi^4 + \cdots \varphi^{2(\tau-1)}) = \sigma^2\left(\frac{1-\varphi^{2\tau}}{1-\varphi^2}\right)$$

a direct implication of (4.7). The second role of mean reversion concerns the impact of short rate movements on long bond prices. In the Vasicek model, a unit fall in the short rate is associated with a rise in the logarithm of the n-period bond price of $(1 + \varphi + \ldots + \varphi^{n-1}) = (1 - \varphi^n)/(1 - \varphi)$, which follows (with some effort) from (4.12). Thus mean reversion attenuates the impact of short rate innovations on long bond prices, an implication we see in the declining volatilities of yield changes with maturity (Table 4.2b). These patterns come from a relatively simple model, but they illustrate the challenges facing a practitioner who would like to value options that vary across both maturities (option and bond). The details depend on the model, but any internally consistent model will place restrictions on the two-dimensional array of option volatilities.

Other theoretical settings introduce additional issues, including departures from Black-Scholes associated with jumps (as in Das's jump model) and stochastic volatility (the CIR and multifactor affine models). We leave these issues for another time and place.

FINAL REMARKS

We have applied a single theoretical approach to a number of bond pricing models, illustrating their solution and the choice of parameter values. The approach has two elements, discrete time and a pricing kernel, neither of which is original to us. The theory is reviewed in Duffie (1992). Applications to bond pricing include Campbell, Lo, and MacKinlay (1997), Sun (1992), and Turnbull and Milne (1991), as well as our work with various coauthors. The models themselves are largely examples from the affine class, whose structure was characterized in continuous-time by Duffie and Kan (1996). We think the affine class of models holds great promise for practitioners. Notably, the number of parameters is linear in both the maturity of the assets and the number of factors, which suggests substantial computational savings over binomial models.

Our catalog of models might leave a practitioner in despair at the range of choices. The choice of models must depend, we think, on the use to which the model is put. If one would like to value bonds, swaps, and short-dated options on them, a relatively simple model might suffice. Practical application will probably dictate that the use of time- or maturity-dependent drift and volatility parameters, perhaps as outlined in our summaries of Ho and Lee (1986) or Heath, Jarrow, and Morton (1992). If one would like to value options on fixed-income instruments over a wide range of maturities, perhaps including options on spreads, the benefits of multifactor models may outweigh the increase in complexity. For out-of-the-money options, jumps and stochastic volatility may play a role. Such models are complicated, but in our view the complications are demanded by the complexity of modern financial markets.

ACKNOWLEDGMENTS

We thank Frank Diebold, Kai Li, and especially Liuren Wu for helpful comments on early versions of this chapter. We also acknowledge a special debt to Stan Zin, whose reliable insight and good humor we have come to rely on. Associated Matlab programs are available at http://www.stern.nyu.edu/~dbackus.

REFERENCES

Backus, D., S. Foresi, K. Li, and L. Wu. (1998). "Accounting for Biases in Black-Scholes," manuscript, Stern School of Business, New York University.

Backus, D., S. Foresi, A. Mozumdar, and L. Wu. (1998). "Predictable Changes in Yields and Forward Rates," NBER working paper No. 6379, January.

Backus, D., S. Foresi, and C. Telmer. (1996). "Affine Models of Currency Pricing," NBER working paper No. 5623, June.

Backus, D., S. Foresi, and S. Zin. (1998). "Arbitrage Opportunities in Arbitrage-Free Models of Bond Pricing," *Journal of Business and Economic Statistics, 16,* 13–26.

Balduzzi, P., S. Das, and S. Foresi. (1998). "The Central Tendency: A Second Factor in Bond Yields," *Review of Economics and Statistics, 80,* 60–72.

Balduzzi, P., S. Das, S. Foresi, and R. Sundaram. (1996). "A Simple Approach to Three-Factor Affine Term Structure Models," *Journal of Fixed Income, 6* (December), 43–53.

Black, F., E. Derman, and W. Toy. (1990). "A One-Factor Model of Interest Rates and Its Application to Treasury Bond Options," *Financial Analysts Journal, 46* (January–February), 33–39.

Brennan, M. and E. Schwartz. (1979). "A Continuous Time Approach to the Pricing of Bonds," *Journal of Banking and Finance, 3,* 133–155.

Campbell, J., A. Lo, and C. MacKinlay. (1996). *The Econometrics of Financial Markets,* Princeton, NJ: Princeton University Press.

Chen, R.R. and L. Scott. (1993). "Maximum Likelihood Estimation for a Multifactor Equilibrium Model of the Term Structure of Interest Rates," *Journal of Fixed Income, 3* (December), 14–31.

Cox, J., J. Ingersoll, and S. Ross. (1985). "A Theory of the Term Structure of Interest Rates," *Econometrica, 53,* 385–407.

Dai, Q. and K. Singleton. (1997). "Specification Analysis of Affine Term Structure Models," manuscript, Stanford University, February; forthcoming, *Journal of Finance.*

Das, S. (1994). "Bond and Option Pricing for Jump-Diffusion Processes," manuscript, Harvard Business School.

Das, S. and S. Foresi. (1996). "Exact Solutions for Bond and Option Prices with Systematic Jump Risk," *Review of Derivatives Research, 1,* 7–24.

Duffie, D. (1992). *Dynamic Asset Pricing Theory,* Princeton, NJ: Princeton University Press.

Duffie, D. and R. Kan. (1996). "A Yield-Factor Model of Interest Rates," *Mathematical Finance, 6,* 379–406.

Duffie, D. and K. Singleton. (1997). "An Econometric Model of the Term Structure of Interest Rate Swap Yields," *Journal of Finance, 52,* 1287–1321.

Gibbons, M. and K. Ramaswamy. (1993). "A Test of the Cox, Ingersoll, Ross Model of the Term Structure," *Review of Financial Studies, 6,* 619–658.

Harvey, A. (1989). *Forecasting, Structural Time Series Models, and the Kalman Filter,* New York: Cambridge University Press.

Harvey, A. (1993). *Time Series Models* (2nd ed.), Cambridge, MA: MIT Press.

Heath, D., R. Jarrow, and A. Morton. (1992). "Bond Pricing and the Term Structure of Interest Rates," *Econometrica, 60,* 225–262.

Ho, T.S.Y. and S.-B. Lee. (1986). "Term Structure Movements and Pricing Interest Rate Contingent Claims," *Journal of Finance, 41,* 1011–1029.

Hull, J. and A. White. (1990). "Pricing Interest-Rate-Derivative Securities," *Review of Financial Studies, 3,* 573–592.

Hull, J. and A. White. (1993). "One-Factor Interest-Rate Models and the Valuation of Interest-Rate Derivative Securities," *Journal of Financial and Quantitative Analysis, 28,* 235–254.

Longstaff, F. and E. Schwartz. (1992). "Interest Rate Volatility and the Term Structure: A Two-Factor General Equilibrium Model," *Journal of Finance, 47*, 1259–1282.

McCulloch, J.H. and H.-C. Kwon. (1993). "US Term Structure Data, 1947–91," manuscript and computer diskettes, Ohio State University.

Pearson, N. and T.S. Sun. (1994). "Exploiting the Conditional Density in Estimating the Term Structure: An Application to the Cox, Ingersoll, and Ross Model," *Journal of Finance, 49*, 1279–1304.

Sun, T.-S. (1992). "Real and Nominal Interest Rates: A Discrete-Time Model and Its Continuous-Time Limit," *Review of Financial Studies, 5*, 581–611.

Turnbull, S. and F. Milne. (1991). "A Simple Approach to Interest-Rate Option Pricing," *Review of Financial Studies, 5*, 87–120.

Vasicek, O. (1977). "An Equilibrium Characterization of the Term Structure," *Journal of Financial Economics, 5*, 177–188.

5

Stochastic Mean Models of the Term Structure of Interest Rates

Pierluigi Balduzzi, Sanjiv Ranjan Das, Silverio Foresi, and *Rangarajan K. Sundaram*

In modeling term-structure dynamics, it is common to specify interest rates as mean-reverting processes with levels which oscillate around a *constant* central value. Some of the most widely studied one-factor models, such as the O-U process of Vasicek (1977), and the square-root process of Cox, Ingersoll, and Ross (CIR; 1985), belong to this category. So too do the two-factor models of Brennan and Schwartz (1979), Longstaff and Schwartz (1992), Schaefer and Schwartz (1984), Pearson and Sun (1994), Pennacchi (1991), and Sun (1992), among others. For a number of theoretical and practical reasons, it appears appropriate to relax this assumption of a constant mean level and to allow for the mean, or more precisely the *central tendency,* to evolve stochastically over time.

From a theoretical standpoint, there is considerable evidence of leptokurtosis ("fat tails") in the distribution of changes in interest rates. This has been addressed in the literature so far by enhancing traditional models with stochastic—or, at least, time-varying—volatility. It is possible that the evidence that has been found in favor of time-varying volatility is simply a consequence of the unrecognized time-variation in the mean level. This issue is especially important for the pricing of options, a process in which the central tendency does not play as crucial a role as the volatility.

On a related note, estimating a model that imposes a constant mean level may overstate the volatility of the short interest rate because changes in the central tendency get lumped into the volatility parameter. Chan, Karolyi, Longstaff, and Sanders (CKLS; 1992) empirically examine several alternative models of the short rate to determine which one-factor model fits the data better. They assume a specification in which the mean level is constant and implement estimation over a 25-year period. Economic regime shifts such as the change in Federal Reserve (Fed) policy in October 1979 imply possible nonstationarity of the parameters driving the interest rate process. Whereas CKLS found no significant impact of the structural break in 1979, Pearson and Sun (1994) suggest that the parameters for the periods before and after the structural break are significantly different.

Finally, there are institutional features that motivate a model with a changing central tendency. Since 1982, the Fed has deemphasized monetary aggregates and emphasized managing interest rates in conducting monetary policy (see Balduzzi, Bertola, & Foresi, 1997; Balduzzi, Bertola, Foresi, & Klapper, 1998). The Fed intervenes almost daily, and, more importantly, also shifts the target level of the overnight Fed funds rate every 3 to 4 weeks on average.[1]

In this chapter, we develop and empirically examine a two-factor model of the term structure of interest rates where the central tendency varies stochastically over time. We build on earlier work on two- and three-factor models by Balduzzi, Das, and Foresi (BDF; 1998) and Balduzzi, Das, Foresi, and Sundaram (BDFS; 1996), respectively, which also posit term structure models with changing central tendency. The main difference relative to BDF is that this chapter derives closed-form solutions for the term structure of

---

[1] The rate of inflation is often cited as a reason for intervention by the Fed. Thus, one would expect changes in the central tendency to be closely related to changes in the rate of inflation.

interest rates and tests these solutions against a cross section of bond prices. The main difference of this chapter relative to BDFS is that it focuses on a two-factor version of the model, which allows us to obtain tractable analytical closed-form solutions. In BDFS, only numerical solutions are available, which makes the three-factor model harder to implement on the data.

The *term structure model* developed in this chapter ignores the possibility that the conditional volatility of the short rate may act as a second factor in bond yields, or that the conditional volatility may be affected by the level of the short rate itself. In fact, we assume the volatility of the short rate to be constant. This approach is motivated by tractability: we are able to derive closed-form solutions for yields of different maturity. Moreover, BDFS show that the stochastic central tendency factor matters at least as much as the conditional volatility in explaining variation in yields of maturity from one to ten years. And, BDF show that a constant-volatility Vasicek model outperforms a CIR model, in two of the four subperiods considered.

In the second part of the chapter, we describe a model of interest-rate dynamics with a changing central tendency. The specification we adopt for the central tendency process is quite general: it admits as special cases a mean-reverting O-U process, and arithmetic Brownian motion. We derive bond pricing equations for the general case. Viewed from an estimation standpoint, these equations have a particularly useful functional form. We then exploit this fact to set up the empirical methodology used in the remainder of the chapter.

Next, we apply this methodology to different models of the interest rate. Using an estimation method analogous to that of CKLS, we show that there is considerable evidence to support the hypothesis of a shifting central tendency; in particular, models with time-varying central tendency fit the data better than those assuming a constant central tendency. This finding raises two natural questions. First, how *important* are central tendency shifts in explaining total variations in interest rates? Second, if a changing central tendency does explain a significant proportion of changes in interest rates, can it also explain the severe leptokurtosis that one associates with the short rate of interest? These questions—the sources of volatility and leptokurtosis—are of obvious importance from the standpoint of pricing options and other derivatives.

To answer these questions, we decompose the changes in interest rates into two parts: those arising from the movement in the central tendency level, and those from other factors such as short-lived fluctuations around the central tendency. (We refer to the latter as "noise.") Using this decomposition, we find that of the total variation in the interest rate, a large percentage is, in fact, accounted for by central tendency shifts. Concerning the second question, however, we find that the central tendency—unlike the short rate—does *not* exhibit a significant degree of leptokurtosis. Indeed, it is closer to being normally distributed, indicating that it may be modeled as a Gaussian process. Excess kurtosis in interest rates thus appears attributable to the noise factors, and not to the shifts in the central tendency.

We employ the bond-pricing equations derived earlier in the chapter to investigate the relationship between the central tendency and the *long* rate of interest (i.e., that of the 10-year T-bond). We find considerable evidence that the two are closely linked. This result is particularly interesting since it shows that by using data only at the short end of the term structure (as we do in our model), we may nevertheless still obtain information about the long end of the rate structure.

Using the same approach as Longstaff and Schwarz (1992), we test the cross-equation restrictions that our model implies for the dynamic behavior of interest rates of different maturities. The test fails to reject the cross-equation restrictions.

Finally, we show that the bond-pricing model under a time-varying central tendency easily outperforms the basic one-factor Vasicek (1977) model with a constant central tendency even when pricing bonds at the short end of the term structure. Our model also compares favorably against other two-factor models, which use the slope of the term structure as the second factor.

THE MODEL

This section is divided into three parts. First, we describe the benchmark process, which is a model of interest-rate dynamics with a *constant* central tendency. Then, we describe a generalization of this benchmark process in which the central tendency may evolve stochastically over time, and derive the corresponding bond-pricing equations. Finally, we describe the empirical methodology used in the remainder of the chapter.

The Benchmark Process

The benchmark process we adopt is the mean-reverting Ornstein-Uhlenbeck (O-U) process introduced in Vasicek (1977). Under this process, the short rate of interest r evolves according to

$$dr = \kappa(\theta - r)dt + \sigma dz \tag{5.1}$$

where κ is the rate of mean reversion, θ is the long run mean of the process, σ is the volatility coefficient, and dz is a standard Wiener increment. We shall refer to the process (5.1) as the *Vasicek model* in the sequel.

Throughout this section, we assume that the long-run mean θ is fixed. Under this condition, we review some of the properties of the bond-pricing solution. The results we describe here are well-known; our exposition is, therefore, correspondingly brief. (For greater detail than we provide here, we refer you to the original paper by Vasicek, 1977).

Let $P(r, \tau; \theta)$ denote the current price of a default-free discount bond with a face value of $1, given that there are τ years to maturity, and the current short rate of interest is r. A standard no-arbitrage argument establishes using Equation (5.1), that P must satisfy the partial differential equation (PDE)

$$[\kappa(\theta - r) - \lambda(\cdot)]P_r - P_\tau + \frac{1}{2}\sigma^2 P_{rr} - rP = 0 \tag{5.2}$$

where $\lambda(\cdot)$ denotes the *market price of interest rate risk,* and the subscripts denote derivatives.[2] Since the bond pays a certain dollar at maturity, it must also satisfy the boundary condition

$$P(r, 0; \theta) = 1 \tag{5.3}$$

[2] The notation $\lambda(\cdot)$ is used to emphasize the fact that the market price of risk could depend on the various parameters of the problem (σ, r, etc.).

Therefore, the price of the bond may be obtained as the solution to Equation (5.2) subject to (5.3). A well-known argument establishes that for the Vasicek model, this solution takes on the form[3]

$$P(r, \tau; \theta) = \exp[A(\tau, \theta) - rB(\tau)]$$

where

$$A(\tau, \theta) = \frac{(B(\tau) - \tau)\left(\dfrac{\kappa(\kappa\theta - \lambda\sigma) - \sigma^2}{2}\right)}{\kappa^2} - \frac{\sigma^2(B(\tau))^2}{4\kappa}$$

and

$$B(\tau) = \frac{1 - e^{-\kappa\tau}}{\kappa}$$

There are two features of this solution that deserve emphasis. First, the parameter θ affects the price of the bond only through the term $A(\cdot)$, and not through the term $B(\cdot)$. Second, the τ-period rate depends on the instantaneous rate only through the term $B(\tau)$. Moreover, from the form of $B(\cdot)$, this dependence is regulated solely by the mean-reversion parameter κ of the interest rate process.

This form of the bond-pricing solution is not unique to the Vasicek model. For example, in the CIR square-root model, where

$$dr = \kappa(\theta - r)dt + \sigma\sqrt{r}dz$$

the bond prices once again have the form (the market price of risk is $\lambda(\cdot) = \lambda r$):

$$P(r, \tau; \theta) = \exp[A(\tau, \theta) - rB(\tau)]$$

---

[3] In the Vasicek model $\lambda(\cdot) = \lambda\sigma$.

In this case, letting $\delta = \sqrt{(\kappa + \lambda)^2 + 2\sigma^2}$, the values for $A(\cdot)$ and $B(\cdot)$ are given by

$$A(\tau, \theta) = \ln\left(\frac{2\delta e^{(\kappa + \delta)\tau/2}}{(\delta + \kappa)(e^{\delta\tau-1}) + 2\delta}\right)^{2\kappa\theta/\sigma^2}$$

$$B(\tau) = \frac{2(e^{\delta\tau} - 1)}{(\delta + \kappa)(e^{\delta\tau-1}) + 2\delta}$$

Note that, like the Vasicek model, the τ-year rate depends on the short rate only through the term $B(\tau)$; however, now $B(\tau)$ depends not only on the mean-reversion parameter κ, but also on risk premium parameter, λ, and the volatility parameter σ.

The Model with a Stochastic Central Tendency

We generalize Equation (5.1) by augmenting it with a stochastic process for the central tendency θ. The augmented model is then described. The bond-pricing equations for this generalized specification are described next. Finally, we examine the implications of allowing θ to follow a jump process.

The Process for the Central Tendency.   As in the benchmark model, we assume that the interest rate process is given by Equation (5.1). However, rather than require the central tendency θ to be constant, we now allow it to evolve stochastically over time. The specification we consider for the θ process is

$$d\theta = (a + b\theta)dt + \eta dw \tag{5.4}$$

where a, b, and η are given constants, and dw is a standard Wiener increment. To complete the description of the model, we must specify the relationship between the Wiener processes z (of the short rate process) and w (of the process for the central tendency). We assume simply that the two processes are correlated with coefficient ρ:

$$dzdw = \rho dt \tag{5.5}$$

Equations (5.1), (5.4), and (5.5) completely specify the augmented model.

The process (5.4) we have adopted for θ is quite general. Two interesting special cases of this specification, which we will have occasion to refer to in the sequel, are the following:

1. *A Mean-Reverting Ornstein-Uhlenbeck Process.* Under a mean-reverting O-U process, θ evolves according to

$$d\theta = \alpha(\beta - \theta)dt + \eta dw \qquad (5.6)$$

   where α regulates the rate of mean reversion, and β is the long-run mean of the θ process. A simple substitution ($\alpha = -b$ and $\beta = -a/b$) shows that (5.6) is just a special case of (5.4).

2. *Arithmetic Brownian Motion.* In an arithmetic Brownian motion process, the evolution of θ is described by

$$d\theta = \alpha dt + \eta dw \qquad (5.7)$$

   where α and η are given constants. Such a process is useful to describe a trending market. Equation (5.7) may be obtained from (5.4) simply by setting $b = 0$.

Bond-Pricing Equations.   Let $P(r, \tau, \theta)$ denote the price in the augmented model, of a discount bond with face value $1 and τ years to maturity, given that the current interest rate is r and the current level of the central tendency is θ. In Appendix 5.1, we show that P has the form

$$P(r,\tau,\theta) = \exp[A(\tau) - rB(\tau) - \theta C(\tau)] \qquad (5.8)$$

where $A(\cdot)$, $B(\cdot)$, and $C(\cdot)$ are all functions that depend on τ, but not on r or θ. The full forms of $A(\cdot)$ and $C(\cdot)$ are described in Appendix A; the function B is given by

$$B(\tau) = \frac{1 - e^{-\kappa\tau}}{\kappa} \qquad (5.9)$$

As expression (5.9) indicates, $B(\cdot)$ depends on the mean-reversion parameter κ of the interest-rate process, but *not* on any of the parameters of the θ process; it is the same whether θ follows a mean-reverting O-U process, an arithmetic Brownian motion process, or any other special case of (5.4). This fact turns out to be especially valuable from an estimation standpoint, as we explain next.

The class of solutions in Equation (5.8) is often denoted as the *exponential-affine* form, following work by Duffie and Kan (1996). All the models we develop in this chapter adhere to this model, even in the case of the jump models discussed next.

A Note on Jump Processes. When the θ-process is specified through (5.4), bond prices take on the functional form (5.8), and the latter, as we have just indicated, will turn out to be valuable for estimation purposes. However, (5.4) also implies that θ has *continuous* sample paths, and the question arises whether our analysis can also be extended to models where θ follows a *jump* process with discontinuous sample paths. The answer turns out to be in the affirmative, but with some qualifications.

To elaborate, suppose θ evolves according to the process

$$d\theta = J(\mu, \gamma^2)\, d\pi(h) \tag{5.10}$$

where $J(\cdot)$ is a given distribution with mean μ and variance γ, and $\pi(h)$ is a Poisson process with intensity h. Suppose further that the process π is independent of the Wiener process z driving the short rate. Under these conditions, we show in Appendix 5.2, that the bond price is approximately given by

$$P(r, \tau, \theta) \approx \exp[A^*(\tau) - rB^*(\tau) - \theta C^*(\tau)] \tag{5.11}$$

where—as in (5.8)—$A^*(\cdot)$, $B^*(\cdot)$, and $C^*(\cdot)$ are all functions that do not depend on r or θ, and B^* and C^* retain the form

$$B^*(\tau) = \frac{1 - e^{-\kappa\tau}}{\kappa}$$

$$C^*(\tau) = \tau - \frac{1 - e^{-\kappa\tau}}{\kappa}$$

The difference between this and the earlier case is that when θ was specified by (5.4), the bond prices (5.8) represented *exact* solutions. On the other hand, the approximation leading to (5.11) appears small in most cases (see Appendix 5.2 for details); to the extent that it is acceptable, much of the sequel is valid even if θ follows the jump process (5.10).[4]

The Econometric Model

We now develop the empirical approach to estimating the process for the mean level and the other parameters of the two-factor model. We employ a Method of Moments (MM) estimator for the empirical work in this chapter. The MM estimator is general and easy to implement. The estimation procedure contains moment conditions modeling processes for both r and θ. While the former process is directly observable from short rate data, the latter is not and needs to be implicitly obtained. We back out information on θ implicitly from bond prices using the theoretical results of the previous subsection.

We use two bonds for this purpose, with maturities τ_1 and τ_2, respectively. Denote their prices by

$$P(r, \tau_1, \theta) = \exp[A(\tau_1) - rB(\tau_1) - \theta C(\tau_1)]$$

and

$$P(r, \tau_2, \theta) = \exp[A(\tau_2) - rB(\tau_2) - \theta C(\tau_2)]$$

These functional forms are based on the material of the previous section. To simplify notation, we suppress dependence on τ in what follows, and use subscripts to differentiate between τ_1 and τ_2. Taking logs and re-arranging these two bond equations to eliminate r, some simple algebra yields:

$$B_1 \log(P_2) - B_2 \log(P_1) = (B_1 A_2 - B_2 A_1) + \theta(B_2 C_1 - B_1 C_2) \tag{5.12}$$

---

[4] Indeed, as is shown in Baz and Das (1996), these analytical approximations to jump-diffusion bond models are extremely accurate for a wide range of such models.

Two observations make (5.12) of particular interest for us:

1. The right-hand side (RHS) of this equation does not contain a term in r; its only stochastic component is that emanating from θ. Since (5.12) is an identity, the left-hand side (LHS) must also be a function solely of θ.

2. The RHS is unobservable, but the LHS is partially observable given the availability of bond price data.

It follows that the observable values on the LHS form a time series of proxies for θ, and, indeed, (5.12) suggests a *linear* function of the LHS for this proxy:

$$\theta = a_0 + a_1[B_1 \log(P_2) - B_2 \log(P_1)] \tag{5.13}$$

What makes this proxy especially attractive is that B_1 and B_2 do *not* depend on the specific parameterization of the θ process; they depend only on the parameter κ of the interest rate process, and are given by

$$B_1 = \frac{1 - e^{-\kappa\tau_1}}{\kappa} \quad \text{and} \quad B_2 = \frac{1 - e^{-\kappa\tau_2}}{\kappa} \tag{5.14}$$

Thus, the proxy process for θ which obtains when (5.14) is substituted in (5.13) is given by

$$\theta = a_0 + a_1\left[\left(\frac{1 - e^{-\kappa\tau_1}}{\kappa}\right)\log(P_2) - \left(\frac{1 - e^{-\kappa\tau_2}}{\kappa}\right)\log(P_1)\right] \tag{5.15}$$

Now, recall that the short-rate process in the augmented model is described by

$$dr = \kappa(\theta - r)dt + \sigma dz$$

By replacing θ in this expression with the proxy process (5.15), the equation for the short rate process becomes:

$$dr = \kappa\left[a_0 + a_1\frac{1}{\kappa}[(1 - e^{-\kappa\tau_1})\log(P_2) - (1 - e^{-\kappa\tau_2})\log(P_1)] - r\right]dt + \sigma dz \tag{5.16}$$

Equation (5.16) may now be used to estimate the four unknown parameters a_0, a_1, κ, and σ.

For the actual estimation, we need to discretize Equation (5.16). Letting Δt denote the length of time between observations, this discretization is given by

$$r_{t+1} - r_t = \kappa(\theta_t - r_t)\Delta t + \sigma\xi_t\sqrt{\Delta t}$$

where the ξ_t are i.i.d. draws from a standard normal distribution. Define

$$\varepsilon_t = r_{t+1} - r_t - \kappa(\theta_t - r_t)\Delta t \qquad (5.17)$$

Similar to CKLS the moment equations for our model are given by:

$$E[\varepsilon_t Z_{t-1}] = 0 \qquad (5.18)$$

$$E[(\varepsilon_t^2 - \sigma^2)Z_{t-1}] = 0 \qquad (5.19)$$

In our application in the following, the instrumental variables are

$$Z = [\text{constant}, r, \log(P_1)] \qquad (5.20)$$

a constant, and lagged values of a short-rate proxy and of the log of a bond price. This provides six moment conditions in four parameters, a_0, a_1, κ, and σ.

Equations (5.15), (5.17) to (5.20) complete the description of the econometric model. When estimating the augmented model with a time-varying central tendency, θ_t is defined by Equation (5.15) above. When estimating the restricted model with a constant mean level, we will simply require that θ be constant.

To sum up the contents of this subsection: We have replaced θ in the process describing the evolution of the short rate with a functional proxy, which is a function of (observable) bond prices, and a parameter κ, which needs to be estimated. This reduces the two-factor model to a model where one factor (the short rate) is observable and the second factor (the central tendency) is latent. Sun (1992) employs an analogous approach in a general equilibrium framework while estimating unobservable parameters. An interesting feature of this approach is that the analytic solution of bond prices has the same functional form for $B(\tau)$ regardless of the precise θ process; therefore, the central tendency is estimable without the need to hang our hat ex-ante on a specific formulation of this process.[5]

DATA AND IMPLEMENTATION

As indicated previously, we use three instrumental variables to generate moment conditions (5.18) to (5.19), a constant, and lagged values of a short-rate proxy and of the log of a bond price. This provides six moment conditions in four parameters, yielding an overidentified system of equations.

In our analysis, the short-rate proxy r in (5.16) is given by the one-month Treasury bill rate from the CRSP riskfree rates file. Zero-coupon bond prices for maturities of one and two years (P_1 and P_2 in Equation (5.16)) were drawn from the Fama-Bliss files on the CRSP database. The monthly data series runs from January 1960 to December 1991.[6] Descriptive statistics are presented in Table 5.1. The usual feature of a high degree of kurtosis clearly exists in the data. Data for the long rate (l) were obtained from CITIBASE. The proxy for the long rate was taken as the yield on the 10-year Treasury bond.[7] The data entails some approximation since data at monthly intervals do not approximate well a continuous time process, nor does the one-month interest rate truly proxy for the instantaneous rate of interest. However, the analysis being carried out concerns to a greater extent the central tendency and not so much the behavior of the short rate itself. Extracting information about the central tendency using the process for the one-month rate, rather than that of

---

[5] Indeed, if one accepts the approximate solution for the jump-process case, a stronger statement is true: that the central tendency is estimable without even the need to choose between the continuous family of processes (5.4) and the discontinuous sample path process (5.10).

[6] Note that this sample period includes the 1964–1989 period investigated by CKLS and Longstaff and Schwartz (1992).

[7] The 10-year rate was used instead of the long bond because the curve is usually flat from this tenor onwards. Additionally, data for the 20- and 30-year bonds were not available for the entire period.

TABLE 5.1. Descriptive Statistics

	r	dr (bp's)	l	dl (bp's)
Mean	0.0601	−0.23	0.0764	0.68
Std. Dev.	0.0275	81	0.0276	32
Skewness	1.030	−0.853	0.594	−0.534
Kurtosis	4.25	11.25	2.82	8.93
Minimum	0.0132	−175	0.0371	−176
Maximum	0.1615	163	0.1532	161
No of Obs	383	382	383	382

Note: The table presents summary details about the one-month T-bill interest rate *(r)* and the changes in this interest rate *(dr)*. Data is also provided on the long rate (10-year bond) which we denote *l*, and the changes in that rate *dl*. The period covered is January 1960 to December 1991. The data frequency is monthly.

the instantaneous rate, should make little difference given that the one month rate must contain as much information about the second factor (related to the mean) as the instantaneous rate does.

Comparison of Models

The estimation was carried out using the MM technique. The results are presented in Table 5.2. Table 5.2a provides the estimates for the benchmark model with a constant mean level. This part of the estimation is identical to that of CKLS except for an additional instrumental variable (the lagged values of the bond price). The parameter values are found to be similar in sign and magnitude to those obtained by CKLS.[8]

Table 5.2b then presents the estimates for the case where the central tendency is allowed to vary. The difference in the χ^2 statistics of the unrestricted and restricted models provides a statistic which, if significant at 1 degree of freedom, indicates that the

---

[8] Note that since the model is estimated by MM, rather than OLS, the estimated value for θ does not need to equal the mean of *r* for the sample period, and in fact the two values differ substantially.

TABLE 5.2. Method of Moments Estimation

a. Constant Mean Model

κ	θ	σ^2	χ^2	D.o.f
0.1027	0.0363	0.0003	20.8088	3
0.36	0.75	7.32		

b. Time-Varying Mean Model

κ	a_0	a_1	σ^2	χ^2	D.o.f
2.8723	−0.0128	−3.2579	0.0004	16.2732	2
3.92	−2.01	−6.03	7.64		

c. Model Comparison

χ^2 diff	P-value
3.5356	0.0601

Note: This table provides parameter estimates for the model specified by Equations (5.1), (5.4). These results are portrayed in Table 5.2b. For the restricted model where the mean is not permitted to vary, Equations (5.1), (5.4) are restated with θ equal to a constant (results in Table 5.2a). The difference in χ^2 values for the two models is distributed χ^2 with one degree of freedom. T-statistics are presented below the parameter estimates. Table 5.2c provides the χ^2 statistic for the comparison of the models with constant mean versus varying mean.

model with a time-varying central tendency provides a better specification. The results in Table 5.2c indicate that such is indeed the case.

There are two other noteworthy features of the results summarized in Table 5.2. First, the *t*-statistics show a dramatic improvement in the augmented model over the restricted model. Second, the estimated value of the mean-reversion coefficient increases sharply when the central tendency is allowed to vary. This is, perhaps, intuitive, and simply reflects the fact that the model captures the tightly banded oscillatory nature of interest rates over a short period of time.

Further Analysis of the Interest-Rate Process

The analysis in the preceding subsection raises a number of questions concerning the relationship between the interest-rate and central tendency processes. For instance, what proportion of the variability in the interest rate process is contributed by changes in the central tendency?

On a related note, how much of the leptokurtosis in changes in the short rate (see Table 5.1) is attributable to changes in the central tendency? We examine these and other questions next.

As a first step, we generated the conditional time series of θ using the estimated parameters, the θ proxy from Equation (5.15), and data on observed bond prices, and found a distinctive (and intuitively appealing) oscillation of the short rate around the central tendency.

Table 5.3 provides some summary statistics regarding the time series of θ. A comparison of these numbers with the analogous statistics obtained for the interest rate process in Table 5.1 further clarifies the relationship between the interest-rate and central-tendency processes. Two aspects of this comparison are particularly interesting:

1. The volatility of r must come from the volatility of θ and other noise factors. When the standard deviations in Tables 5.1 and 5.3 are compared, it can be seen that more than 50% of the variation in dr comes from $d\theta$. This answers the first of the two questions.

2. Concerning the second question, Table 5.3 implies that the distribution of θ is close to normal, since the skewness is low

TABLE 5.3. Descriptive Statistics for the Mean Rate

	Mean	Std. Dev.	Skewness	Kurtosis	Minimum	Maximum
θ	0.0586	0.0239	0.613	2.90	0.0181	0.1307
$d\theta$ (bp's)	0.35	49	−0.275	6.04	−230	195

Note: This table provides summary statistics for the time series of the conditional mean rate of interest obtained by the estimation of Equation (5.16).

and kurtosis is very close to 3. In addition, the kurtosis of $d\theta$ is dramatically reduced from that of dr. There is, therefore, little evidence of leptokurtosis in the distribution of θ. This indicates that while regular Gaussian changes in interest rates may be attributed to changes in the central tendency, the larger shocks originate from the noise component and not from the changes in θ.[9]

Tables 5.1 and 5.3 also reveal some other intuitively desirable properties of the θ-process. For one thing, the mean value of θ in Table 5.3 is close to that of r from Table 5.1. This is as it should be, given that θ is, after all, the mean of the r process. Moreover, the maximum and minimum values of θ lie within the corresponding range for r. Finally, we would expect the central tendency to be less volatile than the short rate, since the former represents the level around which the latter oscillates. A comparison of the standard deviation of changes in these rates from Tables 5.1 and 5.3 reveals that this is, indeed, the case.

Finally, a word on the robustness of the empirical methodology. To test the sensitivity of the estimation procedure to the choice of bonds used to generate the proxy for θ, all ten possible combinations of two bonds of maturities 1 to 5 years were tried, and no significant difference in the process for θ was found. This is interesting since models assuming constant central tendency have typically shown dramatic differences in results for varying choices of bonds (for example, see Pearson and Sun (1994), Table V).

---

[9] The finding that θ consists of draws from a Gaussian distribution also provides some further prescriptive intuition regarding the definition of a process to describe the short interest rate. Two alternative approaches can be employed: a one-factor model with a diffusion and jump component (see Das and Forese [1996]), or a two-factor model with one factor being the level change and the other the change in central tendency (as in this chapter, for example). From an empirical point of view it is hard to distinguish between the two. The choice between the two models rests largely on the available data and empirical methods. The former approach has the advantage of only requiring the time series of interest rates (and not bond prices) to which maximum-likelihood methods can be applied. However, the estimation of jump-diffusion processes is tricky, and estimated variances are often negative (see Press [1967]). In contrast, the latter approach is easier to implement and provides robust parameter estimates, even though additional bond price data are required.

The Central Tendency and the Long Rate

We next explore the nature of the relationship between the central tendency θ and the long rate of interest l. Preliminary evidence concerning the relationship between l and θ may be obtained from Tables 5.1 and 5.3. Table 5.1 summarizes the behavior of the long rate, while Table 5.3 presents properties of the estimated central tendency process. A comparison of these tables reveals that the variance, skewness, and kurtosis levels for the two processes are quite similar.

Finally, Table 5.4 presents the correlation matrix of the interest rate processes. The matrix shows the existence of a significantly stronger relationship between changes in the central tendency $d\theta$ and changes in the long rate dl (a correlation coefficient of 0.47) than between $d\theta$ and changes in the short rate dr (a coefficient of 0.25).

Tests of Cross-Sectional Model Restrictions

So far the analysis has invoked the time series properties of the data. We now test whether the inferred central tendency series also meets the cross-sectional requirements of the bond pricing model. For the purpose of specificity, we consider the case where the central tendency follows the Ornstein-Uhlenbeck process

$$d\theta = \alpha(\beta - \theta)dt + \eta dw$$

As we have seen, the bond price has the form

$$P(r, \tau, \theta) = \exp[A(\tau) - rB(\tau) - \theta C(\tau)]$$

TABLE 5.4. Correlation Matrix for $d\theta$, dr, dl

	$d\theta$	dr	dl
$d\theta$	1.0000	0.2454	0.4721
dr	0.2454	1.0000	0.4202
dl	0.4721	0.4202	1.0000

The full form of $A(\cdot)$ may be found in Appendix 5.1; the functions B and C are given by

$$B(\tau) = \frac{1 - e^{-\kappa\tau}}{\kappa}$$

$$C(\tau) = \frac{\alpha(1 - e^{-\kappa\tau}) + \kappa e^{-\alpha\tau}(1 - e^{\alpha\tau})}{\alpha(\alpha - \kappa)}$$

Note that $dB(\tau)/d\kappa < 0$ and $dC(\tau)/d\kappa > 0$: stronger reversion of r to its central tendency reduces the loading associated with r, but increases the loading associated with θ.

Since $\log(P) = A - rB - \theta C$, we must have

$$\Delta\log(P) = -B\,\Delta r - C\Delta\theta$$

Let

$$\varepsilon_{t+1}(\tau) = \log[P_{t+1}(\tau) - \log[P_t(\tau)] + B(\tau)[r_{t+1} - r_t] + C(\tau)[\theta_{t+1} - \theta_t]$$

where $\tau = 1, 2, 3, 4, 5$ indexes the bond maturity. We employ the MM to estimate the parameters (κ, α) embedded in $B(\tau)$ and $C(\tau)$. The parameter κ is the rate of mean reversion of the short rate, and α is the rate of mean reversion of the central tendency. Similar to Longstaff and Schwartz (1992), the moment conditions used in the estimation are given by

$$E[\varepsilon_t(\tau)Z_{t-1}] = 0; \quad \tau = 1, 2, 3, 4, 5$$

where $Z = [\text{constant}, \Delta r]$. Therefore, we obtain $N = 2 \times 5 = 10$ moment conditions in $K = 2$ parameters, and the objective function value in the MM estimation is then distributed χ^2 with $N - K = 8$ degrees of freedom. If the cross-sectional restrictions are met, then the χ^2 statistic should not be different from zero in a statistical sense. The results of the estimation which are provided in Table 5.5 show that this is in fact the case.[10]

---

[10] It is worth noting that the value of κ estimated in this cross-equation test is much lower than that estimated in the time-series tests. Hence, the information contained in the cross-section of bond prices regarding the dynamics of the short rate differs

TABLE 5.5. Cross-Sectional Test of Model Fit

	α	κ	$\chi^2(8)$	p-Value
Coefficient	0.1884	0.5563	10.29	0.2448
T-statistic	1.2845	2.9279		

BOND PRICING BENCHMARKS

Even though there is evidence that the mean interest rate is time-varying, this feature may be of limited economic significance if there is little difference in price predictability relative to, say, a one-factor model. We can document the performance of a model with time varying central tendency relative to classic pricing benchmarks. First, we compare our extended two-factor Vasicek model versus the one-factor Vasicek model. Then, we compare it with the two-factor Schaefer-Schwartz (1984) model.

As in the previous tests, the data employed are the prices of zero-coupon bonds for maturities of 1, 2, 3, 4 and 5 years.

Comparison with a One-Factor Model

We compare our extended mean shifting Vasicek model with the basic one-factor model. The procedure employed is as follows. The metric of performance for our two-factor model (denoted M2) versus the one-factor model (M1) is the root mean squared price prediction error (RMSE). To obtain the parameters to be employed in the bond pricing equation, we first estimate the interest rate processes. For the model M1 (see Section 5.1), the parameters are found to be

$$\kappa = 0.1027 \qquad \theta = 0.0363 \qquad \sigma = 0.0173$$

In the case of the model M2 (see Econometric Models on pages 137 to 140) we estimate the parameters to be

$$\kappa = 2.8723 \qquad \sigma = 0.028$$

---

from the short-rate dynamics directly observable from the data. So far, the joint estimation of the process for dr together with the cross-equation restrictions for different-maturity bonds has been problematic, and it is the object of ongoing research.

Using the generated time series for θ we estimate the mean-reverting O-U process $d\theta = \alpha(\beta - \theta)\,dt + \eta\,dw$ to obtain the following parameters[11]

$$\alpha = 0.0481 \qquad \text{ß} = 0.0685 \qquad \eta = 0.01122$$

The pricing equation for model M1 is the Vasicek bond pricing formula:

$$P(r,\tau) = \exp[A(\tau) - rB(\tau)]$$

$$A(\tau) = \frac{(B(\tau) - \tau)\left(\kappa\dfrac{(\kappa\theta - \lambda\sigma) - \sigma^2}{2}\right)}{\kappa^2} - \frac{\sigma^2 B(\tau)^2}{4\kappa}$$

$$B(\tau) = \frac{1 - \exp(-\kappa\tau)}{\kappa}$$

The pricing equation for model M2 is provided in Appendix 5.1. We consider the mean-reverting case for the central tendency. The correlation between the dr process and the $d\theta$ process is found to be 0.25 (see Table 5.4).

The measure for the prediction error is computed over all bonds for all time periods. For each month end we have the prices of discount bonds of maturities 1, 2, 3, 4, and 5 years. We have five observations per month for 383 months which yield a total number of observations equal to 1915. The root mean squared error is computed to be

$$\text{RMSE} = \sqrt{\frac{1}{N}\sum_{i=1}^{N}[P_i - A_i]^2}$$

where $N = 1915$, P_i is the model predicted price, and A_i is the actual price for the ith observation. This measure provides an adequate metric with which to compare the fit of the models.

---

[11] For this estimation, we use the two-stage least squares instrumental variable version of the MM rather than the Generalized Method of Moments, because the errors in the model are theoretically normally distributed. The power of this estimation procedure is greater. We also carried out the procedure using estimates from the GMM estimation and found for both models M1 and M2, that the mean squared errors were greater.

To use the pricing models, we still need to obtain parameter values for the market price of risk (λ). To do so, for each model, we search over different values of λ until we minimize the prediction errors (RMSE). We then compare the two models given the best choice of the market risk parameter for each model.

In Table 5.6 we present the results for the above analysis. We computed the values of the RMSE for the values of λ, which minimized the RMSE for model M2 ($\lambda_2 = -1.85$), and for model M1 ($\lambda_1 = -0.60$). The fit of the models is compared for the entire period.

The following observations can be made. The RMSE of model M2 is vastly less than that of model M1. The fact that the optimal value of λ is different for the two models may indicate that in model M2 the single price of risk actually captures two prices of risk, for changes in the mean and the changes in the short rate. In model M2, we have assumed that the risk from mean shifts is not priced. Extension of the model to include another price of risk will only improve the fit of the model. Thus the model in this chapter provides a powerful alternative to other one-factor models.

Comparison with a Two-Factor SS Model

The model chosen for comparison is the Schaefer and Schwartz (SS) two-factor model. The two factors they use are the consol rate or the

TABLE 5.6. Comparison of Bond Pricing Models

Bond Maturity (years)	One-Factor Vasicek $\lambda = -0.60$	Two-Factor Mean-Shifting Model $\lambda = -1.85$	Two-Factor Schaefer-Schwartz $\lambda = -0.70$
1	0.8371	0.5601	0.5673
2	1.7118	0.8471	0.8305
3	2.5419	1.0337	1.0556
4	3.3886	1.2448	1.2796
5	4.2839	1.4438	1.5781
All	2.8258	1.0709	1.11836

Note: This table documents the mean errors and root mean squared errors for bond price prediction by the one- and two-factor models for the period 1960–1991. The errors are per dollar 100 bond. RMSE = Root Mean Square Error. The subscript denotes the model.

long rate, and the spread, which is the difference between the long rate and the short rate. The reason that the spread is used is that it is empirically known to be orthogonal to the long rate, and this makes estimation easier. Their model is specified as

$$ds = m(\mu - s)dt + \gamma dz_1$$

$$dl = \beta_2 dt + \sigma \sqrt{l} dz_2$$

$$dz_1 dz_2 = 0$$

(5.21)

(5.22)

where s is the spread, l is the long rate, m is the coefficient of mean reversion for the spread, μ is the long run mean of the spread, γ is the variance coefficient for the spread, σ is the variance coefficient for the long rate, and β_2 is an unspecified drift term which does not enter their bond pricing equation. SS assume that the long-rate risk is not priced and that the market price of risk of the spread is λ, which is an implicit parameter determined as the value that minimizes price prediction error. As earlier, we denote with ε_s and ε_l the residual terms for the discretized versions of Equations (5.1) and (5.2). To estimate the two equations, we employ an MM approach using the following moment conditions

$$0 = E[\varepsilon_s Z_{t-1}]$$

$$0 = E[(\varepsilon_s^2 - \gamma^2)Z_{t-1}]$$

$$0 = E[\varepsilon_l Z_{t-1}]$$

$$0 = E[(\varepsilon_l^2 - \sigma^2 l)Z_{t-1}]$$

$$0 = E\left[\left(\varepsilon_s \varepsilon_l - \rho \sigma \gamma \sqrt{l}\right)Z_{t-1}\right]$$

The parameter estimates are

$m = 1.9102$	$\mu = -0.0171$	$\gamma = 0.0255$
$\beta_2 = -0.0001$	$\sigma = 0.0433$	$\rho = 0.1196$

The value of ρ is small and statistically insignificant, which is to be expected in the light of past work. Under this specification SS derive the price of the bond with maturity τ to be

$$P(s,l,\tau) = X(s,\tau)Y(l,\tau)$$

$$X(s,\tau) = \exp[C(\tau) - sD(\tau)]$$

$$C(\tau) = \frac{(D-\tau)\left(m\dfrac{(m\mu - \lambda\gamma) - \gamma^2}{2}\right)}{m^2} - \frac{\gamma^2 D^2}{4m}$$

$$D(\tau) = \frac{1 - \exp(-m\tau)}{m}$$

$$Y(l,\tau) = \exp[A(\tau) - lB(\tau)]$$

$$A(\tau) = \left[\frac{2\alpha e^{(\hat{s}+\alpha)\tau/2}}{(\hat{s}+\alpha)(e^{\alpha\tau} - 1) + 2\alpha}\right]^2$$

$$B(\tau) = \frac{2(e^{\alpha\tau} - 1)}{(\hat{s}+\alpha)(e^{\alpha\tau} - 1) + 2\alpha}$$

$$\alpha = \sqrt{\hat{s}^2 + 2\sigma^2}$$

where $\hat{s}$ is implicitly defined by the following equation:

$$\frac{l_0\hat{\mu} - \sigma^2}{\hat{\mu}^2\tau}(1 - e^{-\hat{\mu}\tau}) + \frac{\sigma^2}{\hat{\mu}} = \frac{l_0\hat{s} - \sigma^2}{\hat{s}^2\tau}(1 - e^{-\hat{s}\tau}) + \frac{\sigma^2}{\hat{s}}$$

Notice that in the definition for $Y(l, \tau)$, we substitute the value of $\hat{s}$ with the contemporaneous value of s itself. This reduces computational complexity. The best fit to bond prices in this model was achieved with a price of risk $\lambda = -0.70$.

A comparison of our model with the SS model is presented in Table 5.6. The measures of performance used are the same as in the previous section. As Table 5.6 shows, the in-sample performance of the two models are virtually the same, with our model doing slightly better in most circumstances.

CONCLUSIONS

In this chapter, we develop a new two-factor model of interest rates. We price bonds for alternative processes of the mean interest rate (central tendency), and provide an empirical methodology to investigate the pricing models. When benchmarked against one- and two-factor models, the model performs well, with the additional feature of being simple to operationalize.

The chapter develops an econometric model for estimating alternative interest rate processes with central tendency shifts. The model has sufficiently general theoretical foundations to enable estimation of the time path of the mean interest rate level without specifying a functional form for the stochastic behavior of the central tendency.

The central tendency experiences frequent changes and the pricing of bonds is significantly affected when this is not taken into account. We compare models of the short interest rate for time varying central tendency versus models assuming constant central tendency. With time-variation in θ, the mean reversion coefficient is understated if the mean is held constant. Much of the variation in the interest rate comes from mean changes and the remainder from random shocks. Finally, the mean appears to be drawn from a normal distribution, and leptokurtosis in the data is largely the outcome of the random noise element in r, possibly indicating that a combined jump-diffusion specification for only r may be the best choice.

Extensions to this work will center around the investigation of bond-option pricing models accommodating varying θ. Such models would provide better pricing for long-term bond options.

APPENDIX 5.1

CLOSED-FORM SOLUTIONS FOR BOND PRICES

Recall that the model under consideration is described by the following pair of equations

$$dr = \kappa(\theta - r)dt + \sigma dz$$

$$d\theta = (a + b\theta)dt + \eta dw$$

where the two diffusion processes are correlated with coefficient ρ

$$dz\, dw = \rho\, dt$$

As usual, let $P(r, \tau, \theta)$ denote the price of a bond with face value \$1 that matures in τ years, when the current short rate is r and the current value of the central tendency is θ. By Ito's Lemma, P must obey the differential equation

$$dP = P_r[\kappa(\theta - r)dt + \sigma\,dz] + \frac{1}{2}P_{rr}\sigma^2 dt - P_\tau dt$$

$$+ P_\theta[(a + b\theta)dt + \eta\,dw] + \frac{1}{2}P_{\theta\theta}\eta^2 dt + P_{\theta r}\sigma\eta\,dz\,dw$$

Assuming that the market price of interest rate (r) risk is equal to λ and that the price of central tendency shift risk is zero, the following no-arbitrage condition must be satisfied

$$E\left(\frac{dP}{dt}\right) - rP = P_r\sigma\lambda$$

where

$$E\left(\frac{dP}{dt}\right) = P_r\kappa(\theta - r) + \frac{1}{2}P_{rr}\sigma^2 - P_\tau + P_\theta(a + b\theta) + \frac{1}{2}P_{\theta\theta}\eta^2 + P_{\theta r}\rho\sigma\eta$$

Using this no-arbitrage condition, we now obtain the following differential equation for the bond price

$$[\kappa(\theta - r) - \lambda\sigma]P_r + \frac{1}{2}\sigma^2 P_{rr} - P_\tau + P_\theta\alpha + \frac{1}{2}P_{\theta\theta}\eta^2 + P_{\theta r}\rho\sigma\eta - rP = 0$$

The boundary condition for this PDE is

$$P(r, 0, \theta) = 1$$

We guess a solution of the form

$$P(r, \theta, \tau) = \exp[A(\tau) - rB(\tau) - \theta C(\tau)]$$

Substituting the derivatives of the posited guess into the equation, and then simplifying by separating terms as coefficients of r and θ we arrive at the following transformation of the PDE

$$0 = r[\kappa B + B_\tau - 1] + \theta[-\kappa B + C_\tau - bC]$$
$$+ [\lambda\sigma B + \frac{1}{2}\sigma^2 B^2 - A_\tau - \alpha C + \frac{1}{2}\eta^2 C^2 + \rho\sigma\eta BC]$$

The equation above in three terms is separable in r and θ. Since it must hold for all values of r, θ, the only way this is possible is if all three terms in square brackets are equal to zero. This results in three separate ordinary differential equations as

$$0 = \kappa B + B_\tau - 1$$
$$0 = -\kappa B + C_\tau - bC$$
$$0 = \lambda\sigma B + \frac{1}{2}\sigma^2 B^2 - A_\tau - \alpha C + \frac{1}{2}\eta^2 C^2 + \rho\sigma\eta BC$$

The boundary condition is that at $\tau = 0$, $P = 1$. This implies that $A = 0$, $B = 0$, $C = 0$. These ODEs may be solved in sequence to obtain the following solutions

$$P(r,\theta,\tau) = \exp[A(\tau) - rB(\tau) - \theta C(\tau)]$$

$$A(\tau) = \frac{-(\eta^2\kappa^2)}{4b^3(b+\kappa)^2} + \frac{e^{2b\tau}\eta^2\kappa^2}{4b^3(b+\kappa)^2} + \frac{ab\kappa + \eta^2\kappa - b\eta\rho\sigma}{b^3(b+\kappa)}$$

$$+ \frac{e^{b\tau}(-ab\kappa - \eta^2\kappa + b\eta\rho\sigma)}{b^3(b+\kappa)} + \frac{\eta(\eta\kappa - b\rho\sigma - \kappa\rho\sigma)}{b(-b+\kappa)(b+\kappa)^2}$$

$$- \frac{ab\kappa^2 + \eta^2\kappa^2 - 2b\eta\kappa\rho\sigma - \eta\kappa^2\rho\sigma + b^2\kappa\lambda\sigma + b\kappa^2\lambda\sigma + b^2\sigma^2 + b\kappa\sigma^2}{b\kappa^3(b+\kappa)}$$

$$+ \frac{-\eta^2\kappa^2 + 2b\eta\kappa\rho\sigma - 2\eta\kappa^2\rho\sigma - b^2\sigma^2 - 2b\kappa\sigma^2 - \kappa^2\sigma^2}{4e^{2\kappa\tau}\kappa^3(b+\kappa)^2}$$

$$+ \frac{\eta^2\kappa^2 - 2b\eta\kappa\rho\sigma - 2\eta\kappa^2\rho\sigma + b^2\sigma^2 + 2b\kappa\sigma^2 + \kappa^2\sigma^2}{4\kappa^3(b+\kappa)^2}$$

$$+ \frac{\dfrac{e^{b\tau}\eta(\eta\kappa - b\rho\sigma - \kappa\rho\sigma)}{b(b-\kappa)(b+\kappa)^2} + \dfrac{ab\kappa^2 + \eta^2\kappa^2 - 2b\eta\kappa\rho\sigma - \eta\kappa^2\rho\sigma + b^2\kappa\lambda\sigma + b\kappa^2\lambda\sigma + b^2\sigma^2 + b\kappa\sigma^2}{b\kappa^3(b+\kappa)}}{e^{\kappa\tau}}$$

$$+ \frac{(2ab\kappa^2 + \eta^2\kappa^2 - 2b\eta\kappa\rho\sigma + 2b^2\kappa\lambda\sigma + b^2\sigma^2)\tau}{2b^2\kappa^2}$$

$$B(\tau) = \frac{1 - e^{-(\kappa\tau)}}{\kappa}$$

$$C(\tau) = \frac{(e^{-(\kappa\tau)} - 1)b + (e^{b\tau} - 1)\kappa}{(b+\kappa)b}$$

For the two special cases of the θ process mentioned on page 135 (Arithmetic Brownian motion and a mean-reverting process), this solution simplifies as below.

Special Case 1:   Arithmetic Brownian Motion

When $a = \alpha$ and $b = 0$, the process for θ reduces to Arithmetic Brownian Motion:

$$d\theta = \alpha dt + \eta dw$$

In this special case, the bond prices function $P(r, \tau, \theta)$ is given by

$$P(r,\theta,\tau) = \exp[A(\tau) - rB(\tau) - \theta C(\tau)]$$

$$A(\tau) = \frac{-\eta^2 + 2\eta\rho\sigma - \sigma^2}{4e^{2\kappa\tau}\kappa^3} + \frac{\eta^2 - 2\eta\rho\sigma + \sigma^2}{4\kappa^3} - \frac{\alpha\kappa + \kappa\lambda\sigma - \eta\rho\sigma + \sigma^2}{\kappa^3}$$

$$+ \frac{(\eta^2 + 2\alpha\kappa + 2\kappa\lambda\sigma - 2\eta\rho\sigma + \sigma^2)\tau}{2\kappa^2} + \frac{(-\eta^2 - \alpha\kappa + \eta\rho\sigma)\tau^2}{2\kappa}$$

$$+ \frac{\eta^2\tau^3}{6} + \frac{\alpha\kappa + \kappa\lambda\sigma - \eta\rho\sigma + \sigma^2 - \eta^2\kappa\tau + \eta\kappa\rho\sigma\tau}{e^{\kappa\tau}\kappa^3}$$

$$B(\tau) = \frac{1 - e^{-\kappa\tau}}{\kappa}$$

$$C(\tau) = \tau - \frac{1 - e^{-\kappa\tau}}{\kappa}$$

Special Case 2:   Mean-Reverting θ Process

A mean-reverting process for θ obtains when θ follows

$$d\theta = \alpha(\beta - \theta)dt + \eta dw$$

where α is the coefficient of mean reversion, and β is the long run central tendency of θ. As explained earlier, the mean-reverting process is simply a special case of the general process which results when $\alpha = -b$ and $\beta = -a/b$. Using this substitution, it can be shown that the following expressions result for bond prices when θ follows a mean-reverting process:

$$P(r,\theta,\tau) = \exp[A(\tau) - rB(\tau) - \theta C(\tau)]$$

$$A(\tau) = \gamma_1(1 - e^{-2\alpha\tau}) - \gamma_2(1 - e^{-\alpha\tau}) - \gamma_3 - \gamma_4 + \gamma_5(1 - e^{-2\kappa\tau})$$

$$+ e^{(\alpha-\kappa)\tau}[\gamma_6 + \gamma_7] - \beta\tau + \frac{\eta^2\tau}{2\alpha^2} + \frac{\lambda\sigma\tau}{\kappa} + \frac{\eta\rho\sigma\tau}{\alpha\kappa} + \frac{\sigma^2\tau}{2\kappa^2}$$

$$\gamma_1 = \frac{\eta^2\kappa^2}{4\alpha^3(\alpha - \kappa)^2}$$

$$\gamma_2 = \frac{-\alpha^2\beta\kappa + \eta^2\kappa + \alpha\eta\rho\sigma}{\alpha^3(\alpha - \kappa)}$$

$$\gamma_3 = \frac{\eta(\eta\kappa + \alpha\rho\sigma - \kappa\rho\sigma)}{\alpha(\alpha - \kappa)^2(\alpha + \kappa)}$$

$$\gamma_4 = \frac{a^2\beta\kappa^2 - \eta^2\kappa^2 - \alpha^2\kappa\lambda\sigma + \alpha\kappa^2\lambda\sigma - 2\alpha\eta\kappa\rho\sigma + \eta\kappa^2\rho\sigma - \alpha^2\sigma^2 + \alpha\kappa\sigma^2}{\alpha\kappa^3(\kappa - \alpha)}$$

$$\gamma_5 = \frac{\eta^2\kappa^2 + 2\alpha\eta\kappa\rho\sigma - 2\eta\kappa^2\rho\sigma + \alpha^2\sigma^2 - 2\alpha\kappa\sigma^2 + \kappa^2\sigma^2}{4(\alpha - \kappa)^2\kappa^3}$$

$$\gamma_6 = \frac{\eta(\eta\kappa + \alpha\rho\sigma - \kappa\rho\sigma)}{\alpha e^{2\alpha\tau}(\alpha - \kappa)^2(\alpha + \kappa)}$$

$$\gamma_7 = \gamma_4 e^{-\alpha\tau}$$

$$B(\tau) = \frac{1 - e^{-\kappa\tau}}{\kappa}$$

$$C(\tau) = \frac{(1 - e^{-\kappa\tau}) + \dfrac{\kappa}{\alpha}e^{-\alpha\tau}(1 - e^{\alpha\tau})}{\alpha - \kappa}$$

APPENDIX 5.2

BOND PRICES WHEN θ FOLLOWS A JUMP PROCESS

This is essentially a two-factor model with the process equations given by

$$dr = \kappa(\theta - r)dt + \sigma dz$$

$$d\theta = J(\mu, \gamma^2)d\pi(h)$$

where J is a normally distributed jump size, with mean μ and variance γ^2, and $d\pi$ is a Poisson arrival process with frequency parameter h. h represents the number of jumps per unit time (in most cases one year). The infinitesimal jump probability is given by hdt. The bond price at time t is denoted $P(r, \theta, t)$. Assume that the bond matures on date T. Applying Ito's Lemma we obtain the differential process for P as

$$dP = P_r[\kappa(\theta - r)dt + \sigma dz] + \frac{1}{2}P_{rr}\sigma^2 dt + P_t dt + [P(r,\theta + J,t) - P(r,\theta,t)]d\pi$$

Assuming that the market price of interest rate (r) risk is equal to λ and that the price of central tendency jump risk is zero, the following no-arbitrage condition must be satisfied

$$E\left(\frac{dP}{dt}\right) - rP = P_r\sigma\lambda$$

where

$$E\left(\frac{dP}{dt}\right) = P_r\kappa(\theta - r) + \frac{1}{2}P_{rr}\sigma^2 + P_t + E[P(r,\theta + J,t) - P(r,\theta,t)]h$$

Therefore applying the no-arbitrage condition above, we obtain the following differential equation for the bond price

$$[\kappa(\theta - r) - \lambda\sigma]P_r + \frac{1}{2}\sigma^2 P_{rr} - P_\tau + E[P(r,\theta + J,t) - P(r,\theta,t)]h - rP = 0$$

where we have replaced t with time to maturity $\tau = T - t$. The boundary condition for the PDE above is

$$P(r,\theta,\tau = 0) = 1$$

We guess that the (approximate) solution is of the form

$$P(r,\theta,\tau) = \exp[A(\tau) - rB(\tau) - \theta C(\tau)]$$

Now,

$$E[P(r,\theta+J,t) - P(r,\theta,t)] = E(e^{A-rB-(\theta+J)C} - e^{A-rB-\theta C})$$

$$= \left(E(e^{-JC}) - 1\right)P$$

$$= \left(\exp\left(-\mu C + \frac{1}{2}\gamma^2 C^2\right) - 1\right)P$$

$$\approx \left(-\mu C + \frac{1}{2}\gamma^2 C^2\right)P$$

The next to last step uses the fact that e^{-JC} is lognormal, while the last line is a first-order Taylor Series approximation which uses the fact that JC is typically small (for instance a jump size of 25 basis points means that $J = 0.0025$). Substituting this into the equation, and also the derivatives of the posited guess solution, and then simplifying by separating terms as coefficients of r and θ we arrive at the following transformation of the PDE:

$$0 = r[\kappa B + B_\tau - 1]$$
$$+ \theta[-\kappa B + C_\tau]$$
$$+ \left[\lambda \sigma B + \frac{1}{2}\sigma^2 B^2 - A_\tau - \mu h C + \frac{1}{2}\gamma^2 C^2 h\right]$$

The equation above in three terms is separable in r and θ. Since it must hold for all values of r, θ, the only way this is possible is if all three terms in square brackets are equal to zero. This results in three separate ordinary differential equations as

$$0 = \kappa B + B_\tau - 1$$
$$0 = -\kappa B + C_\tau$$
$$0 = \lambda \sigma B + \frac{1}{2}\sigma^2 B^2 - A_\tau - \mu h C + \frac{1}{2}\gamma^2 C^2 h$$

The boundary condition is that at $\tau = 0$, $P = 1$. This implies that $A = 0$, $B = 0$, $C = 0$. These ODEs are solved in sequence. First, solve the equation subject to the condition $B(\tau = 0) = 0$. The solution is

$$B(\tau) = \frac{1 - e^{-\kappa\tau}}{\kappa}$$

Substituting this solution into equation, we can solve for $C(\tau)$ subject to the condition $C(\tau = 0) = 0$. The solution is

$$C(\tau) = \tau - \frac{1 - e^{-\kappa\tau}}{\kappa}$$

Finally substitute the expressions for $(B(\tau), C(\tau))$ into the equation, which is solved subject to the condition $A(\tau = 0) = 1$ to give the value of $A(\tau)$ as follows:

$$A(\tau) = \frac{\gamma^2 h + \sigma^2}{4\kappa^3} - \frac{\gamma^2 h + \sigma^2}{4e^{2\kappa\tau}\kappa^3} - \frac{h\kappa\mu + \kappa\lambda\sigma + \sigma^2}{\kappa^3}$$
$$+ \frac{(\gamma^2 h + 2h\kappa\mu + 2\kappa\lambda\sigma + \sigma^2)\tau}{2\kappa^2} - \frac{h(\gamma^2 + \kappa\mu)\tau^2}{2\kappa}$$
$$+ \frac{\gamma^2 h\tau^3}{6} + \frac{\dfrac{h\kappa\mu + \kappa\lambda\sigma + \sigma^2}{\kappa^3} - \dfrac{\gamma^2 h\tau}{\kappa^2}}{e^{\kappa\tau}}$$

$$B(\tau) = \frac{1 - e^{-\kappa\tau}}{\kappa}$$

$$C(\tau) = \tau - \frac{1 - e^{-\kappa\tau}}{\kappa}$$

Therefore the bond price is given by the expression:

$$P(r, \theta, \tau) = \exp[A(\tau) - rB(\tau) - \theta C(\tau)]$$

where A, B, and C are defined in their respective equations above.

ACKNOWLEDGMENT

We are grateful to Pedro Santa Clara, Marti Subrahmanyam, René Stulz, Bruce Tuckman, and seminar participants at the University of Illinois at Urbana-Champaign, Carnegie-Mellon University, University of Southern California, University of Pennsylvania, Harvard University, University of Michigan, Cornell University, University of Chicago, the Eastern Finance Conference at Boston, and the American Finance Association at Chicago for helpful comments.

REFERENCES

Balduzzi, P., G. Bertola, and S. Foresi. (1997). "A Model of Target Changes and the Term Structure of Interest Rates," *Journal of Monetary Economics, 39,* 223–249.

Balduzzi, P., G. Bertola, S. Foresi, and L. Klapper. (1998). "Interest Rate Targeting and the Dynamics of Short-Term Rates," *Journal of Money, Credit, and Banking, 30,* 26–50.

Balduzzi, P., S. Das, and S. Foresi. (1998). "The Central Tendency: A Second Factor in Bond Yields," *Review of Economics and Statistics, 80,* 62–72.

Balduzzi, P., S. Das, S. Foresi, and R. Sundaram. (1996). "A Simple Approach to Three-Factor Affine Models of the Term Structure," *Journal of Fixed Income, 6,* 43–53.

Baz, J. and S. Das. (1996). "Analytical Approximations of Term Structure Models: A Numerical Analysis," *Journal of Fixed Income, 6*(1), 78–86.

Brennen, M.J. and E.S. Schwartz. (1979). "A Continuous Time Approach to the Pricing of Bonds," *Journal of Banking and Finance, 3*(2), 133–156.

Chan, K.C., G.A. Karolyi, F.A. Longstaff, and A.B. Sanders. (1992). "An Empirical Comparison of Alternative Models of the Short-Term Interest Rate," *Journal of Finance, 47*(3), 1209–1228.

Cox, J.C., J.E. Ingersoll, and S.A. Ross. (1985b). "A Theory of the Term Structure of Interest Rates," *Econometrica,* 385–407.

Das, S. and S. Foresi. (1996). "Exact Solutions for Bond and Option Prices with Systematic Jump Risk," *Review of Derivatives Research, 1*(1), 7–24.

Duffie, D. and R. Kan. (1996). "A Yield Factor Model of Interest Rates," *Mathematical Finance, 6*(4), 379–406.

Longstaff, F.A. and E.S. Schwartz. (1992). "Interest Rate Volatility and the Term Structure: A Two-Factor General Equilibrium Model," *Journal of Finance, 47*(4), 1259–1282.

Pearson, N.D. and T.S. Sun. (1994). "Exploiting the Conditional Density in Estimating the Term Structure: A Two-Factor General Equilibrium Model," *Journal of Finance, 49,* 1279–1304.

Pennacchi, G.G. (1991). "Identifying the Dynamics of Real Interest Rates and Inflation: Evidence Using Survey Data," *Review of Financial Studies*, 4(1), 53–86.

Press, J.S. (1967). "A Compound Events Model for Security Prices," *Journal of Business*, 40, 317–335.

Schaefer, S.M. and E.S. Schwartz. (1984). "A Two-Factor Model of the Term Structure: An Approximate Analytical Solution," *Journal of Financial and Quantitative Analysis*, 19(4), 413–424.

Sun, T.S. (1992). "Real and Nominal Interest Rates: A Discrete-Time Model and Its Continuous-Time Limit," *Review of Financial Studies*, 5(4), 581–611.

Vasicek, O. (1997). "An Equilibrium Characterization of the Term Structure," *Journal of Financial Economics*, 5, 177–188.

6

Interest Rate Modeling with Jump-Diffusion Processes

Sanjiv Ranjan Das

The choice of jump-diffusion as the stochastic process for interest rates is a natural one. Information flows affect interest rates continuously in small amounts, best described by diffusion processes. Yet, on the rare occasion, surprise information events have large economic impact, causing interest rates to jump. Composite jump-diffusion processes therefore do quite well in describing the movements in interest rates.

This chapter summarizes some of the research in this area, all of which are of recent origin. There is now a burgeoning literature that develops theoretical bond pricing models for jump-diffusion processes (see Ahn & Thompson, 1988; Attari, 1997; Babbs & Webber, 1995; Backus, Foresi, & Wu, 1997; Baz & Das, 1996; Burnetas & Ritchken, 1996; Chacko, 1996a, 1996b; Das, 1995, 1997; Das & Foresi, 1996; Heston, 1995; Naik & Lee, 1993; Shirakawa, 1991 for a range of theoretical models). In contrast, little empirical work has been done, though the evidence does point to the good fit of this class of models (see Chacko, 1996a, 1996b; Chahal & Wang, 1995; Das, 1997; Moreno & Pena, 1995; Naik & Lee, 1993).

The paucity of the literature stems most likely from the fact that the mathematics of mean-reverting jump-diffusion processes is somewhat intractable. Jump-diffusion models for equities and exchange rates do not admit mean-reversion and hence are simpler to use (see Ball & Torous, 1983, 1985; Bates, 1996; Jorion, 1988; Merton, 1976). The absence of mean reversion essentially implies that the terminal density of the underlying is not dependent on the specific time at which jumps occur. When mean-reversion is introduced, this becomes relevant, and if n jumps occur, then the moments of the jump-diffusion distribution will critically depend on when these jumps occur or how they are distributed in time.

The other problem facing researchers is that of making inferences about jumps from discrete data. The aliasing problem raises its ugly head, and prevents distinction of these processes from other plausible pure-diffusion ones. While econometricians are slowly proceeding toward a solution of this problem, we are far from it at the present moment.

Nevertheless, changes in interest rates evidence substantial levels of skewness and kurtosis. These features are easy to capture if jump-diffusion processes are used. Table 6.1 summarizes a time series of the 1-month Treasury bill rate for the period 1986–1996. The presence of skewness and kurtosis is undeniable. Gaussian models are unable to capture this feature, and the addition of a jump process is a logical way to accomplish it.

TABLE 6.1. Descriptive Statistics of the 1-Month Treasury Bill Rate (r), and Changes in the Rate (dr)

Statistic	r	dr
Mean	5.45%	0.0003
Std. Dev.	1.63	0.0576
Skewness	0.13	−0.328
Kurtosis	−0.85	12.99

In the following sections, we will develop theoretical models starting with equilibrium modeling, and a description of closed-form solutions. Then, we shall proceed on to an investigation of jump-diffusion models of the no-arbitrage type, resulting from extensions of the Heath, Jarrow, and Morton (1990) paradigm.

A JUMP-DIFFUSION EQUILIBRIUM MODEL OF THE TERM STRUCTURE

Equilibrium Set-Up

This section develops the equilibrium process for the interest rate in a Cox, Ingersoll, and Ross (1985a) economy. The exposition here is a summarization of the model developed by Ahn and Thompson (1988).

We begin by assuming a standard economy with a representative agent whose preferences follow a log-utility function. A single production process Q characterizes the economy, and its stochastic process is a square-root diffusion

$$\frac{dQ}{Q} = \mu Y dt + \sigma_1 \sqrt{Y} dz_1$$

where μY is the drift term, $\sigma_1^2 Y$ is the variance coefficient and dz_1 is a standard Wiener increment. The economy is driven by a single state variable (Y) which in turn obeys a jump-diffusion process

$$dY = (a + bY) dt + \sigma_2 \sqrt{Y} dz_2 + J(.) d\pi(h)$$

(6.1)

where $(a + bY)$ is the drift, $\sigma_2^2 Y$ is the variance, and dz_2 is a Wiener increment correlated with dz_1 through correlation parameter ξ. The jump term $J(.)$ takes on positive value with probability 1. $|J| \in (0, \infty)$. Jumps arrive at rate h per unit time (one year) through the Poisson process $\pi (h)$. We assume that the jump size and arrival are uncorrelated with the diffusion processes in the economy, and that the parameters (a, b, σ_2) are such that $Y >> 0$.

Assume a representative agent whose happiness derives from the utility of consumption. The residual wealth balance in this economy will be determined by the production less consumption (C_t) in each period. Hence the stochastic process for wealth (W_t) is

$$dW = W \frac{dQ}{Q} - C\,dt$$

$$= (\mu WY - C)dt + \sigma_1 W \sqrt{Y}\,dz_1$$

The agent maximizes expected utility subject to the wealth process through the following additive preference function

$$E_t \left[\int_0^\infty \exp(-\rho t) \ln(C_t)dt \right]$$

where $E(.)$ is the expectations operator, and ρ is the time-preference parameter. This standard optimal control problem for the log investor has been solved by Merton (1971) resulting in the following separable (in the state variable and wealth) value function

$$H(W,Y,t) = \frac{\exp(-\rho t)}{\rho} \ln(W) + G(Y,t)$$

where $H(W,Y,t)$ is the indirect utility function, and $G(Y,t)$ is a function of Y alone, not W. The optimal consumption under this framework is ρW. Substituting this into the process for wealth gives us

$$dW = (\mu Y - \rho)W\,dt + \sigma_1 W \sqrt{Y}\,dz_1 \qquad (6.2)$$

Interest Rate Process

For the purposes of this chapter, we are interested in deriving the equilibrium interest rate process. Theorem 1 in Cox, Ingersoll, and Ross relates the riskless rate of interest to the expected rate of change of marginal utility. Given the logarithmic utility function, the riskless interest rate is given by the mean production rate less its variance,

$$r = \mu Y - \sigma_1^2 Y = (\mu - \sigma_1^2)Y$$

Applying Ito's Lemma we get the differential process for r

$$dr = r_Y dY + r_t dt + \frac{1}{2} r_{YY} (dY)^2$$

$$= (\mu Y - \sigma_1^2) \left[(a + bY)dt + \sigma_2 \sqrt{Y} dz_2 + J d\pi \right]$$

where the subscripts stand for derivatives, and by isomorphism, assuming that the state variable Y is the only state variable, we can write down the final process for the interest rate

$$dr = k(\theta - r)dt + \sigma dz + J d\pi(h) \tag{6.3}$$

where θ is the long-run mean of the interest rate process and k is the rate of mean reversion. The diffusion process dz has volatility coefficient σ. The reader will recognize that the interest rate process mimics the structure of the technology process in this economy.

Risk Premia

We have derived the equilibrium interest rate process in a simple jump-diffusion version of the CIR economy. To price assets in this economy, we need to determine the form of the risk premium so as to obtain the risk-neutral process under which all contingent claims and other assets may be valued using simple expectations. Standard asset-pricing has established that assets may be priced using a pricing kernel (denoted m), and that the following Euler equation must always hold in equilibrium

$$E[m \cdot R] = 1$$

where m is the pricing kernel or marginal rate of substitution of consumption or indirect utility. R is one plus the rate of return on the asset (denoted F) in question. Therefore, we may write

$$\lim_{dt \downarrow 0} E \left[\frac{H_W(t + dt)}{H_W(t)} \frac{F(t + dt)}{F(t)} \right] = 1$$

Therefore,

$$E\left[\left(1+\frac{dH_W}{H_W}\right)\left(1+\frac{dF}{F}\right)\right]=1$$

$$E\left[\frac{dH_W}{H_W}+\frac{dF}{F}+\frac{dH_W}{H_W}\frac{dF}{F}\right]=0$$

and rearranging results in

$$E\left(\frac{dF}{F}\right)=-E\left(\frac{dH_W}{H_W}\right)-E\left(\frac{dH_W}{H_W}\frac{dF}{F}\right)$$

From Theorem 1 in CIR (1985b), we know that $rdt=-E\left(\dfrac{dH_W}{H_W}\right)$, hence

$$E\left(\frac{dF}{F}\right)=rdt-E\left(\frac{dH_W}{H_W}\frac{dF}{F}\right)$$

$$=rdt-\text{cov}\left(\frac{dH_W}{H_W},\frac{dF}{F}\right)-E\left(\frac{dH_W}{H_W}\right)E\left(\frac{dF}{F}\right)$$

$$=rdt-\text{cov}\left(\frac{dH_W}{H_W},\frac{dF}{F}\right)+o(dt^2)$$

$$=rdt+\text{cov}\left(-\frac{dH_W}{H_W},\frac{dF}{F}\right)$$

We shall go on to prove that the second term in the expression above, the risk premium, is linear in the state variable Y. Since the asset in question, $F(Y)$ has a differential process given by

$$dF=\frac{\partial F}{\partial Y}dY+\frac{1}{2}\frac{\partial^2 F}{\partial Y^2}(dY)^2$$

The first term in dF is stochastic and the second term is a constant. Hence,

$$\text{cov}\left(-\frac{dH_W}{H_W},\frac{dF}{F}\right)=\text{cov}\left(-\frac{dH_W}{H_W},dY\right)\frac{F_Y}{F}$$

It remains to be shown that the term

$$\text{cov}\left(-\frac{dH_W}{H_W}, dY\right)$$

is of the form $\lambda(.)Y$ (i.e., linear in Y). Since we have already derived

$$H(W,Y,t) = \frac{1}{\rho}e^{-\rho t}\ln(W) + G(Y,t)$$

we can easily derive

$$H_W = \frac{1}{\rho}e^{-\rho t}\frac{1}{W}$$

Then, using Ito's Lemma we derive

$$dH_W = \frac{1}{\rho}e^{-\rho t}\left(\frac{-dW}{W^2}\right) + o(dt)$$

It follows then that

$$-\frac{dH_W}{H_W} = \frac{dW}{W}$$

and finally,

$$\text{cov}\left(-\frac{dH_W}{H_W}, dY\right) = \text{cov}\left(\frac{dW}{W}, dY\right)$$
$$= Y \times \sigma_1\sigma_2 \times corr(z_1, z_2)dt$$
$$= \lambda(.)Y\, dt$$

the last result is obtained using Equations (6.1) and (6.2). Finally, we can write the expected return on asset F as

$$E\left(\frac{dF}{F}\right) = \left(r + \lambda(.)Y\frac{F_Y}{F}\right)dt \tag{6.4}$$

which we then exploit in order to price contingent claims for this Cox-Ingersoll-Ross economy. The same relationship may be written by replacing Y with r when we assume that the short rate is the single factor driving the entire economy (i.e., the bond price is written as $F(r,t,T)$, where T is the maturity of the bond). The time to maturity is written as $\tau = T - t$.

Bond Pricing

The interest rate process is the same as derived in Equation (6.3). Using Ito's Lemma, changes in the bond price may be written as

$$dF = k(\theta - r)F_r dt + \sigma\sqrt{r}F_r dz + F_t dt + \frac{1}{2}F_{rr}\sigma^2 rdt + [F(r+J,t) - F(r,t)]d\pi$$

Substituting this expression in Equation (6.4), and substituting r in place of Y results in the partial differential equation

$$0 = [k(\theta - r) - \lambda r]F_r - F_\tau dt + \frac{1}{2}F_{rr}\sigma^2 r - rF + hE[F(r+J,t) - F(r,t)] \tag{6.5}$$

The boundary condition for pricing bonds is that the discount bond pays off a dollar at maturity (i.e., when $\tau = 0$). Guess a solution of the form $F(r, \tau) = \exp[A(\tau) - rB(\tau)]$. Inserting this solution in Equation (6.5) separates the partial differential equation into two ordinary differential equations:

$$0 = r\left\{(k+\lambda)B + B_\tau + \frac{1}{2}\sigma^2 B^2 - 1\right\} + \left\{-k\theta B - A_\tau + hE[e^{-JB} - 1]\right\}$$

Since $r \neq 0$ in general, the two bracketed differential equations above must be equal to zero separately. We solve them subject to the conditions $A(0) = 0$ and $B(0) = 0$. The final solution for the bond pricing model with jumps turns out to be

$$F(r,\tau) = \exp[A(\tau) - rB(\tau)]$$

$$A(\tau) = \int \left[-k\theta B(\tau) + hE\left[e^{-JB(\tau)} - 1 \right] \right] d\tau$$

$$B(\tau) = \frac{2(e^{\gamma\tau} - 1)}{(e^{\gamma\tau} - 1)(\gamma + k + \lambda) + 2\gamma}$$

$$\gamma = \sqrt{(k+\lambda)^2 + 2\sigma^2}$$

Therefore, including jumps, we arrive at an equilibrium solution for the term structure. The yield curve is simply the function $Y(\tau) = -\frac{1}{\tau}\ln[F(r,\tau)]$. Since there is a single factor, all yields are perfectly correlated.

A PRICING KERNEL REPRESENTATION

More general models may be derived by directly assuming a pricing kernel for the economy. The pricing kernel (M_t) in continuous time is a stochastic process that satisfies the Euler equations for asset pricing

$$1 = E_t[M_t \times (1 + R_t)]$$

where R_t is the return on any asset. In this section, we review the model developed by Das and Foresi (1996). They assume the pricing kernel to be

$$-\frac{dm}{m} = rdt + \lambda dz + \lambda_J[dN - hdt]$$

where λ is the price of diffusion risk and λ_J is the price of jump risk. The terms $[dN - hdt]$ form a compensated jump point process with dN occurring with frequency h per year. Consistent with the property of pricing kernels, we can verify that $E[-dm/m] = rdt$. Also note that $E(dN) = hdt$ and $E(dN^2) = hdt$.

Assume that the interest rate follows an Ornstein-Uhlenbeck process enhanced with a jump

$$dr = k(\theta - r)dt + \sigma dz + J d\pi$$

and the bond price is given by the function $F(r, \tau)$ defined the same way as in the preceding section. The differential process for the bond price will be

$$dF = k(\theta - r)F_r dt + \sigma F_r dz - F_\tau dt + \frac{1}{2}F_{rr}\sigma^2 r dt + [F(r+J,t) - F(r,t)]d\pi(h)$$

so that the expectation is

$$E(dF) = k(\theta - r)F_r dt - F_\tau dt + \frac{1}{2}F_{rr}\sigma^2 dt \qquad (6.6)$$

$$+ hE[F(r+J,t) - F(r,t)]dt \qquad (6.7)$$

Using the Euler equation we may write for the bond price F

$$E\left[\left(\frac{m+dm}{m}\right)\left(\frac{F+dF}{F}\right)\right] = 1$$

$$E\left[\frac{dm}{m} + \frac{dF}{F} = \frac{dm}{m}\frac{dF}{F}\right] = 0$$

Rearranging gives

$$E\left(\frac{dF}{F}\right) = E\left(-\frac{dm}{m}\right) - E\left(\frac{dm}{m}\frac{dF}{F}\right)$$

$$= rdt + E\left(-\frac{dm}{m}\frac{dF}{F}\right)$$

$$= rdt + E\left[\lambda\frac{F_r}{F}\sigma + h\lambda_J\frac{[F(r+J) - F(r)]}{F}\right]dt \qquad (6.8)$$

$$E\left(\frac{dF}{F}\right) = \left[r + \lambda\frac{F_r}{F}\sigma + \lambda_J qh\right]dt$$

where $q = E[F(r + J) - F(r)]$. Substituting from Equation (6.6) into (6.8) results in a differential equation for the bond price, which may then be solved to realize the solution.

$$P(r, \tau) = e^{A(\tau) + rB(\tau)}$$

$$B(\tau) = \frac{e^{-k\tau} - 1}{k}$$

$$A(\tau) = \int \left[(k\theta - \lambda \upsilon)B(\tau) + \frac{1}{2}\upsilon^2 B(\tau)^2 + qh^* \right] d\tau$$

$$q[B(\tau)] = E(e^{JB(\tau)} - 1)$$

$$h^* = h(1 - \lambda_J)$$

This concludes the treatment of equilibrium jump-diffusion models of the term structure. In the following sections, we shall explore the development of models in the no-arbitrage class.

JUMP MODELS IN A DISCRETE HEATH-JARROW-MORTON (HJM) FRAMEWORK

The first paper in this class of models is Shirakawa (1991). In this section, we provide a very simple direct approach to implementing these models along the lines of Das (1995).

A SIMPLE APPROACH TO JUMP DISCRETIZATION

Since we plan to implement a jump-diffusion version of the HJM model, we need to find a discretization scheme to mimic this process. Given that the jump and diffusion are independent, we may develop lattices separately for each component and then put these lattices together. The product space of the diffusion lattice and jump lattice provides the complete lattice for our model. To start with, we note that the diffusion part of the process may be discretized by means of a binomial tree as is usually done.

Next, we develop a model for discretizing a Poisson distribution. When a binomial process consists of a large number of trials (n), and the probability (p) of an "on" (i.e., jump) is low as compared to an "off," we get the Poisson distribution in the limit, if the expected number of "ons" (i.e., np is also low [Feller, 1950]). A trinomial process captures both the jump probability and jump size in a simple structure which converges to the Poisson limit.

To demonstrate that the discrete scheme converges to the continuous time jump process, we look at the moments of the discrete jump process in the limit and then see if they coincide with those from a continuous time derivation. Assume the following jump process for variable J with initial value 0 and three possible outcomes from a branching process

$$J = \begin{cases} \mu + \gamma \\ 0 \\ \mu - \gamma \end{cases}$$

and the corresponding probabilities are

$$p = \begin{cases} \dfrac{\lambda dt}{2} \\ 1 - \lambda dt \\ \dfrac{\lambda dt}{2} \end{cases}$$

where dt is a small interval of time. Computation shows that

$$E(J) = \lambda \mu dt$$

The variance is

$$Var(J) = \lambda(\mu^2 + \gamma^2)dt - \lambda^2 \mu^2 dt^2$$
$$\approx \lambda(\mu^2 + \gamma^2)dt$$

because we can ignore terms in dt^k, $k > 1$ since they are very small. Likewise, further computation gives

$$\text{Skewness } (J) = \frac{E[(J - E[J])^3]}{Var(J)^{3/2}} = \frac{1}{\sqrt{dt}}\left[\frac{\lambda(\mu^3 + 3\mu\gamma^2)}{(\lambda[\mu^2 + \gamma^2])^{3/2}}\right]$$

$$\text{Kurtosis } (J) = \frac{E[(J - E[J])^4]}{Var(J)^2} = \frac{1}{dt}\left[\frac{\lambda(\mu^4 + 6\mu^2\gamma^2 + \gamma^4)}{(\lambda[\mu^2 + \gamma^2])^2}\right]$$

We shall now show that these moments coincide with those of a pure jump process when derived formally in continuous time. Start with a stochastic process for J

$$dJ = g(\mu, \gamma^2)dQ(\lambda), \quad J_0 = 0$$

where $g(\mu, \gamma^2)$ is the jump magnitude coming from a distribution with mean μ and variance γ^2. The Poisson process $Q(\lambda)$ has intensity λ. The conditional moments of J may be derived by solving the Kolmogorov backward equation (KBE) for the characteristic function $F(J,T; s \mid J_0, t = 0)$ and then using it to find the moments. This gives the characteristic function over an interval T. The KBE (derived using the jump version of Ito's Lemma) is

$$0 = \lambda E[F(J + g) - F(J)] - \frac{\partial F}{\partial T}$$

with boundary condition

$$F(J, T = 0; s) = e^{isJ}, \quad i = \sqrt{-1}$$

The solution to this differential equation is

$$F(J, T; s) = \exp[isJ + \lambda TE(e^{isJ} - 1)]$$

The nth moment is equal to

$$\frac{1}{i^n}\left[\frac{\partial^n F}{\partial s^n}\right]_{s=0}$$

Setting $J_0 = 0$, and repeatedly using the formula above we can get the moments. The first moment is (noting that now $F(s = 0) = 1$)

$$\frac{1}{i}\left[\frac{\partial F}{\partial s}\right]_{s=0} = \left\{F\left[iJ_0 + \lambda TE\left(iJe^{isJ}\right)\right]\right\}_{s=0}$$

$$= \lambda E(J)T$$

Since we can set our time interval T to be equal to the small interval dt and we know that $E(J) = \mu$, we find that we get exactly the same first moment as that from the discrete time model in the limit. This is simply equal to

$$\frac{1}{i}\left[\frac{\partial F}{\partial s}\right]_{s=0} = \lambda \mu dt$$

Now we can compute the second moment too. First,

$$\frac{\partial^2 F}{\partial s^2} = F\left[\lambda TE\left(-J^2 e^{isJ}\right)\right] + F\left[iJ_0 + \lambda TE\left(iJe^{isJ}\right)\right]^2$$

Therefore,

$$\frac{1}{i^2}\left[\frac{\partial^2 F}{\partial s^2}\right]_{s=0} = \lambda TE(J^2) + \lambda^2 T^2 E(J)^2$$

Hence, the variance is

$$\frac{1}{i^2}\left[\frac{\partial^2 F}{\partial s^2}\right]_{s=0} - \left(\frac{1}{i}\left[\frac{\partial F}{\partial s}\right]_{s=0}\right)^2 = \lambda TE(J^2)$$

$$= \lambda(\mu^2 + \gamma^2)dt$$

which again coincides with the discrete model limit. Similar calculations for the skewness and kurtosis show that those moments also coincide with the discrete time limits.

Thus, the scheme for the jump provides a limit with moments that coincide with those of a Poisson process. Adding this to the scheme for the diffusion gives the jump-diffusion model we use in the paper. Hence, a hexanomial tree arises because it is the natural product space of the jump (trinomial) and diffusion (binomial).

The Discrete HJM Model with Skewness and Kurtosis

The HJM model is a comprehensive framework for the pricing of interest rate sensitive securities in an arbitrage-free manner. Starting with the known current term structure of forward rates, the HJM model allows the imposition of a wide range of stochastic dynamics describing the future evolution of the forward curve. Usual implementations have considered a wide choice of volatility functions for the diffusion that drives the stochastic process. In this chapter, we tack on a jump process and demonstrate that the dynamics and the theory required may be seamlessly extended for the jump process.

The HJM model employs the well-known results of Harrison and Pliska (1981) that state that the discounted prices of assets must follow a martingale to ensure the absence of arbitrage. Here, we develop a pricing lattice on which the forward curve dynamics are chosen under a probability measure that ensures that the security prices are martingales. Hence, the HJM approach ensures no arbitrage, and in what follows, we derive analytically the conditions that sustain the model, with the enhancement for jump processes.

The standard HJM diffusion model fits a lattice to the existing term structure of interest rates and the known term structure of volatility. Shirakawa (1991) developed a jump-diffusion version of this model. Das (1995) develops a similar model such that the term structures of volatility, skewness, and kurtosis may be easily fitted. Derivative securities display the impact of all these moments and hence the model is practically useful.

This section presents a simple version of these papers. The model allows fitting of all moments greater than the mean, namely the variance, skewness, and kurtosis of forward rates at all maturities. Market participants are interested in trading not only interest rate volatility, but also skewness and kurtosis by speculating on the shape of the volatility smile.

Since the model is developed in discrete-time, it is essential to stipulate a discrete time interval, which we denote as h. Whereas it is also possible to index h such that we employ time intervals of varying length, we shall assume without loss of generality that the intervals are all of equal length. In the model, we will be using risk-neutral pricing methods (see Harrison & Pliska, 1981), and therefore we assume the existence of a probability measure Q, under which the prices of all interest-sensitive assets will follow a martingale.

To accommodate a term structure of skewness and kurtosis, the forward rate process may be written as follows. At each trading date t, the forward rates for all future maturities $T > t$ follow the stochastic difference equation

$$f(t+h,T) = f(t,T) + \alpha(T)h + \sigma(T)\sqrt{h}X_1 + J[\mu(T),\gamma^2(T)]N(\bar{\lambda}), \forall T \qquad (6.9)$$

$f(t,T)$ is the one period forward rate at time T, as observed at time t. The drift coefficient of the process is α (.), and the Gaussian coefficient is σ (.). We assume that they are bounded. $X_1(.)$ and $J(.)$ are random shocks to the process and are assumed to be distributed as

$$X_1 \sim N(0,1)$$

$$J(T) = \begin{cases} \mu(T) + \gamma(T) & \text{with probability} \quad \frac{1}{2} \\ \mu(T) - \gamma(T) & \text{with probability} \quad \frac{1}{2} \end{cases}$$

X_1 and J are independent random variables. The discrete process above mimics the behavior of a continuous-time jump-diffusion process. Hence, the first noise term above represents the diffusion component, and the second term represents the jump, which takes values $(\mu + \gamma)$ or $(\mu - \gamma)$. Therefore, the jump has mean μ and variance γ^2. $N(\bar{\lambda})$ is an indicator function (representing a point process) taking on the value 1 on rare occasions with probability driven by the parameter $\bar{\lambda}$. $\bar{\lambda}$ is the probability parameter of a jump in unit time, and hence the probability of a jump in any time interval $\approx \bar{\lambda}h$. We assume an infinite number of forward rates in the interval $[0,T]$. Notice that every forward rate at maturities T has a designated volatility parameter $\sigma(T)$, a skewness coefficient $\mu(T)$, and a kurtosis coefficient $\gamma(T)$. Hence, the term structures for all three moments, as well as the initial term structure of forward rates forms the initial input for the model.

The "spot" rate of interest is defined to be $r(t) = f(t,t)$. We shall denote riskless bonds as $P(r,\tau)$, where $\tau = T - t$, and T is the bond's maturity date. The model's objective is to develop a risk-neutral lattice for pricing riskless debt. The riskless interest rates lattice is generated by solving for the risk-neutral drifts so that all interest rate sensitive securities are martingales. This ensures that the lattice is free from arbitrage.

We assume the existence of a risk-neutral measure under which the prices of securities are martingales. We shall denote this as measure Q in order to distinguish it from the physical probability measure P.[1] In order to derive the risk-neutral process, we proceed as in Heath, Jarrow, and Morton (1990).

As shown in Das (1995), the arbitrage-free dynamics of the term structure imply the following for the drift term $\alpha(.)$

$$\sum_{i=\frac{t}{h}+1}^{\frac{T}{h}-1} \alpha(ih) = \frac{1}{h^2} \ln\left(E_Q\left[\exp\left\{ -\sum_{i=\frac{t}{h}+1}^{\frac{T}{h}-1} \left[\sigma(ih)X_1\sqrt{h} + J(ih)N(\bar{\lambda}) \right]h \right\} \right] \right) \qquad (6.10)$$

The expectation is taken over the joint outcomes for the diffusion and jump shocks, and is in hexanomial space. Once the $\alpha(.)$s are computed analytically, the recombining tree is generated. Note that since neither $\sigma(.)$ nor $J(.)$ are functions of the forward rate, the tree will recombine. Pricing of term structure securities proceeds by discounting cash flows on the tree. This also suggests empirical extraction of the term structures of skewness and kurtosis is possible, allowing traders to obtain implied skewness and kurtosis. We explore the derivation of this in detail next.

---

[1] This is not to be confused with the bond price $P(r,\tau)$.

The point process N takes on the value 1 with probability $1 - e^{-\bar{\lambda}h}$. Therefore, we can write

$$
N = \begin{cases} 0 & \text{with probability} \quad 1 - \bar{\lambda}h + o(h) \\ 1 & \text{with probability} \quad \bar{\lambda}h + o(h) \\ >1 & \text{with probability} \quad o(h) \end{cases}
$$

For notational convenience, let $\lambda = \bar{\lambda}h$. In the process above, jumps occur rarely, which we achieve by choosing a low value for $\lambda \in (0,1)$, and then we may choose the parameters μ and γ to provide the necessary skewness and kurtosis. The parameter μ will govern skewness in the model and the parameter γ will drive kurtosis. λ is the jump frequency parameter, which also acts as the mixing parameter providing the composite distribution of (X_1, J).

Assuming a continuous compounding convention, we can write out the expressions for the bond price as

$$
P(t,T) = \exp\left[-\sum_{i=\frac{t}{h}}^{\frac{T}{h}-1} f(t,ih)h \right]
$$

$$
f(t,ih) = f(0,ih) + \sum_{j=0}^{i-1}\left[\begin{array}{l} \alpha(jh,ih)h + \sigma(ih)X_1[(j+1)h]\sqrt{h} \\ +J[(j+1)h]N[(j+1)h] \end{array} \right]
$$

(6.11)

Define the spot rate of interest $r(t)$ as

$$
r(t) = f(t,t)
$$

We define a money market account (numeraire) and assume it is traded. This account is the balance of a reinvested dollar at the spot rate over time.

$$
B(t) = \exp\left[\sum_{i=0}^{\frac{t}{h}-1} r(ih)h \right] = \exp\left[\sum_{i=0}^{\frac{t}{h}-1} f(ih,ih)h \right]
$$

An exact set of six bonds can be used to span the uncertainty at each node, and thus a unique replication is also achieved. The unique spanning of the state space ensures that markets are complete. Therefore, completeness of markets ensures a unique martingale measure for the pricing of securities. Utilizing this specification allows us to compute the drift terms $\alpha(t,T)$ consistent with the martingale condition. Define the process for discounted bonds as follows, using the numeraire $B(t)$

$$Z(t,T) = \frac{P(t,T)}{B(t)}$$

In the absence of arbitrage, the prices of discounted assets follows a martingale under the measure Q, that is,

$$E_t^Q\left[\frac{Z(t+h,T)}{Z(t,T)}\right] = 1$$

Proceeding as in Amin and Bodurtha (1995), we can write

$$\frac{B(t+h)}{B(t)} = \exp[r(t)h] = \exp[f(t,t)h]$$

and

$$\frac{P(t+h,T)}{P(t,T)} = \frac{\exp\left[-\sum_{j=\frac{t}{h}+1}^{\frac{T}{h}-1} f(t+h,jh)h\right]}{\exp\left[-\sum_{j=\frac{t}{h}}^{\frac{T}{h}-1} f(t,jh)h\right]}$$

$$= \exp\left[f(t,t)h - \sum_{j=\frac{t}{h}+1}^{\frac{T}{h}-1}(f(t+h,jh)-f(t,jh))h\right]$$

Combining the equations above, we arrive at the following expression:

$$\frac{Z(t+h,T)}{Z(t,T)} = \exp\left[-\sum_{j=\frac{t}{h}+1}^{\frac{T}{h}-1}[\alpha(t,jh)h + \sigma(jh)X_1((j+1)h)\sqrt{h} + \frac{1}{h}(T-t)J((j+1)h)N((j+1)h)]h\right]$$

Taking expectations under the risk-neutral measure on both sides and equating to 1 (i.e., using the martingale condition, $E_t^Q\left[\frac{Z(t+h,T)}{Z(t,T)}\right] = 1$) results in Equation (6.10).

A Simple Numerical Example

The scheme presented above may be implemented quite easily. The following example illustrates the simplicity of the implementation. Assume a world of three periods. Each period is of length 1 year (i.e., $h = 1$). The details of the continuously compounded forward rate curve are as follows:

T	f(0,T)	σ(T)	μ(T)	γ(T)
1	0.08	0.015	0	0.02
2	0.09	0.020	0.001	0.03
3	0.10	0.025	0.002	0.03

This table states that the forward rates $f(0,T)$ at time 0 for the three years are 8%, 9%, and 10%, respectively. The parameters for the forward rates correspond to the equation of motion for the forward rates given in (6.9). Hence the term structure of diffusion volatility is driven by σ (T), $\forall T$. The skewness and kurtosis term structures are given by μ (T) and γ (T), respectively. We shall also assume that the probability of a jump in any year is 20% (i.e., we set $\lambda = 0.2$).

The prices of zero-coupon bonds of maturity T are denoted by $P(T) = \exp\left[-h\sum_{t=1}^{T} f(0,t)\right]$ and simple computations reveal that the vector for these bond prices is

$$P(T) = \begin{pmatrix} 0.923116 \\ 0.843665 \\ 0.763379 \end{pmatrix}$$

The branching process for the jump-diffusion model results in a hexanomial tree (6-way branching model). Note that, at time 0 there are three elements in the initial forward rate vector. After moving ahead one period, two periods are remaining, and each of the 6 nodes will have two elements in the forward rate vector. Applying Equation (6.9), we find that the 6 nodes will appear as

$$
\begin{bmatrix}
\begin{pmatrix} f(1,2)\,(1) \\ f(1,3)\,(1) \end{pmatrix} \\
\begin{pmatrix} f(1,2)\,(2) \\ f(1,3)\,(2) \end{pmatrix} \\
\begin{pmatrix} f(1,2)\,(3) \\ f(1,3)\,(3) \end{pmatrix} \\
\begin{pmatrix} f(1,2)\,(4) \\ f(1,3)\,(4) \end{pmatrix} \\
\begin{pmatrix} f(1,2)\,(5) \\ f(1,3)\,(5) \end{pmatrix} \\
\begin{pmatrix} f(1,2)\,(6) \\ f(1,3)\,(6) \end{pmatrix}
\end{bmatrix}
=
\begin{bmatrix}
\begin{pmatrix} f(0,2)+\alpha(1,2)+\sigma(2)+\mu(2)+\gamma(2) \\ f(0,3)+\alpha(1,3)+\sigma(3)+\mu(3)+\gamma(3) \end{pmatrix} \\
\begin{pmatrix} f(0,2)+\alpha(1,2)+\sigma(2) \\ f(0,3)+\alpha(1,3)+\sigma(3) \end{pmatrix} \\
\begin{pmatrix} f(0,2)+\alpha(1,2)+\sigma(2)+\mu(2)-\gamma(2) \\ f(0,3)+\alpha(1,3)+\sigma(3)+\mu(3)-\gamma(3) \end{pmatrix} \\
\begin{pmatrix} f(0,2)+\alpha(1,2)-\sigma(2)+\mu(2)+\gamma(2) \\ f(0,3)+\alpha(1,3)-\sigma(3)+\mu(3)+\gamma(3) \end{pmatrix} \\
\begin{pmatrix} f(0,2)+\alpha(1,2)-\sigma(2) \\ f(0,3)+\alpha(1,3)-\sigma(3) \end{pmatrix} \\
\begin{pmatrix} f(0,2)+\alpha(1,2)-\sigma(2)+\mu(2)-\gamma(2) \\ f(0,3)+\alpha(1,3)-\sigma(3)+\mu(3)-\gamma(3) \end{pmatrix}
\end{bmatrix}
$$

and the probabilities of the 6 nodes are given by the following vector

$$
p =
\begin{pmatrix}
\frac{\lambda}{4} \\
\frac{1-\lambda}{2} \\
\frac{\lambda}{4} \\
\frac{\lambda}{4} \\
\frac{1-\lambda}{2} \\
\frac{\lambda}{4}
\end{pmatrix}
$$

All the parameters are known, but for the appropriate values of $\alpha(1,2)$ and $\alpha(1,3)$, which we solve for employing the Equation (6.10). To start with, we need to find $\alpha(1,2)$ such that the values of two-period zero-coupon bonds may be computed on the tree so that they equal the value of $P(2)$. This requires solving

$$
P(2) = \exp[-f(0,1)]\sum_{i=1}^{6} \exp[-f(1,2)(i)] \times p(i)
$$

The solution to this equation is

$$\alpha(1,2) = 8.98 \times 10^{-5}$$

Likewise, we set up the equation for $\alpha(1,3)$

$$P(3) = \exp[-f(0,1)]\sum_{i=1}^{6} \exp[-f(1,2)(i) - f(1,3)(i)] \times p(i)$$

to which the solution is

$$\alpha(1,3) = 0.000682$$

Substituting these values back into the forward rate equations results in the values of the forward rate curve at the 6 nodes at time $T = 1$

$$\begin{bmatrix} \begin{pmatrix} 0.14109 \\ 0.15768 \end{pmatrix} \\ \begin{pmatrix} 0.11009 \\ 0.12568 \end{pmatrix} \\ \begin{pmatrix} 0.08109 \\ 0.09768 \end{pmatrix} \\ \begin{pmatrix} 0.10109 \\ 0.10768 \end{pmatrix} \\ \begin{pmatrix} 0.07009 \\ 0.07568 \end{pmatrix} \\ \begin{pmatrix} 0.04109 \\ 0.04768 \end{pmatrix} \end{bmatrix}$$

We are now ready to move onto the final period. Each of the 6 nodes branches into a further 6 nodes. Hence at the end of the final period we would expect to see 36 nodes. It turns out (see Das, 1995) that the hexanomial tree evidences recombination of nodes, and the number of nodes at each time step does not grow very rapidly because of this. In fact, the number of distinct nodes at the final step is only 18, not 36.[2]

---

[2] To see this, first consider the jump process by itself. After one step the possible values, ignoring time dependence notation, are $\mu + \gamma$, 0, and $\mu - \gamma$. The possible values

For each node at the final step there will be only one remaining forward rate in the term structure (i.e., $f(2,3)$). To make matters clear, let us focus on the first node of the 6 nodes at the penultimate step. We had computed the term structure to be

$$\begin{pmatrix} 0.14109 \\ 0.15768 \end{pmatrix}$$

The price of a two-period zero-coupon bond at this time would be

$$\exp[-0.14109 - 0.15768] = 0.700633$$

After one period this node branches into 6 nodes

$$\begin{bmatrix} f(2,3)\,(1) \\ f(2,3)\,(2) \\ f(2,3)\,(3) \\ f(2,3)\,(4) \\ f(2,3)\,(5) \\ f(2,3)\,(6) \end{bmatrix} = \begin{bmatrix} f(1,3) + \alpha(2,3) + \sigma(3) + \mu(3) + \gamma(3) \\ f(1,3) + \alpha(2,3) + \sigma(3) \\ f(1,3) + \alpha(2,3) + \sigma(3) + \mu(3) - \gamma(3) \\ f(1,3) + \alpha(2,3) - \sigma(3) + \mu(3) + \gamma(3) \\ f(1,3) + \alpha(2,3) - \sigma(3) \\ f(1,3) + \alpha(2,3) - \sigma(3) + \mu(3) + \gamma(3) \end{bmatrix}$$

with the same 6 probabilities as before. We can solve for $\alpha(2,3)$ from

$$0.700633 = \exp[-0.14109] \times \sum_{i=1}^{6} \exp[-f(2,3)(i)] \times p(i)$$

---

after another step are $2\mu + \gamma$, $\mu + \gamma$, 2μ, 0, $\mu - \gamma$, and $2\mu - 2\gamma$. Note that there are 6 distinct values, not 9, since an up jump followed by no jump gives the same value as no jump followed by an up jump, an up jump followed by a down jump gives the same value as a down jump followed by an up jump, and so on. Now consider the diffusion process as well. There are four sets of the 6 jump nodes to deal with, an up-up move from the diffusion, an up-down move, a down-up move, and a down-down move. But since a move of σ followed by a move of $-\sigma$ leaves value unchanged, as does a move of $-\sigma$ followed by a move of σ, the up-down set of 6 jump nodes has the same values as the down-up set of 6 jump nodes. Hence there are only three distinct set of 6 jump nodes, or 18 nodes in total.

and the solution is

$$\alpha(2,3) = -8.1 \times 10^{-8}$$

As a result, the 6 values of the final forward rate from the first node are

$$\begin{pmatrix} 0.214682 \\ 0.182682 \\ 0.154682 \\ 0.164682 \\ 0.132682 \\ 0.104682 \end{pmatrix}$$

This calculation was undertaken for the branching from the first of the 6 nodes at the penultimate stage. Similar computations for the remaining 5 nodes reveal that all the values of $\alpha(2,3)$ are the same. The following table provides the forward rate term structures emanating from each of the 6 nodes at the penultimate stage

From Node 1	From Node 2	From Node 3
$\begin{pmatrix} 0.214682 \\ 0.182682 \\ 0.154682 \\ 0.164682 \\ 0.132682 \\ 0.104682 \end{pmatrix}$	$\begin{pmatrix} 0.182682 \\ 0.150682 \\ 0.122682 \\ 0.132682 \\ 0.100682 \\ 0.072682 \end{pmatrix}$	$\begin{pmatrix} 0.154682 \\ 0.122682 \\ 0.094682 \\ 0.104682 \\ 0.072682 \\ 0.044682 \end{pmatrix}$

From Node 4	From Node 5	From Node 6
$\begin{pmatrix} 0.164682 \\ 0.132682 \\ 0.104682 \\ 0.114682 \\ 0.082682 \\ 0.054682 \end{pmatrix}$	$\begin{pmatrix} 0.132682 \\ 0.100682 \\ 0.072682 \\ 0.082682 \\ 0.050682 \\ 0.022682 \end{pmatrix}$	$\begin{pmatrix} 0.104682 \\ 0.072682 \\ 0.044682 \\ 0.054682 \\ 0.022682 \\ -0.00532 \end{pmatrix}$

Thus the entire lattice is set up, such that

- The lattice is arbitrage-free (i.e., the prices of bonds obtained by discounting cashflows on the lattice are equal to those obtained by discounting cashflows using the initial term structure of forward rates).

- The scheme enables the computation of risk-neutral drift terms $\alpha(t,T)$ such that no-arbitrage conditions are met.
- Inspection of the final sets of forward rates will reveal that altogether there are only 18 distinct rates, not 36, showing the economy obtained from recombination.
- The lattice has been derived by fitting three term structures of risk: volatility risk, skewness risk, and kurtosis risk. Hence, the jump-diffusion model captures more details than the pure diffusion HJM model.

CONCLUSION

We derived both equilibrium and no-arbitrage models of the term structure when the underlying process driving its evolution was assumed to be of the jump-diffusion type. While this made the analysis more complex than that of pure diffusion models, the results were still derivable. This chapter attempts to present simplified versions of the Cox-Ingersoll-Ross and Heath-Jarrow-Morton models when extended to jump-diffusions.

Using jump-diffusions quite understandably allows accommodation of the skewness and kurtosis features that are empirically ubiquitous in term structures of interest rates. Derivative claims are certainly priced differently in the presence of higher-order moments, and the final model of this chapter offers a simple discrete time approach to building a hexanomial tree to make such pricing possible in a practical manner. By fitting the term structures of variance, skewness, and kurtosis, the model provides a rich framework for modeling bonds and options.

ACKNOWLEDGMENT

I owe special thanks to Silverio Foresi whose published work with me forms a large part of the review undertaken here.

REFERENCES

Ahn, C.M. and H.E. Thompson. (1988). "Jump-Diffusion Processes and Term Structure of Interest Rates," *Journal of Finance, 43*(1), 155–174.

Amin, K. and J. Bodurtha. (1995). "Discrete-Time Valuation of American Options with Stochastic Interest Rates," *Review of Financial Studies, 8*(1), 193–234.

Attari, M. (1997). "Discontinuous Interest Rate Processes: An Equilibrium Model for Bond Option Prices," working paper, University of Madison, Wisconsin (Ph.D. dissertation, University of Iowa).

Babbs, S.H. and N.J. Webber. (1995). "A Theory of the Term Structure with an Official Short Rate," working paper, University of Warwick.

Backus, D., S. Foresi, and L. Wu. (1997). "Macroeconomic Foundations of Higher Order Moments in Bond Yields," working paper, New York University.

Balduzzi, P., G. Bertola, and S. Foresi. (1992). "A Model of Target Changes and the Term Structure of Interest Rates," working paper, New York University.

Ball, C. and W.N. Torous. (1983). "A Simplified Jump Process for Common Stock Returns," *Journal of Financial and Quantitative Analysis, 18*(1), 53–65.

Ball, C. and W.M. Torous. (1985). "On Jumps in Common Stock Prices and Their Impact on Call Option Pricing," *Journal of Finance, 40*(1), 155–173.

Bates, D.S. (1996). "Jumps and Stochastic Volatility: Exchange Rate Processes Implicit in DM Options," *Review of Financial Studies, 9*(1), 69–107.

Baz, J. and S. Das. (1996). "Analytical Approximations of the Term Structure for Jump-Diffusion Processes: A Numerical Analysis," *Journal of Fixed Income, 6*(1), 78–86.

Bremaud, P. (1981). "Point Processes and Queues," Springer-Verlag.

Brenner, R., R. Harjes, and K. Kroner. (1996). "Another Look at Models of the Short-Term Interest Rate," *Journal of Financial and Quantitative Analysis, 31*(1), 85–107.

Burnetas, A.N. and P. Ritchken. (1996). "On Rational Jump Diffusion Models in the Flesaker-Hughston Paradigm," working paper, Case Western Reserve University.

Chacko, G. (1996a). "A Stochastic Mean/Volatility Model of Term Structure Dynamics in a Jump-Diffusion Economy," unpublished manuscript, Harvard Business School.

Chacko, G. (1996b). "Multifactor Interest Rate Dynamics and Their Implications for Bond Pricing," unpublished manuscript, Harvard Business School.

Chahal, M. and J. Wang. (1995). "Jump Diffusion Processes and Emerging Stock and Bond Markets: An Investigation Using Daily Data," working paper, Georgia State University, Atlanta.

Cox, J.C., J.E. Ingersoll, and S.A. Ross. (1985a). "An Intertemporal General Equilibrium Model of Asset Prices," Econometrica, 363–384.

Cox, J.C., J.E. Ingersoll, and S.A. Ross. (1985b). "A Theory of the Term Structure of Interest Rates," Econometrica, 385–407.

Das, S. and S. Foresi. (1996). "Exact Solutions for Bond and Option Prices with Systematic Jump Risk," Review of Derivatives Research, 1(1), 7–24.

Das, S.R. (1995). "A Direct Discrete-Time Approach to Poisson-Gaussian Bond and Option Pricing in the Heath-Jarrow-Morton Model," NBER technical working paper No. 212, forthcoming Journal of Economic Dynamics and Control.

Das, S.R. (1997). "Discrete Time Bond and Option Pricing for Jump-Diffusion Processes," Review of Derivatives Research, 1(3), 211–243.

Das, S.R. and R.K. Sundaram. (1997). "Of Smiles and Smirks: A Term Structure Perspective," working paper, National Bureau of Economic Research, working paper No. 5976.

Feller, W. (1950). "An Introduction to Probability Theory and Its Applications," New York: John Wiley & Sons.

Harrison, J.M. and S. Pliska. (1981). "Martingales and Stochastic Integrals in the Theory of Continuous Trading," Stochastic Processes and Their Applications, 11, 215–260.

Heath, D., R. Jarrow, and A. Morton. (1990). "Bond Pricing and the Term Structure of Interest Rates: A Discrete Time Approximation," Journal of Financial and Quantitative Analysis, 25, 419–440.

Heston, S. (1995). "A Model of Discontinuous Interest Rate Behavior, Yield Curves and Volatility," working paper, Washington University, St. Louis.

Jorion, P. (1988). "On Jump Processes in the Foreign Exchange and Stock Markets," Review of Financial Studies, 1(4), 427–445.

Kushner, H. (1967). "Stochastic Stability and Control," New York: Academic Press.

Merton, R.C. (1971). "Optimal Portfolio and Consumption Rules in a Continuous-Time Model," Journal of Economic Theory, 3, 373–413.

Merton, R.C. (1976). "Option Pricing When Underlying Stock Returns Are Discontinuous," Journal of Financial Economics, 3(1/2), 125–144.

Moreno, M. and J.I. Penas. (1995). "On the Term Structure of Interbank Interest Rates: Jump-Diffusion Processes and Option Pricing," working paper, Universidad Carlos III de Madrid.

Naik, V. and M.H. Lee. (1993). "The Yield Curve and Bond Option Prices with Discrete Shifts in Economic Regimes," working paper, University of British Columbia.

Shirakawa, H. (1991). "Interest Rate Option Pricing with Poisson-Gaussian Forward Rate Curves," *Mathematical Finance*, 1(4), 77–94.

Vasicek, O. (1977). "An Equilibrium Characterization of the Term Structure," *Journal of Financial Economics*, 5, 177–188.

PART III

Other Risk Factors

Parts I and II have dealt exclusively with the modeling of interest rate risk. But many fixed income securities are subject to risks coming from other sources of uncertainty. This part addresses some of the most important of these risk factors.

Consider a security that pays $\{f_t(z_t)\}$ at times $t = 1, \ldots, T$ where f_t is some function of a risk factor z_t. If the interest rate at time s is r_s, then the value of the security is given by

$$\sum_{t=1}^{T} E\left[f_t(z_t)e^{-\int_0^t r_s ds} \right]$$

where the expectation is taken with respect to the risk-neutral probability measure.

If the interest rate process and the additional risk factor are independent, the value of the security can be rewritten as

$$\sum_{t=1}^{T} E[f_t(z_t)]E\left[e^{-\int_0^t r_s ds} \right] = \sum_{t=1}^{T} E[f_t(z_t)]d_t$$

where d_t is the discount factor at time t. If, in addition, one is willing to take the market discount factors as given, then it is clear from the above equation that one does not need a term structure model to price this security: one need only model the other risk factor and discount the appropriate expectations at market observable rates.

In many important applications, however, the additional risk factor is very dependent on interest rates. For example, prepayments on mortgages vary inversely with rates and tax-exempt rates vary directly with taxable rates. Credit risk, or default events can also vary with rates. One simple example would be the liabilities of a company whose profit tends to depend on the level of rates (e.g., financial institutions). Another example would be the counter-party risk of a swap. Credit losses from a swap occur only if the counter-party defaults and the swap has positive value. But, of course, whether the swap has positive value or not depends on the level of rates at the time.

The discussion in the previous paragraph indicates that, in general, one needs to model the interaction between the interest rate process and any other risk factors present. In particular, one needs a term structure model on which to build a complete model. But, as discussed in the introduction to Part II, one must be careful to choose the model appropriate for the application. In developing a model to price mortgage-backed securities, for example, one would spend more time and effort on how prepayments vary with interest rates than on the term structure model in isolation. Similarly, the strength of one's model of the interaction between default, exchange rates, or municipal yield spreads and interest rates would be a much larger determinant of profitability in these respective businesses than one's choice among reasonable term structure models.

Chapter 7 reviews the literature on modeling credit risk. Chapters 8 and 9 discuss prepayment risk, that is the risk that borrowers will choose to exercise their options to repay mortgage principal outstanding and no longer be obliged to pay interest at the original mortgage rate. Chapter 10 reviews the relationship between rates on municipal or tax-exempt bonds and rates on taxable bonds. Chapter 11 presents some models of exchange rate behavior.

7

Some Elements of Rating-Based Credit Risk Modeling

David Lando

Default risk must be one of the oldest sources of financial risk that one can think of and yet there has been a surge of interest in the area in the 1990s. It is difficult to say why this surge did not come earlier, but now that it is here one can look for some reasons:

- Risk management of financial institutions is becoming increasingly complex and relies more and more on quantitative methods. The quantitative revolution in pricing and hedging market risk is beginning to spill over into credit risk management and it is likely that banks will use increasingly sophisticated quantitative credit risk models to allocate capital internally and to convince regulators that capital adequacy standards are being met.

- Credit derivatives are becoming more popular as a low transaction cost means of diversifying loan portfolios and perhaps as part of a general tendency toward derivatizing wider classes of risk. The idea behind such derivatives is typically to allow a bank to diversify without having to give up its core customer base which may have a strong regional concentration or a large concentration in a specific industry. The pricing and hedging of credit derivatives is impossible without a solid modeling framework.

The models we build to handle credit risk are centered around modeling credit events (e.g., defaults or downgrades) and payments on contracts made at such events. When choosing a modeling framework, it is important to keep in mind what the purpose of the model is. Different models have advantages in different areas and an attempt to single out a single framework as generally superior is misguided. The key issues that credit risk models have to address include:

- *Pricing bank loans and corporate bonds.* The fact that these types of loans exist is reason enough to study their pricing. But they serve a special role of basic building blocks for modeling credit risk in many applications, in much the same way that zero-coupon bonds are used to set up a term structure of default-free bonds from which term structure derivatives can be priced. At a more fundamental theoretical level, the pricing of corporate bonds is intimately linked with questions of optimal capital structure and the study of conflicting interest between different creditors in a firm.

- *Risk management.* Our models should be able to quantify risks associated with having credit risky instruments in a portfolio. The difficult question here is not only describing the stochastic behavior of prices but also to describe and measure correlation between price movements.

- *Pricing credit derivatives.* Credit derivatives are contracts whose pay-out depend either on certain underlying credit events (such as default or downgrade) or measures of credit quality for example, the yield spread between an A-rated bond and a Treasury bond with similar payment structure. In this area, implied modeling is key: The ability to calibrate a model against observed data and price complicated structures off the model is the primary objective.

The main focus of this chapter is on understanding the idea of calibrating a rating-based model using a low-dimensional modification of a known transition (or generator) matrix. This chapter is not intended as a survey but to put the chapter in a context, it does provide an introduction to a few basic ideas in credit risk modeling. The list of references is far from complete. A much more complete view of the literature would be obtained by consulting the references in papers such as Anderson and Sundaresan (1997), Cooper and Martin (1996), Duffie and Singleton (1997), Jarrow and Turnbull (1995), Lando (1997), Leland (1994), and Schönbucher (1998).

CONNECTIONS BETWEEN DEFAULT PROBABILITY AND SPREADS

A first step that is important when modeling credit risk is to know the connections between spreads in forward rates and default probabilities. First, recall a little interest rate mathematics: Throughout, we let $B(t,T)$ denote the price at time t of zero-coupon bond maturing at year T. The yield using discrete time (annual) compounding is

$$y(0,t) = \left(\frac{1}{B(0,t)}\right)^{\frac{1}{t}} - 1$$

and the yield using continuous compounding is

$$y_c(0,t) = -\frac{1}{t} \log B(0,t)$$

The forward rate at time t seen from 0 (discrete time) is

$$f(0,t) = -\frac{B(0,t)}{B(0,t+1)} - 1$$

and in continuous time the instantaneous forward rate at time t seen from 0 is

$$f(0,t) = \frac{\partial}{\partial t} \log B(0,t)$$

The exact same quantities can be defined for a defaultable zero-coupon bond. Let $v^i(0,t)$ denote the price of zero-coupon bond maturing at t issued by a firm i. The credit spreads are obtained by taking differences: The yield spread is then defined as

$$ys^i(0,t) = y^i(0,t) - y(0,t)$$

and the forward spread is

$$fs^i(0,t) = f^i(0,t) - f(0,t)$$

and the continuous time versions may be defined this way as well.

To establish a connection between spreads and default probabilities we must have a model for the pricing of risky bonds. The cleanest picture is obtained in the case of the following very simple model for pricing the risky bond at time 0: Let the (random) default time of the firm be denoted τ. Now consider a defaultable zero-coupon bond with maturity t, whose recovery in the event of default is equal to a constant δ, received at the time of maturity. This is equivalent to receiving at the default time a fraction δ of a Treasury bond maturing at the same time as the defaulted bond. We let the probability of the firm surviving past t be denoted $S^i(0,t)$, that is, if our underlying probability measure is P, we have

$$S^i(0,t) = P(\tau > t)$$

A simple pricing formula for the risky bond is then given as

$$v^i(0,t) = \delta B(0,t) + (1-\delta)B(0,t)S^i(0,t) \tag{7.1}$$

with the obvious interpretation that the bondholder always gets at least the discounted value of the recovery and—if the firm survives—the remaining value is received as well. The assumptions underlying this expression could be that P is a risk neutral measure obtained in some underlying arbitrage-free model and that under this risk neutral measure the default event is independent of the evolution of the variables governing the pricing of riskless bonds. One could also merely assume risk neutrality. What is important is that this simple pricing formula has a structure general enough to capture the essential structure of many model setups.

In the case where recovery is 0, the price simplifies to the expression

$$v^i(0,t) = B(0,t)S^i(0,t)$$

The issue of stripping out such a price is a delicate one and information from credit swaps may have to be added in practice to get enough pricing information to use for the calibration. For more on decomposing an observed spread into default probability and recovery rate, see Das and Sundaram (1998). The one year conditional default probability between time t and $t+1$ (i.e., the probability) computed at time 0, of default before $t+1$ given survival up to and including time t is given by

$$\frac{S^i(0,t) - S^i(0,t+1)}{S^i(0,t)}$$

and rewriting this using our pricing formula gives us

$$\frac{S^i(0,t) - S^i(0,t+1)}{S^i(0,t)} = 1 - \frac{S^i(0,t+1)}{S^i(0,t)}$$

$$= 1 - \frac{v^i(0,t+1)}{v^i(0,t)} \frac{B(0,t)}{B(0,t+1)}$$

$$= 1 - \frac{1 + f(0,t)}{1 + f^i(0,t)}$$

$$\approx f^i(0,t) - f(0,t)$$

Hence we see that forward spreads in discrete time are (almost) conditional default probabilities. To get an exact relationship, consider the continuous time case. Before computing the spread, recall that any distribution on the positive reals which has a density can be expressed as a function of its hazard rate h defined as

$$h(t) = \frac{f(t)}{1 - F(t)}$$

where $f(t)$ is the density of the distribution and $F(t)$ is the distribution function. From this it follows that

$$S^i(t) = \exp\left(-\int_0^t h(s)ds\right)$$

Now consider the forward spread:

$$-\frac{\partial}{\partial t}\log v^i(0,t) - f(0,t) = -\frac{\partial}{\partial t}\log\left(P(\tau \geq t)\right)$$

$$= \frac{-\frac{\partial}{\partial t}P(\tau \geq t)}{P(\tau \geq t)}$$

$$= \frac{f}{1-F}$$

which is precisely the hazard rate of τ. The hazard rate gives conditional default intensities in the following sense:

$$P\left(\tau \in (t, t+\Delta t) \mid \tau \geq t\right) \approx h(t)\Delta t$$

Note the conditioning information: We are looking at the conditional default probability given only the information of survival up to time t. The central element of *reduced form* models (or *intensity* models) is the conditional default probability given survival *and* additional information which may have been collected up to time t.

SOME NOTES ON REDUCED-FORM MODELING

Rating-based models are typically formulated as a special case of reduced-form models. The fundamental object of modeling in these models is the stochastically varying instantaneous rate of default (i.e., the intensity λ). Let information at time t be represented by F_t. Then, heuristically, λ is F_t-adapted process such that[1]

---

[1] For precise definitions of this and a review of some of the results, see for example Lando (1997).

$$P(\tau \in (t, t + \Delta t) \mid F_t) \approx \lambda(t) 1_{\{\tau > t\}} \Delta t$$

Under some technical conditions (see Duffie, 1998), Duffie and Singleton (1997) and Lando (1998) that need not worry us here it is the case that the survival probability over a given horizon T is given by

$$S(0, T) = E \exp\left(-\int_0^T \lambda(s) \, ds\right)$$

Note that this is of the same functional form as the formula for a bond price computed from the spot rate process r

$$B(0, T) = E \exp\left(-\int_t^T r(s) \, ds\right)$$

Expressing the bond price in terms of the (instantaneous) forward rate

$$B(0, T) = \exp\left(-\int_0^T f(0, s) \, ds\right)$$

and comparing with the form of the survival probability in terms of its hazard rate

$$S(0, T) = \exp\left(-\int h(s) \, ds\right)$$

we note the analogy between, on one hand, spot rates and forward rates in bond pricing and, on the other hand, intensities and hazard rates in survival probability modeling. This analogy is fundamental in the approach developed by Duffie, Schroder, and Skiadas (1996), Duffie and Singleton (1997), and Lando (1994, 1998) which is able to handle dependence between the stochastic intensity and the spot rates very easily and essentially reduce the computation of prices of defaultable claims to the same form as that of default-free bonds. This makes it technically appealing from the viewpoint of computation and the advantages are perhaps more clear when computing prices of credit derivatives, see for example Schönbucher (1998). But there are empirical reasons as well for taking this path: Given the observation that spreads in forward rate curves are (in the case of zero recovery) the same as the hazard rates and that in particular the spread in the spot rates is equal to the intensity, it is clear that the spreads in the short end on yields will be strictly positive as long as there is a positive intensity of default. In the classical approach, taken in the works by Black and Scholes (1973) and Merton (1974), the spread in the short end goes to zero. To see this, note that if we assume that the value of a firm's equity starts out at a positive level S_0 and if default is defined as the first time the equity hits zero, then one has the following limiting result

$$\lim_{h \to 0} \frac{P(\tau \le h)}{h} = \lim_{h \to 0} \frac{\log P(\tau \ge h)}{h} = 0 \tag{7.2}$$

This fact makes short spreads go to zero in the short end.[2] To see this, think of the case with constant r and zero recovery

$$v(0,h) = B(0,h)P(\tau \ge h)$$

where v is price of defaultable zero-coupon bond. The yield spread is

$$-\frac{\log v(0,h)}{h} = y(0,h) - \frac{\log P(\tau \ge h)}{h}$$

and inserting the result from (7.2) shows that spreads go to 0. The empirical difficulties of diffusion models for firm value in explaining spreads on corporate bonds, as noted for example in Jones, Mason, and Rosenfeld (1984), might be attributed to this fact. Introducing small fixes such as stochastic interest rates will not change this by much. More drastic features such as introduction of strategic debt service by the equity holders and absolute priority violations may partially remedy this (see, for example, Anderson & Sundaresan, 1996). Another immediate fix is to apply

---

[2] In the Black-Scholes-Merton formulation, one has to assume that the firm has a value larger than the face value of debt to get this result. Otherwise the yield goes to infinity.

a jump-diffusion model for the asset value of the firm. This is done, for example, in Zhou (1997).

It may seem that there is a huge difference in economic content between, on one hand, modeling default as the first time the issuer's assets fall below a certain level and on the other hand modeling default as a Poisson-like process in which the default event is not specified directly as a condition on the firm's assets (or cash flows).[3] Results of Duffie and Lando (1998) show, however, that using a classical approach in a model in which there is imperfect observation of the firm's assets, assumed to follow a diffusion process, default becomes a Poisson-like process whose intensity process may be characterized and computed explicitly in certain cases. The yield spread in the short end then becomes strictly positive and the size of the spread reflects not only asset value but also the quality of information on the firm that bondholders have.

APPROACHES USING RATINGS

One of the simplest ways of having a stochastically varying default intensity is to let a finite state space Markov chain—representing for example a rating—modulate the intensity. We will from now on focus primarily on using ratings and for illustrational purposes we will look at a pricing model which uses *only* ratings, as in Jarrow, Lando, and Turnbull (1997). We will explain the idea behind calibration of such a model and give three examples based on modifying an underlying generator matrix of a continuous-time Markov chain. For more on calibration of rating based models, see Das and Tufano (1996), Kijima (1998), and Kijima and Komoribayashi (1998). Rating-based models which include stochastically varying transition intensities were introduced in Lando (1994, 1998) and recent contributions include Arvanitis, Gregory, and Laurent (1999), T. Li (1997), and Nakazato (1997).

We think now of a rating system for pricing corporate debt or perhaps indices of corporate debt. The example chosen here is one where only the rating category matters. In practice, more advanced

---

[3] Note however, that the intensity of default may well depend on the firm's assets in a reduced-form model.

methods and more explanatory variables will have to be added, but the calibration method discussed here is important in these frameworks as well.

The rating process is modeled as a Markov chain whose basic ingredients are a *state space*—often labeled $\{1, 2, \ldots, K\}$, where one should think of 1 as the top rating (AAA, say) and K as default—and a *transition matrix*

$$P = \begin{pmatrix} p_{11} & p_{12} & \cdots & & p_{1K} \\ p_{21} & p_{22} & \cdots & \cdots & p_{2K} \\ \vdots & \vdots & \ddots & \vdots & \vdots \\ p_{K1} & p_{K2} & \cdots & \cdots & p_{KK} \end{pmatrix} \tag{7.3}$$

Here, p_{ij} is the probability that the Markov chain which is currently in state i will be in state j next period. All entries in the transition matrix are non-negative and the rows sum to one

$$\sum_{j-1}^{K} p_{ij} = 1$$

Formally, let η_n denote the rating at time n. Then

$$\text{Prob}(\eta_n = j \mid \eta_0 = i_0, \eta_1 = i_1, \ldots, \eta_{n-1} = i) = \text{Prob}(\eta_n = j \mid \eta_{n-1} = i) = p_{ij}$$

The key property to note (the Markov property) is that only the rating at time $n - 1$ and *not* the entire history is relevant for determining the probability of being in rating j at time n. From the one-period transition matrix, we get transition probabilities over several periods by multiplying the transition matrix with itself

$$\text{Prob}(\eta_n = j \mid \eta_0 = i) = p_{ij}^{(n)}$$

where $p_{ij}^{(n)}$ is the ij^{th} entry of P^n.

There are two key assumptions underlying this many period transition phenomenon: Time-homogeneity and the Markov property.

The Markov property has already been described above. Non-homogeneity occurs if a separate matrix is used for each period (but we still have the Markov property). The multiperiod matrix will then have to be indexed by both the starting date and the ending date of the period over which we consider transitions. The length of the period is not sufficient. In this case the Markov property would be captured by the semi-group property of transition matrices

$$P(s,u) = P(s,t)P(t,u)$$

whenever $s < t < u$. This means that the state at a certain time is still sufficient for determining the transition probabilities in the future but the transition probabilities are changing over (calendar) time. An example where even the Markov property breaks down would be a case where the number of time periods spent in the current rating or the precise level of the previous rating entered into the probability. One can then regain the Markov property by enlarging the state space but this is costly in terms of new parameters that are introduced into the model.

However, we will look at the case where the Markov property holds and we are interested in trying to deduce the implied transition probabilities from market prices. In principle, it is possible to imply out parameters from a homogeneous Markov chain implied by prices if we have known recovery rates (or known expected recovery rates) in our model for bond prices given by (7.1): To see this, note from (7.1) that for each starting rating category and each time to maturity t we have

$$S^i(0,t) = \frac{v^i(0,t) - \delta B(0,t)}{(1-\delta)B(0,t)}$$

Since (expected) recovery rates are assumed known, we can observe the implied survival probabilities. To get the discrete-time transition probabilities, first note that

$$p_{iK} = 1 - S^i(0,1)$$

Then note that

$$S^i(0,t) = \sum_{j=1}^{K-1} p_{ij} S^j(1,t) \tag{7.4}$$

$$= \sum_{j=1}^{K-1} p_{ij} S^j(0,t-1) \tag{7.5}$$

where we used time-homogeneity to replace $S^j(1,t)$—the probability of surviving past t given rating j at time 1—by $S^j(0,t-1)$. This gives one new equation in the transition probabilities from category i for each time to maturity, since for fixed i and $t \geq 2$ we get

$$S^i(0,t) = p_{i1} S^1(0,t-1) + \cdots p_{i,K-1} S^{K-1}(0,t-1)$$

Hence from K maturities we get all the parameters $p_{i1}, \ldots, p_{iK}$ from this system. This procedure is then repeated for every rating category.

When trying to do this in practice one could replace one equation by the restriction that the probabilities sum to one but even then there is no guarantee that the solution is positive as probabilities should be. This reflects the fact that time-homogeneity is much too restrictive. Why not then assume a general nonhomogeneous structure? The problem is that the unknown parameters cumulate quickly. For each new maturity that we consider, we have as many new equations as there are rating categories (i.e., $K-1$), but we have $(K-1)^2$ new parameters to determine.

Therefore, the real world attempts of calibrating a model often introduce nonhomogeneity by finding a low dimensional modification of a known homogeneous Markov chain such that we only add as many parameters for each maturity as we can actually determine from the data using a known base matrix.

To illustrate this approach, assume that a one-period transition matrix P is given as in (7.3). This matrix will be our base matrix. In Jarrow, Lando, and Turnbull (1997) it is based on empirically observed transitions but it need not be in a general approach. The key is that it is *known* and that implied default probabilities for different maturities will be obtained from this matrix by a low dimensional modification. Throughout, we will assume that there exists a matrix

$$\Lambda = \begin{pmatrix} -\lambda_1 & \lambda_{12} & \cdots & & \lambda_{1K} \\ \lambda_{21} & -\lambda_2 & \cdots & \cdots & \lambda_{2K} \\ \vdots & \vdots & \ddots & \vdots & \vdots \\ \lambda_{K1} & \lambda_{K2} & \cdots & \cdots & -\lambda_K \end{pmatrix}$$

with

$$\sum_{j \in \{1,\ldots,K\} \setminus \{i\}} \lambda_{ij} = \lambda_i$$

$$\lambda_i \geq 0, \quad i = 1,\ldots,K$$

such that

$$\exp(\Lambda) = P$$

The goal is to create a family of transition matrices $(Q(0,t))_{t > 1}$ such that the implied default probabilities for each maturity t are matched by the corresponding entries in the last column of $Q(0,t)$. The general procedure is as follows: Let implied survival probabilities for rating category i over a time horizon t be denoted $S^i(t)$, so that the implied default probability is $1 - S^i(t)$.

1. Let $Q(0,0) = I$.
2. Given $Q(0,t)$. Choose $Q(t,t+1)$ such that $Q(0,t)Q(t,t+1)$ satisfies $(Q(0,t+1))_{iK} = 1 - S^i(t+1)$, for $i = 1, \ldots, K-1$.
3. Go to step 2.

What distinguishes the methods is the way in which step 2 is performed. Throughout we will consider an example with a rating system consisting of 4 categories A, B, C, D with D denoting default. For our example (which is purely for illustration), we let P be given as

P	A	B	C	D
A	0.95	0.03	0.01	0.01
B	0.1	0.7	0.1	0.1
C	0.1	0.2	0.4	0.3
D	0	0	0	1

and the associated generator Λ is

Λ	A	B	C	D
A	−0.0539	0.0350	0.0125	0.0064
B	0.1126	−0.3889	0.19037	0.0859
C	0.1369	0.3795	−0.9612	0.4448
D	0	0	0	0

For comparison we also list the two period transition matrix obtained by squaring P

$P(0,2)$	A	B	C	D
A	0.9065	0.0515	0.0165	0.0255
B	0.175	0.513	0.111	0.201
C	0.155	0.223	0.181	0.441
D	0	0	0	1

Assume that from prices of bonds we have deduced the following implied default probabilities

	A	B	C
$1 - S^i(0,1)$	0.02	0.12	0.35
$1 - S^i(0,2)$	0.045	0.215	0.490

We now show different ways of modifying P (based on modifications of Λ) such that the implied default probabilities are matched. Note that the procedure does not match transition probabilities other than those to default. If further contracts are available—such as default swaps protection against downgrades—a higher dimensional modification of P can be used to fit not only implied default probabilities but also implied transitions probabilities between non-default categories. In each procedure, we let

$$Q(0,1) = \exp(\Lambda(0))$$
$$Q(1,2) = \exp(\Lambda(1))$$

where $\Lambda(0)$ is a modification of Λ depending on $\pi_1 = (\pi_{11}, \pi_{12}, \pi_{13})$ and $\Lambda(2)$ is a modification of Λ depending on $\pi_2 = (\pi_{21}, \pi_{22}, \pi_{23})$ and we determine the parameter such that

$$(Q(0,1))_{i,D} = 1 - S^i(0,1), \quad i = A, B, C$$

$$(Q(0,2))_{i,D} = (Q(0,1)Q(1,2))_{i,D} = 1 - S^i(0,2), \quad i = A, B, C$$

The extension to several periods is obvious. In each case, we need to check whether the modified generator still is non-negative in its off-diagonal elements, so that we still have a generator matrix. Once this is checked, the matrix exponential will automatically give us a transition probability matrix.

Method 1: Modifying Default Intensities

In this method, we modify the default column of the generator matrix by letting

$$\begin{aligned}
\lambda_{AD}(0) &= \pi_{11} \cdot 0.0064 \\
\lambda_{BD}(0) &= \pi_{12} \cdot 0.0859 \\
\lambda_{CD}(0) &= \pi_{13} \cdot 0.4448
\end{aligned}$$

where $\pi_{11}, \pi_{12}, \pi_{13}$ are all strictly positive. The diagonal elements need modification too so that the matrix remains a generator with rows summing to zero

$$\begin{aligned}
\lambda_{AA}(0) &= -0.0539 - (\pi_{11} - 1) \cdot 0.0064 \\
\lambda_{BB}(0) &= -0.3889 - (\pi_{12} - 1) \cdot 0.0859 \\
\lambda_{CC}(0) &= -0.9612 - (\pi_{13} - 1) \cdot 0.4448
\end{aligned}$$

$\Lambda(1)$ is computed similarly using $(\pi_{21}, \pi_{22}, \pi_{23})$ instead of $(\pi_{11}, \pi_{12}, \pi_{13})$. Solving the matching conditions numerically, we obtain the following values

$$\begin{aligned}
(\pi_{11}, \pi_{12}, \pi_{13}) &= (2.4998, 1.2158, 1.2116) \\
(\pi_{21}, \pi_{22}, \pi_{23}) &= (2.6725, 0.7884, 1.1486)
\end{aligned}$$

The associated implied transition probability matrices are

$Q(0,1)$	A	B	C	D
A	0.940879	0.0295479	0.00957321	0.02
B	0.098418	0.68669	0.0948917	0.12
C	0.0956735	0.189793	0.364534	0.35
D	0	0	0	1

$Q(0,2)$	A	B	C	D
A	0.888184	0.0512025	0.0156132	0.045
B	0.170443	0.510694	0.103864	0.215
C	0.144236	0.209551	0.156213	0.49
D	0	0	0	1

Method 2: Modifying Rows of the Generator

This method is the one proposed in Jarrow, Lando, and Turnbull (1997, see Equation (2.19) on page 495), but in there a numerical approximation of the transition matrix using the generator is used to solve for the adjustment parameters. The advantage of the numerical approximation is that it gives linear equations which of course can be solved analytically. But the procedure requires fairly small time intervals and the resulting matrix is not guaranteed to be a transition matrix (but see Kijima and Komoribayashi (1998) for a modified procedure). Here we do not use a linear approximation. Hence the transition matrix property is guaranteed, but we can only solve numerically: Let

$$\Lambda(0) = \begin{pmatrix} -0.0539 \cdot \pi_{11} & 0.0350 \cdot \pi_{11} & 0.0125 \cdot \pi_{11} & 0.0064 \cdot \pi_{11} \\ 0.1126 \cdot \pi_{12} & -0.3889 \cdot \pi_{12} & 0.19037 \cdot \pi_{12} & 0.0859 \cdot \pi_{12} \\ 0.1369 \cdot \pi_{13} & 0.3795 \cdot \pi_{13} & -0.9612 \cdot \pi_{13} & 0.4448 \cdot \pi_{13} \\ 0 & 0 & 0 & 0 \end{pmatrix}$$

for strictly positive values of $\pi_{11}, \pi_{12}, \pi_{13}$. $\Lambda(1)$ is computed similarly using $(\pi_{21}, \pi_{22}, \pi_{23})$ instead of $(\pi_{11}, \pi_{12}, \pi_{13})$. The resulting parameters are

$$(\pi_{11}, \pi_{12}, \pi_{13}) = (1.8988, 1.1606, 1.2925)$$

$$(\pi_{21}, \pi_{22}, \pi_{23}) = (1.4754, 0.7005, 1.6628)$$

and the associated transition matrices are

$Q(0,1)$	A	B	C	D
A	0.908042	0.0547708	0.0171868	0.02
B	0.112348	0.667519	0.100133	0.12
C	0.115383	0.223701	0.310916	0.35
D	0	0	0	1

$Q(0,2)$	A	B	C	D
A	0.847867	0.090461	0.0166715	0.045
B	0.166842	0.556799	0.0613593	0.215
C	0.162213	0.266138	0.0816494	0.49
D	0	0	0	1

Method 3: Modifying Eigenvalues of the Transition Probability Matrix

Finally, we consider a case studied first in Lando (1994, 1998). We assume that P (and therefore also Λ) are diagonalizable, we let B denote a matrix of eigenvectors of P, and we let D denote a diagonal matrix of eigenvalues of Λ. Hence we have

$$\Lambda = BDB^{-1}$$

and we now let

$$\Lambda(0) = B\Pi(0)DB^{-1}$$

where $\Pi(0)$ is a diagonal matrix with diagonal elements $(\pi_{11}, \pi_{12}, \pi_{13})$ and 0, where the value 0 should correspond to the eigenvalue of zero in the generator. The same procedure is used for $\Lambda(1)$. In our example, this gives the following value of parameters:

$$(\pi_{11}, \pi_{12}, \pi_{13}) = (1.4124, 1.18906, 1.3326)$$

$$(\pi_{21}, \pi_{22}, \pi_{23}) = (1.2601, 0.9561, 2.8896)$$

where the order of parameters here are chosen such that π_{11} modifies the (numerically) largest eigenvalue. The associated transition matrices are

$Q(0,1)$	A	B	C	D
A	0.935037	0.0336963	0.0112667	0.02
B	0.112148	0.652385	0.115467	0.12
C	0.113185	0.230881	0.305933	0.35
D	0	0	0	1

$Q(0,2)$	A	B	C	D
A	0.886296	0.0518704	0.0168333	0.045
B	0.175185	0.478481	0.131333	0.215
C	0.161481	0.263352	0.0851667	0.49
D	0	0	0	1

One needs to check in this method that the modified generator is indeed a generator. The rows are guaranteed to sum to zero, but off-diagonal elements may become negative. This is a potential problem of the method. The advantage is the fact that the equation solving for the parameter vectors π_1 and π_2 are linear and can therefore be solved explicitly. To see this, let b_{jK}^{-1} denote the $(j,K)'th$ entry of B^{-1}, where we assume that the $K'th$ eigenvalue of the generator is 0. One may check that $b_{iK}b_{KK}^{-1} = 1$. Defining $\beta_{ij} = -b_{ij}b_{jK}^{-1}$ we can write the probability of no default before time 1 as

$$1 - P(0,1)_{i,K} = \sum_{j=1}^{K-1} \beta_{ij} \exp\left(d_j(1)\right)$$

where $d_j(i) = d_1\pi_{1i}$ and since β_{ij} is known for every i,j this system of equations determines $(d_1(1), \ldots, d_{K-1}(1))$, and therefore π_1. Now consider the survival probability for two periods. Rewrite as before

$$S^i(0,2) = \sum_{j-1}^{K-1} P_{ij}(0,1) S^i(1,2)$$

and use the fact that there are only $K - 1$ new parameters to determine here, namely the constants $(d_1(2), \ldots, d_{K-1}(2))$ entering into the expression $S^j(1, 2)$. Fortunately, there are also $K - 1$ equations, which are linear in the variables exp $(d_j(2))$, $j = 1, \ldots, K - 1$. The procedure is then repeated for maturity three years and so forth. The problem using this method in practice is finding a good base matrix. Empirical generators seem to have too small default intensities for high-rated issuers and this leads to strange results and possibly no solutions to the calibration. The key assumption for the procedure to work is that there exists a common basis of eigenvectors for the implied transition matrices of all maturities. Arvanitis, Gregory, and Laurent (1999) present results supporting this assumption. For the simplification and connection with affine models which are obtained in rating based models by using this representation in continuous time, see Lando (1994, 1998).

CREDIT SWAPS

Given a calibrated intensity model of default, such as the rating-based model of the previous section, one may proceed to price credit derivatives. One of the most popular credit derivatives is the credit default swap (or credit swap) whose basic idea is to protect the holder of the swap against default on an underlying *reference* security. As we will see, with a known recovery rate the credit default swap can be priced just knowing the default probabilities and therefore the particular choice of calibration method is irrelevant. However, by changing the credit event to include a downgrade to a non-default category, the calibration method will matter. In technical terms, this is because we are only calibrating to a subset of securities which does not span all sources of uncertainty in our model.

In a credit default swap, the protection buyer pays a fixed coupon $c(T)$ every period (typically every 3 or 6 months.) T is the maturity date of the contract—the size of the constant payment naturally depends on the length of the swap contract. The payment continues until which ever comes first: default or maturity of the credit swap. If default occurs before the maturity of the swap, there is (in the case of cash settlement) a payment from the protection seller to the protection buyer usually equal to the difference between the notional amount of the bond and the recovery value (based for example on an average quote among dealers in the immediate post-default market). As with ordinary swaps, the fixed side payment is set so that the contract value at initiation is zero. In abstract terms, the cash flow of the contract is as follows: The payment at a coupon date i for the protection buyer is

$$c(T)1_{\{\tau>i\}}$$

The payment of the protection seller is equal to at time τ

$$(1-\delta)1_{\{\tau\leq T\}}$$

To find $c(T)$ such that the cash flows of the two sides are equal assuming known survival probabilities under the pricing measure, we find assuming a constant interest rate r

$$c(T) = \frac{(1-\delta)E\left[e^{-rt}1_{\{\tau\leq T\}}\right]}{\sum_{i=1}^{n}e^{-ni}E\left[1_{\{\tau>i\}}\right]}$$

which can be readily calculated and is easy to generalize to cases with stochastic interest rates and dependence between interest rates and default intensities. To see the formula illustrated in the example of the previous section, consider a two-period default swap entered into at time 0, and with a maturity at date 2. The protection buyer pays $c(2)$ at date 1 if there is no default and $c(2)$ again at date 2 if there is no default at or before time 2. If default happens at (or before) time 1 the protection buyer receives $1-\delta$ where δ is the recovery of face value and the same applies at date 2. If the default date denotes τ then it is clear that the value of the cash flow paid by the protection buyer is

$$c(2)B(0,1)Q(\tau>1)+c(2)B(0,2)Q(\tau>2)$$

The value of the cash flow paid by the protection seller is

$$(1-\delta)B(0,1)Q(\tau=1)+(1-\delta)B(0,2)Q(\tau=2)$$

The swap premium is then the value of $c(2)$ for which these two cash flows have the same value. Note that we do not consider the default risk of the parties to the contract but focus on the reference security. We also ignore for simplicity the effects of accrued interest if default happens between coupon dates. For the example of the previous section, the premium $c(2)$ as a function of initial rating assuming a continuously compounded interest rate of 5%, a recovery of 50%, and a notional amount of 100 is

	A	B	C
$c(2)$	1.159	6.466	21.28

In practice, as swaps are becoming sufficiently liquid, the observed prices are used to generate their own implied term structures supplementing scarce data on defaultable bonds.

It is clear that one could generalize to swaps insuring against a downgrade in addition to a default such that the protection seller would receive a specified amount in the event of a transition to a category lower than a certain boundary. In the procedure above, simply define the relevant credit event and modify the payment accordingly. In this case, prices will reflect the fact that transition probabilities between nondefault categories depended on the calibration method, as can be seen by comparing the implied transition matrices. There is clearly significant variation in the probabilities of ending in category C over, say, a two-year time period. This dependence is not surprising given that we only fitted default probabilities.

The intensity framework (and in particular the ratings-based approach) generalizes easily to a first-to-default type swap contract, in which there is a basket of reference securities. The loss on the first of the reference securities to default is then covered by the swap contract. The framework developed to handle such contracts is also relevant for taking credit risk of the parties to the credit swap into account. The advantage of reduced form models here is that intensities of baskets behave very nicely in that the sum of the intensities is the intensity of the first default.

ACKNOWLEDGMENT

I am grateful to Morten Bai Andersen and Brian Huge for helpful discussions.

REFERENCES

Anderson, R. and S. Sundaresan. (1996). "Design and Valuation of Debt Contracts," *Review of Financial Studies, 9,* 37–68.

Arvanitis, A., J.K. Gregory, and J.-P. Laurent. (1998). "Building Models for Credit Spreads," *Journal of Derivatives* (Spring), 27–43.

Black, F. and M. Scholes. (1973). "The Pricing of Options and Corporate Liabilities," *Journal of Political Economy, 81,* 637–654.

Cooper, I. and M. Martin. (1996). "Default Risk and Derivative Products," *Applied Mathematical Finance, 3,* 53–74.

Das, S. and R. Sundaram. (1998). "A Direct Approach to Arbitrage-Free Pricing of Credit Derivatives," *Management Science* (forthcoming).

Das, S. and P. Tufano. (1996). "Pricing Credit Sensitive Debt When Interest Rates and Credit Spreads Are Stochastic," *Journal of Financial Engineering, 5,* 161–198.

Duffie, D. (1998). "First-to-Default Valuation," working paper, Graduate School of Business, Stanford University, and Institute de Finance, Universté de Paris, Dauphine.

Duffie, D. (1999). "Credit Swap Valuation," *Financial Analysts Journal, 55* (January–February), 73–87.

Duffie, D. and D. Lando. (1998). "Term Structures of Credit Spreads with Incomplete Accounting Information," working paper, Stanford University and University of Copenhagen.

Duffie, D., M. Schroder, and C. Skiadas. (1996). "Recursive Valuation of Defaultable Securities and the Timing of Resolution of Uncertainty," *Annals of Applied Probability, 6,* 1075–1090.

Duffie, D. and K. Singleton. (1997). "Modeling Term Structures of Defaultable Bonds," *Review of Financial Studies.*

Jarrow, R., D. Lando, and S. Turnbull. (1997). "A Markov Model for the Term Structure of Credit Spreads," *Review of Financial Studies, 10,* 481–523.

Jarrow, R. and S. Turnbull. (1995). "Pricing Options on Financial Securities Subject to Default Risk," *Journal of Finance, 50,* 53–86.

Jones, E., S. Mason, and E. Rosenfeld. (1984). "Contingent Claims Analysis of Corporate Capital Structures: An Empirical Investigation," *The Journal of Finance, 39,* 611–625.

Kijima, M. (1998). "Monotonicities in a Markov Chain Model for Valuing Corporate Bonds Subject to Credit Risk," *Mathematical Finance, 8,* 229–247.

Kijima, M. and K. Komoribayashi. (1998). "A Markov Chain Model for Valuing Credit Risk Derivatives," *Journal of Derivatives,* Fall, 97–108.

Lando, D. (1994). "Three Essays on Contingent Claims Pricing," Ph.D. Thesis, Cornell University.

Lando, D. (1997). "Modeling Bonds and Derivatives with Default Risk," in M. Dempster and S. Pliska (Eds.), *Mathematics of Derivative Securities*, 369–393, Cambridge University Press.

Lando, D. (1998). "On Cox Processes and Credit Risky Securities," *Review of Derivatives Research, 2*, 99–120.

Leland, H. (1994). "Corporate Debt Value, Bond Covenants, and Optimal Capital Structure," *Journal of Finance, 49*, 1213–1252.

Merton, R. (1974). "On The Pricing of Corporate Debt: The Risk Structure of Interest Rates," *The Journal of Finance, 29*, 449–470.

Nakazato, D. (1997). "Gaussian Term Structure Model with Credit Rating Classes," working paper, The Industrial Bank of Japan.

Schönbucher, P. (1998). "The Term Structure of Defaultable Bond Prices," *Review of Derivatives Research, 2*, 161–192.

Zhou, C. (1997). "A Jump Diffusion Approach to Modeling Credit Risk and Valuing Defaultable Securities," working paper, Federal Reserve Board.

8

Anatomy of Prepayments: The Salomon Brothers Prepayment Model

Lakhbir Hayre and *Arvind Rajan*

Prepayment projections are at the center of all mortgage security valuation and analysis. Since Salomon Brothers pioneered the development of the Street's first prepayment model in the mid-1980s,[1] such models have come to be widely used to obtain prepayment projections and indeed, are critical for valuation techniques such as option-adjusted spread (OAS) analysis.

At the same time, most market participants are well aware that projecting prepayments is not an exact science. While a large body of data now exists on prepayments, it still only partially covers the range of economic and interest rate environments that is possible over the term of a mortgage-backed security (MBS). As with any econometric model, the basic premise is that the conditions and

[1] See *The Salomon Brothers Prepayment Model: Impact of the Market Rally on Mortgage Prepayments and Yields,* Salomon Brothers Inc., September 4, 1985.

216

relationships observed in the past will hold going forward. The experience of the refinancing waves of 1991 through 1993, when prepayment models generally were perceived to have failed to predict the high speeds actually observed, has led to a fair degree of investor skepticism about such models. We feel that while many prepayment models indeed proved deficient during the past few years, skepticism about such models is partly due to the fact that they tend to be "black boxes"; thus, human nature being what it is, the models receive little credit, even when they are right.

These considerations suggest that a prepayment model should possess two critical characteristics. First, it needs to be based on fundamental relationships that are likely to persist over time, rather than just on a statistical fit to the data. Second, the model and its projections, and the assumptions that they are based on, should be easily understandable by users. With these caveats in mind, Salomon Brothers has developed a completely new prepayment model. Among its key features are the following:

- The model is modular and transparent, with the different components of the model corresponding to well-known prepayment causes (home sales, refinancings, etc.).

- The model applies to all mortgage types. While different mortgage types may vary in the relative importance of these components and borrower characteristics, the fundamental causes of prepayments apply to all types.

- Each component is well formulated and depends in a logical and rigorous manner on the variables likely to influence mortgagor behavior or response.

- Within each component, relationships can be easily modified, to explore the effects of unanticipated demographic or mortgage market changes on prepayments and hence on MBS value.[2]

This chapter presents a general discussion of prepayment behavior and describes how this behavior is captured by the new Salomon Brothers prepayment model. The model has been fit

---

[2] Readers who have access to Salomon Brothers's analytic system, the Yield Book, can use the "Dials" facility to do this.

using data from the past 15 years; despite the myriad economic environments and mortgage market changes, the same model accurately predicts prepayments over the whole of this period. We must stress this critical point, because a widespread perception exists that, for example, the refinancing experiences of 1986–1987 and 1991–1993 were very different, and hence cannot be accurately described by the same model. The new Salomon Brothers Prepayment Model demonstrates that an approach that is, first, comprehensive in incorporating the different reasons for prepayments and, second, uses fundamental and hence long-lasting relationships between variables and prepayments rates can be robust and reliable over time.

DISSECTING PREPAYMENTS

What causes prepayments? Most readers are familiar with mortgages and home ownership in general and hence with the various reasons for prepayments. We will use five categories to classify prepayments:

1. *Home Sales.* The sale of a home generally will lead to the prepayment of a mortgage. Exceptions will arise if the home has a Federal Housing Administration or Veterans Administration (FHA/VA) loan and the new buyer decides to assume the existing loan or if the home happens to be one that does not carry a mortgage.

2. *Refinancings.* The second major cause of prepayments refers to mortgagors taking advantage of lower rates by refinancing out of an existing loan into a new one. As we will discuss shortly, this is the most volatile component of speeds, and constitutes the bulk of prepayments when speeds are very high.

3. *Defaults.* A prepayment caused by a foreclosure and subsequent liquidation of a mortgage. This is a relatively minor component in most cases, averaging less than 0.5% per year for moderately seasoned loans, and is close to zero for very seasoned loans.

4. *Curtailments.* Some mortgagors are in the habit of sending in more than the scheduled payment each month, as a form of

forced savings and to build up equity in their homes faster. Such extra payments, referred to as partial prepayments or curtailments, show up as prepayments of principal and, for fixed-rate loans (with a fixed monthly payment), shorten the loan maturity. Data from mortgage servicers (and the observed weighted-average maturity (WAM) shortenings on Federal National Mortgage Association (FNMA) and Federal Home Loan Mortgage Corporation (FHLMC) pools, from which average curtailment rates can be estimated) indicate that, for new and moderately seasoned loans, curtailments typically amount to less than 0.5% per year.

5. *Full Payoffs.* Evidence exists that many mortgagors pay off their mortgage completely when it is very seasoned and the remaining loan balance is small (Carliner & D'Alessandris, 1992). Full payoffs also can occur because of the destruction of the home from natural disasters such as hurricanes and earthquakes. In general, full payoffs are negligible until the loans are very seasoned. For 30-year loans, FHA data on loans more than 20 years old suggests that the combination of curtailments and full payoffs averages several percent per year.

The various components, and their relative importance and evolution over time, are illustrated in Figure 8.1. This figure shows prepayment speeds on 1977 origination Government National Mortgage Association (GNMA) 8s, along with the turnover rate on existing homes, which is obtained by dividing the number of existing homes sold in a given month[3] by the estimated number of single-family homes in the United States at that time (based on U.S. Census Bureau data). The average turnover rate has hovered around 6% per year, and this figure can be considered a baseline prepayment rate for mortgages. This average turnover rate explains the prepayment rate of 6% per year for seasoned loans assumed by the Public Security Association (PSA)'s benchmark 100% PSA rate.

During the first half of the 1980s, mortgage rates were high (generally in the teens), leading to a substantial proportion of assumptions on the GNMA 8s. This resulted in the prepayment rate

[3] This data is provided by the National Association of Realtors. Note that we are using the actual, rather than the seasonally adjusted number of homes sold.

FIGURE 8.1. Turnover Rate on Existing Homes and Speeds on 1977 GNMA 8s, 1980–Present

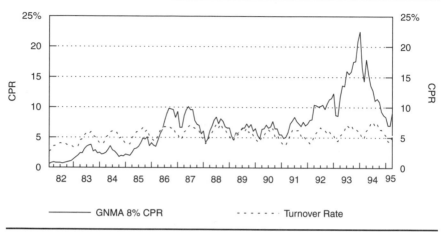

CPR Constant prepayment rate.
Source: Salomon Brothers, Inc. National Association of Realtors and U.S. Census Bureau.

on GNMA 8s being below the turnover rate for existing homes. In 1986 and early 1987, a period of heavy refinancing activity, speeds on the GNMA 8s jumped to well above the turnover rate. However, the weighted-average coupon (WAC) on the GNMA 8s is 8.5%, while mortgage rates in 1986 and 1987 were generally 9% or higher; this discrepancy suggests that the 1977 GNMA 8s experienced *cash-out refinancings* in 1986 and 1987, as some homeowners, inspired by the sharp drop in mortgage rates from 1985 to 1986, refinanced into larger loans to make use of the equity in their homes, even if it meant a small increase in the loan rate.

From 1988 through early 1991, speeds on the GNMA 8s tracked the turnover rate quite closely, on average being about 1% to 2% constant prepayment rate (CPR) higher. This trend indicates that over this period speeds were due mostly to home sales, few assumptions occurred (because the balances on the underlying loans, originated in 1977, were by then small compared with the cost of a new home), and some curtailments occurred. Defaults were quite low (below 0.25% CPR, according to Office of Housing and Urban Development (HUD) data), reflecting the fact that few loans default once they are seasoned more than 10 years.

Starting in late 1991, the 1977 GNMA 8s begin to experience refinancings, reflecting declining mortgage rates. Note, however, that the 1977 GNMA 8s did not experience the sky-high prepayment rate of newer coupons, probably because the small remaining balances on 1977 loans reduced the incentive to refinance the loans.

Structure of the Prepayment Model

The Salomon Brothers Prepayment Model is additive in form, consisting of submodels for each of the sources of prepayments discussed above. The first two submodels, for home turnover and refinancings, contribute most of the projected speed. In the next few sections, we describe these two components in more detail, in particular identifying the variables that drive them.

HOUSING SALES: THE BASIC DRIVER OF PREPAYMENTS

In the absence of refinancings, prepayments will be due mostly to home sales, as Figure 8.1 illustrates. Hence, the critical component of discount speeds is housing turnover.

While a number of housing industry statistics are published each month, the one that is most relevant for prepayment analysis is *sales of existing homes.* While other statistics, such as housing starts or new home sales, often receive more publicity, they do not have the direct relationship with prepayments that existing home sales do; unless the mortgage is assumed or the home has no mortgage, the sale of an existing home leads to a prepayment.

Table 8.1 shows existing home sales from 1978 to the present. Also shown are mortgage rates, total single-family housing stock and the turnover rate on existing homes (the number of homes sold as a percentage of the stock).

Annual turnover rates on existing homes generally have hovered between 5% and 7%, with somewhat lower rates in the early 1980s, when high mortgage rates and a severe recession severely depressed sales volume. While mortgage rates do affect housing activity through affordability levels, note that economic growth and the business cycle seem to be equally important factors. For example, the turnover rate in 1986 was about the same as that in 1993, despite

TABLE 8.1. Housing Turnover Rates, 1978–Present

Year	Avg. Mtg. Rate	Sales of Exst. Homes[a]	Est. SF Housing Stock[a]	Turnover Rate
1978	9.64%	3.99	51.84	7.70%
1979	11.19	3.83	52.72	7.26
1980	13.77	2.97	53.60	5.55
1981	16.64	2.42	54.27	4.46
1982	16.09	1.99	54.95	3.62
1983	13.23	2.70	55.63	4.85
1984	13.87	2.83	56.31	5.02
1985	12.42	3.31	56.99	5.82
1986	10.18	3.47	57.67	6.02
1987	10.20	3.44	58.35	5.89
1988	10.33	3.51	59.03	5.95
1989	10.32	3.35	59.70	5.60
1990	10.13	3.21	60.38	5.32
1991	9.25	3.22	61.06	5.27
1992	8.40	3.52	61.74	5.70
1993	7.33	3.80	62.42	6.09
1994	8.36	3.95	63.10	6.26

[a] In millions. SF Single family.
Note: Total housing stock is estimated by using U.S. Census Bureau data on detached single-family residences.
Source: FHLMC, National Association of Realtors, U.S. Census Bureau and Salomon Brothers Inc.

mortgage rates being several hundred basis points higher in 1986. The turnover rate in 1994, while slightly higher than those in the mid-1980s, was still lower than those in the late 1970s, when mortgage rates were significantly higher.

Projecting Housing Turnover

If housing turnover largely drives speeds on discount MBSs, then we need to understand how turnover rates vary over different interest rate cycles. Mortgage rates clearly affect the overall level of home turnover and hence speeds, and most prepayment models use an ad hoc adjustment to vary discount speeds as interest rates change. To establish a sounder basis for estimating prepayment speeds resulting from home sales, Salomon Brothers has developed an innovative model for projecting housing turnover rates.

We discuss the main features of the model in Appendix 8.1. The model is fitted to historical data over the past 15 years. Its projections include the influence of current interest rates as well as the lingering influence of the recent interest rate history on the present level of home sales.

Figure 8.2 depicts the turnover model's fit to actual data, as well as its turnover predictions for various interest rate changes. The model realistically captures mortgagors' real-life response to interest-rate changes. For example, if rates rise by 1.5% and hold steady, it projects that turnover rates will fall initially but subsequently revert toward historical means as consumers adjust to the

FIGURE 8.2. Actual and Projected Housing Turnover Rates, 1983–2008P

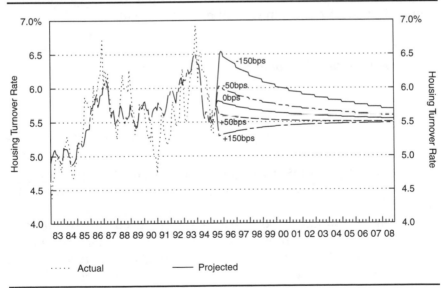

P Salomon Brothers Inc. projections.

Source: National Association of Realtors, U.S. Census Bureau and Salomon Brothers Inc.

FIGURE 8.3. Seasonal Adjustments for Existing Home Sales, 1985–Present

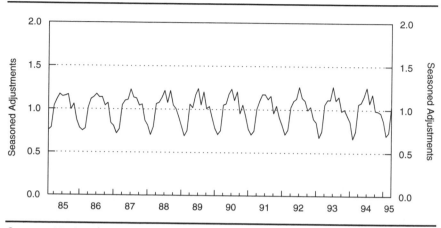

Source: National Association of Realtors.

new economic situation. Conversely, a drop in rates leads to an initial surge in turnover, followed by a gradual drop, as satiation of demand causes a reversion toward historical means.

Seasonal Variation in Home Sales

Home sales volume exhibits a pronounced but consistent seasonal pattern, which obviously passes through to prepayment speeds. The extent and consistency of the seasonal cycle is indicated in Figure 8.1; it is also shown in Figure 8.3, which demonstrates the monthly seasonal adjustments calculated by the National Association of Realtors (NAR) for existing home sales from 1980 to the present.[4]

As one might expect, the seasonal highs occur in the summer and the lows in the winter, with the school year calendar and the weather the driving forces behind the seasonal cycle. MBS investors need to be aware of the magnitude of the seasonal variation. There is

[4] The NAR uses the U.S. Census Bureau's X-11 statistical program to estimate seasonal adjustments.

almost a two-to-one ratio between summer highs and winter lows and some significant month-to-month changes. Table 8.2 shows a weighted-average seasonal factor for each month, based on the past 27 years of NAR adjustments, along with the change from the previous month.

The largest one-month change is from February to March, when home sales typically increase by about 37%. In the fall and winter months, a series of double-digit percentage declines occurs until the seasonal cycle reaches its low in January.

While these adjustments can form the basis for incorporating seasonal factors in prepayment projections, readers should be aware of one or two complications. First, in reporting sales volume to the NAR, local realtors do not consistently define a sale. The majority defines a sale as a closing, which implies an immediate mortgage prepayment, but some fraction (the NAR is not sure as to the number) defines it as a sales contract, which implies a mortgage prepayment a couple of months later. Second, depending on the servicer and servicing agreement, for some closings that take place near the

TABLE 8.2. Estimated Seasonal Adjustments for Sales of Existing Homes

Month	Seasonal Adjustment	Pct. Change from Previous Month
Jan	0.70	−15%
Feb	0.77	19
Mar	1.05	+37
Apr	1.09	+4
May	1.14	+5
Jun	1.23	+8
Jul	1.11	−10
Aug	1.16	+5
Sep	0.99	−15
Oct	1.02	+3
Nov	0.91	−10
Dec	0.83	−10

Sources: National Association of Realtors and Salomon Brothers Inc.

end of the month, the prepayment may not actually show up in pool factors until the following month.

The Salomon Brothers Prepayment Model starts with the NAR adjustments and uses historical correlations between home sales changes and discount speed changes to derive monthly seasonal factors for each agency.

HOUSING TURNOVER AND PREPAYMENT RATES

Given an overall level of housing turnover, how do specific loan or borrower characteristics affect resulting prepayment speeds? Among the most important characteristics are loan seasoning (which in addition to age depends on other features such as whether the loan was originated as a purchase or a refinancing, the points paid, etc.), the loan coupon relative to prevailing mortgage rates, relative loan balance, and last but not least, loan type.

The Seasoning Process

A large fraction of currently outstanding MBSs are new discounts, many of which were originated in the refinancing waves of 1992 and 1993. A critical question for MBS investors concerns the rate at which the underlying loans will season.

The current industry standard, the PSA aging ramp, assumes that loans season linearly over the first 30 months. In fact, as is by now fairly well established, loan seasoning is a complex process that depends on a number of factors and will differ depending on whether the mortgagor is contemplating moving versus refinancing. We will discuss the seasoning process for refinancings in the next section; here we discuss the seasoning process as it pertains to home turnover.

The Base Seasoning Ramp. This factor refers to the core age-dependent part of the seasoning process. The transaction costs incurred in a home purchase are substantial, amounting to several percent of the purchase price. Most home purchases therefore are followed by a quiescent settling-in period, when the family avoids

FIGURE 8.4. Seasoning Patterns for Conventional Discounts

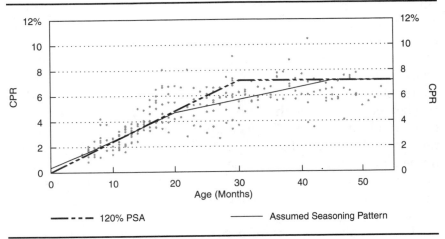

CPR Constant prepayment rate.

Note: Data points represent seasonally adjusted speeds for FNMA 30-year discounts centered around −150 basis points relative coupon.

Source: Salomon Brothers Inc.

relocation unless compelled by circumstances. Hence prepayments associated with newly originated purchase loans are initially quite small, and increase to the "natural" level implied by the housing turnover rate gradually over a *seasoning period.*

Self-selection by borrowers implies that the length of this period depends on the type of loan, but we illustrate the basic form in Figure 8.4, which shows speeds on discount conventional 30-year MBSs as a function of age. Also shown is an appropriate multiple of the industry-standard PSA curve. The base seasoning ramp typically starts above the PSA curve in the initial months of the mortgage, but then drops below it, leading to the so-called PSA *elbow,* which is most pronounced around the age of 30 months. This type of seasoning ramp leads to high initial PSAs, which then decrease but eventually increase until the collateral is fully seasoned.

A number of other effects that vary with age are superimposed on the basic seasoning ramp. The most important of these effects are as follows.

The Percentage of Refinanced Loans in the Pool.   The presence of a substantial number of refinanced loans in a mortgage pool can indicate higher prepayments during the seasoning period. It could be argued that refinanced loans should season faster than purchase loans, because many of the elements that determine seasoning (a growing family, expanding income, etc.) are already developed to some extent in a refinanced loan. The very act of purchase sends a much stronger message than a refinancing that the mortgage holder plans to put down some "roots." Moreover, the circumstances that tend to make the purchasers of a home unwilling/unable to move immediately, such as a high loan-to-value ratio (LTV), the fresh memory of the "joys" of moving and the typically higher transaction costs of relocation continue to distinguish purchase loans from refinanced loans.

However, the view that refinanced loans season faster is not universally held. Homeowners who plan to move in the near future can now refinance into a balloon or adjustable-rate mortgage (ARM). Therefore some speculation has occurred as to whether mortgage holders refinancing into 30-year loans nowadays might actually be sending the opposite message, namely that they plan to stay awhile.

On balance, we believe that a high percentage of refinancings is still likely to lead to a somewhat faster seasoning process. The fixed-rate 30-year mortgage has retained its popularity as the refinancing vehicle of choice for mortgagors with an existing 30-year loan. For example, in 1993 the percentage of 30-year conventional mortgage holders refinancing into another 30-year fixed-rate loan was 52%, compared with 57% in 1986. This comparison suggests that the characteristics of borrowers refinancing into a 30-year loan were not substantially different in 1993 than in 1986.

However, the data to prove this theory is limited. The loans refinanced in 1991 and 1992 were themselves subject to refinancings in 1992–1993. Data from the 1986–1987 refinancing episodes do suggest faster seasoning for refinanced loans, but care has to be taken in separating the effects of seasoning from other factors such as a strong housing market and the amount of points paid. In Figure 8.5, we compare the seasoning ramp of the FNMA 30-year 9.5% pass-throughs backed by mortgages originated respectively in the fourth quarters of 1986 and 1987. Other characteristics, such as points

FIGURE 8.5. Seasoning Ramp of FNMA 30-Year 9.5s Backed by Mortgages Originated in 4Q 86 versus 4Q 87

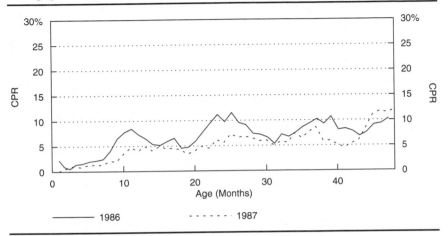

CPR Constant prepayment rate.
Source: Salomon Brothers Inc.

paid, are comparable, yet the 1986 cohort, with a higher percentage of refinancings at origination, prepaid faster.

The data available for discount collateral originated after 1992 seems inconclusive on the distinction between the seasoning rates of refinanced versus purchased loans. Future speeds on these loans should help to resolve the issue. In the meantime, our model conservatively projects a slightly higher trajectory of prepayments during the seasoning period based on the percentage of refinancings at origination.

The "Points" Effect.   Another distinguishing feature useful in predicting seasoning characteristics is the estimated points paid at origination. It has become common for lenders to offer loans with differing amounts of points. At one extreme are "low-point" or "no-point" loans, with which the borrower accepts a higher coupon rate in exchange for a lower down payment. As discussed later in the section on refinancings, such borrowers tend to be "fast" refinancers. At the other extreme, borrowers can pay extra points to obtain a lower coupon rate. Both theory and empirical evidence indicate that borrowers who choose to put down points to lower their rates are signaling an intent to stay for some period of time. Although the number of points paid is not part of the available data for agency mortgage pools, we can estimate it from the difference between the prevailing mortgage rate at the time of origination and the WAC of the pool.

Figure 8.6 compares FNMA 7s (with WACs of around 7.60% to 7.70%) originated in April and September 1992. Mortgage rates in early 1992 were around 8.50% to 8.80%, suggesting that borrowers paid substantial points to obtain mortgages with rates below 8%. By the late summer, mortgage rates were close to 8%, indicating that the September 1992 FNMA 7s contain mostly "normal point" loans. The April 1992 FNMA 7s have prepaid much more slowly in PSA terms than the September 1992 FNMA 7s. Even on a CPR basis, the April 1992 FNMA 7s have been slower, despite their extra six months of seasoning.

The Salomon Brothers Prepayment Model uses the difference between the rates prevailing at the origination date of the loans and their WAC to deduce the points paid and their effect on turnover and seasoning behavior.

FIGURE 8.6. The Effect of Points Paid on Discount Speeds

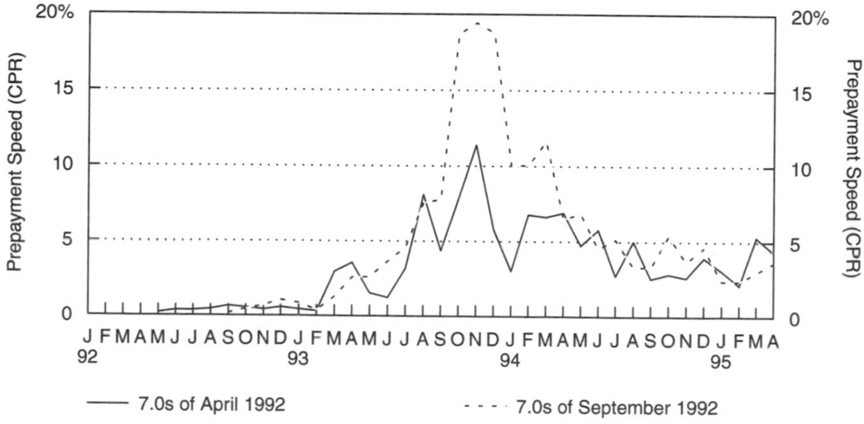

Source: Salomon Brothers Inc.

The Lock-In Effect: Disincentive and Assumability

Lock-in refers to the disincentive to move due to the existing loan being a discount, so that a new home would also entail a higher mortgage rate; for FHA/VA loans, which are assumable, the effect is stronger because even if the current homeowner decides to move, the new buyer may well decide to assume the existing loan. While the lock-in effect is often considered part of the seasoning process, it is worth a separate discussion, because of its importance and because it depends on factors other than age.

It is possible that low speeds on newer discounts, which appear to reflect a lock-in effect, could well be caused by other factors such as the points effect discussed above. Given that this is not the case for a particular cohort of discount loans and that the lower speeds are in fact due to a lock-in effect, how do we model the effect? Common sense suggests that over time, as inflation makes the price of a new home larger relative to the existing loan balance, both the disincentive to move and (in the case of FHA/VA loans) the likelihood of a new buyer assuming the existing loan will diminish over time. In fact, a straightforward economic argument shows that the disincentive to move (and the incentive to refinance) is a function of two quantities:

1. The present value cost per dollar of changing from an existing loan rate of C to a new loan rate M, which we estimate as

$$1 - \frac{C}{M} \times \frac{1 - (1+M)^{-(\text{TERM}-\text{AGE})}}{1 - (1+C)^{-\text{TERM}}} \tag{8.1}$$

where C and M are expressed as monthly decimals, TERM is the original loan term, and AGE is the number of months since loan origination; and

2. The amortized loan balance as a proportion of the likely amount of a new loan (that is, the amortized inflation-adjusted balance of the existing loan). We estimate this as

$$\frac{(1+C)^{\text{TERM}} - (1+C)^{\text{AGE}}}{INF \times [(1+C)^{\text{TERM}} - 1]} \tag{8.2}$$

where INF is a deflator based on the cumulative housing inflation rate from the mortgage origination date to the present. Figure 8.7 shows a plot of the amortized loan balance, the inflation deflater (1/INF), and the combined value (Equation (8.2)), assuming a 360-month original term and an inflation rate of 5% per year.

In essence, we are assuming that the lock-in effect is a function of the relative coupon differential between the loan rate and current rates and that it diminishes over time because of housing inflation (and to a lesser extent, amortization).

Figure 8.8 illustrates the effects of inflation, amortization and assumability using GNMA 7.5s and 9s issued in the 1970s and 1980s. The 1987 7.5 GNMAs, newer discounts that were attractive to assume throughout the late 1980s, had the slowest seasoning ramp, whereas the 1986 9s, which were less attractive to assume, seasoned within the first three years of origination. In contrast, the 1970s coupons experienced brisk prepayments throughout the late 1980s, with even the 1975 7.5s reflecting diminished lock-in and assumability because of several years of above-average housing inflation along with regular amortization.

The Salomon Brothers Prepayment Model calculates the LTV throughout the life of the mortgage, using it to compute the negative impact of lock-in and assumability on prepayments.

FIGURE 8.7. Amortized Inflation-Adjusted Loan Balance Over Time

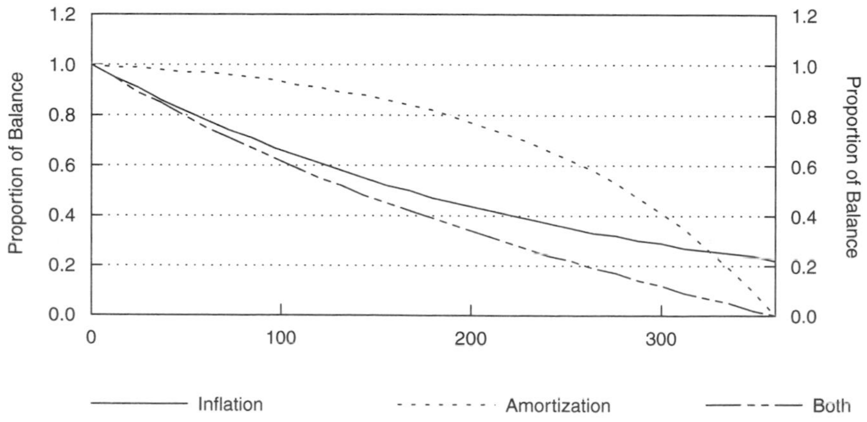

Source: Salomon Brothers Inc.

FIGURE 8.8. GNMA 7.5s and 9s, 1970s versus 1980s Originations

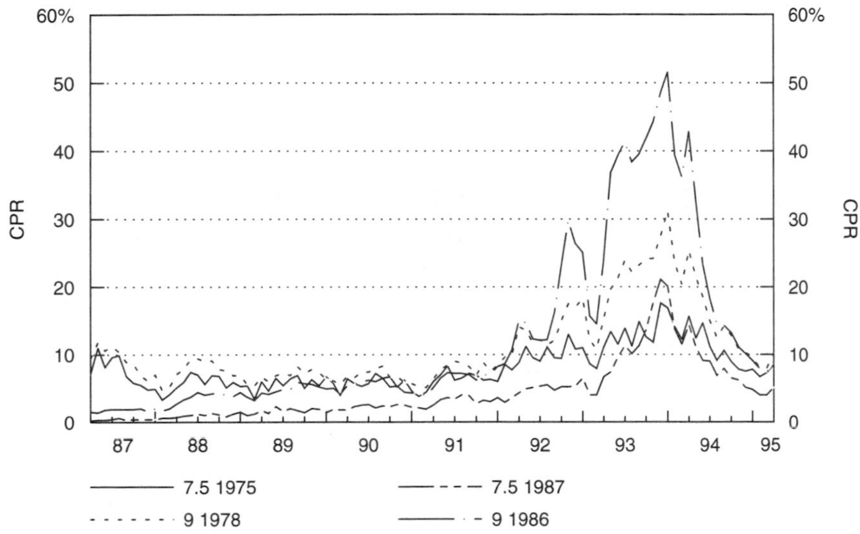

CPR Constant prepayment rate.
Source: Salomon Brothers Inc.

Housing Inflation and Geographical Factors

Apart from the lock-in effect, housing inflation also can affect the ability of a homeowner to move. Rapid price appreciation leads to a quick increase in the amount of equity in the home, which can spur "trade-up" moves, as well as reflect a generally vigorous housing market. In contrast, price depreciation will dampen the ability to move and overall housing activity.[5]

To a large extent, observed differences in speeds between geographical areas often reflect differences in the current state of the housing markets in the respective areas. Such differences are often transient. For example, the Pacific Northwest has had one of the most active housing markets over the past few years; ten years ago, because of recessions in the lumber and aircraft industries, it had

[5] This observation also applies, of course, to the ability to refinance a loan.

one of the slowest.[6] This observation indicates that care should be taken in applying geographical adjustments to projections on a long-term basis, unless long-term underlying factors are behind geographic differences. An example of the latter would be California speeds, which because of the demographics of California's population, might be expected to be typically faster than the average.

Recognizing the highly specific and transitory nature of inflation and regional economic conditions on prepayments, we have based the Salomon Brothers prepayment model on an expected rate of national housing inflation derived from the demographic outlook and historical trends. Specific adjustments to this basic projection may be made where warranted after careful analysis of the data underlying certain pools or deals on a case-by-case basis.

Loan Type

Observed speeds on discounts tend to vary by loan type; for example, balloon discounts typically prepay faster than conventional discounts, which in turn usually prepay faster than GNMA discounts. A large proportion of these differences result from differences in the loan characteristics described above. However, even after controlling for the latter, a residual difference often remains resulting from self-selection or demographics. For example, observed speeds and anecdotal evidence from originators indicate that borrowers who select balloon loans often expect to move again soon, leading to a higher base-line mobility rate (as well as faster seasoning) than the average.

An example of such loan-specific differences may be found by comparing FNMA 30-year 8% mortgages from 1992 with FHLMC 5-year 7% balloons from the same origination year, as shown in Figure 8.9. While the overall pattern of prepayments is the same for the two classes, the shorter seasoning ramp and the higher overall level of turnover rates (a balloon mortgage is often chosen by borrowers who intend to move in a relatively short period of time) are indications of the fundamental differences engendered because of the characteristics of the loan type.

---

[6] See *Regional Differences in Mortgage Prepayments,* Salomon Brothers Inc., August 1984.

FIGURE 8.9. The Effect of Loan Type: Speeds on FNMA 30-Year 8s and 5-Year FHLMC Balloon 7s

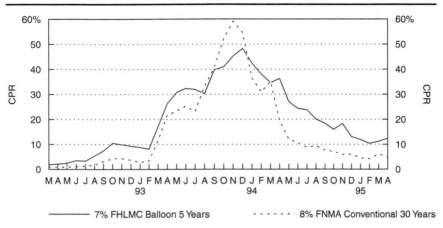

CPR Constant prepayment rate.
Source: Salomon Brothers Inc.

The Salomon Brothers model was developed first to take full advantage of universal mortgage characteristics to explain as much of the variation in prepayments as possible. However, the model also reflects the specific characteristics of each loan type, provided they satisfy the following carefully observed conditions:

- Systematic differences in prepayments between the loan type and other loan types persist after variations due to the universal variables common to all types have been removed.

- The differences may be explained logically by differences in the nature of the loan terms, regulations, borrower characteristics, geography, and so on; and

- The differences are consistent over the period for which data is available for the loan type, and the model as amended provides a superior fit (by statistical and other measures) to the data.

A consistent application of these principles has led to a family of models that are identical in their fundamental structure for the full universe of mortgage instruments, including GNMA, FNMA and non-agency mortgages, with 30-year and 15-year maturities as well as 5- to 7-year balloon and ARM products. Yet, each is custom-fit to predict the idiosyncrasies of the prepayments of the individual instrument it represents with the precision expected of an independently developed model.

REFINANCING BEHAVIOR

Very high prepayment speeds are primarily due to refinancings. Housing turnover by itself will rarely lead to prepayment rates above 10% to 12% CPR. Hence, an accurate modeling of prepayments during market rallies such as those from 1991–1993, when speeds sometimes exceeded 60% CPR, requires a sound understanding of refinancing behavior.

A refinancing is an economic prepayment and can be thought of as an exercise of a call option on the existing loan by the mortgagor. However, traditional option theory is of limited use in analyzing refinancings, because mortgagor behavior seems to represent an inefficient exercise of the option. This observation is illustrated in Figure 8.10, which shows prepayment rates versus refinancing incentive at two different points in time.[7]

Both sets of speeds display the familiar "S-curve" known to all mortgage analysts. This curve is an approximation to the "0–1" step-function that represents an efficient option exercise by the mortgagor; that is, do not refinance if the savings from a refinancing is less than some hypothetical transaction cost and refinance otherwise. A striking feature of Figure 8.10 from an option-theoretic point of view, albeit one very familiar to anyone who has looked at prepayment speeds, is the difference between the speeds in November 1993 and August 1994; for the same refinancing incentive, speeds in August 1994 were one third to one half of what they were nine months earlier. This phenomenon, whereby refinancing rates decline over time even if no change occurs in the refinancing incentive, is known as *burnout*. This term, often misunderstood and sometimes controversial, is typically understood to mean that a pool of mortgages that experienced previous exposure

---

[7] As discussed in the box on pages 238–239, we use the ratio of the coupon on the refinanced loan to the refinancing rate to measure refinancing incentive.

FIGURE 8.10. Prepayment Rates on FNMAs versus Refinancing Incentive, November 1993 and August 1994

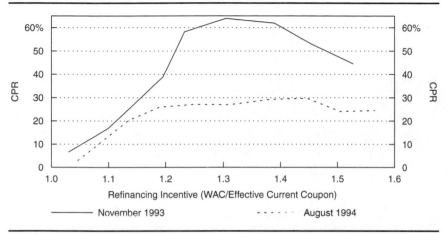

CPR Constant prepayment rate.
Source: Salomon Brothers Inc.

to refinancing opportunities will have lower refinancing rates than a pool with no such prior exposure. It also explains why the speeds in Figure 8.10 actually begin to decline for higher refinancing incentives; these coupons have had greater past exposure to refinancing opportunities.

The market's belief in burnout was severely shaken in the refinancing waves of 1991–1993, when speeds on many coupons remained at stubbornly high levels, or even increased, during successive waves. Furthermore, the speeds of many high-premium coupons from the early 1980s, which were considered completely burnt out, more than doubled in this period. We show this pattern in Figure 8.11, for 1983 origination FNMA 12s and 13s.

The FNMA 12s and 13s experienced a heavy round of refinancings in 1986 and 1987, and then, from 1988 to early 1991, gradually stabilized at an average speed of around 18% CPR. Two additional factors seemed to confirm the heavy hand of burnout. First, for much of the 1988–1990 period mortgage rates averaged about 10%, around the same level prevailing at the time of the first spike in 1986; however, speeds on the FNMA 12s and 13s were roughly one third of the peak values in 1986. Second, speeds on the FNMA 12s

FIGURE 8.11. Prepayment Speeds on FNMA 12s and FNMA 13s

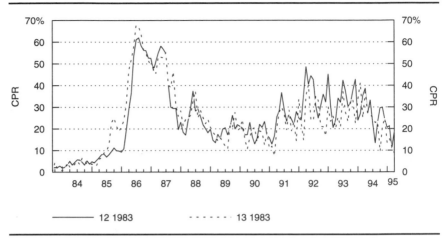

CPR Constant prepayment rate.

Source: Salomon Brothers Inc.

averaged about the same as those on the FNMA 13s, despite the roughly 100-basis-point higher coupon on the 13s. Hence, the jumps in speeds for the FNMA 12s and 13s in 1991 and 1992 are difficult to understand in the context of burnout and amount of refinancing incentive.

We feel that burnout, and refinancing patterns in general, are best modeled within a behavioral or statistical framework.

How Do We Measure Refinancing Incentive?

The traditional measure of refinancing incentive has been the difference, or spread, between the WAC and prevailing mortgage rates. This measure is simple and easily understood. However, the experience in the 1991–1993 refinancing waves suggested that refinancing from a 9% loan to a 7% one was not quite the same as refinancing from a 12% loan to a 10% one. The fact that 9% to 7% represents a significantly bigger percentage savings than 12% to 10% was cited as a reason that some spread-based prepayment models underpredicted refinancing levels for this period.

A straightforward argument shows that, in present value terms, the savings per dollar from refinancing a loan with rate C to a new loan at a rate M is

$$\frac{C}{M} \times \frac{1-(1+M)^{-(\text{TERM}-\text{AGE})}}{1-(1+C)^{-\text{TERM}}} - 1 \tag{8.3}$$

where C and M are expressed as monthly decimals, TERM is the original term of the existing loan in months and AGE is the number of months since origination. If the mortgage loan is still in the first half of its term, Equation (8.3) can be approximated by

$$\frac{C}{M} - 1$$

which argues for using a ratio rather than a difference to measure refinancing incentive. Some data from FHLMC seems to offer further evidence for using the ratio.[8] For refinancings from 1986 to 1994, FHLMC examined the rates on the refinanced loan and on the new loan. Its analysis showed that while the average difference, C-M, between the new and old loan rates has been narrower in the past few years than in 1986–1987, the average ratio, C/M, was pretty constant (at around 1.30). Of course, it is possible that this evidence just reflects a more efficient mortgage market, with borrowers now willing to refinance for a lower coupon differential

In reality, different mortgagors will look at the potential savings from a refinancing in different ways. Furthermore, the possibility of being able to refinance from, say a 30-year loan into a 15-year loan, means that the mortgagor can consider a complex mix of rates and monthly payments. We have chosen to base our refinancing function on the ratio rather than difference (with the refinancing rate M reflecting both 30-year rates and shorter-maturity refinancing alternatives), for two reasons. First, from Equation (8.3), basic economic arguments imply using the ratio. Second, and perhaps more important, it allows us to fit speeds well in both the 1986–1987 and 1991–1993 refinancing waves, something difficult to do if we use the spread difference to measure refinancing incentive.

---

[8] See "Secondary Mortgage Markets," *Mortgage Market Review*, FHLMC, 1994.

Explaining Refinancing Patterns Using a Statistical Approach

In previous publications, one of the authors has outlined a statistical approach to describing refinancing patterns (e.g., Hayre, 1994). Appendix 8.2 gives a mathematical description of this approach. Its basic elements are as follows.

Diverse Pool of Mortgagors.   The mortgagors in a given pool are assumed to differ in their intrinsic propensity to refinance. The simplest case is to assume that each person is either a "slow" or a "fast" refinancer. At the other extreme, we could assume that there is a continuous spectrum of borrower types. Different borrower types have different response rates (likelihoods of refinancing) for a given level of refinancing incentive, as illustrated in Figure 8.12.

All of the refinancing curves in Figure 8.12 have the familiar empirically observed S-shaped curve that speeds tend to follow and that is displayed in Figure 8.10. The refinancing rate is low for a low incentive, accelerates as the incentive increases (the "cuspy" part of the refinancing curve) and levels off, as further incentive increases seem to have little incremental impact. However, the rate at which the refinancing response rate rises with incentive, and the cuspiness or steepness of the curve, varies according to borrower type.

FIGURE 8.12. Refinancing Curves for Different Borrower Types (WAC Weighted-Average Coupon)

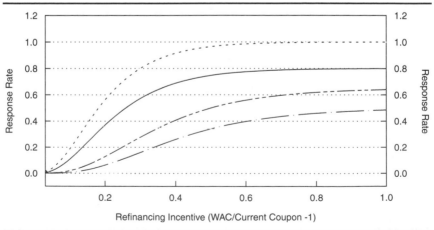

The observed refinancing rate for the pool will be the average of the refinancing rates for the different categories of borrowers, weighted by the proportion of the pool in that category in that particular month. For example, if in month one half the mortgagors are "slow" refinancers with a refinancing rate (for a given level of refinancing incentive) of 2% per month, and the other half are "fast" refinancers with a rate of 18% per month, then the expected refinancing rate for the pool in month one will be 10%.[9]

Evolution of the Pool over Time.   As the pool undergoes refinancings, faster refinancers will leave the pool at a faster rate. For example, in the simple slow/fast case discussed above, 18% of the fast refinancers, but only 2% of the slow refinancers, will leave the pool each month. Hence the slow refinancers will form an increasingly larger proportion of the remaining population, and other things being equal, the refinancing rate of the pool will gradually slow down toward the 2% rate of the slow group.[10] This gradual slowdown in the pool refinancing rate, caused solely by the change in the pool's composition as faster refinancers leave at a faster rate, is what we term *burnout*.

The Media Effect and the Migration of Borrowers.   We have assumed that the intrinsic refinancing propensity of a borrower does not change over time. The experience of the past few years has made it fairly obvious that this is not the case. Borrower propensities can change for a variety of reasons:

- A blitz of media publicity about refinancing opportunities after a big market rally (especially pronounced when rates hit generational lows in 1992 and 1993);
- More proactive mortgage lenders when refinancing rates are at attractive levels; or

---

[9] In general, the pool refinancing rate is the expected value across the probability distribution of borrower types and is given by Equation (8.4) in the Appendix 8.2.

[10] Equation (8.5) in Appendix 8.2 gives a mathematical model of the evolution of the population mix. A detailed examination of the slow/fast case is given in the Salomon Brothers publication "A Simple Statistical Framework for Modeling Burnout and Refinancing Behavior," Lakhbir Hayre, *Journal of Fixed Income*, December 1994.

- Dormant accumulated changes in the personal circumstances of borrowers who did not refinance in the past (improved credit, more equity in the home, etc.).

The first two reasons will lead to a higher overall level of refinancings, while the combination of all three will lead to a pickup in the speeds of even very seasoned, burnt-out coupons, as illustrated by the FNMA 12s and 13s in Figure 8.11.

This phenomenon has been labeled the *media effect*. In terms of our statistical framework, it can be modeled as a shift in the distribution of borrowers toward a higher average refinancing propensity, which can temporarily overwhelm the downward trend in average refinancing propensity resulting from burnout.

How do we actually capture the media effect? Clearly, it will be high when a widespread impression prevails that mortgage rates are low relative to "historical levels." At the same time, the recent rather than the distant past will tend to weigh more in people's minds. The Salomon Brothers Prepayment Model uses a comparison of current mortgage rates to a weighted average of past rates to estimate the media effect. Figure 8.13 shows 30-year mortgage rates, a weighted average of past mortgage rates and the ratio of the two.

FIGURE 8.13. Modeling the Media Effect: A Comparison of Current and Historical Mortgage Rates, 1983–1994

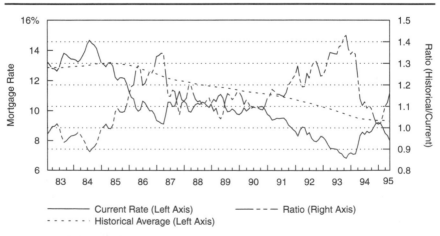

Source: Salomon Brothers Inc.

The ratio of the historical average rate to the current rate has been an excellent indicator of the level of refinancing activity. The ratio first peaked in the spring of 1986, had a slightly higher peak in early 1987, then remained relatively low until early 1991, before reaching a series of ever higher peaks through the end of 1993, faithfully following the refinancing waves that occurred in this period.

Capturing a Complex Combination of Effects

The interaction of refinancing incentive, burnout and the media effect can be seen in Figure 8.14, which shows historical speeds on 1991 FNMA 8.5s, 9s and 9.5s.

In 1992 and 1993, mortgage rates followed a consistent pattern of hitting a multiyear low, briefly stabilizing or slightly backing up, before declining again to hit another multiyear low, and in October 1993 culminating in the lowest rates seen for almost 30 years. This led to a corresponding pattern in prepayment speeds. Speeds would

FIGURE 8.14. Speeds on 1991 Origination FNMA 8.5s, 9s, and 9.5s, and 30-Year Mortgage Rates

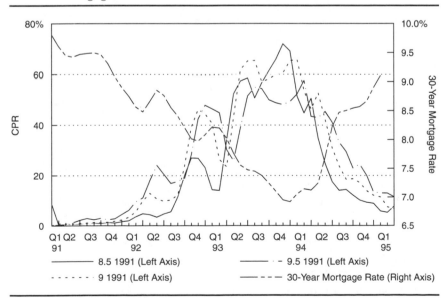

Source: Salomon Brothers Inc.

spike as rates declined, then start declining as rates stabilized or backed up—even though ample refinancing incentive still remained—as burnout began to play a role. However, a new multiyear low, and the media publicity it generated, led to a new and higher spike. Burnout was still present, as exemplified by the 8.5s' prepaying at higher rates than the 9.5s in 1993, but its effect was fairly weak in the refinancing frenzy that occurred during this time.

Figure 8.15 shows projected speeds for the three coupons in Figure 8.14. A comparison of Figures 8.14 and 8.15 shows a close match between the actual and projected speeds, indicating that the Salomon Brothers Prepayment Model faithfully captures this complex combination of effects driving speeds in this period.

Two more graphs illustrate the changing effect over time of refinancing incentive, burnout and the media effect. Figure 8.16 shows actual and projected speeds on 1990 origination FNMA 7-year balloons. Speeds on this coupon started accelerating in early 1992 and stayed well over 50% CPR for most of the period from the fall of 1992

FIGURE 8.15. Projected Speeds on 1991 FNMA 8.5s, 9s, and 9.5s

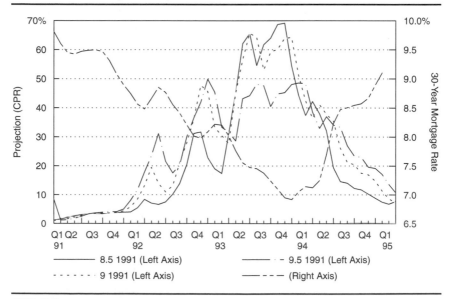

CPR Constant prepayment rate.

Source: Salomon Brothers Inc.

FIGURE 8.16. Actual and Projected Speeds on 1990 FNMA 7-Year Balloons

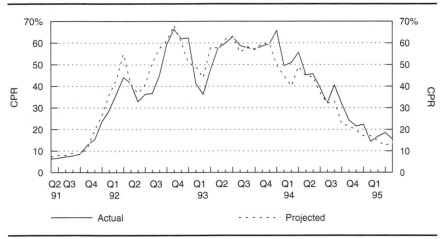

CPR Constant prepayment rate.
Source: Salomon Brothers Inc.

to early 1994, suggesting a close balancing of increases in refinancing incentive, burnout and the media effect.

Finally, Figure 8.17 shows actual and projected speeds on 1980 GNMA 11s, a seasoned coupon that has seen its share of interest rate and economic cycles, not to mention several refinancing waves. This coupon went through its first refinancing wave in 1986 and early 1987, then settled into a typical burnt-out state for several years before beginning a series of spikes in 1991, and finally entered a sustained decline in speeds in early 1994. The projected speeds closely track the actual ones for most of the 14-year period shown in Figure 8.17, suggesting that, despite the widespread perception of fundamental changes in the mortgage markets, a well-formulated model can withstand the test of ages.

The Effect of Relative Loan Size

The combination of refinancing incentive, burnout and the media effect explain a large proportion of the refinancing patterns seen

FIGURE 8.17. Actual and Projected Speeds on 1980 Origination GNMA 11s

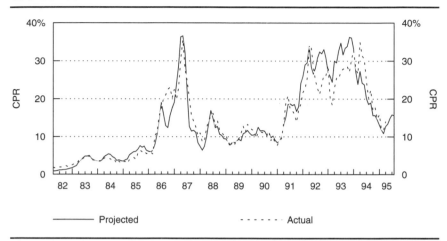

CPR Constant prepayment rate.
Source: Salomon Brothers Inc.

during the past few years. One feature not captured is the slower response of very seasoned loans, which is illustrated in Figure 8.18.

Although the 1978 FNMA 9s had a mild degree of refinancing exposure in 1986–1987, essentially all three coupons had no burnout prior to 1992. Despite this, the 1978 9s experienced significantly lower prepayment rates during 1992 and 1993 than the 1986 9s, which in turn were a little slower than the 1991 9s. This pattern is repeated for other coupons and sectors and is particularly pronounced for GNMAs; in the refinancing waves of 1992 and 1993, 1986–1987 origination GNMA 8s through 9.5s prepaid at between 70% to 80% of newer (90 and onward originations) coupons, while 1970s origination 8s through 9s prepaid at only 50% of the newer coupons.

An explanation for the dampened refinancing rates of older coupons is not difficult to find. If a loan was taken out some time ago, housing inflation has made its balance small relative to current levels. If the loan is fairly seasoned, amortization has accentuated this process; for a loan halfway through its term (which means mid-1980s originations in the case of 15-year MBSs) the amortized loan balance will be about 80% of the original balance (not counting any

FIGURE 8.18. Speeds on 1978, 1986, and 1991 FNMA 9s

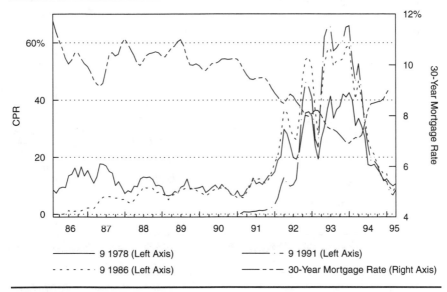

CPR Constant prepayment rate.
Source: Salomon Brothers Inc.

curtailments). Given that a refinancing involves some fixed costs, as well as some general hassle and paperwork, obviously a smaller incentive exists to refinance a low-balance loan.

The Salomon Brothers Prepayment Model uses Equation (8.2) which gives the amortized, inflation-adjusted value of a $1 mortgage taken out a specified time ago[11] as the basis for dampening the refinancing responses of seasoned loan.[12] Figure 8.19 shows projections for the coupons in Figure 8.18; the adjustment based on Equation (8.2) captures the differentials quite well.

---

[11] This quantity can also be thought of as an estimated current LTV as a fraction of the original LTV. Figure 8.7 provides a graph of this fraction as a function of loan age.

[12] Note that this approach assumes that all the loans of a particular type originated at a given time had the same loan balances. If we know that a particular cohort has an average original loan balance different from the average for that origination period, this information can of course be combined with Equation (8.2) in adjusting the refinancing response.

FIGURE 8.19. Capturing Differences in Loan Balances: Projected Speeds on 1978, 1986, and 1991 FNMA 9s

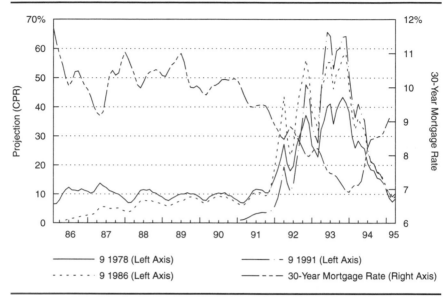

9 1978 (Left Axis)   9 1991 (Left Axis)

- - - - - - 9 1986 (Left Axis)   - - - - 30-Year Mortgage Rate (Right Axis)

Source: Salomon Brothers Inc.

Amortization differences also explain why speeds on mid-1980s 15-year MBSs were slower during the recent refinancing waves than similar vintage 30-year MBSs. The slower 15-year speeds have sometimes been attributed to their smaller original loan balances vis-à-vis 30-year loans. However, speeds on post-1990 origination 15-year MBSs were just as fast as their 30-year peers. A more likely explanation is the faster amortization of 15-year loans; whereas the mid-1980s 30-year loans had very little principal amortization by 1992, the 15-year loan balances were down to about 80% of the original. This differential is captured by the amortization component in Equation (8.2), as illustrated in Figure 8.20, which shows actual and projected speeds for 1986 origination 15-year and 30-year FNMA 9s.

Seasoning Patterns for Newer Loans

In the previous section, we have discussed the dampened refinancing responses of older loans. What about newer loans? The fact that

FIGURE 8.20. Capturing Amortization Differences: Actual and Projected Speeds on 1986 15-Year and 30-Year FNMA 9s

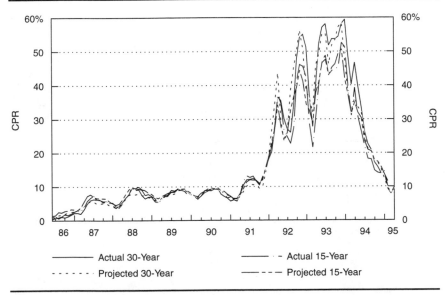

CPR Constant prepayment rate.
Source: Salomon Brothers Inc.

a loan was taken out fairly recently will tend to dampen refinancing rates. However, as became apparent in 1992 and 1993, if sufficient refinancing incentive exists, speeds can accelerate sharply even for relatively new loans.

Figure 8.21 shows speeds of premiums by age and degree of refinancing incentive and makes clear the accelerated seasoning curve for well in-the-money mortgages.

We use a refinancing seasoning curve that starts out above zero (to reflect the fast PSAs of very new premiums) and shortens as the refinancing incentive increases. Figure 8.22 shows actual and projected speeds for 1992 origination FNMA 8s. Actual speeds on these coupons reached 60% CPR in the fall of 1993, although they were barely more than a year old. The "elastic" seasoning ramp in the model allows projections to match these high actual speeds.

The "Points" Effect. Another reason for the high speeds on newer premiums in 1992 and 1993 is that many were originated as

FIGURE 8.21. Speeds of FNMAs by Age and Refinancing Incentive

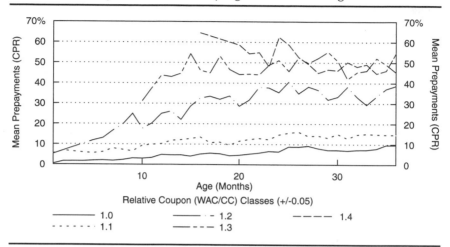

WAC Weighted-average coupon.
Source: Salomon Brothers Inc.

FIGURE 8.22. Actual and Projected Speeds for 1992 FNMA 8s, 1992-1Q 95

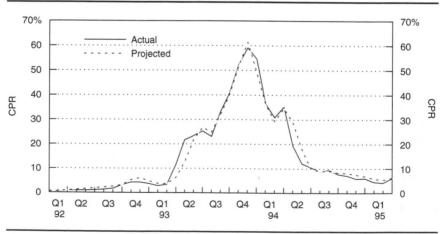

CPR Constant prepayment rate.
Source: Salomon Brothers Inc.

"low-point" or "no-point" loans, with the borrower paying a higher coupon rate to reduce or eliminate refinancing costs. This practice not only leads to a very sharp seasoning ramp, but also means that the mortgagor only needs a minor drop in rates to refinance again into another "no-point" loan. If a particular collateral is identified as consisting of such loans, then a very sharp seasoning ramp and an accelerated base refinancing curve is needed.

However, care has to be taken in identifying no-point loans. An above-market loan rate could either mean a no-point loan, or it could indicate credit or other difficulties; the latter may imply lower rather than faster prepayment levels for that segment of borrowers. Indeed, small amounts of premium pass-throughs have been originated at above-market rates since the late 1980s, but they did not prepay abnormally faster in the refinancing waves of 1992–1993—if anything, they showed slightly *slower* refinancing rates than other comparable premiums.

The evidence therefore suggests that prepayments of mortgages originated above market rates would reflect the combined behavior of two very different types of borrower: (1) opportunistic refinancers who jump at the first refinancing opportunity, causing elevated prepayments in the initial years of the life of the pool; and (2) borrowers who could not get loans at or below market rate and who might depress prepayments over the longer term to some degree.

At the other extreme are the borrowers who pay high points to secure a below-market loan rate. As discussed in the previous section, the evidence indicates that such borrowers have a slow seasoning period as far as housing turnover is concerned. Is there evidence that such borrowers have a slow refinancing seasoning period as well?

Our analysis of the data clearly shows that they do. Indeed, as Figure 8.6 illustrates with 1992 origination FNMA 7s, "high-point" coupons did prepay more slowly in the refinancing waves of 1992–1993. As with other origination-related effects, the "curing" and seasoning process will, over time, eliminate these effects, so that their impact on the prepayments of say, a 10-year-old mortgage pool, should be small to negligible.

As mentioned earlier, our estimate of the points paid is based on the difference between the gross coupon and the prevailing mortgage rate at the time of origination. The Salomon refinancing submodel then takes account of "high-points" and "no-points" effects by appropriately adjusting the mortgage pool's refinancing response and rate of seasoning. Our application of the effect is careful and conservative, because substantial variation in mortgage rates across regions and originators reduces the accuracy of our estimate of points paid, diluting its predictive power.

PREPAYMENT MODELS: A USER'S GUIDE

While MBS investors often display a degree of skepticism about the long-term predictive power of prepayment models, they have little choice but to use them—key valuation measures, such as OASs and effective durations, cannot be calculated without a prepayment model. Given this imperative, what do users need to be aware of concerning the uses, misuses and limitations of prepayment models?

Some Basic Properties of Model Projections

Figure 8.23 shows historical speeds and projections for a FNMA 8% pass-through under three assumed interest rate scenarios: rates unchanged; rates up by 200 basis points; and rates down 100 basis points.[13] The numbers shown are the vectors of monthly projections from the model. There are several points to note from Figure 8.23:

- *The Conditional Nature of Projections.* Projections from a prepayment model are *for a specified path of interest rates.* In other words, projections are conditional upon the realization of the prescribed path of interest rates—a path which in reality is never going to be *exactly* realized. While this observation will not be news to most investors, two implications are worth noting. First, prepayment projections should always be obtained for a variety of bullish and bearish interest rate scenarios. Second, in evaluating the accuracy of a model, it is necessary to determine what its projections were for interest

---

[13] We are assuming parallel shifts in interest rates.

FIGURE 8.23. Prepayment Projections for a FNMA 8%, 1992–2021

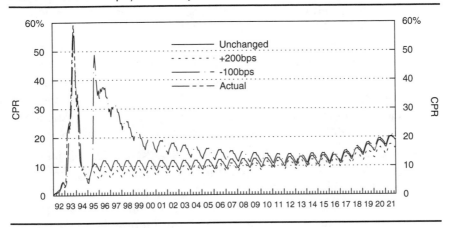

CPR Constant prepayment rate.
Source: Salomon Brothers Inc.

rate scenarios approximating those which actually occurred. While many models did fail to accurately predict the high speeds that occurred in 1991–1994, investors should remember that mortgage rates fell by approximately 300 basis points between 1990 and 1993; hence, the relevant predictions from 1990 would be those for a 300-basis-point drop in rates.

- *Use Long-Term Projections with Care.* Even if interest rates were to stay unchanged forever, prepayments (actual and projected) would still differ over time, for a variety of reasons. Premium speeds tend to decline over time because of burnout; newer discount speeds tend to increase as a result of seasoning. On a month-to-month basis, seasonal factors can lead to double-digit percentage changes. Changes in speeds over time will be even greater in changing interest rate scenarios. For convenience and practicality, a long-term average of the projected speeds is typically reported as the model's projection.[14] The somewhat obvious point here is that a single

[14] The long-term projection is a weighted average of the vector of month-by-month projections. The method used in the Salomon Brothers model is to find the single speed that gives the same average life as the vector; another common method is to find the single speed that gives the same yield as the vector.

long-term projected speed is inadequate for most investors. Figure 8.24 shows the vector and the long-term average speed for the FNMA 8s in the "down-100" scenario.

The long-term average projection is below model projections for the first few years and above in later years. For an investor analyzing, for example, a short-term Collateralized Mortgage Obligation (CMO) bond, the long-term projection can be quite misleading. Yet a surprising proportion of investors still seem to evaluate MBSs using a single speed.

- *Noise: The Random Component of Speeds.* Model projections represent a statistical estimate of the *expected* prepayment rates along a specified path of interest rates. Hence, random variation ("noise") means that actual month-to-month speeds will differ from projections even if the model is perfectly accurate (in this context, "perfectly accurate" just means that the average deviation will be zero). This is a particularly important point for CMO or Interest Only/Principal Only (IO/PO) deals; even for relatively large deals, the random errors can be significant (Bykhovsky & Hayre, 1992).

Our analysis shows that the effect of purely random variation in speeds has almost no impact on OASs of pass-throughs and a minimal impact for IOs and POs. In other words, if the model is accurate

FIGURE 8.24. Monthly Projections and the Long-Term Average for FNMA 8s, 1995–2021 (CPR Constant Prepayment Rate)

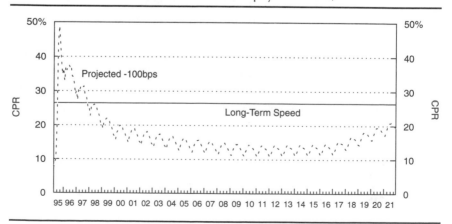

on average, then the averaging over many interest rate paths involved in OAS calculations minimizes the effect of noise.

Of course, no model is ever likely to be perfectly accurate for any length of time; projections incorporate a number of assumptions (explicitly or implicitly) about various factors (such as housing sales rates and housing inflation) which are unlikely to hold forever. In the next section, we discuss ways of quantifying the impact of systematic errors.

Prepayment Risk: Partial Prepayment Durations

We use the term prepayment risk to signify the risk that the market price will reflect prepayment assumptions that differ from model projections. This risk measure is distinct from the risk associated with interest rate movements causing changes in prepayments. We note that prepayment risk may arise either because actual prepayments are substantially different from projected levels (for example, because of structural changes in the mortgage finance industry and housing market) or because market expectations about prepayment prospects differ from model projections.

A useful measure of prepayment risk is the concept of *prepayment duration*. This was defined in an earlier Salomon Brothers publication (1992) as the percentage change in price, holding OAS constant, for a given percentage deviation in speeds from some defined base level projections. The base level could be the straight model projections, or some market-implied multiple of the projections, for example, the multiple of the projections that would equalize OASs on the IO and PO of a chosen benchmark strip issue.

An extension of this concept is to calculate partial prepayment durations; that is, price sensitivity with respect to deviations from the projections for a specific component of speeds. One can define partial prepayment durations for any of the important variables discussed in the previous few sections. In general, the most important ones are the following:

- *Housing Turnover Rate.* The impact of higher- or lower-than-projected home sales.
- *Refinancing Rate.* The impact of refinancing rates being higher- or lower-than-projected refinancing rates.

FIGURE 8.25. Prepayment Component Partial Durations

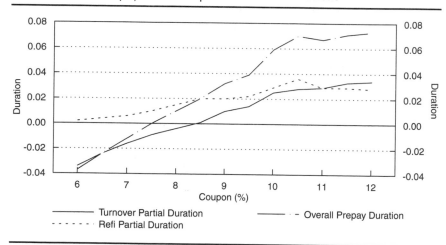

Source: Salomon Brothers Inc.

We have computed overall prepayment durations as well as partial durations associated with these two components using the new Salomon Brothers prepayment model projections as the base. Figure 8.25 shows prepayment durations and partial prepayment component durations for these two components for a range of representative FNMA 30-year pass-throughs.[15]

The durations represent the estimated change in price for a 1% change in prepayments associated with the total prepayment or prepayment component. From the formula in footnote 20, if slower than expected speeds lead to an increase in price the prepayment duration will be positive. Note that the current coupon for the calculations in Figure 8.25 is approximately 7.5%. We may draw a number of interesting observations from these durations.

---

[15] The durations are calculated by

$$D_c = \frac{P_{-10} - P_{+10}}{20P_0} \cdot 100$$

where D_c = Prepayment partial duration w.r.t. component C
P_d = Price when projections for component C are changed by d% in Salomon Brothers prepayment model, holding OAS constant.

The overall prepayment durations and partial durations for the turnover component are negative for discounts and current coupons, while they are positive for the premiums. This is because slower-than-projected speeds hurt mortgage pass-throughs in discount scenarios but help them when they are premiums. However, the partial durations for the refinancing component are always positive, because the refinancing component is zero except in premium scenarios, in which lower prepayments lead to higher prices. Newer premiums that have had less exposure to refinancing opportunity have the highest durations, because refinancing represents the largest component of prepayments for such coupons. Note that the overall prepayment duration is approximately, although not exactly, the sum of the partial durations for the turnover and refinancing components.

The durations are most significant for deep discounts (about −0.03 for the turnover component) and substantial premiums (about +0.03 each for the turnover and the refinancing components). These levels imply a price change of roughly one tick per 1% change in prepay component projections.

For seasoned premiums, the partial durations for the turnover and refinancing components are more or less of equal importance. While this pattern should not be surprising, given that long-term projections for each of those components is roughly the same (around 6%–10% CPR), it may come as a revelation to investors accustomed to thinking of refinancing rates as posing the major prepayment risk for premiums. At the same time, the partial durations associated with deep discounts for the turnover component are quite high, suggesting that there is substantial prepayment risk associated with that sector. The risk is accentuated by substantial recent divergence in predictions about the strength of the housing market and the seasoning rates of discounts among Street firms.[16]

If desired, these prepay components may be dissected further, and partial durations computed for other more specific factors:[17]

---

[16] The actual price risk could be thought of as the product of the partial duration with some measure of dispersion or volatility for the projected prepayment component. Disagreement and uncertainty among market players would tend to increase the volatility of the component's projected levels.

[17] Readers who have access to Salomon Brothers's *Yield Book* will recognize these as some of the "Dials" available for customizing the prepayment model.

- *Turnover Seasoning Length.* The length of time after origination required for seasoning of the turnover component.
- *The Refinancing Elbow.* The degree of refinancing incentive at which refinancing rates begin to accelerate.
- *Steepness (or "Cuspiness") of the Refinancing Curve.* The slope of the refinancing response curve.
- *Refinancing Amplitude.* Peak speeds when premium coupons are first exposed to significant refinancing opportunities.
- *Degree of Burnout.* The rate at which speeds slow down after a refinancing peak.

These more elaborate measures can be very useful in certain contexts, such as risk management or in evaluating complex mortgage derivatives.

SUMMARY AND CONCLUSIONS

The projection of prepayments is a maturing field that has benefited from the varied and rapidly changing market environment over the past 15 years and the intensive attention paid to it by researchers and investors. The best prepayment models of the future will be those that have absorbed and incorporated the lessons learned during this process, benefiting from past information while fully recognizing its limitations when predicting the future. In other words, a good model should fit past prepayment data well, but at the same time it should account for the recent secular shifts in mortgage marketplace and mortgage-holders' behavior.

We have presented a model that remains consistent with past observed behavior, while incorporating the best available understanding of the processes that underlie the behavior of today's mortgage holder. Our model is *modular* (projections are additive, incorporating the different well-known causes of prepayments), *universal* (designed to handle virtually all mortgage types) and *transparent* (relationships among the different components of the projections are visible to and alterable by the user). The design should help dispel investor skepticism about the intelligence behind the model's predictions.

Prepayments due to *home sales, refinancings, curtailments, full pay-offs,* and *defaults* are individually modeled using economically and behaviorally sound relationships with underlying independent variables such as age, mortgage rates and home prices. The subtler individual differences within a mortgage type related to *seasonality, refinancing percentage at origination, points paid at origination, lock-in,* and *assumability,* among others, are superimposed on a fundamental projection of housing turnover rates to produce a realistic projection of the home-sales component of prepayments. A statistical approach to modeling the refinancing decision of the mortgage-holder leads to an economically sound methodology to project the refinancing component. Such a projection naturally incorporates the observed characteristics of refinancing behavior such as *seasoning, burnout,* and the *media effect.*

The combination of these carefully sculpted submodels produces projections that are universal in consistency across mortgage types and yet are highly specific to the salient characteristics of the individual mortgage security. The model provides a powerful tool to value and compare mortgages across and within sectors of the mortgage market.

APPENDIX 8.1

THE SALOMON BROTHERS HOUSING TURNOVER MODEL

As discussed in the section on home sales, housing turnover may be defined as the ratio of existing (single-family) home sales to single-family housing stock. This definition makes the relationship of housing turnover rates to prepayment speeds very clear. Hence, Salomon Brothers has performed a careful analysis of housing turnover rates over the past 15 years, leading to a deeper understanding of the factors that affect home sales and to a model that may be used to project turnover rates into the future under different interest rate scenarios. This Appendix outlines the latter, which forms a submodel of the Salomon Brothers prepayment model.

We believe that explicitly modeling home turnover rates offers a number of advantages. It leads to a more dynamic and realistic depiction of the evolution of turnover and hence prepayment rates over time, capturing in particular the path dependence of such rates. For example, if a sudden and sustained rise in mortgage rates occurs, an initial drop in home sales (and hence in speeds) will take place, but eventually pent-up demand and a gradual adjustment to the higher mortgage rates will lead to a pickup in sales and in speeds (as happened, for example, in the first half of the 1980s). The model also allows easier sensitivity testing; for example, what happens if for a given level of interest rates, home inflation is significantly different from historical norms? Finally, an explicit projection for the housing turnover rate furthers our goal of increasing the transparency of the prepayment model; users can determine for themselves if they agree with the model's projections for home turnover rates along given interest rate paths.

Factors Affecting Housing Turnover

Demographics and population mobility, as well as macroeconomic and social factors all combine to influence home sales:

- *Affordability.* This refers to the home buyer's ability to make a monthly mortgage payment. Affordability can be approximated by the ratio of median income to the median monthly mortgage payment on a median home. Affordability is often cited as an important predictor of home sales, and correctly so. However, the effect of affordability is subtler than first appears, in that home sales depend not only on the current affordability of housing, but also on the recent history of affordability. For example, when mortgage rates rallied after hitting all-time highs above 16% in 1981–1982, the pickup in home sales was immediate. Turnover averaged 4.85% and 5.02% in 1983 and 1984, respectively, although affordability was still quite low by historical standards, with rates still several hundred basis points above mean 1970s levels. It is likely that pent-up demand for housing from prospective buyers who could not afford a house in 1981–1982 was a factor.

- *Desirability.* Another socioeconomic factor that helps explain historical variations in turnover is the desirability of homeownership. We use this term in a general sense, to include a perception of the likely economic return from buying a home and a perception as to whether it is currently prudent to do so. In our model, the variable influencing this desirability is the prospective inflation in home prices, for which a good proxy might be a weighted average of nominal home price changes in recent years. High levels of price inflation, which tend to lower the *real* (inflation-adjusted) mortgage interest rate are acknowledged in the literature as a key factor behind the sharp rise in turnover rates from 1973 to 1978, which bucked the sustained drop in affordability during the same period.[18]

- *Consumer Confidence.* This is another important influence on housing activity. However, although using this variable would improve the historical fit of our model, we have chosen not to use it, as we do not want to attempt to predict its levels going forward.

The Estimation of Turnover

There are two intersecting populations of prospective buyers or movers: those who desire to buy or trade up and those that can afford to do so. The basic behavioral assumption behind the model is that the turnover rate is determined by the size of the intersection of these two groups. The size of the groups depends upon the levels of desirability and affordability, respectively. We capture these levels with two factors, an *affordability factor* that depends upon the median income, median home price and mortgage rates, as described above, and a *desirability factor* that incorporates the effects of home price inflation. The model also accounts for pent-up demand, or the lack of demand due to past interest rates, by carrying forward an affordability "deficit" or "surplus" from previous periods.

For our projections, we make the assumption that income and home prices change at the same rate over time; hence, changes in affordability are just a function of changes in mortgage rates.

A discussion of the model's fit to actual data as well as its predictions for various interest rate scenarios is included in the section on home sales (see Figure 8.2 and accompanying commentary). As shown there, the model manages to capture historical variations quite well and also provides realistic projections of the impact of interest rate changes on future housing turnover levels.

---

[18] See, for example, *Urban Economics*, E.S. Mills and B.W. Hamilton, Scott Foresman and Company, Chapter 10.

APPENDIX 8.2

A GENERAL STATISTICAL FRAMEWORK FOR MODELING REFINANCING BEHAVIOR

Let x be a measure of refinancing incentive. Assume that, for a given x, the likelihood of a refinancing varies from person to person. Let θ be a parameter that characterizes a mortgagor's propensity to refinance, and let $p(x; \theta)$ = the probability of a refinancing, given x and θ. Let $f_0(\theta)$ = initial probability distribution of θ across the population of borrowers. If x_1 = refinancing incentive in month one, then the refinancing rate in month one will be $\bar{p}_1$ = average of $p(x_1; \theta)$ across the distribution of θ

$$\bar{p}_1 = E[p(x_1; \theta)] = \int_{-\infty}^{\infty} p(x_1; \theta) f_0(\theta) d\theta$$

Evolution of the Distribution of θ

Mortgagors with a higher propensity to refinance will leave the population at a faster rate. The survival rate in month one of a "type θ" mortgagor is $[1 - p(x_1; \theta)]$, and it follows that the new distribution of θ at the end of month one is

$$f_1(\theta) = A_1(x_1)(1 - p(x_1; \theta))f_0(\theta)$$

where $A_1(x_1)$ is a normalizing constant given by

$$A_1(x_1) = \left[\int_{-\infty}^{\infty} (1 - p(x_1; \theta)) f_0(\theta) d\theta \right]^{-1}$$

Repeating this argument, it can be seen that if x_n is the refinancing incentive in month n, then the refinancing rate in month n will be

$$\bar{p}_n = \int_{-\infty}^{\infty} p(x_n; \theta) f_{n-1}(\theta) d\theta \tag{8.4}$$

where $f_{n-1}(\theta)$ is the distribution at the beginning of the month. The distribution of θ at the end of the month is given by

$$f_n(\theta) = A_n(1 - p(x_n; \theta))f_{n-1}(\theta)$$

$$= A_n(1 - p(x_n; \theta))(1 - p(x_{n-1}; \theta))\ldots(1 - p(x_1; \theta))f_0(\theta) \qquad (8.5)$$

$$= A_n Q_n f_0(\theta)$$

where $Q_n = (1 - p(x_n; \theta))(1 - p(x_{n-1}; \theta)) \ldots (1 - p(x_1; \theta))$ and A_n is a normalizing constant given by

$$A_n = \left[\int_{-\infty}^{\infty} Q_n f_0(\theta) d\theta \right]^{-1}$$

Burnout

Note that, from Equation (8.5), as the population undergoes refinancings, the population distribution will shift toward those with the lowest propensities to refinance (or highest survival likelihoods). Hence, even for a constant refinancing incentive, the refinancing rate will decline, at a rate proportional to the average across θ of the cumulative survival factor Q_n (note the similarity to the traditional Wall Street practice of modeling burnout using some sort of pool factor).

Changes in Intrinsic Propensities: The Media Effect

Thus far, we have assumed that, for any given mortgagor, the basic propensity to refinance remains unchanged; that is, an individual's θ does not change. The evidence from the refinancing waves of 1991–1993 suggests that borrowers' propensity to refinance does change. The combination of media publicity about low mortgage rates and resulting refinancing opportunities, proactive originators, and dormant changes in personal circumstances (for example, improved credit or equity) can lead to a distributional change in θ.

This phenomenon, which has been labeled the "media effect," can be modeled as a second influence in the evolution of the probability distribution $f_n(\theta)$. Thus, each month, the distribution of θ across the population can change because of two factors:

1. Refinancings removing faster refinancers from the population at a faster rate ("burnout"). This will lead a decline in the average propensity to refinance.

2. A migration of some borrowers from "slower" to "faster" categories ("media effect"), leading to an increase in the average propensity to refinance. The migration rate can be a function of the history of interest rates, and a variety of ways exist to implement the effect on the distribution of θ.

A simple version of this framework, in which θ can take only two values (so that mortgagors are either "slow" or "fast"), has been discussed in more detail in a previous Salomon Brothers publication (1994).

REFERENCES

Bykhovsky, M. and L. Hayre. (1992). "Fact and Fantasy About Collateral Speeds," *Journal of Portfolio Management*.

Carliner, S. and D. D'Alessandris. (1992). "Home Owner Mobility and Mortgage Prepayments," *Housing Economics*.

Hayre, L. (1994). "A Simple Statistical Framework for Modeling Burnout and Refinancing Behavior," *Journal of Fixed Income*.

Salomon Brothers Inc. (1992). *Beyond Duration: Dimensions of Mortgage Risk*.

9

The Pricing and Hedging of Mortgage-Backed Securities

A MULTIVARIATE DENSITY ESTIMATION APPROACH

Jacob Boudoukh, Matthew Richardson, Richard Stanton,
and *Robert F. Whitelaw*

The mortgage-backed security (MBS) market plays a special role in the U.S. economy. Originators of mortgages (S&Ls, savings and commercial banks) can spread risk across the economy by packaging these mortgages into investment pools through a variety of agencies, such as the Government National Mortgage Association (GNMA), Federal Home Loan Mortgage Corporation (FHLMC), and Federal National Mortgage Association (FNMA). Purchasers of MBS are given the opportunity to invest in virtually default-free

This chapter is based closely on the paper, "Pricing Mortgage-Backed Securities in a Multifactor Interest Rate Environment: A Multivariate Density Estimation Approach," *Review of Financial Studies* (Summer 1997, Vol. 10, No. 2, pp. 405–446).

interest-rate contingent claims that offer payoff structures different from U.S. Treasury bonds. Due to the wide range of payoff patterns offered by MBS and their derivatives, the MBS market is one of the largest as well as fastest growing financial markets in the United States. For example, this market grew from approximately $100 million outstanding in 1980 to about $1.5 trillion in 1993.

Pricing of mortgage-backed securities is a fairly complex task, and investors in this market should clearly understand these complexities to fully take advantage of the tremendous opportunity offered. Pricing MBS may appear fairly simple on the surface. Fixed-rate mortgages offer fixed nominal payments; thus, fixed-rate MBS prices will be governed by pure discount bond prices. The complexity in pricing of MBS is due to the fact that typically residential mortgage holders have the option to prepay their existing mortgages; hence, MBS investors are implicitly writing a call option on a corresponding fixed-rate bond. The timing and magnitude of cash flows from MBS are therefore uncertain. While mortgage prepayments occur largely due to falling mortgage rates, other factors such as home owner mobility and home owner inertia play important roles in determining the speed at which mortgages are prepaid. Since these non-interest rate related factors that affect prepayment (and hence MBS prices) are difficult to quantify the task of pricing MBS is quite challenging.

This chapter develops a non-parametric method for pricing MBS. Much of the extant literature (e.g., Schwartz & Torous, 1989) employs parametric methods to price MBS. Parametric pricing techniques require specification and estimation of specific functions or models to describe interest rate movements and prepayments. While parametric models have certain advantages, any model for interest rates and prepayments is bound to be only an approximation of reality. Non-parametric techniques such as the multivariate density estimation (MDE) procedure that we propose, on the other hand, estimates the relation between MBS prices and fundamental interest rate factors directly from the data. MDE is well suited to analyzing MBS because, although financial economists have good intuition for what the MBS pricing fundamentals are, the exact models for the dynamics of these fundamentals is too complex to be determined precisely from a parametric model. For example, while it is standard to assume at least two factors govern interest rate movements, the time series dynamics of these factors and the interactions between them are not well understood. In contrast, MDE has the potential to capture the effects of previously unrecognized or hard to specify interest rate dynamics on MBS prices.

In this chapter, we first describe the MDE approach. We present the intuition behind the methodology and discuss the advantages and drawbacks of non-parametric approaches. We also discuss the applicability of MDE to MBS pricing in general and to our particular application.

We then apply the MDE method to price weekly TBA (to be announced) GNMA securities[1] with coupons ranging from 7.5% to 10.5% over the period 1987–1994. We show that at least two interest rate factors are necessary to fully describe the effects of the prepayment option on prices. The two factors are the interest rate level, which proxies for the moneyness of the prepayment option, the expected level of prepayments, and the average life of the cash flows; and the term structure slope, which controls for the average rate at which these cash flows should be discounted. The analysis also reveals cross-sectional differences among GNMAs with different coupons, especially with regard to their sensitivities to movements in the two interest rate factors. The MDE methodology captures the well-known negative convexity of MBS prices.

Finally, we present the methodology for hedging the interest rate risk of MBS based on the pricing model in this chapter. The sensitivities of the MBS to the two interest rate factors are used to construct hedge portfolios. The hedges constructed with the MDE methodology compare favorably to both a linear hedge and an alternative non-parametric technique. As can be expected, the MDE methodology works especially well in low interest rate environments when the GNMAs behave less like fixed maturity bonds.

MORTGAGE-BACKED SECURITY PRICING: PRELIMINARIES

Mortgage-backed securities represent claims on the cash flows from mortgages that are pooled together and packaged as a financial

---

[1] A TBA contract is just a forward contract, trading over the counter. More details are provided in the next section.

asset. The interest payments and principal repayments made by mortgagees, less a servicing fee, flow through to MBS investors. MBS backed by residential mortgages are typically guaranteed by government agencies such as the GNMA and FHLMC or private agencies such as FNMA. Because of the reinsurance offered by these agencies MBS investors bear virtually no default risk. Thus, the pricing of an MBS can be reduced to valuing the mortgage pool's cash flows at the appropriate discount rate. MBS pricing then is very much an issue of estimating the magnitude and timing of the pool's cash flows.

However, pricing an MBS is not a straightforward discounted cash flow valuation. This is because the timing and nature of a pool's cash flows depends on the prepayment behavior of the holders of the individual mortgages within the pool. For example, mortgages might be prepaid by individuals who sell their homes and relocate. Such events lead to early repayments of principal to the MBS holders. In addition, MBS contain an embedded interest rate option. Mortgage holders have an option to refinance their property and prepay their existing mortgages. They are more likely to do so as interest rates, and hence refinancing rates, decline below the rate of their current mortgage. This refinancing incentive tends to lower the value of the mortgage to the MBS investor because the mortgages' relatively high expected coupon payments are replaced by an immediate payoff of the principal. The equivalent investment alternative now available to the MBS investor is, of course, at the lower coupon rate. Therefore, the price of an MBS with, for example, a 8% coupon is roughly equivalent to owning a default-free 8% annuity bond and writing a call option on that bond (with an exercise price of par). This option component induces a concave relation between the price of MBS and the price of default-free bonds (the so called "negative convexity").

MBS Pricing: An MDE Approach

Modeling and pricing MBS involves two layers of complexity: (1) modeling the dynamic behavior of the term structure of interest rates, and (2) modeling the prepayment behavior of mortgage holders. The standard procedure for valuation of MBS assumes a particular stochastic process for term structure movements and uses specific statistical models of prepayment behavior. The success of this approach depends crucially on the correct parameterization of prepayment behavior and on the correct model for interest rates. We propose here a different approach that directly estimates the relation between MBS prices and various interest rate factors. This approach circumvents the need for parametric specification of interest rate dynamics and prepayment models.

The basic intuition behind the MDE pricing technique we propose is fairly straightforward. Let a set of m variables, denoted by x_t, be the underlying factors that govern interest rate movements and prepayment behavior. The vector x_t includes interest rate variables (e.g., the level of interest rates) and possible prepayment specific variables (e.g., transaction costs of refinancing). The MBS price at time t, denoted as $P_{mb,t}$, is a function of these factors and can be written as

$$P_{mb,t} = V(x_t, \theta)$$

where $V(x_t, \theta)$ is a function of the state variables x_t, and the vector θ is a set of parameters that describe the interest rate dynamics and the relation between the variables x_t and the prepayment function. The vector θ includes variables such as the speed with which interest rates tend to revert to their long run mean values and the sensitivity of prepayments to changes in interest rates. Parametric methods in the extant literature derive the function V based on equilibrium or no-arbitrage arguments and determine MBS prices using estimates of θ in this function. The MDE procedure, on the other hand, aims to directly estimate the function V from the data and is not concerned with the evolution of interest rates or the specific forms of prepayment functions.

The MDE procedure starts with a similar basic idea as parametric methods: That MBS prices can be expressed as a function of a small number of interest rate factors. MBS prices are expressed as a function of these factors plus a pricing error term. The error term allows for the fact that model prices based on any small number of pricing factors will not be identical to quoted market prices. There are several reason why market prices can be expected to deviate from model prices. First, bid prices may be asynchronous with respect to the interest rate quotes. Furthermore, the bid-ask spreads for the MBS in this chapter generally range from $\frac{1}{32}$nd to $\frac{4}{32}$nds, depending on the liquidity of the MBS. Second, the MBS prices used in this chapter refer to prices of unspecified mortgage pools in the marketplace (see p. 277). To the extent that the universe of pools changes from period to period, and its composition may not be in the agent's information set, this introduces an error into the pricing equation. Finally, there may be pricing factors that are not specified in the model. Therefore, we assume observed prices are given by

$$P_{mb,t} = V(x_t) + \varepsilon_t \qquad (9.1)$$

where ε_t represent the aforementioned pricing errors. A well-specified model will yield small pricing errors. Examination of ε_t based on our model will therefore enable us to evaluate its suitability in this pricing application.

The first task in implementing the MDE procedure is to specify the factors that determine MBS prices. To price MBS we need factors that capture the value of fixed cash flow component of MBS and refinancing incentives. The particular factors we use here are the yield on 10-year Treasury notes and the spread between the 10-year yield and the 3-month T-bill yield. There are good reasons to use these factors for capturing the salient features of MBS. The MBS analyzed in this paper have 30 years to maturity; however, due to potential prepayments and scheduled principal repayments, their expected lives are much shorter. Thus, the 10-year yield should approximate the level of interest rates which is appropriate for discounting the MBS's cash flows. Further, the 10-year yield has a correlation of 0.98 with the mortgage rate (see Table 9.1 and Figure 9.1). Since the spread between the mortgage rate and the MBS's coupon determines the refinancing incentive, the 10-year yield should prove useful when valuing the option component.

The second variable, the slope of the term structure (in this case, the spread between the 10-year and 3-month rates) provides information on two factors: the market's expectations about the future path of interest rates, and the variation in the discount rate over short and long horizons. Steep-term structure slopes imply lower discount rates for short-term cash flows and higher discount rates for long-term cash flows. Further, steep-term structures may imply

TABLE 9.1. Summary Statistics

Coupon:	7.5%	8.0%	8.5%	9.0%	9.5%	10.0%	10.5%
GNMA Prices							
Mean	93.132	95.578	97.876	100.084	102.204	104.347	106.331
Max.	105.156	106.563	107.500	108.281	109.469	110.938	112.719
Min.	78.375	81.625	83.656	86.531	89.531	92.688	95.750
Vol.	6.559	6.287	5.831	5.260	4.722	4.294	3.978
Correlations							
7.5%	1.000	0.998	0.993	0.986	0.981	0.983	0.977
8.0%	0.998	1.000	0.997	0.992	0.987	0.987	0.979
8.5%	0.993	0.997	1.000	0.998	0.995	0.993	0.982
9.0%	0.986	0.992	0.998	1.000	0.999	0.995	0.983
9.5%	0.981	0.987	0.995	0.999	1.000	0.997	0.985
10.0%	0.983	0.987	0.993	0.995	0.997	1.000	0.994
10.5%	0.977	0.979	0.982	0.983	0.985	0.994	1.000

	Long Rate	Spread	Mortgage Rate
Interest Rates			
Mean	7.779	2.119	9.337
Max.	10.230	3.840	11.580
Min.	5.170	−0.190	6.740
Vol.	1.123	1.101	1.206
Correlations			
Long rate	1.000	−0.450	0.980
Spread	−0.450	1.000	−0.518
Mortgage rate	0.980	−0.518	1.000

Note: Summary statistics for prices of TBA contracts on 7.5% to 10.5% GNMAs, the long rate (10-year), the spread (10-year minus 3-month), and the average mortgage rate. All data are weekly from January 1987 through May 1994. Interest rates are in percent per year.

FIGURE 9.1. Mortgage Rates and Interest Rates

Note: The yield on the "on-the-run" 10-year treasury note and the average 30-year mortgage rate, from January 1987 to May 1994.

increases in future mortgage rates, which should decrease the likelihood of mortgage refinancing.

Multivariate Density Estimation Issues

This subsection explains the details of the multivariate density estimation technique proposed in this chapter. To understand the issues involved, suppose that the error term in Equation (9.1) is uniformly zero and that we have unlimited data on the past history of MBS prices. Now suppose that we are interested in determining the fair price for a MBS with a particular coupon and prepayment history at a particular point in time when, for example, the 10-year yield is 8% and the slope of the term structure is 1%. In this case, all we have to do is look back at the historical data and pick out the price of an MBS with similar characteristics at a point in time historically when the 10-year yield was 8% and the slope of the term structure was 1%. While this example illustrates the simplicity of the underlying idea behind the MDE procedure, it also highlights the sources of potential problems in estimation. First, for reasons discussed in the last subsection, it is unrealistic to assume away the error terms. Second, in practice we do not have unlimited historical data, and a particular economic scenario, such as an 8% 10-year yield and a 1% term structure slope, may not have been played out in the past. The estimation technique therefore should be capable of optimally extracting information from the available data.

The MDE procedure characterizes the joint distribution of the variables of interest, in our case the joint distribution of MBS prices and interest rate factors. We implement MDE using a kernel estimation procedure.[2] In our application, the kernel estimator for MBS prices as a function of interest rate factors simplifies to:

$$
\hat{P}_{mb,c}(r_l, r_l - r_s) = \frac{\sum_{t=1}^{T} P_{mb,c,t} K\left(\frac{r_l - r_{l,t}}{h_{r_l}}\right) K\left(\frac{[r_l - r_s] - [r_{l,t} - r_{s,t}]}{h_{r_l - r_s}}\right)}{\sum_{t=1}^{T} K\left(\frac{r_l - r_{l,t}}{h_{r_l}}\right) K\left(\frac{[r_l - r_s] - [r_{l,t} - r_{s,t}]}{h_{r_l - r_s}}\right)}
\tag{9.2}
$$

where T is the number of observations, $K(\cdot)$ is a suitable kernel function and h is the window width or smoothing parameter. $\hat{P}_{mb,c}(r_l, r_l - r_s)$ is our model price for a MBS with coupon c when the long rate is r_l and the term structure slope is $r_l - r_s$. $P_{mb,c,t}$ is the market price of the tth observation for the price of a MBS with coupon c. Note that the long rate at the time of observation t is $r_{l,t}$ and the term structure slope is $r_{l,t} - r_{s,t}$.

The econometrician has at his or her discretion the choice of $K(\cdot)$ and h. It is important to point out, however, that these choices are quite different from those faced by researchers employing parametric methods. Here, the researcher is not trying to choose

---

[2] For examples of MDE methods for approximating functional forms in the empirical asset pricing literature, see Pagan and Hong (1991), Harvey (1991), and Ait-Sahalia (1996). An alternative approach to estimating nonlinear functionals in the derivatives market is described by Hutchinson, Lo, and Poggio (1994). They employ methods associated with neural networks to estimate the nonlinear relation between option prices and the underlying stock price.

functional forms or parameters that satisfy some goodness-of-fit criterion (such as minimizing squared errors in regression methods), but is instead characterizing the joint distribution from which the functional form will be determined.

One popular class of kernel functions is the symmetric beta density function, which includes the normal density, the Epanechnikov (1969) "optimal" kernel, and the commonly used biweight kernel as special cases. Results in the kernel estimation literature suggest that any reasonable kernel gives almost optimal results, though in small samples there may be differences (Epanechnikov, 1969). In this chapter, we employ an independent multivariate normal kernel, though it should be pointed out that our results are relatively insensitive to the choice of kernel within the symmetric beta class. The specific functional form for the $K(\cdot)$ that we use is:

$$K(z) = (2\pi)^{-\frac{1}{2}} e^{-\frac{1}{2}z^2}$$

where z is the appropriate argument for this function.

The other parameter, the window width, is chosen based on the dispersion of the observations. For the independent multivariate normal kernel, Scott (1992) suggests the window width

$$\hat{h}_i = k_i \hat{\sigma}_i T^{\frac{-1}{m+4}}$$

where $\hat{\sigma}_i$ is the standard deviation of the ith variable (i.e., i may denote either variable r_l or $r_l - r_s$), m is the dimension of the variables, which in our case is 2, and k_i is a scaling constant often chosen via a cross-validation procedure. In our application we need to choose two such scaling constants, one for the long rate r_l and one for the term structure slope $r_l - r_s$. Note that the window width is larger when the variance of the variable under consideration is larger in order to compensate for the fact that observations are, on average, further apart. This window width (with $k_i = 1$) has the appealing property that, for certain joint distributions of the variables, it minimizes the asymptotic mean integrated squared error of the estimated density function. Unfortunately, our data are serially correlated and therefore the necessary distributional properties are not satisfied.

We employ a cross-validation procedure to find the k_i that minimizes the estimation error. To implement cross-validation, the implied MDE price at each data point is estimated using the entire sample, except for the actual data point and its nearest neighbors.[3] We identify the k_i's that minimize the mean-squared error between the observed price and the estimated kernel price. Once the k_i's are chosen based on cross-validation, the actual estimation of the MBS prices and analysis of pricing errors involves the entire sample.

To gain further intuition into the estimation procedure, note that Equation (9.2) takes a special form; the estimate of the MBS price can be interpreted as a weighted average of observed prices:

$$\hat{P}_{mb,c}(r_l^*, r_l^* - r_s^*) = \sum_{t=1}^{T} w_i(t) P_{mb,c,t} \tag{9.3}$$

where

$$w_r(t) = \frac{K\left(\dfrac{r_l^* - r_{l,t}}{h_{r_l^*}}\right) K\left(\dfrac{[r_l^* - r_s^*] - [r_{l,t} - r_{s,t}]}{h_{r_l^* - r_s^*}}\right)}{\sum_{t=1}^{T} K\left(\dfrac{r_l^* - r_{l,t}}{h_{r_l^*}}\right) K\left(\dfrac{[r_l^* - r_s^*] - [r_{l,t} - r_{s,t}]}{h_{r_l^* - r_s^*}}\right)}$$

Note that to determine the MBS price when the interest rate factors are $(r_l^*, r_l^* - r_s^*)$ the kernel estimator assigns to each observation t a weight $w_r(t)$ that is proportional to the "distance" (measured via the kernel function) between the interest rate factors at the time of observation $t(r_{l,t}, r_{l,t} - r_{s,t})$ and the current interest rate factors. The attractive idea behind MDE is that these weights are not estimated in an ad hoc manner, but instead depend on the true underlying distribution (albeit estimated) of the relevant variables. Thus, if the current state of the world, as measured by the state vector $(r_l^*, r_l^* - r_s^*)$, is not close to a particular point in the sample, then this sample price is given little weight in estimating the current price. Note, however, that MDE can give weight (possibly inconsequential) to all observations, so that the price of the MBS with $(r_l^*, r_l^* - r_s^*)$ also takes into account MBS prices at surrounding interest rates. This will help

---

[3] Due to the serial dependence of the data, we performed the cross-validation omitting one year of data, for example, six months in either direction of the particular data point in question.

average out the different ε errors in Equation (9.1) from period to period. Although our application utilizes only two factors, MDE will average out effects of other factors if they are independent of the two interest rate factors. Thus, for any given long rate r_l^* and a given short rate r_s^*, there is a mapping to the MBS price $P_{mb}(r_l^*, r_l^* - r_s^*)$. These prices can then be used to evaluate how MBS prices move with fundamental interest rate factors.

While the MDE procedure has the advantage that it does not require explicit functional specification of interest rate dynamics and prepayment models, it does have certain drawbacks. The most serious problem with MDE is that it is data intensive. Much data are required in order to estimate the appropriate weights which capture the joint density function of the variables. The quantity of data which is needed increases quickly in the number of conditioning variables used in estimation. How well MDE does at estimating the relation between MBS prices and the interest-rate factors is then an open question, since the noise generated from the estimation error can be substantial.[4]

Another problem with MDE is that the procedure requires covariance stationarity of the variables of interest. For example, when we use only two interest rate factors, the MDE procedure does not account for differences in prices MBS when the underlying pools have different prepayment histories. For this reason the MBS procedure is most suitable for pricing TBA securities which are most commonly used for new originations rather than for seasoned MBS. Accounting for *seasoning* of a mortgage or a mortgage pool's *burnout* will require additional factors that are beyond the scope of this chapter.

A few comments are in order, however, to provide some guidance on how these factors could be accounted for when one is interested in pricing seasoned MBS. First, one could potentially take account of a mortgage pool's seasoning by nonlinearly filtering out any time dependence. Estimation error aside, this filtering would be effective as long as the seasoning is independent of the other state variables. Second, in order to incorporate path dependence due to a

---

[4] Boudoukh, Richardson, Stanton, and Whitelaw (1997) perform simulation exercises in an economy governed by two factors and some measurement error in reported prices. Within this (albeit simple) environment, the MDE methodology performs quite well.

pool's burnout, the only viable way would be to employ a state variable which captures this dependence. For example, Boudoukh, Richardson, Stanton, and Whitelaw (1997) and Richard and Roll (1989) describe several variables that might be linked closely with *burnout*. Because the strength of the MDE procedure estimation of nonlinear relations, all that is required is that these variables span the appropriate state space.

DATA DESCRIPTION

Mortgage-backed security prices were obtained from Bloomberg Financial Markets covering the period January 1987 to May 1994. Specifically, we collected weekly data on 30-year fixed-rate Government National Mortgage Association (GNMA) MBS, with coupons ranging from 7.5% to 10.5%.[5] The prices represent dealer-quoted bid prices on GNMAs of different coupons traded for delivery on a *to be announced* (TBA) basis.

The TBA market is most commonly employed by mortgage originators who have a given set of mortgages that have not yet been pooled. However, trades can also involve existing pools on an unspecified basis. Rules for the delivery and settlement of TBAs are set by the Public Securities Association (PSA); (see, for example, Bartlett, 1989, for more details). For example, an investor might purchase $1 million worth of 8% GNMAs for forward delivery next month. The dealer is then required to deliver 8% GNMA pools within 2.5% of the contracted amount (i.e., between $975,000 and $1,025,000), with specific pool information to be provided on a TBA basis (just prior to settlement). This means that, at the time of the agreed-upon-transaction, the characteristics of the mortgage pool to be delivered (e.g., the age of the pool and its prepayment history) are at the discretion of the dealer. Nevertheless, for a majority of the TBAs, the delivered pools represent newly issued pools.

---

[5] Careful filters were applied to the data to remove data reporting errors using prices reported in the *Wall Street Journal*. Furthermore, data are either not available or sparse for some of the GNMA coupons during the period. For example, in the 1980s, 6% coupon bonds represent mortgages originated in the 1970s, and not the more recent issues which are the focus of this paper. Thus, data on these MBS were not used.

With respect to the interest rate series, weekly data for the 1987–1994 period were collected on the average rate for 30-year mortgages (collected from Bloomberg Financial Markets),[6] and the yields on the 3-month Treasury bill and 10-year Treasury note (provided by the Board of Governors of the Federal Reserve).

Data Characteristics

Before describing the pricing results and error analysis for MBS using the MDE approach, we briefly describe the environment for interest rates and mortgage rates during the sample period, 1987–1994.

Since the mortgage rate represents the available rate at which homeowners can refinance, it plays an especially important role with respect to the prepayment incentive. Figure 9.1 graphs the mortgage rate for 1987 through 1994. From 1987 to 1991, the mortgage rate varied from 9% to 11%. In contrast, from 1991 to 1994, the mortgage rate generally declined from 9.5% to 7%.[7]

For pricing GNMA TBAs, it is most relevant to understand the characteristics of the universe of pools at a particular point in time. That is, the fact that a number of pools have prepaid considerably may be irrelevant if newly originated pools have entered into the MBS market since the MBS from new originations are the one typically delivered in TBA contracts. To get a better idea of the time series behavior of the GNMA TBAs during this period, Figure 9.2 graphs an artificially constructed index of all the originations of 7.5% to 10.5% GNMA pools from January 1983 to May 1994.[8]

There is a wide range of origination behavior across the coupons. As mortgage rates moved within a 9% to 11% band between 1987 to 1991, Figure 9.2 shows that GNMA 9s, 9.5s, 10s, and

---

[6] Bloomberg's source for this rate is "Freddie Mac's Primary Mortgage Market Survey," which reports the average rate on 80% of newly originated 30-year, first mortgages on a weekly basis.

[7] Note that the MBS coupon rate is typically 50 basis points less than the interest rate on the underlying mortgage. The 50 basis points are retained to cover the servicing fee and reinsurance cost.

[8] The dollar amount outstanding for each coupon is normalized to 100 in January 1987. Actual dollar amounts outstanding in that month were $10,172, $27,096, $10,277, $63,392, $28,503, $15,694, and $5,749 (in millions) for the 7.5%–10.5% coupons, respectively.

FIGURE 9.2. GNMA Originations

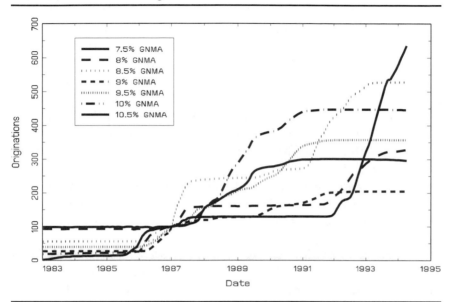

Note: Originations of 7.5% to 10.5% GNMAs from January 1983 to April 1994. The dollar amount outstanding is normalized to 100 in January 1987.

10.5s were all newly originated during this period. Consistent with the decline in mortgage rates in the post-1991 period, GNMA 7.5s, 8s, and 8.5s originated while the GNMA 9s to 10.5s became seasoned issues. Thus, in terms of the seasoning of the pools most likely to be delivered in the TBA market, there are clearly cross-sectional differences between the coupons.

Figure 9.2 shows that there are several reasons for choosing the TBA market during the post-1986 time period to investigate MBS pricing using the MDE methodology. First, during 1985 and 1986, interest rates dramatically declined, leading to mortgage originations for a wide variety of coupon rates. Thus, the GNMA TBAs in 1987–1994 correspond to mortgage pools with little prepayment history (i.e., no *burnout*) and long maturities. In contrast, prior to this period, the 7.5% to 10.5% GNMAs were backed by mortgages originated in the 1970s and thus represented a different security (in both maturity and prepayment levels). Second, MDE pricing requires joint stationarity between MBS prices and the interest rate variables.

This poses a potential problem in estimating the statistical properties of any fixed maturity security, since the maturity changes over time. Recall that the TBA market refers to unspecified mortgage pools available in the marketplace. Thus, to the extent that there are originations of mortgages in the GNMA coupon range, the maturity of the GNMA TBA is less apt to change from week to week. Figure 9.2 shows that this is the case for the higher coupon GNMAs pre-1991, and for the low coupon GNMAs post-1991. Of course, when no originations occur in the coupon range (e.g., the GNMA 10s in the latter part of the sample), then the maturity of the available pool will decline. In this case, the researcher may need to add variables to capture the maturity effect and possibly any prepayment effects. In our analysis, we choose to limit the dimensionality of the multivariate system, and instead focus on the relation between MBS prices and the two interest rate factors.

Table 9.1 provides ranges, standard deviations, and cross-correlations of GNMA prices and mortgage and interest rates during the 1987–1994 period. Absent prepayments, MBS are fixed-rate annuities, and the dollar volatility of an annuity increases with the coupon. In contrast, from Table 9.1, we find that the lower coupon GNMAs are more volatile than the higher coupon GNMAs. The lower volatility of the higher coupon GNMAs is due to the embedded call option of MBS. The important element of the option component for MBS valuation is the refinancing incentive. For most of the sample (especially 1990 on), the existing mortgage rate lies below 10.5% and the prepayment option is at- or in-the-money.[9] Historically, given the costs associated with refinancing, a spread of approximately 150 basis points between the old mortgage rate and the existing rate is required to induce rapid prepayments.[10]

---

[9] Figure 9.1 also graphs one of the interest rate factors, the 10-year yield. There is a difference in the level between the two series (i.e., on average 1.56%), representing the cost of origination, the option value, and the bank profits, among other factors.

[10] See Bartlett (1989) and Breeden (1991) for some historical evidence of the relation between prepayment rates and the mortgage spread. Note that in the 1990s the threshold spread required to induce refinancing has been somewhat lower—in some cases, 75 to 100 basis points. Some have argued that this is due to the proliferation of new types of mortgage loans (and ensuing marketing efforts by the mortgage companies) (Bartlett, 1989), though it may also be related to aggregate economic factors, such as the implications of a steep term structure.

The lack of seasoning aside, this would suggest that the higher coupon GNMAs began to prepay in the early 1990s.

As mentioned, Figure 9.1 graphs the 10-year yield against the mortgage rate. During the 1987 to 1994 period, there are multiple observations of particular interest rates. Since these multiple observations occur at different points of the sample, this will help MDE isolate the potential impact of additional interest rate factors, as well as reduce maturity effects not captured by the MDE pricing (see *Characteristics of Mortgages* above). Similarly, while the spread between the 10-year yield and the 3-month rate is for the most part positive, there is still variation of the spread during the period of an order of magnitude similar to the underlying 10-year rate (see Table 9.1). Moreover, the correlation between these variables is only −0.45, indicating that they potentially capture independent information, which may be useful for pricing GNMAs.

EMPIRICAL RESULTS

This section implements the MDE procedure and investigates how well the model prices match market prices.

One-Factor Pricing

As a first pass at the MBS data, we describe the functional relation between GNMA prices and the level of interest rates (the 10-year yield). As an illustration, Figure 9.3 graphs the estimated 9% GNMA price with the actual data points. The smoothing factor, which is chosen by cross-validation, is 0.35 (i.e., $k_i = 0.35$).

Several observations are in order. First, the figure illustrates the well-known negative convexity of MBS. Specifically, the MBS price is convex in interest-rate levels at high interest rates (when it behaves more like a straight bond), yet concave at low interest rates (as the prepayment option becomes in-the-money). Second, the estimated functional relation is not smooth across the entire range of sample interest rates. Specifically, between 10-year yields of 7.1% to 7.8%, there is a *bump* in the estimated relation. While this feature is most probably economically spurious, it reflects the fact that the

FIGURE 9.3. Market Prices and One-Factor Model Prices

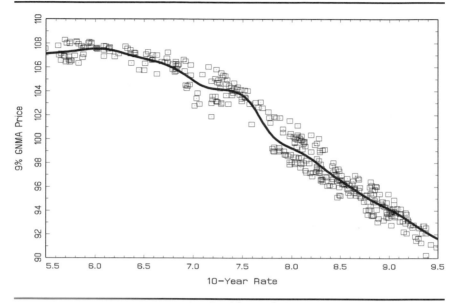

Note: Observed weekly prices and estimated prices from a one-factor (long rate) MDE model for a 9% GNMA for the period January 1987 to May 1994.

observed prices in this region are high relative to the prices at nearby interest rates. Increasing the degree of smoothing eliminates this bump at the cost of increasing the pricing errors. The source of this variation, which could be missing factors, MDE estimation error, or structural changes in the mortgage market, is investigated further below. Third, there is a wide range of prices at the same level of interest rates. For example, at a 10-year yield of 8%, prices of GNMA 9s vary from 98% to 102% of par. Is this due to the impact of additional factors, measurement error in GNMA prices, MDE estimation error, or some other phenomenon?

Table 9.2 provides some preliminary answers to this question, reporting summary statistics on the pricing errors (defined as the difference between the MDE estimated price and the observed MBS price) for the 7.5% to 10.5% GNMAs. As seen from a comparison between Tables 9.1 and 9.2, most of the volatility of the GNMA price can be explained by a 1-factor kernel using the interest rate level. For example, the volatility of the 9% GNMA is $5.26, but its residual

TABLE 9.2. One-Factor GNMA Pricing

Coupon:	7.5%	8.0%	8.5%	9.0%	9.5%	10.0%	10.5%
Pricing Errors							
Mean	0.003	0.006	0.007	0.010	0.010	0.010	0.009
Mean Abs.	0.529	0.605	0.649	0.679	0.660	0.597	0.666
Vol.	0.703	0.747	0.800	0.832	0.824	0.767	0.841
Autocorr.	0.861	0.898	0.918	0.927	0.921	0.917	0.916
Pricing Error Regression Analysis							
Const.	3.226	3.613	3.887	3.857	3.721	3.249	2.755
	(3.190)	(3.413)	(4.133)	(4.419)	(4.402)	(4.028)	(4.320)
Long rate	−0.963	−1.062	−1.130	−1.117	−1.074	−0.942	−0.805
	(0.887)	(0.941)	(1.135)	(1.216)	(1.210)	(1.119)	(1.216)
(Long rate)^2	0.069	0.075	0.080	0.078	0.075	0.066	0.057
	(0.059)	(0.063)	(0.075)	(0.081)	(0.080)	(0.075)	(0.082)
R^2	0.028	0.026	0.023	0.020	0.018	0.017	0.011
Joint test	2.795	2.157	1.709	1.441	1.327	1.228	0.707
p-value	0.247	0.340	0.426	0.487	0.515	0.541	0.702
AC(e)	0.853	0.891	0.913	0.923	0.916	0.912	0.914
Const.	0.491	0.236	0.411	0.607	0.887	1.137	1.494
	(0.148)	(0.194)	(0.212)	(0.211)	(0.194)	(0.165)	(0.135)
Spread	−0.673	−0.373	−0.446	−0.605	−0.948	−1.234	−1.582
	(0.275)	(0.330)	(0.365)	(0.374)	(0.342)	(0.286)	(0.261)
(Spread)^2	0.165	0.098	0.095	0.120	0.199	0.261	0.328
	(0.074)	(0.090)	(0.101)	(0.103)	(0.094)	(0.079)	(0.072)
R^2	0.072	0.020	0.033	0.068	0.145	0.276	0.401
Joint test	6.480	1.281	2.608	5.916	14.102	34.899	79.195
p-value	0.039	0.527	0.271	0.052	0.001	0.000	0.000
AC(e)	0.848	0.895	0.914	0.920	0.904	0.877	0.847

Note: Summary statistics and regression analysis for the pricing errors from a one-factor (long rate) MDE GNMA pricing model. The regression analysis involves regressing the pricing errors on linear and squared explanatory variables. Heteroscedasticity and autocorrelation consistent standard errors are reported in parentheses below the corresponding regression coefficient. AC(e) is the autocorrelation of the residuals from the regression.

volatility is only $0.83. However, while 1-factor pricing does well, it clearly is not sufficient as the pricing errors are highly autocorrelated (from 0.861 to 0.927) for all the GNMA coupons. Though this autocorrelation could be due to measurement error induced by the MDE estimation, it does raise the possibility that there is a missing factor. In addition, the residuals are highly correlated across the seven different coupon bonds (not shown in the table). Thus, the pricing errors contain substantial common information.

This correlation across different GNMAs implies that an explanation based on idiosyncratic information (such as measurement error in prices) will not be sufficient. Combined with the fact that the magnitude of the bid-ask spreads in these markets lies somewhere between $\frac{1}{32}$nd and $\frac{4}{32}$nds, clearly measurement error in observed prices cannot explain either the magnitude of the pricing errors with 1-factor pricing (e.g., $2 – $3 in some cases) or the substantial remaining volatility of the errors (e.g., $0.70 to $0.84 across the coupons).

Table 9.2 investigates the impact of additional interest rate factors. We run a regression of the pricing errors on the level and squared level to check whether any linear or nonlinear effects remain. For the most part, the answer is no. The level has very little explanatory power for the pricing errors, with R^2s ranging from 1.1% to 2.8%. Moreover, tests of the joint significance of the coefficients cannot reject the null hypothesis of no explanatory power at standard significance levels. Motivated by our earlier discussion, we also run a regression of the pricing errors for each GNMA on the slope of the term structure (the spread between the 10-year yield and the 3-month yield) and its squared value. The results strongly support the existence of a second factor, with R^2s increasing with the coupon from a low of 2.0% to 40.1%. Furthermore, this second factor comes in nonlinearly as both the linear and nonlinear terms are large and significant.

Most interesting is the fact that the slope of the term structure has its biggest impact on higher coupon GNMAs. This suggests an important relation between the prepayment option and the term structure slope. Due to the relatively lower value of the prepayment option, low coupon GNMAs behave much like straight bonds. Thus, the 10-year yield may provide enough information to price these MBS. In contrast, the call option component of higher coupon

GNMAs is substantial enough that the duration of the bond is highly variable. Clearly, the slope of the term structure provides information about the variation in yields across these maturities; hence, its additional explanatory power for higher coupon GNMAs. The negative coefficient on the spread implies that the 1-factor MDE is underpricing when the spread is high. In other words, when spreads are high, and short rates are low for a fixed long-rate, high-coupon GNMAs are more valuable than would be suggested by a 1-factor model. The positive coefficients on the squared spread suggest that the relation is nonlinear, with a decreasing effect as the spread increases. Note that in addition to information about variation in discount rates across maturities, the spread may also be proxying for variation in expected prepayment rates that is not captured by the long rate.

Two-Factor Pricing

Motivated by the results in Table 9.2, it seems important to consider a second interest rate factor for pricing MBS. Therefore, we describe the functional relation between GNMA prices and two interest rate factors, the level of interest rates (the 10-year yield) and the slope of the term structure (the spread between the 10-year yield and the 3-month yield). In particular, we estimate the pricing functional given in Equation (9.1) for each of the GNMA coupons. For comparison purposes with Figure 9.3, Figure 9.4 graphs the 9% GNMA against the interest rate level and the slope. The smoothing factor for the long rate is fixed at the level used in the one-factor pricing (i.e., 0.35), and the cross-validation procedure generates a smoothing factor of 1.00 for the spread.

The well-known negative convexity of MBS is very apparent in Figure 9.4. However, this functional form does not hold in the northwest region of the figure, that is, at low spreads and low interest rates. The explanation is that the MDE approach works well in the regions of the available data, but extrapolates poorly at the tails of the data and beyond. Figure 9.5 graphs a scatter plot of the interest rate level against the slope. As evident from the figure, there are periods in which large slopes (3%–4%) are matched with both low interest rates (in 1993–1994) and high interest rates (in

FIGURE 9.4. Two-Factor Model Prices of 9% GNMA

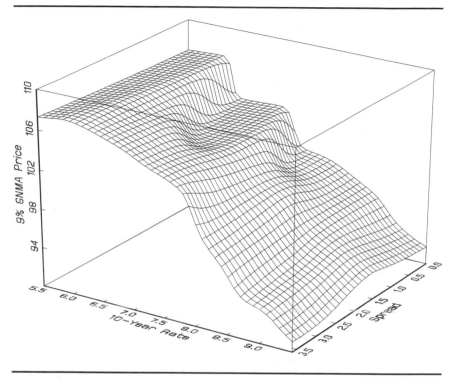

Note: The price of a 9% GNMA as a function of the pricing factors: the long rate and the spread. The pricing functional is estimated using the MDE approach and weekly data from January 1987 to May 1994.

1988). However, few observations are available at low spreads joint with low interest rates. Thus, the researcher needs to be cautious when interpreting MBS prices in this range.

Within the sample period, the largest range of 10-year yields occurs around a spread of 2.70%. Therefore, we take a slice of the pricing functional for the 8%, 9%, and 10% GNMAs, conditional on this level of the spread. Figure 9.6 graphs the relation between GNMA prices for each of these coupons against the 10-year yield. Several observations are in order. First, the negative convexity of each MBS is still apparent even in the presence of the second factor. Though the *bump* in the functional form is still visible, it has

FIGURE 9.5. Interest Rates and Spreads

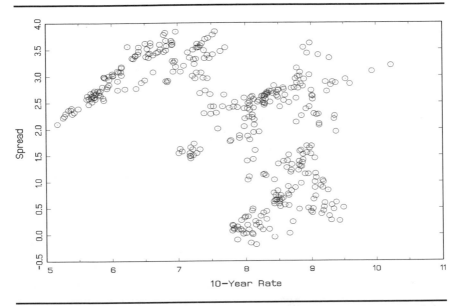

Note: A scatter plot of the pairs of data available for the 10-year rate and the spread between the 10-year rate and the 3-month rate, from January 1987 to May 1994.

been substantially reduced. Thus, multiple factors do play a key role in MBS valuation. Second, the price differences between the various GNMA securities narrow as interest rates fall. This just represents the fact that higher coupon GNMAs are expected to prepay at faster rates. As GNMAs prepay at par, their prices fall because they are premium bonds, thus reducing the differential between the various coupons. Third, the GNMA prices change as a function of interest rates at different rates depending on the coupon level, that is, on the magnitude of the refinancing incentive. Thus, the effective duration of GNMAs varies as the moneyness of the prepayment option changes.

The results of the one-factor pricing analysis and Figures 9.5 and 9.6 suggest the possible presence of a second factor for pricing MBS. To understand the impact of the term structure slope, Figure 9.7 graphs the various GNMA prices against interest rate levels,

FIGURE 9.6. GNMA Prices across Coupons

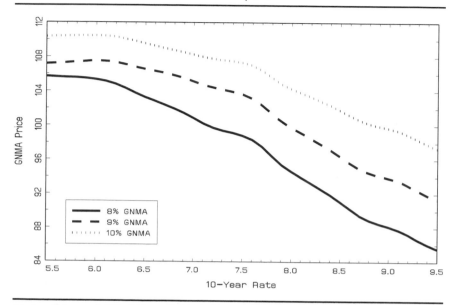

Note: Prices of 8%, 9%, and 10% GNMAs for various interest rates, with the spread fixed at 2.70%, as estimated via the MDE approach using weekly data from January 1987 to May 1994.

conditional on two different spreads (2.70% and 0.30%).[11] Recall that the slope of the term structure is defined using the yield on a full-coupon note, not a 10-year zero-coupon rate. As a result, positive spreads imply upward sloping full-coupon yield curves and even more steeply sloping zero-coupon yield curves. In contrast, when the spread is close to zero, both the full-coupon and zero-coupon yield curves tend to be flat. Thus, holding the 10-year full-coupon yield constant, short-term (long-term) zero-coupon rates are lower (higher) for high spreads than when the term structure spread is low.

In terms of MBS pricing, note that at high interest rate levels, the option to prepay is out-of-the-money. Consequently, many of the cash flows are expected to occur as scheduled, and GNMAs have long expected lives. The appropriate discount rates for these

---

[11] The spreads and interest rate ranges are chosen to coincide with the appropriate ranges of available data, to insure that the MDE approach works well.

FIGURE 9.7. GNMA Prices at Different Spreads

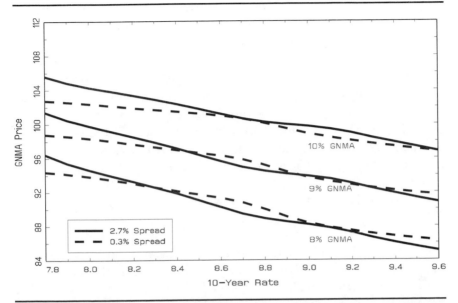

Note: Prices of 8%, 9%, and 10% GNMAs for various interest rates, with the spread fixed at 2.70% and 0.30%, as estimated via the MDE approach using weekly data from January 1987 to May 1994.

cash flows are therefore longer-term zero-coupon rates. Consider first the effects on the price of an 8% GNMA. Since this security has its cash flows concentrated at long maturities, its price should be lower for higher spreads, just as we observe in Figure 9.7. On the other hand, the option component of the 10% GNMA is much closer to being at-the-money, even for the highest interest rates shown in the figure. Hence, at these interest rates, 10% GNMA prices do not follow the same ordering as 8% GNMAs vis-à-vis the level of the spread.

As interest rates fall, prepayments become more likely, and the expected life of the MBS falls for GNMAs of all coupons. As this life declines, the levels of the shorter-term zero-coupon rates become more important for pricing. In this case, high spreads imply lower discount rates at the relevant maturities, for a fixed 10-year full-coupon yield. Consequently, when the GNMAs are priced as shorter-term securities due to high expected prepayments, high spreads imply higher prices for all coupons. This implication is illustrated in Figure 9.7. While prices always increase for declining long rates, the increase is much larger when spreads are high. For the 8% GNMA, this effect causes the prices to cross at a long rate of approximately 8.3%, while for the 10% GNMA it causes the pricing functionals to diverge further as rates decrease. The effect in Figure 9.7 is primarily driven by changes in expected cash flow life. The 10-year yield proxies for the moneyness of the option, the expected level of prepayments, and the average life of the cash flows. The addition of the second factor, the term structure slope, also controls for the average rate at which these cash flows should be discounted.

To understand the impact of two-factor pricing more clearly, Table 9.3 provides an analysis along the lines of Table 9.2 for one-factor pricing, reporting summary statistics on the pricing errors for the 7.5% to 10.5% GNMAs. The addition of a second interest rate factor reduces the pricing error volatility across all the GNMA coupons (i.e., from $0.70 to $0.65 for the 7.5s, $0.83 to $0.61 for the 9s, and $0.84 to $0.52 for the 10.5s). Most interesting, the largest reduction in pricing error volatility occurs with the higher coupon GNMAs, which confirms the close relation between the slope of the term structure and the prepayment option. Table 9.3 also investigates whether there is any remaining level or slope effect on the two-factor MBS prices. We run nonlinear regressions of the pricing errors on the level and the slope separately. Neither the level nor the slope have any remaining economic explanatory power for the pricing errors, with R^2s ranging from 3.6% to 4.5% for the former and R^2s under 1.0% for the latter. The tests of joint significance of the coefficients exhibit marginal significance for the level, suggesting that reducing the smoothing parameter will generate a small improvement in the magnitude of the pricing errors.

HEDGING INTEREST RATE RISK

Hedging Methodology

This section illustrates how to hedge the interest rate risk of MBS using the pricing model presented here. Since there are two interest

TABLE 9.3. Two-Factor GNMA Pricing

Coupon:	7.5%	8.0%	8.5%	9.0%	9.5%	10.0%	10.5%
Pricing Errors							
Mean	0.018	0.020	0.022	0.023	0.025	0.023	0.018
Mean Abs.	0.503	0.489	0.499	0.494	0.483	0.412	0.396
Vol.	0.646	0.616	0.627	0.623	0.613	0.532	0.523
Autocorr.	0.832	0.843	0.859	0.869	0.864	0.840	0.819
Pricing Error Regression Analysis							
Const.	3.470	3.924	4.193	4.188	4.088	3.559	3.002
	(2.751)	(2.784)	(3.112)	(3.064)	(2.924)	(2.228)	(1.875)
Long rate	−1.036	−1.150	−1.215	−1.207	−1.176	−1.030	−0.878
	(0.763)	(0.754)	(0.830)	(0.814)	(0.780)	(0.605)	(0.526)
$(\text{Long rate})^2$	0.075	0.082	0.085	0.085	0.082	0.072	0.062
	(0.051)	(0.049)	(0.054)	(0.053)	(0.051)	(0.040)	(0.036)
R^2	0.041	0.045	0.043	0.040	0.039	0.042	0.036
Joint test	4.775	5.846	5.185	5.059	4.608	5.332	3.792
p-value	0.092	0.054	0.075	0.080	0.100	0.070	0.150
AC(e)	0.825	0.834	0.852	0.865	0.856	0.833	0.814
Const.	0.124	0.096	0.082	0.093	0.117	0.151	0.210
	(0.200)	(0.182)	(0.175)	(0.171)	(0.178)	(0.171)	(0.151)
Spread	−0.203	−0.158	−0.105	−0.105	−0.126	−0.183	−0.308
	(0.279)	(0.265)	(0.265)	(0.255)	(0.243)	(0.210)	(0.177)
$(\text{Spread})^2$	0.057	0.045	0.028	0.027	0.031	0.046	0.081
	(0.072)	(0.068)	(0.069)	(0.065)	(0.061)	(0.052)	(0.043)
R^2	0.009	0.006	0.002	0.002	0.003	0.009	0.027
Joint test	0.665	0.486	0.172	0.173	0.270	0.777	3.474
p-value	0.717	0.784	0.917	0.917	0.874	0.678	0.176
AC(e)	0.830	0.841	0.857	0.868	0.862	0.836	0.809

Note: Summary statistics and regression analysis for the pricing errors from a two-factor (long rate, spread) MDE GNMA pricing model. The regression analysis involves regressing the pricing errors on linear and squared explanatory variables. Heteroscedasticity and autocorrelation consistent standard errors are reported in parentheses below the corresponding regression coefficient. AC(e) is the autocorrelation of the residuals from the regression.

rate factors that are important for pricing MBS we need two fixed-income assets to hedge out interest rate risk. The hedging instruments we use are a 3-month T-bill and a 10-year treasury note futures contract. Let ω_{t-bill} and $\omega_{futures}$ denote the appropriate positions in T-bills and T-note futures contracts respectively to hedge the interest rate risk of one unit of a MBS. The hedge position taken in each of the instruments should ensure that

$$\omega_{t-bill}\frac{\partial P_{t-bill}}{\partial r_l} + \omega_{futures}\frac{\partial P_{futures}}{\partial r_l} = -\frac{\partial P_{mb}}{\partial r_l}$$

$$\omega_{t-bill}\frac{\partial P_{t-bill}}{\partial(r_l-r_s)} + \omega_{futures}\frac{\partial P_{futures}}{\partial(r_l-r_s)} = -\frac{\partial P_{mb}}{\partial(r_l-r_s)}$$

where $\frac{\partial P}{\partial r_l}$ and $\frac{\partial P}{\partial(r_l-r_s)}$ are the sensitivities of these instruments with respect to the long rate r_l and slope of the term structure $r_l - r_s$. The equations specify that the sensitivity of MBS price to changes in the long rate and the slope of the term structure are exactly offset by the corresponding sensitivities of the hedged positions.

Solving for ω_{t-bill} and $\omega_{futures}$ gives

$$\omega_{t-bill} = \frac{-\dfrac{\partial P_{mb}}{\partial(r_l-r_s)}\dfrac{\partial P_{futures}}{\partial r_l} + \dfrac{\partial P_{mb}}{\partial r_l}\dfrac{\partial P_{futures}}{\partial(r_l-r_s)}}{\dfrac{\partial P_{t-bill}}{\partial r_l}\dfrac{\partial P_{futures}}{\partial(r_l-r_s)} - \dfrac{\partial P_{t-bill}}{\partial(r_l-r_s)}\dfrac{\partial P_{futures}}{\partial r_l}} \tag{9.4}$$

$$\omega_{futures} = \frac{-\dfrac{\partial P_{mb}}{\partial r_l}\dfrac{\partial P_{t-bill}}{\partial(r_l-r_s)} + \dfrac{\partial P_{mb}}{\partial(r_l-r_s)}\dfrac{\partial P_{t-bill}}{\partial r_l}}{\dfrac{\partial P_{t-bill}}{\partial r_l}\dfrac{\partial P_{futures}}{\partial(r_l-r_s)} - \dfrac{\partial P_{t-bill}}{\partial(r_l-r_s)}\dfrac{\partial P_{futures}}{\partial r_l}} \tag{9.5}$$

Using Equations (9.4) and (9.5), these hedged portfolios then can be constructed *ex ante* based on the econometrician's estimate of the partial derivatives of the three fixed-income assets with respect to the two factors. These estimates can be generated from historical data (prior to the forming of the hedge) using kernel estimation. For example, an estimate of $\frac{\partial P_{mb}}{\partial r_l}$ can be calculated from Equation (9.2) using

$$
\frac{\partial P_{mb}}{\partial r_l} = \frac{\sum_{t=1}^{T} P_{mb,t} K'\left(\frac{r_l - r_{l,t}}{h_{r_l}}\right) K\left(\frac{[r_l - r_s] - [r_{l,t} - r_{s,t}]}{h_{r_l - r_s}}\right)}{\sum_{t=1}^{T} K\left(\frac{r_l - r_{l,t}}{h_{r_l}}\right) K\left(\frac{[r_l - r_s] - [r_{l,t} - r_{s,t}]}{h_{r_l - r_s}}\right)}
$$

$$
\frac{\sum_{t=1}^{T} P_{mb,t} K\left(\frac{r_l - r_{l,t}}{h_{r_l}}\right) K\left(\frac{[r_l - r_s] - [r_{l,t} - r_{s,t}]}{h_{r_l - r_s}}\right) \sum_{t=1}^{T} K'\left(\frac{r_l - r_{l,t}}{h_{r_l}}\right) K\left(\frac{[r_l - r_s] - [r_{l,t} - r_{s,t}]}{h_{r_l - r_s}}\right)}{\left[\sum_{t=1}^{T} K\left(\frac{r_l - r_{l,t}}{h_{r_l}}\right) K\left(\frac{[r_l - r_s] - [r_{l,t} - r_{s,t}]}{h_{r_l - r_s}}\right)\right]^2}
$$

where $K'(z) = -(2\pi)^{-\frac{1}{2}} z e^{-\frac{1}{2}z^2}$. Unfortunately, it is difficult to estimate the derivative accurately (see Scott, 1992); therefore, we average the estimated derivative with price sensitivities estimated over a range of long rates or slopes. For example, we calculate the elasticity

$$
\frac{\Delta P_{mb}}{\Delta r_l} = \frac{P_{mb}(r_l^a) - P_{mb}(r_l^b)}{r_l^a - r_l^b}
$$

for two different pairs of interest rates, (r_l^a, r_l^b) and average these values with the kernel derivative. The points are chosen to straddle the interest rate of interest. Specifically, we use the 10th and 20th nearest neighbors along the interest rate dimension within the sample, if they exist, and the highest or lowest interest rates within the sample if there are not 10 or 20 observations with higher or lower interest rates. The return on the hedged portfolio is then given by

$$
\frac{P_{mb,t+1} + \hat{\omega}_{t-bill}(P_{1,t+1} - P_{1,t}) + \hat{\omega}_{futures}(P_{2,t+1} - P_{2,t})}{P_{mb,t}}
$$

where it is assumed that the investor starts with one unit of GNMAs at time t. The hedged portfolio can then be followed through time and evaluated based on its volatility and correlation with the fixed-income factors, as well as other factors of interest.[12]

Hedging Analysis

We conducted an out-of-sample hedging exercise over the period January 1990 to May 1994 to evaluate the hedge performance. Starting in January 1987, approximately three years of data (150 weekly observations) were used on a weekly rolling basis to estimate the MBS prices and interest rate sensitivities as described above. For the T-bill and T-note futures, we assume that they move one-for-one with the short rate and long rate, respectively. This assumption simplifies the analysis and is a good first-order approximation. For each rolling period, several different hedges were formed for comparison purposes:

1. To coincide with existing practice, a linear hedge of the GNMAs against the T-note futures was estimated using rolling regressions. The hedge ratio is given by the sensitivity of the MBS price changes to futures price changes.

2. Breeden (1991) suggests a roll-up/roll-down approach to computing hedge ratios. Specifically, the hedge can be formed for a GNMA by computing the ratio between the T-note futures price elasticity and the GNMA price elasticity. (The GNMA price elasticity of, say, an 8% GNMA is calculated from the difference between the prices of 8½% and a 7½% GNMA. We investigate hedging of 8%, 9%, and 10% GNMAs using GNMAs with 7.5% through 10.5% coupons.)

3. We investigate the two-factor MDE hedge described by the portfolio weights given in Equations (9.4) and (9.5).

4. To the extent that the second factor (the slope) seems to play a small role in pricing it is possible that the slope factor may not be important for hedging. To evaluate this, we employ a

---

[12] The method described here forms an instantaneous hedge, which in theory would require continuous rebalancing. For an alternative hedge based on horizon length, see Boudoukh, Richardson, Stanton, and Whitelaw (1995).

one-factor MDE hedge using the T-note futures and GNMA as a function of only the 10-year yield.

Table 9.4 compares the performance of the four hedges for the 8%, 9%, and 10% GNMAs over the 1990 to 1994 sample period. Consider first the 10% GNMA. The unhedged GNMA return has a volatility of 0.414% (41.4 basis points) on a weekly basis. The two-factor MDE hedge reduces the volatility of the portfolio to 26.1 basis points weekly. In contrast, the one-factor MDE hedge, the roll-up/roll-down hedge and linear hedge manage only 30.0, 29.4, and 34.9 basis points, respectively. The 10% GNMA is the most in-the-money in terms of the refinancing incentive, and it is comforting to find that, in the GNMA's most nonlinear region, the MDE approach works well.

Figure 9.8 illustrates how the volatility of the hedged and unhedged returns move through time. While the volatility of the unhedged returns declines over time, this pattern is not matched by the hedged returns. To quantify this evidence Table 9.4 breaks up the sample into four subperiods: January 1990–February 1991, March 1991–April 1992, May 1992–June 1993, and July 1993–May 1994. The most telling fact is that the MDE approach does very well in the last subperiod relative to the other hedges (19.2 versus 39.4 basis points for the roll-up/roll-down approach). This is a period in which massive prepayments occurred in the first part of the period. Due to these prepayments, 10% GNMAs are much less volatile than in previous periods. Thus, the linear and roll-up/roll-down approaches tended to overhedge MBS, resulting in large exposures to interest rate risks. This might explain some of the losses suffered by Wall Street during this period.

On the other hand, the MDE approach does not fare as well in the first two subperiods. For example, the one- and two-factor hedges have 38.8 and 29.6 basis points of volatility respectively versus the unhedged GNMA's volatility of 48.1 basis points in the second subperiod. In contrast, the roll-up/roll-down hedge has only 26.4 basis points of volatility. The explanation is that the MDE procedure does not extrapolate well beyond the tails of the data. During the first and second subperiod, the rolling estimation period faces almost uniformly higher interest rate levels than the out-of-sample

TABLE 9.4. Hedging Results

Period	GNMA	Linear	Roll-Up Roll-Down	MDE 1-Factor	MDE 2-Factor
8% GNMA					
1/90–5/94	68.3	35.0	27.6	30.0	29.4
1/90–2/91	85.5	26.9	27.6	27.8	30.1
3/91–4/92	72.2	30.5	31.7	34.8	32.1
5/92–6/93	61.3	37.7	25.9	29.3	27.8
7/93–5/94	45.5	43.2	24.8	26.9	27.2
$\sigma\Delta r_l, \Delta (r_1 - r_s)$	59.0	15.0	6.8	6.1	4.3
$\sigma\Delta r_l$	59.0	15.0	6.8	6.1	4.2

Period	GNMA	Linear	Breeden	MDE 1-Factor	MDE 2-Factor
9% GNMA					
1/90–5/94	53.0	36.8	24.6	29.3	25.6
1/90–2/91	73.9	24.3	23.5	26.0	27.2
3/91–4/92	55.2	32.3	25.8	38.1	28.2
5/92–6/93	43.8	46.4	25.3	29.3	25.3
7/93–5/94	23.8	39.6	23.7	19.7	20.8
$\sigma\Delta r_l, \Delta (r_1 - r_s)$	41.1	18.7	1.2	5.5	3.9
$\sigma\Delta r_l$	41.1	18.6	0.7	5.3	0.1
10% GNMA					
1/90–5/94	41.4	34.9	29.4	30.0	26.1
1/90–2/91	58.2	24.0	22.3	27.6	27.8
3/91–4/92	48.1	33.8	26.4	38.8	29.6
5/92–6/93	34.8	44.6	29.2	29.5	27.8
7/93–5/94	20.3	32.2	39.4	18.8	19.2
$\sigma\Delta r_l, \Delta (r_1 - r_s)$	28.6	16.4	11.3	5.9	5.4
$\sigma\Delta r_l$	28.6	16.4	11.3	5.7	1.4

Note: Results of hedging the 8%, 9%, and 10% GNMAs with various methods. Each method's hedge ratios are calculated using the past 150 weeks, for the next week. Hence the hedging period is January 1990 through May 1994. The methods are (i) GNMA—the total volatility of an open position (no hedging) in basis points, (ii) linear—hedging via linear regression on T-note futures returns, (iii) roll-up/roll-down—a method which infers hedge ratios from contemporaneous market prices of near coupon MBS, (iv) MDE—hedge ratios determined via a one-factor (long rate only) and two-factor (long rate and spread) models, trading in T-note futures and T-bills in the corresponding hedge ratios. The last two rows provide a measure of the quantity of interest rate risk (two factor risk or one factor risk), which remains using each method's hedging results. In all cases the numbers in the tables represent the standard deviation of weekly returns in basis points.

FIGURE 9.8. Returns under Alternative Hedging Procedures

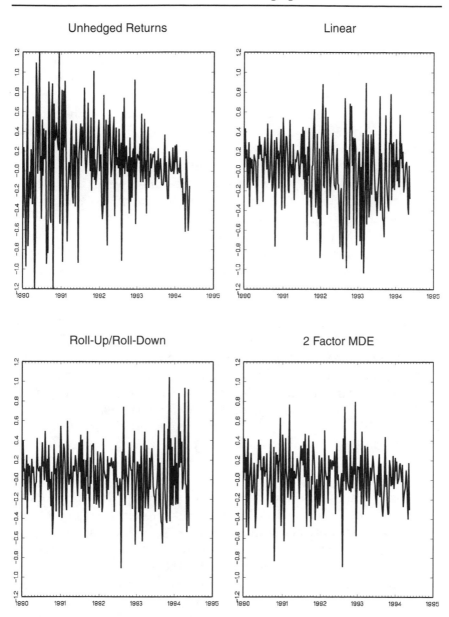

Note: Results from hedging the 10% GNMA using a rolling regression method, where "Linear" is hedging via linear regression of returns on T-note futures, "Roll-Up/Roll-Down" infers hedge ratio from market prices of near coupon MBS, and "2 Factor MDE" uses the two factor MDE approach. The y-axis is return expressed in percentage.

forecast. Thus, hedge ratios were calculated for sparse regions of the data.

Recall that the MDE two-factor hedge reduces the volatility to 65% of the unhedged GNMA's volatility. Since the hedging was performed on an out-of-sample basis, there is no guarantee that the remaining variation of the GNMA's return is free of interest-rate exposure. Table 9.4 provides results from a linear regression of the GNMA unhedged and hedged portfolio's return on changes in the interest rate level (i.e., $\Delta r_{l,t}$) and movements in the terms structure slope (i.e., $\Delta(r_{l,t} - r_{s,t})$). It gives the volatility of each portfolio due to interest rate and term structure slope movements. For example, the volatility of the explained portion of the 10% GNMA due to the interest rate level and slope is 28.6 basis points a week; in contrast, the MDE two-factor hedged 10% GNMA's interest rate risk exposure is only 5.4 basis points. Note that the roll-up/roll-down and linear hedges face much more exposure—11.3 and 16.4 basis points, respectively.[13]

So far, we have described the results for hedging the 10% GNMA. Table 9.4 also provides results for the 8% and 9% GNMAs. Essentially, the patterns are very similar to the 10%, except that the MDE approach fares less well relative to the roll-up/roll-down approach. To understand why this is the case, note that the 8% and 9% GNMAs have a lower refinancing incentive. The bonds therefore behave more like a straight bond, and are more volatile (see Table 9.1). Thus, because the negative convexity of the GNMAs is less prevalent for the 8% and 9% coupons, one explanation for why the MDE approach to hedging GNMAs fares relatively less well with lower coupons is that estimation error is more important. In fact, the roll-up/roll-down method actually produces a lower volatility of the hedged GNMA portfolio than the MDE two-factor approach for both the 8% and 9% GNMAs (27.6 versus 29.4 basis points for the 8%s and 24.6 versus 25.6 basis points for the 9%s).

Multiple factors become less important from a hedging perspective as the GNMA coupon falls (e.g., compare the 8% to 10%). This is to be expected, since we argued that the term structure slope plays a role in pricing as the moneyness of the prepayment option changes

---

[13] For completeness we also report the volatility of the returns due only to movements in the long rate. These results are very similar to those discussed above, suggesting that most of the volatility on a weekly basis is attributable to variation in the long rate.

through time. The subperiod analysis confirms the intuition based on our findings for the 10% GNMAs. While the relative hedging performance of the various approaches is still related to the sub-periods, it is less prevalent for the lower coupon GNMAs. The MDE approach fares relatively best in periods with substantial nonlinear-ities, for example, the 10% GNMAs during July 1993 to May 1994. The large prepayments which induced 10% GNMA prices to fall (ce-teris paribus) did not occur for the 8% GNMAs. After all, the 8% GNMAs are backed by 8.5% mortgages, and the lowest 30-year fixed-rate mortgage only briefly dropped below 7%.

Of particular interest, both the MDE approach and the roll-up/roll-down hedges substantially reduce the interest rate expo-sure of their 8% and 9% GNMA hedge portfolios. For example, for the 8% (9%) GNMA, the unhedged GNMA has 59.0 (41.1) basis point of volatility due to the interest rate factors, while the MDE and roll-up/roll-down approaches have only 4.3 (3.9) and 6.8 (1.2) basis points respectively.

CONCLUSION

This chapter presents a nonparametric model for pricing mortgage-backed securities and hedging their interest rate risk exposures. In-stead of postulating and estimating parametric models for both interest rate movements and prepayments, as in previous ap-proaches to mortgage-backed security valuation, we directly esti-mate the functional relation between mortgage-backed security prices and the level of economic fundamentals. This approach can yield consistent estimates without the need to make the strong as-sumptions about the processes governing interest rates and prepay-ments required by previous approaches.

We implement the model with GNMA MBS with various coupons. We find that MBS prices can be well described as a func-tion of the level of interest rates and the slope of the term structure. A single interest rate factor, as used in most previous mortgage val-uation models, is insufficient. The relation between prices and in-terest rates displays the usual stylized facts, such as negative convexity in certain regions, and a narrowing of price differentials as interest rates fall. Most interesting, the term structure slope

plays an important role in valuing MBS via its relation to the interest rate level and the refinancing incentive associated with a particular MBS. We also find that the interest rate hedge established based
on our model compares favorably with existing methods.

On a more general note, the MDE procedure will work well (in a
relative sense) under the following three conditions. First, since
density estimation is data intensive, the researcher either needs a
large data sample or an estimation problem in which there is little
disturbance error in the relation between the variables. Second, the
problem should be described by a relative low dimensional system,
since MDE's properties deteriorate quickly when variables are
added to the estimation. Third, and especially relevant for comparison across methods, MDE will work relatively well for highly
nonlinear frameworks. As it happens, these features also describe
derivative pricing. Hence, while the results we obtain here for
GNMAs are encouraging, it is likely that the MDE approach would
fare well for more complex derivative securities. Though the TBA
market is especially suited for MDE analysis due to its reduction of
the maturity effect on bonds, it may be worthwhile investigating the
pricing of interest only (IO) and principal only (PO) strips, and collateralized mortgage obligations (CMOs). Since the relation between
the prices of these securities and interest rates is more highly nonlinear than that of a GNMA, a multifactor analysis might shed light
on the interaction between various interest rate factors and the underlying prices. The advantage of the MDE approach is its ability to
capture arbitrary nonlinear relations between variables, making it
ideally suited to capturing the extreme convexity exhibited by many
derivative mortgage-backed securities.

REFERENCES

Ait-Sahalia, Y. (1996). "Nonparametric Pricing of Interest Rate Derivative Securities," *Econometrica, 64,* 527–560.

Bartlett, W.W. (1989). *Mortgage-Backed Securities: Products, Analysis,
Trading.* New York: Institute of Finance.

Boudoukh, J., M. Richardson, R. Stanton, and R.F. Whitelaw. (1995). "A
New Strategy for Dynamically Hedging Mortgage-Backed Securities," *Journal of Derivatives, 2,* 60–77.

Boudoukh, J., M. Richardson, R. Stanton, and R.F. Whitelaw. (1997). "Pricing Mortgage-Backed Securities in a Multifactor Interest Rate Environment: A Multivariate Density Estimation Approach," *Review of Financial Studies, 10,* 405–446.

Breeden, D.T. (1991). "Risk, Return and Hedging of Fixed Rate Mortgages," *Journal of Fixed Income, 1,* 85–107.

Epanechnikov, V. (1969). "Nonparametric Estimates of Multivariate Probability Density," *Theory of Probability and Applications, 14,* 153–158.

Harvey, C. (1991). "The Specification of Conditional Expectations," working paper, Fuqua School of Business.

Hutchinson, J.M., A.W. Lo, and T. Poggio. (1994). "A Nonparametric Approach to Pricing and Hedging Derivative Securities via Learning Networks," *Journal of Finance, 49,* 851–889.

Pagan, A. and Y.S. Hong. (1991). "Non-Parametric Estimation and the Risk Premium," in W. Barnett, J. Powell, and G. Tauchen (Eds.), *Semiparametric and Nonparametric Methods in Econometrics and Statistics,* Cambridge: Cambridge University Press.

Richard, S.F. and R. Roll. (1989). "Prepayments on Fixed-Rate Mortgage-Backed Securities," *Journal of Portfolio Management, 15,* 74–82.

Schwartz, E.S. and W.N. Torous. (1989). "Prepayment and the Valuation of Mortgage-Backed Securities," *Journal of Finance, 44,* 375–392.

Scott, D.W. (1992). *Multivariate Density Estimation: Theory, Practice, and Visualization,* New York: John Wiley & Sons.

10

The Muni Puzzle

EXPLANATIONS AND IMPLICATIONS FOR INVESTORS

John M.R. Chalmers

The coupons and original issue discount on a municipal bond are exempt from Federal tax, which would appear to be a large benefit relative to the returns earned on U.S. government bonds which are subject to Federal taxes. Surprisingly, the extent to which the pricing of municipal bonds reflects the tax-exemption benefit declines sharply with the maturity of the tax-exempt bond. For example, suppose that U.S. government bonds currently offer a yield of 10% and the top marginal tax rate is 40%. A reasonable guess at comparable tax-exempt yields would be 6%, since that would provide the same after-tax return to investors in the highest tax bracket. On average, this analysis is consistent with observed short-term bond markets. However, long-term tax-exempt yields are higher than would be predicted by this calculation. For example, there are times when 20-year municipals offer 95% of comparable maturity Treasuries, or for the example above 9.5% when Treasuries offer 10%. This poses the *muni puzzle*. That is, while short-term tax-exempt yields fall into line with expectations, long-term tax-exempt bond yields appear to be too high relative to yields on taxable bonds. Despite widespread knowledge of its existence, the muni puzzle persists even though it seems clear that municipal bonds provide a greater after-tax return to investors subject to high marginal tax rates.

The persistence of the muni puzzle challenges our understanding of the impact that taxes have on bond returns. If the starting point is that there is no free lunch in this $1.3 trillion muni market, the goal in this chapter is to inspect the lunch basket to understand why it includes something extra, at what appears to be, no extra charge. To this end, the muni puzzle is described and a list of candidates is arranged to explain the muni puzzle. In many cases these explanations must be evaluated by the investor to account for individual's risk tolerance, tax, and liquidity requirements.

To begin it is instructive to briefly describe several of the terms and tax laws that apply to the municipal bond market. These terms frame an understanding of the choices available to municipal bond investors. This is followed by a discussion of the framework in which the muni puzzle is analyzed. I then describe explanations to the muni puzzle and evidence that either supports or refutes these solutions to the puzzle. While in the end there is not a definitive solution to the muni puzzle, this chapter will serve as a checklist that allows investors to systematically evaluate the benefits and costs of investing in the municipal bond market.

THE TAX LAW AND INVESTING IN MUNICIPAL BONDS

While the tax law was allegedly simplified by the Tax Reform Act of 1986 the environment for municipal bonds gained several layers of complication. Distinctions such as those between private activity bonds and governmental purpose bonds, bank-eligible bonds versus nonbank eligible, provide complicated terrain. From an investor's perspective, these changes can provide opportunities in a market where, depending upon the investor's circumstances, there may exist bonds that are better values than others given an investor's risk preferences, investment goals, and tax situation. Many of the

tax issues are intertwined with credit issues since the type of issuers entitled to the most straightforward tax-exemption are those
that repay bonds from a property tax levy rather than project revenues. The most recent changes to the Tax Code in the Taxpayer Re-
lief Act of 1997 do little to change the existing rules and regulations
from a municipal bond investors' perspective. The change in the
capital gains tax rates, while important, are not unique the muni
market and the bulk of municipal bond changes relax detailed regulations for bond issuers.

For investors the Tax Code defines an important distinction between governmental purpose bonds and private activity bonds.
Governmental purpose bonds are issued by school districts, states,
and other entities and usually are general obligation (GO) bonds
secured by the taxing authority of the issuer. The proceeds from
governmental bonds must be used to fund essential government
services, such as schools, highways, government buildings, and gov-
ernmentally owned and operated water and sewer facilities. In contrast, private activity bonds are issued by entities like private
universities, nonprofit hospitals, airport authorities, housing authorities and are usually secured by revenues from the project that
is being funded. Examples of projects that may qualify for tax-
exempt financing as private activity bonds include airports, civic
centers, privately run electrical utilities, mass commuting facilities, low income housing bonds, and nonprofit universities and hospitals identified as 501(C)(3) organizations. These types of bonds
will often be referred to as revenue bonds to reflect the source of
repayment.

To investors, the importance of the private activity bond label
has two dimensions. Most obvious is that tax-exempt coupons from
private activity bonds are subject to the Alternative Minimum Tax
while governmental purpose bonds are not subject to the Alternative Minimum Tax. In addition to the direct cost of making the
Alternative Minimum Tax payment, compliance with the provisions
in the Tax Code is likely to impose significant accounting and legal
expense on investors. A more subtle cost involves the continuing
tax-exempt status of a given municipal bond. Tax-exempt private activity bonds are encumbered by reams of technical rules which
must be complied with to obtain and maintain tax-exempt status. To
enforce the regulations regarding the issue and use of municipal

bonds, the Internal Revenue Service has the ability to render a bond's payments retroactively taxable. This risk is greater with private activity bonds issues, if for no other reason, because compliance with the set of rules imposed is more complicated.

Despite the costs and risks, private activity bonds do present opportunities to investors who are not subject to the Alternative Minimum Tax, comfortable visiting their tax accountant, and careful to buy private activity bonds from scrupulous issuers. Opportunities result since the returns to private activity bonds are in general higher than the returns to similar governmental purpose bonds. Finally, it is worth mentioning investment opportunities available to corporate investors. In particular, some smaller bond issuers qualify for small issue exemptions which allow governmental purpose bonds to be held by banks while simultaneously allowing interest expenses to be deducted from taxable income. The so-called "bank eligible" sector of the muni market is attractive to banks but probably not attractive to other investors. In addition, all corporations retain the right to hold small quantities of municipal bonds and simultaneously deduct interest expense. This is a potential opportunity for corporations with ready access to the debt market and a steady stream of taxable income.

A FRAMEWORK FOR STUDYING THE MUNI PUZZLE

The intuitive notion behind comparisons of relative yields is that investors, who have decided to purchase a bond, will choose the bond that provides the largest after-tax return. This idea suggests that Equation (10.1) describes the relation between municipal and government bond yields

$$y_M(N) = (1 - \tau)y_G(N) \tag{10.1}$$

That is, $y_M(N)$, the municipal par-bond yield for maturity N, is given by one minus the tax rate of the marginal bond holder, $1 - \tau$, times $y_G(N)$, the taxable government par-bond yield for maturity N. Where a par-bond yield is defined as the coupon rate that enables a bond to sell at par. Par-bond yields are convenient because they allow direct comparisons of cash flows from taxable and tax-exempt bonds.

Furthermore, if held to maturity, par-bonds will never realize capital gains or losses which simplifies issues related to differences in the tax treatment of capital gains and losses for taxable and tax-exempt bonds. Given that $y_M(N)$ and $y_G(N)$ are observable, an implied tax rate, $\tau^i(N)$, can be calculated

$$\tau^i(N) = 1 - \frac{y_{m,t}(N)}{y_{G,t}(N)} \tag{10.2}$$

The implied tax represents the tax rate at which an investor would be indifferent between the tax-exempt and taxable bond if all else is equal.

An important question is whose marginal tax rate matters. Fama (1977) argues that, because banks were legally able to deduct interest expense incurred to carry municipal bonds from taxable income, banks would borrow at an effective rate of $(1 - \tau_c)y_G(N)$ and invest in tax-exempt bonds earning $y_M(N)$. Therefore, arbitrage activity by banks would ensure that Equation (10.1) holds and τ should equal to the top marginal corporate tax rate. Except for the bank eligible bonds mentioned above, the Tax Reform Act of 1986 eliminated this arbitrage opportunity for banks. However, the tax code continues to allow all nonfinancial U.S. corporations to hold up to 2% of their assets in tax-exempt bonds and simultaneously deduct the interest on attributed debt from their taxable income. In aggregate, this implies that substantial arbitrage opportunities for corporations exist if the implied tax rate is less than the highest marginal corporate tax rate.

Consistent with the Fama (1977) prediction, Jordan and Pettway (1985), Poterba (1986), and Jordan and Jordan (1990) show that *short-term* tax-exempt bond yields are, on average, equal to one minus the highest marginal corporate tax rate times the short-term taxable yield. However, Arak and Guentner (1983), Poterba (1986), among many others, find that *long-term* municipal bond yields tend to be much higher than predicted by Fama (1977). This is the muni puzzle.

Figure 10.1 illustrates the muni puzzle. As described, the yield spread between tax-exempt and taxable yields decreases with maturity. Alternatively, if the yield spread narrows with maturity, implied tax rates calculated from the taxable and tax-exempt yields

FIGURE 10.1. Two Perspectives on the Muni Puzzle: Relative Yields and Implied Tax Rates

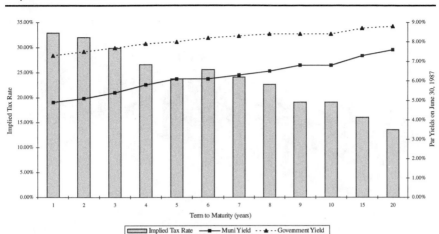

Note: Term structure estimates from June 30, 1987, provide a representative set of par bond yield curve estimates for the Government and pre-refunded municipal bond samples. Implied tax rates are calculated from the par bond yield estimates.

decline with maturity. Depicting the muni puzzle as a declining term structure of implied tax rates is a convenient way to view the puzzle over time. Figure 10.2 plots the term structure of implied tax rates from 1973 to 1999. Figure 10.2 shows that the declining term structure of implied tax rates is present in every year, but 1991, from 1973 to 1999. The muni puzzle is a pervasive empirical fact.

There are several hypotheses designed to explain the muni puzzle. Most of these theories focus on properties of municipal bonds that increase the required rate of return of long-term tax-exempt bonds relative to long-term taxable bonds. The next section explores several explanations for the muni puzzle.

EXPLANATIONS FOR THE MUNI PUZZLE

Any explanation for the muni puzzle must be able to explain two aspects of the puzzle. The solution must allow the relation between

FIGURE 10.2. Historical Term Structure of Implied Tax Rates
(1973–1999)

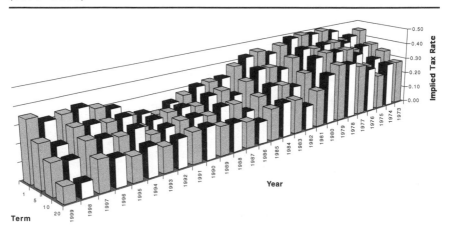

Note: Annual average implied tax rates for 1, 5, 10, and 20 year maturities. From 1973 to 1983 these data are calculated by Poterba (1986) from Salomon Brothers' prime grade municipal yield curves in the *Analytical Record of Yields and Yield Spreads*. From 1984 to May 1999 Aaa-AAA monthly yield curves are provided by Municipal Market Data, a Thomson Financial Municipals Group Company.

muni and taxable yields to conform to the theory at the short-end of the term structure while explaining higher municipal yields at the long-end of the term structure. Possible explanations of the muni puzzle as well as discussion of related evidence follow:

1. Default risk is substantially more important in the pricing of long-term municipal bonds.
2. Standard municipal call options require additional return relative to taxable bonds.
3. Tax-exemption induces additional systematic risk in municipal bonds.
4. Taxes affect taxable yields less than we think.
5. Liquidity and transaction costs are substantially higher in the municipal market.

6. The federal government's option to rescind the tax-exempt status of municipal bonds is especially costly for long-term municipal bonds.

7. Tax-timing options are more valuable in long-term taxable bonds.

8. Clientele effects dominate pricing in the municipal bond market.

Differences in Default Risk and Call Options

Obvious differences between tax-exempt and taxable bonds provide a natural starting point for an investigation into the muni puzzle. One clear difference between municipals and Treasuries is that while municipal defaults are possible, U.S. government bond default is unthinkable. Not surprisingly, a widely cited explanation for high relative municipal yields is that municipal default risk exceeds the default risk of corporate and U.S. treasury bonds. Another common explanation relies upon differences in the standard call provisions included in taxable and tax-exempt bond issues. Municipal bonds usually provide the issuer the option to call bonds 10 years from the date of issue, while government bonds are normally noncallable. Because differences in default risk and call options have the potential to raise required municipal yields relative to comparable maturity Treasuries, these explanations have received considerable attention and to varying degrees are used to explain the muni puzzle.

Chalmers (1998) studied the relative yields of U.S. treasury bonds and municipal bonds that are secured by U.S. government bonds. These special municipal bonds are called pre-refunded municipal bonds. Pre-refunded municipal bonds are tax-exempt bonds that have been defeased by an escrow of non-callable U.S. government securities. Roughly speaking, defeased means that the debt has been paid, even though the debt has not been retired. The defeasance escrow is structured in a manner such that principal and interest payments received from the escrowed portfolio of U.S. government securities meet or exceed (without reinvestment) the payments required over the remaining life of the refunded municipal bonds. Given that defeased bonds are secured by U.S. government securities, it is reasonable to assume that defeased municipal bonds are nominally riskless.[1]

Another advantage of studying pre-refunded bonds is that they are effectively noncallable bonds. Despite the fact that most long-term municipal bonds include a 10-year call provision when they are issued, uncertainty imbedded in the call options is resolved when bonds are refunded. Usually, the escrow trustee is instructed to exercise the call option at the first available call date with certainty, any resulting call premium is included in the cost of the refunding escrow. Therefore, at the refunding date, the call date becomes the bond's effective maturity date and the redemption price (par plus the call premium) is the defeased bond's new maturity price. If a bond is escrowed to maturity, the maturity date and maturity payment maintain the original terms of the bond, with the exception that, any call options are canceled on the date of the defeasance.[2]

Given these arguments, government bonds and pre-refunded bonds are nominally riskless. Since most U.S. government securities are issued without any call options a sufficiently large sample of noncallable government bonds can be studied. The special characteristics of this sample imply that if default risk or call provisions explain the muni puzzle then this sample of pre-refunded bonds should not display the same characteristics illustrated in Figure 10.2.

Using government bond data from CRSP and pre-refunded bond data from J.J. Kenny, par bond yields for 1 to 10, 15 and 20 years are estimated for the taxable and tax-exempt markets. Using these government and municipal yields implied tax rates are calculated once a month from January 1984 through August 1991 for each of the maturities.

---

[1] There exists one case in Wedowee, Alabama, in which a defeased municipal bond was placed in technical default. For details see Chalmers (1998).

[2] In 1986, Kansas City attempted to exercise unused call provisions in an escrowed to maturity issue and extract excess escrow funds by redeeming bonds early, but this transaction never transpired. Despite new contracts that explicitly cancel call provisions in escrowed to maturity issues, municipal bond traders suggest that some investors remain wary of escrowed to maturity issues. See Fabozzi, Fabozzi, and Feldstein (1995) p. 36.

Figure 10.3 provides a time-series perspective on the degree to which the muni puzzle exists in the sample of pre-refunded municipal bonds by showing the time-series of implied tax rates has been downward sloping in the sample. Figure 10.3 plots 92 monthly coefficient estimates from the OLS cross-sectional regression of the implied tax rate on term to maturity,

$$\tau^{i}(N) = \alpha + \beta_{2} Term(N) + \varepsilon(N) \tag{10.3}$$

Figure 10.3 plots the intercept term, α, the slope of term structure of implied tax rates, β_{2}, and error bars $\pm$ two standard errors around β_{2}.

FIGURE 10.3. Shape of the Term Structure of Implied Tax Rates

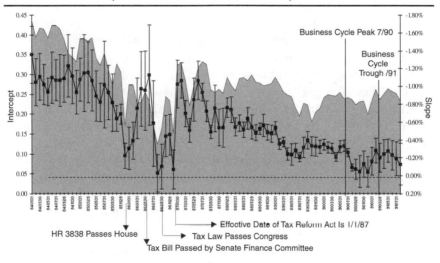

Note: (Right-hand scale refers to the estimated slope coefficients with the least negative slopes at the bottom.) Equation (10.4) is estimated in 92 separate OLS cross-sectional regressions and the intercepts and slope coefficients are plotted below. Implied tax rates, $\tau^{i}(N)$, are calculated with the pre-refunded municipal and the government par bond yields. Each cross-sectional regression has 12 observations. The intercept, α, is shaded. The slope, β_{2}, is plotted with boxes connected by a line and surrounded by error bars that mark $\pm$ two standard errors. The NBER business cycle peak and trough which fall in the time series interval are noted, as are four important tax law events which occurred.

$$\tau^{i}(N) = \alpha + \beta_{2} Term(N) + \varepsilon(N)$$

In each cross-section regression the maturity, N, is equal to $1, 2, \ldots,$ 10, 15, and 20 years.

In Figure 10.3, the slope of the term structure of implied tax rates is consistently negative and significant. It is also notable that the slope has become less negative in the period following the Tax Reform Act of 1986. Furthermore, during the economic downturn and times of tax law uncertainty it appears that implied tax rates are lower for all maturities and the differences across maturities are less pronounced. For example, periods of radical change in the tax law such as December 1985 (House passes tax bill), May 1986 (Senate Finance Committee approves a tax bill), September 1986 (Tax Reform Act is passed into law), and December 31, 1986 (last day prior to effective date of Tax Reform Act) and the lone economic downturn during the sample period are months where the short-term implied tax rate estimate, α, is at its lowest levels and the slope estimate, β_2, is more likely to be insignificantly different from zero. When uncertainty looms, the municipal yield curve appears to revert toward the shape and level of the taxable yield curve.

The fundamental result is that effectively default-free non-callable taxable and tax-exempt yields display the same qualitative relation observed in yield comparisons that utilize riskier, callable municipal bonds. Controlling for default risk and call provisions by selecting a specialized sample of U.S. government secured municipal bonds, the term structure of non-callable default-free municipal bonds is steeper than the U.S. Treasury term structure. That is, the tax rate that would make an investor indifferent between a taxable bond and a tax-exempt bond declines with term to maturity. These results, combined with similar evidence in Ang, Peterson, and Peterson (1985) and Gordon and Malkiel (1981), imply that differences in default risk and call options do not explain the declining term structure of implied tax rates.

From an investor's perspective, these results imply that if it is default risk or call provisions that have kept you out of the municipal market this concern is probably overrated. Not mentioned up to this point is the fact that the yields of these pre-refunded bonds tend to be greater than yields on AAA rated municipal bonds. This strange fact from Chalmers (1995) implies that if you are buying highly rated municipals you can obtain pre-refunded bonds that are secured by Treasuries and receive slightly higher yields.

Pre-refunded municipal bonds appear to be very high quality investments. However, because of the genesis of most pre-refunded bonds, it is difficult to find pre-refunded bonds with de facto maturities longer than 7 to 8 years.

Systematic Risk and Yields on Municipals

Skelton (1983) provides intuition and Piros (1987) and Heaton (1986) formalize the systematic risk hypothesis. The basic idea of the systematic risk hypothesis is that the tax-exemption feature itself induces systematic risk in municipal bonds. As a result, long-term municipal bonds have larger betas and have higher required rates of return. The intuition for the systematic risk hypothesis follows.

When the economy is good, investors have high taxable income and face high marginal tax rates. As a result, the expected after-tax cash flows from a taxable bond decline because marginal tax rates increase. When the economy is bad, investors have less taxable income and face lower marginal tax rates. As a result, expected after-tax cash flows from a taxable bond increase because marginal tax rates decrease. So the after-tax cash flows from a taxable bond provide for more return when the economy is bad and less return when the economy is good. This is an attractive payoff relative to the payoffs from a municipal bond because you receive higher returns when you can put them to a highly valued use.

Studies that have examined this hypothesis have found little support. However, the issues raised by this analysis are relevant to some investors.

Taxes Affect Taxable Bond Yields Less Than We Think

Green (1993) argues that dealer arbitrage activities *within* the market for *taxable bonds* substantially reduce the impact that taxes have on long maturity taxable bond prices. Green's model formalizes the idea that portfolios of taxable bonds can be formed to provide *pre-tax cash flows* that are identical to the cash flows from a taxable coupon bond, while the *after-tax cash flows* from the portfolios are preferred to the after-tax cash flows from the coupon bond. The most tractable result of the model is that synthetic zero coupon bonds can be created that are taxed only at maturity (rather than every year) by carefully constructing portfolios of coupon bonds. These "tax-advantaged" zero coupon bonds then impact the pricing of the coupon bonds. As a result, the impact that taxes have on the pricing of taxable bonds is less than the analysis in the previous section would suggest. Empirical evidence in Green (1993) and Chalmers (1995) finds that Green's model cannot be rejected.

Green's model depends on the fact that there is no arbitrage between the municipal and taxable markets (e.g., there is no bank arbitrage). However, if this model is correct it implies that investors facing high marginal tax rates but without access to the sophisticated financial technology necessary to implement the portfolio strategies in Green's model, may strongly prefer long-term municipals over taxable bonds.

Liquidity Differences

Table 10.1 presents data to support the presumption that the Treasury bond market is more liquid than the municipal bond market. Average daily trading volume of Treasuries is $193 billion, while for the entire municipal bond market trading volume is estimated at $3 billion per day. At least as important, the trading volume for Treasuries is spread over only 230 different issues of bills, notes, and bonds. Contrast the structure of the Treasury market with the municipal bond market which is comprised of an estimated 1.2 million distinct bonds with vast heterogeneity in terms of security, maturity, coupon, and applicable tax rules. As a result, the muni market is a thin market where most bonds are unlikely to trade at all on a given day. The thinness of the municipal market raises the question of whether the additional yield paid on long-term bonds is compensation for the illiquid nature of the bonds.

No one can yet answer this question. However, quick back of the envelop calculations would imply that size of the premium received on a long-term municipal bond would be a very large liquidity premium to be paid to the holder of the municipal bond. However, there is no question that liquidity in the municipal market is expensive relative to the other taxable bond markets. Therefore, as an investor

TABLE 10.1. Relative Size and Components of the U.S. Bond
Market (1995)

Security Type	Par Value (billions)	Daily Volume (billions)	Outstanding Issues	Number of Issuers
U.S. Treasury bills, notes & bonds	$3,292	$193.2	208 Notes and Bonds 32 Bills	1
Municipal bonds	1,301	3.0	1.2 Million CUSIPS	50,000
Corporate bonds[a]	1,823	NA	40–50,000[c]	4,500[c]
Mortgage backed[b]	1,570	45.0	NA	3

[a] Includes U.S.-based and non-asset backed corporate issues.
[b] Includes only GNMA, FNMA, and FHLMC mortgage-backed securities.
[c] Rough estimates by Moodys' Investor Services.
Sources: Public Securities Association, Monthly Statement of the Public Debt,
Moodys' Investors Services, Federal Reserve Board, Fabozzi and Fabozzi
(1995) p. 155.

you may want to avoid municipal bonds if you are likely to sell
bonds prior to maturity. On the other hand, if you have structured a
bond portfolio to meet the needs of college or retirement and you
are a buy and hold investor these liquidity costs are not borne by
you but you may benefit from them because other investors' liquidity demands force municipal bond issuers to pay higher yields.

The Government's Option to Rescind Tax-Exemption

Another explanation considers the U.S. government's option to rescind the tax-exemption feature of municipal bonds. In 1988, the
Supreme Court ruled in South Carolina v. Baker that the U.S. government has a right to tax interest on municipal bonds (Poterba,
1989). Since options with longer time to expiration are more valuable, the characteristics of the government's option are consistent
with the observed relative yields.

The likelihood that the municipal bond tax-exemption is removed is remote. However, the 1996 presidential election brought to

the fore several flat tax proposals which contained provisions that would have eliminated the taxation of government bonds. The pricing of municipal bonds would suffer in this situation simply because the unique feature that they enjoy would have been made common. While the likelihood of a new flat tax proposal being enacted also seems remote, it is certainly a risk worthy of consideration.

For municipal investors, these risks are probably unavoidable. However, while the risk of tax law change is very real it must be measured against the returns relative to taxable bonds.

Tax-Timing Options

Tax-timing options quantify the value of an investors ability to realize capital losses and deduct those losses from taxable income, while avoiding the realization of gains. The ability to control your realization of losses and gains for tax purposes has value because it affects your after-tax cash flow. The tax-timing options in municipal bonds are less valuable than those imbedded in government bonds because of the fact that municipal bonds purchased at a premium in the secondary market are treated differently than premium taxable bonds.

While both tax-exempt and taxable bonds purchased at a discount in the secondary market accrue taxable capital gains at the time of sale or maturity, the premium over par paid for a taxable bond may be amortized and taken as an annual tax deductible loss over the life of the bond. While the purchaser of a premium municipal bond must amortize the bond's basis, the amortized premium *cannot* be taken as an expense for tax purposes. If the premium municipal bond is subsequently sold, the basis for computing capital gains or losses is the depreciated basis not the original purchase price. Constantinides and Ingersoll (1984) have pointed out that this difference in the tax treatment of premium bonds results in an inferior tax-timing option on municipal bonds selling at a premium. Empirically, Jordan and Jordan (1990) find that the basic features of a tax-timing option are potentially important factors in explaining the relative yields.

The impact of tax-timing options should be considered jointly with liquidity issues because exercising tax-timing options requires trading. The extent to which the inferior tax-timing options will impact the value of municipal bonds to your portfolio will largely depend on your individual investment goals. For example, if you are a buy and hold investor choosing between taxable and tax-exempt bonds these issues are unlikely to be important unless you hold large quantities of bonds and can trade at low cost.

Clientele Effects

A popular hypothesis, supported by Mussa and Kormendi (1979) and Kidwell and Koch (1983) implies that investors in different marginal tax brackets have distinct maturity preferences, or preferred habitats. The marginal tax rates of the clientele at each maturity lead to implied tax rates that decline with maturity. There is a great deal of evidence that the holders of municipal bonds at various maturities do differ. However, the clientele story begs the question of why more high tax bracket investors do not purchase long-term municipals and push the yields down.

The clientele explanation should not dissuade investors from purchasing municipal rather than taxable bonds. If an investor finds himself in a high tax bracket for the foreseeable future, and clientele effects explain the muni puzzle, that investor is not assuming any hidden risk. Rather, he stands to benefit from the advantageous pricing of long-term municipal bonds.

CONCLUSIONS

To a large extent, my description of preceding explanations to the muni puzzle reflect the degree to which these issues have been explored. Liquidity costs, the costs of government tax changes, tax-timing options, and Green's explanation all deserve more careful exploration. However, investors are already in a position to evaluate the importance of most of these issues in the context of their personal investment situations. The municipal bond market does allow investors in some situations to make choices that are clearly better given the yields that are available. The decision of how much better will depend to a large extent on how the prior eight issues impact an individual's investment plan. If one has short-term liquidity needs then it is perhaps too costly to take advantage of the higher yielding municipals. If one expects that one's tax rate may fall in the next year then again long-term municipals may be less attractive. These are issues that one would want to consider in designing your bond portfolio.

While there is no clear solution to the muni puzzle, it is perhaps comforting that default risk and call options do not appear to be critical factors in the pricing of long-term municipals. Furthermore, with the exception of changes in the Federal tax status of municipal interest other candidate explanations to the muni puzzle can be evaluated for consistency with the goals of one's investment portfolio.

ACKNOWLEDGMENTS

This chapter is based on Chalmers, 1998, "Default Risk Cannot Explain the Muni Puzzle: Evidence from Municipal Bonds That Are Secured by U.S. Treasury Obligations," the *Review of Financial Studies*, V. 11, n. 2. Portions are printed with the permission of the *Review of Financial Studies*. I thank J.J. Kenny and Municipal Market Data for their generous donation of data.

REFERENCES

Ang, J., D. Peterson, and P. Peterson. (1985). "Marginal Tax Rates: Evidence from Nontaxable Corporate Bonds: A Note," *Journal of Finance*, 40(1), 327–332.

Arak, M. and K. Guentner. (1983). "The Market for Tax-Exempt Issues: Why Are the Yields So High? *Natioinal Tax Journal*, 36(2), 145–162.

Chalmers, J.M.R. (1995). "The Relative Yields of Tax-Exempt and Taxable Bonds: Evidence from Municipal Bonds That Are Secured by U.S. Government Obligations," Ph.D. dissertation, University of Rochester.

Chalmers, J.M.R. (1998). "Default Risk Cannot Explain the Muni Puzzle: Evidence from Municipal Bonds That Are Secured by U.S. Treasury Obligations," *The Review of Financial Studies*, 11(2), 281–308.

Constantinides, G.M. and J.E. Ingersoll, Jr. (1984). "Optimal Bond Training with Personal Taxes," *Journal of Financial Economics*, 13, 299–335.

Fabozzi, F.J. and T.D. Fabozzi. (1995). *The Handbook of Fixed Income Securities* (4th ed.), Burr Ridge, IL: Irwin Professional Publishing.

Fama, E.F. (1977). "A Pricing Model for the Municipal Bond Market," unpublished manuscript, University of Chicago.

Gordon, R.H. and B.G. Malkiel. (1981). "Corporation Finance," *How Taxes Affect Economic Behavior*, Henry J. Aaron and Joseph A. Pechman (Eds.), Washington, DC: Brookings Institution.

Green, R.C. (1993). "A Simple Model of the Taxable and Tax-Exempt Yield Curves." *The Review of Financial Studies, 6*(2), 233–264.

Jordan, B. and S.D. Jordan. (1990). "Tax-Timing Options and the Relative Yields on Municipal and Taxable Bonds," working paper, University of Missouri-Columbia.

Jordan, B. and R. Pettway. (1985). "The Pricing of Short-Term Debt and the Miller Hypothesis: A Note," *The Journal of Finance, 40,* 589–594.

Kidwell, D.S. and T.W. Koch. (1983). "Market Segmentation and the Term Structure of Municipal Yields," *Journal of Money, Credit and Banking, 18*(4), 482–494.

Miller, M. (1977). Debt and Taxes, *Journal of Finance, 32,* 261–275.

Mussa, M.L. and R.C. Kormendi. (1979). *The Taxation of Municipal Bonds.* Washington, DC: American Enterprise Institute.

Poterba, J.M. (1986). "Explaining the Yield Spread between Taxable and Tax-Exempt Bonds," in H. Rosen (Ed.), *Studies in State and Local Public Finance,* Chicago: University of Chicago Press.

Poterba, J.M. (1989). "Tax Reform and Market for Tax-Exempt Debt," *Regional Science and Urban Economics, 19,* 537–562.

11

Models of Currency Option Pricing

Gurdip Bakshi and *Zhiwu Chen*

With the increasing globalization of world financial markets, derivative products linked to exchange rates are assuming a new importance. There are a large number of exchange-rate-linked products in the marketplace. One purpose of this chapter is to review existing models of currency option pricing. Another purpose is to present some directions in which this work can be fruitfully extended. For example, given recent fluctuations in currency volatility, Garman and Kohlhagan's (1983) constant-currency-volatility assumption is becoming untenable in foreign exchange option markets. There is abundant empirical evidence, both formal and informal, that exchange rate volatility is highly autocorrelated and varies stochastically over time (e.g., Bates, 1995). Further evidence on the failure of the Garman-Kohlhagan option model can be established from the shapes of implied volatility curves, which tend to exhibit pronounced smile patterns. This seems true not only across option moneyness, but also across option terms to expiration. The shape of the volatility curves are not time-homogenous either: they are sometimes downward sloping, sometimes U-shaped, and at other times upward sloping (e.g., Bakshi & Chen, 1997; Bates, 1996). While it is widely understood that a constant-volatility formula is likely to fail empirically (in both pricing and hedging), the Garman-Kohlhagan model is, for a lack of alternatives, still the most widely used currency-option valuation formula.

In generalizing the constant-volatility assumption, we follow Bakshi and Chen (1997), Bates (1996), Chesney and Scott (1987), Heston (1993), and Melino and Turnbull (1990). That is, we let the volatility of exchange rate depreciation follow a mean-reverting diffusion process that is correlated with the exchange rate depreciation. This change to the Garman-Kohlhagan framework fundamentally alters the properties of the *risk-neutral* distribution of the exchange rate. Under realistic parameter values, this distribution is (1) fat-tailed, (2) peaked at short maturities, and (3) skewed to the left or the right (depending on the correlation between volatility and exchange-rate shocks). Such a distribution is in sharp contrast with the symmetric and slightly positively skewed lognormal distribution assumed in the Garman-Kohlhagan model. For practical implementations, the resulting option formula is parsimonious with four structural parameters and can be expressed solely in terms of observable economic entities. In addition, all useful derivatives such as option delta, vega, rho, and gamma are analytically obtainable, making hedging and option trading strategies easily achievable in an internally consistent manner. Furthermore, the new option formula inherits the intuitive structure of its constant-volatility counterpart: the call price is the spot exchange rate multiplied by the option delta minus the discounted strike price multiplied by a risk-neutral probability (for the call option to expire in-the-money). Given these appealing features, the stochastic-volatility option model presented here is likely to become a better-performing alternative to the Garman-Kohlhagan model.

Given that foreign exchange rates tend to exhibit sharp moves, options on higher exchange rate moments are also useful and beneficial to currency risk managers. It is thus of interest to examine such more general foreign-exchange claims. To do so, we keep the stochastic currency volatility assumption and posit an option payoff that is a power function (with $1 - \alpha$) of the spot exchange rate. As the payoff is nonlinear and smooth in α, a wide variety of payoff structures are spanned by this contract. When α is restricted to zero, it admits, as a special case, the commonly considered plain vanilla option contract (i.e., Garman-Kohlhagan). In the limit as $\alpha \to 1$, the log contract of Neuberger (1994) results. In principle, we can accommodate payoffs written on any central or non-central moment of the spot rate distribution. More precisely, when $\alpha = -1$, we can price the option on *volatility*; when $\alpha = -2$, the option on *skewness*; and when $\alpha = -3$, an option contingent on *kurtosis*. This can be done outside of the restrictive log-normal setting. When α is a positive integer, the payoff is concave in the spot rate and such a contract can also be accommodated and priced. Given the smoothness of the payoff function and its differentiability in the exercise region beyond $\alpha > 1$, the so-called *asymmetric power contract* possesses the desirable property that all claims in this parametric family can be delta- and gamma-hedged more easily than the traditional option contracts.

Another application concerns investing in foreign equity market-related instruments. For example, when domestic investors purchase foreign equity options, the ultimate payoff has an exchange rate element in it. In pricing such foreign equity linked contracts, we assume a realistic forcing structure for the spot exchange rate and the underlying equity price. More specifically, the foreign equity price is driven by two autonomous components: one related to the foreign equity volatility and the other due to exchange rate volatility. In this framework with stochastic volatility, we consider the pricing of a quanto in two steps. First, convert the dollar payoff into the currency in which the equity is denominated. This payoff in foreign currency needs to be priced from the perspective of the foreign investor (i.e., the conditional expectations should involve a martingale measure dependent on the foreign interest rate). In the next step, re-convert the foreign currency price of the quanto back into dollars using the current spot exchange rate.

Finally, in the spirit of Margrabe (1978) we also consider an outperformance option contingent on two exchange rates. This option contract is exercised when the difference between the *depreciation rates* exceeds zero. The exact payoff is the maximum depreciation-rate differential (the strike is set to zero for simplicity). In pricing this exotic option contract, we assume that (1) each exchange rate is driven by a proportional stochastic process and (2) the two exchange rates are dynamically correlated and driven by a common (stochastic) volatility factor. But the impact of stochastic volatility on the respective exchange rate movements is asymmetric with a scaling factor of their own. As the contract is on the depreciation rate, the option price is independent of the spot exchange rates. In fact, the option price is linear in two probability functions: each probability is solely a function of the spot exchange rate volatility. We show that this option contract has zero spot-price delta and zero spot-price gamma.

The rest of the chapter is divided into four parts. We first introduce the Garman and Kohlhagan currency option model. We then develop a formula for currency options when exchange rate volatility is stochastic. Examples of exchange-rate exotics are presented next. Concluding remarks are offered last.

THE GARMAN-KOHLHAGAN CURRENCY OPTION MODEL

To address the key issues in this chapter, denote the dollar price of a unit of foreign currency (say, Swiss franc) by $S(t)$ and the short-term interest rate in the United States (Switzerland) by $r(r^*)$. To streamline the development of the currency option models, we will typically specify, at the outset, the dynamics of the spot exchange rate and the exchange rate volatility under the martingale (risk-neutral) measure. This means that we will ignore the micro foundations for the spot exchange rate process. As is evident from the recent work of Bakshi and Chen (1997), however, the exchange rate processes we posit in this chapter are not only reasonable, but also supportable by dynamic equilibrium international economies.

Let us first consider the premier Garman and Kohlhagan (1983) currency option model, which is based on two building blocks: (1) the interest rates at home and abroad are time-invariant constants (the term structure of interest rates is flat); and (2) the spot exchange rate is governed by a one-dimensional Markov process

$$\frac{dS(t)}{S(t)} = [r - r^*]dt + \sigma d\omega_s(t) \qquad S(0) > 0 \qquad (11.1)$$

where σ is the constant volatility of the exchange rate depreciation. In this simple model, the standard Brownian motion, $\omega_s(t)$, is the sole stochastic source of variation in the exchange rate. Using Ito's lemma and the moment generating function of $\ln[S(t+T)]$, the expectation and variance of the future (log) exchange rate are

$$E_t^Q\{\ln[S(t+T)]\} = \ln[S(t)] + (r - r* - \frac{1}{2}\sigma^2)T \tag{11.2}$$

$$Var_t^Q\{\ln[S(t+T)]\} = \sigma^2 T \tag{11.3}$$

Also notice that by the martingale restriction, we must have

$$S(t) - E_t^Q\{S(t+\tau)e^{-(r-r*)\tau}\} = 0 \tag{11.4}$$

where $E_t^Q\{.\}$ denotes conditional expectation under the risk-neutral pricing measure. That is, the currency price at time t is precisely the conditional expectation of the future currency value when proper drift restrictions are imposed on the exchange rate dynamics. Clearly, the exchange rate process postulated in Equation (11.1) is Black-Scholes like, but the exogenous drift rate is the instantaneous interest rate differential.

Let $C(t,\tau;K)$ be the European call option price on the spot exchange rate with strike price K and τ periods to expiration. Given the Markovian nature of the valuation problem, it is well known that the option price can only be a function of $S(t)$ and t. Based on standard results from Ito calculus, the call price satisfies the valuation equation

$$\frac{1}{2}\sigma^2 S^2 \frac{\partial^2 C}{\partial S^2} + [r - r*]S\frac{\partial C}{\partial S} - \frac{\partial C}{\partial \tau} - rC = 0 \tag{11.5}$$

subject to the terminal condition $C(t+\tau,0;K) = \max\{0, S(t+\tau) - K\}$. As made explicit by Garman-Kohlhagan, $C(t,\tau)$ can be viewed as an option on an asset with dividend-yield $r*$. With this analogy, the price of the call option is

$$C(t,\tau;K) = S(t)e^{-r*\tau}N(d_1) - Ke^{-r\tau}N(d_2) \tag{11.6}$$

where defining

$$d_1 \equiv \frac{1}{\sigma\sqrt{\tau}} \ln\left[\frac{S(t)e^{-r^*\tau}}{Ke^{-r\tau}}\right] + \frac{1}{2}\sigma\sqrt{\tau} \tag{11.7}$$

$$d_2 \equiv d_1 - \sigma\sqrt{\tau} \tag{11.8}$$

and $N(d) \equiv \frac{1}{2\pi}\int_{-\infty}^{d} e^{-\frac{z^2}{2}} dz$ is the standard normal distribution function. The currency option formula in Equation (11.6) has an intuitive interpretation: the first term is the present value of the future spot exchange rate conditional on the option expiring in-the-money, and the second term is the present value of the strike price. The put option price, denoted $P(t,\tau;K)$, can be recovered from the put-call parity for currency claims

$$P(t,\tau;K) = C(t,\tau;K) + Ke^{-r\tau} - S(t)e^{-r^*\tau} \tag{11.9}$$

which can be seen from the following spanning identity: $\max(0,S(t+\tau)-K) - \max(0,K-S(t+\tau)) = S(t+\tau) - K$.

To understand the Garman-Kohlhagan currency option model better, we can take the partial derivative of the option price with respect to each of the underlying entities. Since the properties of the put option price are obtainable from the put-call parity in (11.9), let us focus on the comparative statics of the call. First, note that the higher the spot exchange rate, the higher the call option price as reflected in the spot price delta

$$\Delta_s(t,\tau) \equiv \frac{\partial C}{\partial S} = e^{-r^*\tau}N(d_1) > 0 \tag{11.10}$$

This is invariably the outcome as both terms on the right hand side of Equation (11.10) are strictly positive. Since $N(d_1)$ is a probability and takes a value between 0 and 1, the call delta is bounded between 0 and $e^{-r^*\tau}$. Clearly, the lower the foreign interest rate r^*, the wider is the upper bound but never beyond 1.

By similarly taking the partial derivative of the call with respect to K, σ, and r, we respectively obtain the strike price delta, the volatility delta (vega), and the interest rate delta

$$\Delta_K(t, \tau) \equiv \frac{\partial C}{\partial K} = -e^{-r\tau} N(d_2) < 0 \qquad (11.11)$$

$$\Delta_\sigma(t, \tau) \equiv \frac{\partial C}{\partial \sigma} = Se^{-r^*\tau} n(d_1)\sqrt{\tau} > 0 \qquad (11.12)$$

$$\Delta_r(t, \tau) \equiv \frac{\partial C}{\partial r} = \tau Ke^{-r\tau} N(d_2) > 0 \qquad (11.13)$$

where $n(z) \equiv \frac{1}{\sqrt{2\pi}} e^{-\frac{z^2}{2}}$ is the density for the normal distribution. Figure 11.1 displays the variation in each of the deltas when $K = 1.50$,

FIGURE 11.1.   Option Prices and Sensitivities

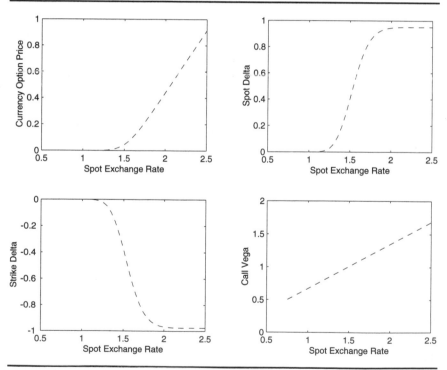

Note: The call option price, the spot delta, the strike delta, and the vega are all based on the Garman Kohlhagan currency option formula. For this benchmark illustration, we fix $K = 1.50$, $\sigma = 15\%$, $r^* = 10\%$ and vary the spot exchange rate between 0.75 and 2.50.

$\sigma = 15\%$, $r = 5\%$, $r^* = 10\%$, and the spot exchange rate is varied between 1.0 and 2.0.

The partial derivatives, or Greeks, are also useful for constructing delta-neutral, or vega-neutral hedging strategies. They tend to play an important role in the execution of option-based trading strategies (such as bull spreads, calendar spreads, and so on) also. To expound on the finer details of such a procedure, suppose an option trader is *short* a currency option with time-t price $C(t,\tau;K)$. Based on the Garman-Kohlhagan model, the short position in the option can be hedged by investing (1) $N(d_1)$ in a foreign zero-coupon bond and (2) $C(t,\tau;K) - N(d_1)e^{-r^*\tau}$ in cash. This position will synthetically replicate the payoff on the target currency option and hence immunize spot price risk. To see the logic behind this assertion let the composite position be $G(t,\tau) = X_0 + X_1 S(t)e^{-r^*\tau} + b_0$ for some weights X_0 and X_1. Expanding via Ito's formula, $dG - E_t^Q(dG) = X_1 e^{-r^*\tau}[dS - E_t^Q(dS)]$. Likewise, for the target option: $dC - E_t^Q(dC) = \Delta_S[dS - E_t^Q(dS)]$. Then using the Δ_s displayed in Equation (11.10) and equating the positions in the replicating and target portfolio proves our assertion that $G(t,\tau)$ spans $C(t,\tau)$. For other strategies, the construction of the hedge has a similar intuitive structure.

The input requirements for implementing the Garman-Kohlhagan currency option model are minimal, which is the main reason for its wide empirical appeal. The option formula and the option deltas basically require (in addition to K and τ): (1) the matching domestic, and foreign yield-to-maturity, (2) the time-t spot exchange rate value, and (3) the exchange rate volatility σ. In practice, the matching yields are culled from liquid Eurocurrency markets, and the spot exchange rate is also in the information set. So, the first two inputs present no difficulties. The exchange rate volatility parameter σ is not directly available, however. For this reason, and for model implementation purposes, practitioners have found it convenient to back-out σ directly from the price of traded options. That is, practitioners assume that the true spot exchange dynamics are those displayed in Equation (11.1) and recover σ from the market price of the currency option, as if the Garman-Kohlhagan model is correct. To formally illustrate how this step is accomplished in practice, let $\hat{C}(t,\tau;K)$ denote the market price of a option with strike price K and term-to-expiration τ. By inserting the current values for

$S(t)$ and the matching τ-period r, and r^* into the model price (11.6), minimize the following criteria

$$\min_{\sigma} [\hat{C}(t,\tau;K) - C(t,\tau;K)]^2 \tag{11.14}$$

for each option contract. This procedure is iterative (say, Newton-Raphson) and converges quickly. Repeating this procedure will, in principle, deliver an implied volatility estimate for each K and for each time t. Implied volatility so recovered, say, from short-term at-the-money options can be used to price and hedge at-the-money long-term options on the same day (in-sample); or, to price short-term at-the-money options on the next day (out-of-sample). Because the implied volatilities are not homogeneous in the strike price or maturity, the shape of implied volatility curve has come to symbolize mis-specification of the Garman-Kohlhagan option formula. For example, a typical volatility smile pattern is downward sloping (or U-shaped): deep out-of-the-money call options have higher implied volatilities than at-the-money and deep in-the-money calls. The volatility smiles reflect the fact that the risk-neutral distributions are unable to accommodate both the skewness and the kurtosis embedded in traded currency option prices. Thus, in summary, better distributional characteristics for the underlying exchange rate dynamics are needed to realistically model currency option prices.

The Garman-Kohlhagan formula is applicable only to European options. Since most options traded on the Philadelphia currency option market are of the American style, this is clearly a shortcoming. For any American option unlikely to be exercised early, the European option formula will nonetheless work. For instance, if the U.S. interest rate exceeds that in the Switzerland (i.e., $r > r^*$), the American call will never be exercised early. When the reverse is true, it renders the early exercise of the American put sub-optimal as well (Grabbe, 1983). For currency options that can be exercised early, we recommend the early exercise approximation proposed by Barone-Adesi and Whaley (1987). Adding the early-exercise premium to the European option price in (11.6) will likely result in a reasonable approximation to the corresponding American option price.

CURRENCY OPTION MODELS BEYOND GARMAN-KOHLHAGAN

The objective of this section is to introduce a simple alternative to the Garman-Kohlhagan currency option formula. This more general alternative is based on stochastic volatility and permits a much richer characterization of the underlying risk-neutral distribution. For this purpose, we continue to maintain the constancy of the yield curve, but modify the spot exchange rate process in Equation (11.1) to the one shown below:

$$\frac{dS(t)}{S(t)} = [r - r^*]dt + \sqrt{V(t)}\,d\omega_s(t) \qquad S(0) > 0 \tag{11.15}$$

$$dV(t) = [\theta_v - \kappa_v V(t)]dt + \sigma_v\sqrt{V(t)}\,d\omega_v(t) \qquad V(0) > 0 \tag{11.16}$$

where $V(t)$ represents the diffusion component of the exchange rate depreciation. As the reader can see, there are now two sources of uncertainty in this extended set-up: (1) the standard Brownian motion shock to the exchange rate (denoted by $\omega_s(t)$) and (2) the standard Brownian notion shock to volatility (denoted by $\omega_v(t)$). Let $\rho \equiv Cov_t[\omega_s(t), \omega_v(t)]$ represent the correlation coefficient between the two standard Brownian motions. Notice that the (risk-neutral) volatility process in (11.16) is an AR-1 process in continuous-time and mean-reverting, which are not implausible features for $V(t)$ to have. Specifically, the structural parameters $\kappa_v > 0, \frac{\theta_v}{\kappa_v} > 0$ and $\sigma_v > 0$ represent the speed of adjustment, the long-run mean, and the variation coefficient of the volatility $V(t)$. For instance, when $\theta_v = 0$, the long-run mean becomes zero; and when $\sigma = 0$, volatility is deterministic. Observe that volatility risk is indeed priced. That is, although risk compensation does not show up explicitly in the volatility process, it is implicitly internalized within the structural parameter κ_v. Under the parametric restriction $\kappa_v = \theta_v = \sigma_v = 0$, the exchange rate volatility becomes time-invariant with the exchange rate dynamics (11.15) and (11.16) reducing to the simpler one in Equation (11.1).

It is useful to grasp how the distributional restrictions in (11.15) and (11.16) can potentially lead to a better performing option pricing model. First, with nonzero ρ, one can control the rate of positive, or negative, skewness in the exchange rate distribution. With $\rho > 0$ ($\rho < 0$), it shifts more probability mass to the right (left) side of the exchange-rate distribution, thus imparting it a positive (negative) skew. This flexibility is quite important: unlike distributions from index options, the implicit exchange rate distribution need not be negatively skewed. Second, the amount of (excess) kurtosis can be regulated by varying the diffusion parameter σ_v. Thus, in principle, both of these generalizations to the stochastic structure should en-richen the valuation framework beyond Garman-Kohlhagan. As argued persuasively by Bakshi and Chen (1997) and Bates (1996), the said features can only help flatten the volatility smile patterns associated with the Garman-Kohlhagan currency option formula. One can thus expect the generalized model (11.15) and (11.16) to bring model option prices closer to market-determined prices.[1]

Currency Option Formula under Stochastic Volatility

To formulate the European option pricing problem under stochastic volatility, again let $C(t,\tau;K)$ denote the price of the call with strike price K and term-to-expiration τ. Given the dynamic structure in Equations (11.15) and (11.16), the call price is jointly Markovian in $S(t)$, $V(t)$, and t. Applying Ito's lemma to the call price and equalizing the drift of

$$\frac{dC(t,\tau)}{C(t,\tau)}$$

---

[1] We could have extended the Garman-Kohlhagan currency model by making the interest rates at home and abroad stochastic. This only alters how the cash flows are discounted. As most traded currency options possess short maturities, the stochastic interest rate generalization is unlikely to modify the distributional characteristics of the state-price density function. For instance, in their empirical inquiry, Bakshi, Cao, and Chen (1997) find that the pricing and hedging performance of the stochastic volatility model with and without the stochastic interest rate feature is virtually the same. In the spirit of their work, the theoretical analysis with stochastic interest rates is omitted.

to $r \, dt$, we have the valuation equation for the call

$$\frac{1}{2} V S^2 \frac{\partial^2 C}{\partial S^2} + [r - r^*] S \frac{\partial C}{\partial S} + \rho \sigma_v V S \frac{\partial^2 C}{\partial S \partial V} + \frac{1}{2} \sigma_v^2 V \frac{\partial^2 C}{\partial V^2}$$
$$+ [\theta_v - \kappa_v V] \frac{\partial C}{\partial V} - \frac{\partial C}{\partial \tau} - rC = 0 \tag{11.17}$$

subject to $C(t + \tau, 0; K) = \max\{0, S(t + \tau) - K\}$. It can be shown that the call option price is

$$C(t, \tau) = S(t) e^{-r^* \tau} \Pi_1(t, \tau) - K e^{-r \tau} \Pi_2(t, \tau) \tag{11.18}$$

where $\Pi_1(t, \tau)$ and $\Pi_2(t, \tau)$ are risk-neutral probabilities, and the precise counterparts of $N(d_1)$ and $N(d_2)$ (displayed in Equations (11.7) and (11.8)). Essentially Π_1 (Π_2) can be interpreted as the price of an Arrow-Debreu security, when the reference measure is forward-adjusted (risk-neutral). Provided the call is exercised, they are just discounted values of a unity payoff. As in Bakshi and Chen (1997) and Heston (1993), to solve for Π_1 and Π_2, one first conjectures the functional form in (11.18). Substituting Equation (11.18) into (11.17) produces two valuation equations for Π_1 and Π_2. Rather than solving the PDEs for Π_1 and Π_2, it is instead convenient to solve for the corresponding characteristic function. This is mostly the case as the terminal condition for the characteristic function is $e^{i\phi \ln[S(t + \tau)]}$, which is mathematically much more tractable. Using the closed-form formulation of the characteristic function, we can now recover each Arrow-Debreu security price by inverse Fourier transformation

$$\Pi_j(t, \tau) = \frac{1}{2} + \frac{1}{\pi} \int_0^\infty \mathrm{Re}\left[\frac{e^{-i\phi \ln[K]} f_j(t, \tau; \phi)}{i\phi}\right] d\phi \qquad j = 1, 2 \tag{11.19}$$

where $\mathrm{Re}[.]$ is a stand-in for the real part of the expression and $i = \sqrt{-1}$ represents a complex number. In other words, by taking the real part of the expression in (11.19) and numerically integrating the characteristic function delivers the price of each Arrow-Debreu security.

Returning to the stochastic volatility option model, we note that the closed-form characteristic function of the state-price density is exponential affine in two factors $V(t)$ and $\ln[S(t)]$, as made exact[2]

$$
\begin{aligned}
f(t,\tau;\phi) = \exp\Bigg\{ &-\frac{\theta_v}{\sigma_v^2}\Bigg[2\ln\Bigg(1-\frac{[\hat{\xi}_v-\kappa_v+i\phi\rho\sigma_v](1-e^{-\hat{\xi}_v\tau})}{2\hat{\xi}_v}\Bigg)+[\hat{\xi}_v-\kappa_v+i\phi\rho\sigma_v]\tau\Bigg] \\
&+\frac{i\phi(i\phi-1)(1-e^{-\hat{\xi}_v\tau})}{2\hat{\xi}_v-[\hat{\xi}_v-\kappa_v+i\phi\rho\sigma_v](1-e^{-\hat{\xi}_v\tau})}V(t)+i\phi(r-r^*)\tau-r\tau+i\phi\ln[S(t)]\Bigg\}
\end{aligned}
$$

(11.20)

where $\hat{\xi}_v = \sqrt{[\kappa_v-i\phi\rho\sigma_v]^2-i\phi(i\phi-1)\sigma_v^2}$. Then the required characteristic functions in Equation (11.19) can be translated from Equation (11.20) as

$$
f_1(t,\tau;\phi) = \frac{f(t,\tau;\phi-i)}{f(t,\tau;-i)}
$$

(11.21)

$$
f_2(t,\tau;\phi) = e^{r\tau}f(t,\tau;\phi)
$$

(11.22)

which completes the description of the closed-form call option formula in Equation (11.18). The price of a European put on the same currency can be deduced from put-call parity.

Several points are noteworthy about this option model. First, letting $\kappa_v = \theta_v = \sigma_v = 0$ and using L'Hopital's rule, $f_1(t,\tau)$ and $f_2(t,\tau)$ become the characteristic functions for the normal density. That is, as expected, in this special case, Π_1 and Π_2 converge respectively to $N(d_1)$ and $N(d_2)$ of the Garman-Kohlhagen option model. Thus, provided the error in estimating the structural parameters is not too large, this model should do as well as the Garman-Kohlhagen model in fitting market option prices. Second, by construction, the option solution applies to the square-root volatility process and to a specific correlation structure between exchange rate depreciation and

---

[2] Recall that $N(d_1)$ and $N(d_2)$ also involve a numerical integration. But as cumulative normal distribution functions are elementary mathematical functions, rational polynominal approximations are readily available. In the present context of the stochastic volatility characteristic functions, the integrand does decays rapidly in ϕ. For most practical purposes, we found that an upper limit of 100 gave accurate results up to 4 digits.

volatility. For other classes of volatility processes, the characteristic functions and hence option formula are not yet available. The Hull and White (1987) option model is an exception, but their model imposes the counterfactual assumption that volatility follows geometric Brownian motion, and is uncorrelated with the spot exchange rate.

Finally, compared to the Garman-Kohlhagan formula, the implementation requirements of this model are more stringent: it requires four additional parameters as inputs (i.e., κ_v, θ_v, σ_v, and ρ). But as each parameter appearing in the currency option formula are readily identified, it facilitates model implementation. To formalize one such implementation strategy, we now follow Bakshi, Cao, and Chen (1997) and explain how the option parameters and $V(t)$ can be jointly backed-out from cross-sectional option prices. Let $\Phi \equiv \{\kappa_v, \theta_v, \sigma_v, \rho\}$ and collect $n = 1, \ldots, N$ (with $N \geq 5$) option prices $\hat{C}(t, \tau_n; K_n)$. Adopt the criterion function

$$\min_{\Phi, V(t)} \frac{1}{N} \sum_{n=1}^{N} \left[\frac{\hat{C}(t_n, \tau_n; K_n)}{C(t, \tau_n; K_n, \Phi)} - 1 \right]^2 \tag{11.23}$$

which will give an estimate of Φ and $V(t)$ for each date t. The estimation methodology is versatile, as one is free to choose any set of option contracts in the procedure (sorted by strike and maturity). Bakshi, Cao, and Chen (1997, 1998) demonstrate that such a treatment enhances the out-of-sample pricing and hedging performance of the option pricing model. In particular, when the structural parameters and the implied volatility backed-out from, say, short-term, at-the-money options are used to price options in the same class on the *next day*, the empirical performance is better. We should expect the implied parameter matrix treatment to serve a similarly useful role in currency option models.

Without conducting an extensive empirical examination, the importance of stochastic volatility can be gauged in the following manner. Set $\theta_v = 0.1568$, $\kappa_v = 7.98$, $\sigma_v = 0.2882$, $\rho = 0.89$, $\sqrt{V} = 5.60\%$, and $\tau = 27$ days. Then, compute the SV model price for various strike prices. Treating these hypothetical option prices to be market prices, generate the Garman-Kohlhagan implied volatilities. Figure 11.2 reveals that the Garman-Kohlhagan model does indeed produce a

FIGURE 11.2. Garman–Kohlhagan Implied Volatility.

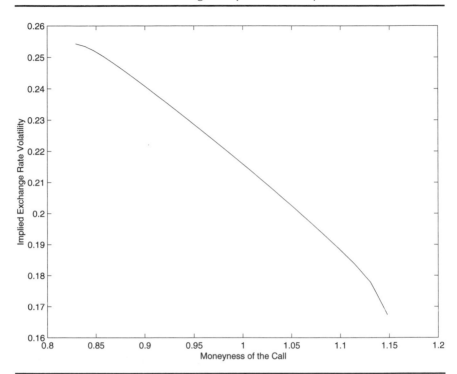

Note: Three steps are followed: (1) Set $r = 5.13\%$, $r^* = 0.81\%$, $S(t) = 0.7461$, $\Theta_\upsilon = 0.1568$, $K_\upsilon = 7.98$, $\sigma_\upsilon = 0.2882$, and $\rho = 0.89$. (2) Compute the option price for different strikes using the SV model price in (18). (3) Invert the implied volatility using the Garman-Kohlhagan currency model. The moneyness of the call is defined as the spot divided by the strike price of the option. In all calculations, τ equals 27 days.

downward-sloping implied volatility curve. Thus, incorporating stochastic volatility should align currency option pricing with the real-life counterparts.

Even under stochastic exchange rate volatility, the hedge ratio's are known analytically—which is theoretically desirable. In the present context, the sources of stochastic variations are two-fold:

(1) the currency risk $S(t)$, and (2) volatility risk $V(t)$. Consequently, there are two option deltas to account for

$$\Delta_S(t,\tau;K) \equiv \frac{\partial C(t,\tau)}{\partial S} = e^{-r^*\tau} \Pi_1 \geq 0 \tag{11.24}$$

$$\Delta_V(t,\tau;K) \equiv \frac{\partial C(t,\tau)}{\partial V} = S(t)e^{-r^*\tau} \frac{\partial \Pi_1}{\partial V} - Ke^{-r\tau} \frac{\partial \Pi_2}{\partial V} > 0 \tag{11.25}$$

where $\frac{\partial \Pi_j}{\partial V} = \frac{1}{\pi} \int_0^\infty \mathrm{Re}\left[(i\phi)^{-1} e^{-i\phi \ln[K]} \frac{\partial f_j}{\partial V}\right] d\phi$. The analytical expressions for the deltas form a convenient basis for constructing delta-neutral and minimum variance hedges. To investigate how such hedges differ from the corresponding ones under the Garman-Kohlhagan currency option model, let us reexamine how to hedge a short position in a call option. As there are two sources of risk, consider a dynamic replicating portfolio consisting of (1) X_1 units of a call option with strike $\overline{K}$ and maturity $\overline{\tau}$ (to control for volatility risk) and (2) X_2 units of the foreign bond (denominated in the foreign currency) and (3) the remainder X_0 in cash. Write $G(t,\tau) = X_0 + X_1 C(t,\overline{\tau};\overline{K}) + X_2 S(t)e^{-r^*\tau}$. Then standard steps yield

$$X_1 \equiv \frac{\Delta_V(t,\tau;K)}{\Delta_V(t,\overline{\tau};\overline{K})} \tag{11.26}$$

$$X_2 \equiv \Delta_S(t,\tau;K) - \Delta_S(t,\overline{\tau};\overline{K}) \frac{\Delta_V(t,\tau;K)}{\Delta_V(t,\overline{\tau};\overline{K})} \tag{11.27}$$

and $X_0 = C(t,\tau) - X_1 C(t,\overline{\tau};\overline{K}) + X_2 S(t)e^{-r^*\tau}$. These positions can be exploited to empirically assess the effectiveness of delta-neutral hedging strategies such as the ones analyzed empirically in Bakshi, Cao, and Chen (1997, 1998). Readers are referred to their papers for further details.

Options on Higher Powers

The framework developed till now is also the key to understanding option contracts contingent on higher exchange rate powers (and moments). To pursue this topic, continue to assume that the exchange rate process is as described in Equations (11.15) and (11.16) and the interest rates at home and abroad are constants. Modify the payoff on the European option to the one shown

$$\hat{C}(t+\tau,0;K) = \max\left(0, \frac{S^{1-\alpha}(t+\tau)}{1-\alpha} - K\right) \tag{11.28}$$

for $-\infty < \alpha < \infty$ and $\hat{C}(t,\tau;K)$ stands for the price of the *asymmetric call option* with strike price K and term-to-expiration τ. The following special cases of the option payoff in (11.28) are appealing:

- When $\alpha \to 1$, the log contract of Neuberger (1994) is obtained as a special case;
- When $\alpha = -1$, we have an option on the second moment; when $\alpha = -2$, an option on the third moment (skewness); when $\alpha = -3$, an option on the fourth moment (kurtosis);
- When $\alpha = 0$, the plain vanilla option contract results.

In either case, the power option will be exercised when $\ln[S(t+\tau)] > \frac{1}{1-\alpha}\ln[(1-\alpha)K]$. The generic price of this option must be

$$\hat{C}(t,\tau) = E_t^Q\left\{e^{-r\tau}\max\left(0, \frac{1}{1-\alpha}S^{1-\alpha}(t+\tau) - K\right)\right\} \tag{11.29}$$

It is easy to verify that (11.29) satisfies the valuation PDE (11.17) subject to (11.28). The analytical solution to the conditional expectation (11.29) is given by

$$\hat{C}(t,\tau) = \frac{1}{1-\alpha}f(t,\tau;-i(1-\alpha))\Pi_1(t,\tau) - Ke^{-r\tau}\Pi_2(t,\tau) \tag{11.30}$$

and the risk-neutral probabilities are

$$\Pi_j(t,\tau) = \frac{1}{2} + \frac{1}{\pi}\int_0^\infty \text{Re}\left[\frac{e^{-\frac{i\phi}{1-\alpha}\ln[K(1-\alpha)]}\hat{f}_j(t,\tau;\phi)}{i\phi}\right]d\phi \tag{11.31}$$

for $j = 1, 2$, with the characteristic functions $\hat{f}_j(t,\tau)$ as displayed

$$\hat{f}_1(t,\tau;\phi) = \frac{f(t,\tau;\phi - i(1-\alpha))}{f(t,\tau;-i(1-\alpha))} \tag{11.32}$$

$$\hat{f}_2(t,\tau;\phi) = e^{r\tau} f(t,\tau;\phi) \tag{11.33}$$

where $f(t,\tau;\phi)$ is as previously displayed in Equation (11.20).

These options can be effective in positioning to variations in higher exchange rate moments. As the model price still depends on the parameter vector Φ and $V(t)$, the model implementation is straightforward.

Step 1. Use the quotes in the FX option markets to estimate Φ and $V(t)$.

Step 2. Use the closed-form option formula in (11.30) to compute the arbitrage-free price. The sensitivities with respect to price and volatility (the deltas) are analogously computable. That is,

$$\frac{\partial \hat{C}(t,\tau)}{\partial S} = \frac{\partial D}{\partial S}\Pi_1 + D(t,\tau)\frac{\partial \Pi_1}{\partial S} - Ke^{-r\tau}\frac{\partial \Pi_2}{\partial S} \geq 0 \tag{11.34}$$

$$\frac{\partial \hat{C}(t,\tau)}{\partial V} = \frac{\partial D}{\partial V}\Pi_1 + D(t,\tau)\frac{\partial \Pi_1}{\partial V} - Ke^{-r\tau}\frac{\partial \Pi_2}{\partial V} > 0 \tag{11.35}$$

which poses no difficulties. In hedging these more general claims, the positions (11.26) and (11.27) are still valid, except that they must be changed to account for a different α.

A CLASS OF EXOTIC FOREIGN EXCHANGE OPTIONS

Models of currency option pricing have other applications of interest. This section discusses two such applications in a stochastic volatility setting. First examined are quantity-adjusted options (quanto options) followed by a class of outperformance options.

Quanto Options

When investors in the United States purchase foreign equity options to hedge or speculate on equities, exposures in currency markets must invariably be dealt with. A U.S. hedge fund manager investing in the U.K. stock market, and desiring downside protection and unfavorable currency fluctuations at the same time now buy *quanto* put options. The quanto option will fix the pound/dollar conversion rate. To see the mechanics behind these options, let $q(t)$ denote the pound price of a stock/index traded in the United Kingdom and r^* the constant interest rate on a pound deposit. Suppose that

$$\frac{dq(t)}{q(t)} = r^* \, dt + \sigma_1 \sqrt{V(t)} \, d\omega_S(t) + \sigma_2 \sqrt{X(t)} \, d\omega_x(t) \tag{11.36}$$

$$\frac{dS(t)}{S(t)} = [r - r^*] dt + \sqrt{V(t)} \, d\omega_S(t) \tag{11.37}$$

$$dV(t) = [\theta_v - \kappa_v V(t)] dt + \sigma_v \sqrt{V(t)} \, d\omega_v(t) \tag{11.38}$$

$$dX(t) = [\theta_x - \kappa_x X(t)] dt + \sigma_x \sqrt{X(t)} \, d\omega_x(t) \tag{11.39}$$

where $S(t)$ is again the spot exchange rate.

Three comments are in order about spot exchange rate and equity price dynamics. First, the rate at which equities are appreciating under the risk-neutral measure is r^*. Second, the equity return volatility is

$$Var\left[\frac{dq(t)}{q(t)}\right] = \sigma_1^2 V(t) + \sigma_2^2 X(t)$$

with the exchange rate volatility, $V(t)$, and the equity volatility, $X(t)$, independent of one another. Having two factors driving equity volatility can induce a more plausible correlation structure between equity returns and the exchange rate depreciation. For example, component shock to equities, ω_x, is uncorrelated with ω_v and ω_S, and $\rho \equiv Cov_t(\omega_S, \omega_v)$. Third, κ_x, θ_x, and σ_x respectively control for the speed of mean-reversion, the mean, and the volatility of the process $X(t)$. By appropriating restricting the structural parameters, both $q(t)$ and $S(t)$ will follow geometric Brownian motions

$$\frac{dq(t)}{q(t)} = r^* dt + \sigma_q d\omega_q(t) \tag{11.40}$$

$$\frac{dS(t)}{S(t)} = [r - r^*] dt + \sigma_s d\omega_s(t) \tag{11.41}$$

which is a special case of corresponding one in (11.36) and (11.37).

Write the dollar price of the quanto option as $H(t,\tau; K_p)$ and let K_p be the strike price in pounds. The dollars payoff on the option must be

$$H(t + \tau, 0; K_p) = \bar{S} \max(q(t + \tau) - K_p, 0) \tag{11.42}$$

for some preset exchange rate $\bar{S}$. As this contract is hedged in pounds, two steps are followed to price this contract. First, convert the random dollar payoff (11.42) into pounds (dividing by $S(t + \tau)$) and value the transformed payoff from the perspective of the foreign investor (i.e., using r^* for discounting). In the next step, reconvert the pound price of option claim into a dollar price using the current spot exchange rate $S(t)$. We can show that the price of the quanto contract is

$$H(t,\tau) = S(t) \bar{S} \left\{ h(t,\tau; i, -i) \Pi_1(t,\tau) - K_p e^{-r^*\tau} \Pi_2(t,\tau) \right\} \tag{11.43}$$

where the expression in curly brackets represents the pound price of the option and

$$\Pi_j(t,\tau) = \frac{1}{2} + \frac{1}{\pi} \int_0^\infty \mathrm{Re} \left[\frac{e^{-i\varphi \ln[K_p]} h_j(t,\tau; \varphi)}{i\varphi} \right] d\varphi \qquad j = 1,2 \tag{11.44}$$

where the characteristic functions $h_1(t,\tau;\varphi)$ and $h_2(t,\tau;\varphi)$ are respectively

$$h_1(t,\tau;\varphi) = \frac{h(t,\tau;i,\varphi-i)}{h(t,\tau;i,-i)} \tag{11.45}$$

$$h_2(t,\tau;\varphi) = e^{r^*\tau}h(t,\tau;i,\varphi) \tag{11.46}$$

and defining the joint characteristic function of the state-price density

$$h(t,\tau;\phi,\varphi) = E_t^Q\left\{e^{-r^*\tau}e^{i\phi\ln[S(t+\tau)]+i\varphi\ln[q(t+\tau)]}\right\}$$

$$= \exp\left[-\frac{\theta_v}{\sigma_v^2}\left[(X_v+b_v)\tau+2\ln\left(1-\frac{(b_v+X_v)(1-e^{-X_v\tau})}{2X_v}\right)\right]\right.$$

$$-\frac{\theta_x}{\sigma_x^2}\left[(X_x+b_x)\tau+2\ln\left(1-\frac{(b_x+X_x)(1-e^{-X_x\tau})}{2X_x}\right)\right] \tag{11.47}$$

$$+\frac{c_v(1-e^{-X_v\tau})V(t)}{2X_v-(b_v+X_v)(1-e^{-X_v\tau})}+\frac{c_x(1-e^{-X_x\tau})X(t)}{2X_x-(b_x+X_x)(1-e^{-X_x\tau})}$$

$$\left.-r^*\tau+i\phi(r-r^*)\tau+i\varphi r+i\varphi\ln[q(t)]+i\phi\ln[S(t)]\right]$$

and $X_v=\sqrt{b_v^2-2\sigma_v^2c_v}$; $b_v\equiv i\phi\sigma_v\rho-\kappa_v$; $c_v\equiv\frac{1}{2}(i\phi)^2-\frac{1}{2}i\phi+\frac{1}{2}i\varphi(i\varphi-1)^2\sigma_1^2$ $-\varphi\phi\sigma_1$. By similarly defining $b_x\equiv i\varphi\sigma_x\sigma_2-\kappa_x$; $c_x\equiv\frac{1}{2}(i\varphi)^2\sigma_2^2-\frac{1}{2}i\varphi\sigma_2^2$ and $X_x\equiv\sqrt{b_x^2-2\sigma_x^2c_x}$ completes the pricing of quanto options under a general framework.

Outperformance Options

Let $S(t)$ and $P(t)$ denote the time-t values of the dollar/pound and the dollar/DM exchange rate. Entitling the option holder the maximum of the difference between the depreciation of the dollar/pound and the dollar/DM exchange rates and zero, the outperformance option has a notional *dollar* payoff: $\max\left(0,\frac{S(t+\tau)}{S(t)}-\frac{P(t+\tau)}{P(t)}\right)$. Observe that it makes sense to define the option payoff relative to the current exchange rates $S(t)$ and $P(t)$. The time-t option price must be

$$\overline{C}(t,\tau) = E_t^Q \left\{ e^{-r\tau} \max\left(0, \frac{S(t+\tau)}{S(t)} - \frac{P(t+\tau)}{P(t)} \right) \right\} \qquad (11.48)$$

To value the contract in (11.48), we need to specify variations in $S(t)$ and $P(t)$. Assume

$$\frac{dS(t)}{S(t)} = [r - r^*]dt + \sigma_s \sqrt{V(t)} d\omega_S(t) \qquad (11.49)$$

$$\frac{dP(t)}{P(t)} = [r - r^*]dt + \sigma_p \sqrt{V(t)} d\omega_P(t) \qquad (11.50)$$

$$dV(t) = [\theta_v - \kappa_v V(t)]dt + \sigma_v \sqrt{V(t)} d\omega_v(t) \qquad (11.51)$$

where r and r^* are again constants and $V(t)$ represents a common volatility factor. The correlation structure between shocks to $S(t)$, $P(t)$, and $V(t)$ is as follows. Denote $\rho_1 \equiv Cov_t(\omega_s, \omega_v)$, $\rho_2 \equiv Cov_t(\omega_p, \omega_v)$, and $\rho_3 \equiv Cov_t(\omega_s, \omega_p)$. It can be shown that the solution for this class of out-performance options is

$$\overline{C}(t,\tau) = \frac{1}{\pi} \int_0^\infty \mathrm{Re}\left[\frac{\bar{f}_1(t,\tau;\phi)}{i\phi} \right] d\phi - \frac{1}{\pi} \int_0^\infty \mathrm{Re}\left[\frac{\bar{f}_2(t,\tau;\phi)}{i\phi} \right] d\phi \qquad (11.52)$$

where the first characteristic function, $\bar{f}_1(t,\tau;\phi)$, has the form

$$\bar{f}_1(t,\tau;\phi) = \exp\left\{ -r^*\tau + \frac{\theta}{\sigma^2}\left[2ln\left(1 - \frac{[\vartheta_1 + \beta_1](1 - e^{-\vartheta_1\tau})}{2\vartheta_1} \right) \right] \right.$$
$$\left. + \frac{\theta}{\sigma^2}[\vartheta_1 + \beta_1]\tau + \frac{2\zeta_1(1 - e^{-\vartheta_1\tau})}{2\vartheta_1 - [\vartheta_1 + \beta_1](1 - e^{-\vartheta_1\tau})} V(t) \right\} \qquad (11.53)$$

with $\beta_1 \equiv \kappa_v - \frac{1}{2}(1 + i\phi)\sigma_s\sigma_v\rho_1 + \frac{1}{2}i\phi\sigma_p\sigma_v\rho_2$

$\vartheta_1 \equiv \sqrt{\beta_1^2 + 2\sigma_v^2\zeta_1}$

$\zeta_1 \equiv \frac{1}{2}(1 + i\phi)\sigma_s^2 - \frac{1}{2}i\phi\sigma_p^2 - \frac{1}{2}(1 + i\phi)^2\sigma_s^2 + \frac{1}{2}\phi^2\sigma_p^2 + (\phi - i)\phi\sigma_s\sigma_p\rho_3$

Similarly

$$\bar{f}_2(t,\tau;\phi) = \exp\left\{-r^*\tau + \frac{\theta}{\sigma^2}\left[2ln\left(1-\frac{[\vartheta_2+\beta_2](2-e^{-\vartheta_2\tau})}{2\vartheta_2}\right)\right]\right.$$

$$\left. + \frac{\theta}{\sigma^2}[\vartheta_2+\beta_2]\tau + \frac{2\zeta_2(1-e^{-\vartheta_2\tau})}{2\vartheta_2-[\vartheta_2+\beta_2](1-e^{-\vartheta_2\tau})}V(t)\right\}$$

(11.54)

where $\beta_2 \equiv \kappa_v - \frac{1}{2}i\phi\sigma_s\sigma_v\rho_1 - \frac{1}{2}(1-i\phi)\sigma_p\sigma_v\rho_2$

$\vartheta_2 \equiv \sqrt{\beta_1^2 + 2\sigma_v^2\zeta_2}$

$\zeta_2 \equiv \frac{1}{2}i\phi\sigma_s^2 + \frac{1}{2}(1-i\phi)\sigma_p^2 + \frac{1}{2}\phi^2\sigma_s^2 - \frac{1}{2}(1-i\phi)^2\sigma_p^2 - (i+\phi)\phi\sigma_s\sigma_p\rho_3$

The constant volatility case obtains when $\kappa_v = \theta_v = \sigma_v = 0$ and $V = 1$ for all t. Under these assumptions the characteristic functions $\bar{f}_1$ and $\bar{f}_2$ converge to that of the normal distribution. As in this option model, the characteristic functions are solely a function of $V(t)$, the spot price deltas and gammas are identically zero. Further

$$\frac{\partial \bar{C}(t,\tau)}{\partial V} = \frac{1}{\pi}\int_0^\infty Re\left[\frac{1}{i\phi}\frac{\partial \bar{f}_1}{\partial V}\right]d\phi - \frac{1}{\pi}\int_0^\infty Re\left[\frac{1}{i\phi}\frac{\partial \bar{f}_2}{\partial V}\right]d\phi$$

(11.55)

which can assume either sign.

CONCLUDING REMARKS

In this chapter, we have examined the pricing of foreign exchange contingent claims. In the model setup, the expected instantaneous percentage change in the exchange rate is always the instantaneous interest rate differential. Unlike in the Garman-Kohlhagan framework, exchange-rate volatility is assumed to change stochastically over time, which fundamentally alters the properties of the risk-neutral distribution of the exchange rate. Under realistic parameter values, this distribution is fat tailed, peaked at short maturities, and skewed to the left or the right (depending on the correlation between volatility and exchange-rate shocks). Such a distribution is in sharp contrast with the symmetric and slightly positively skewed lognormal distribution assumed in the Garman-Kohlhagan model. All the resulting valuation formulas are parsimonious with four structural parameters and expressed solely in terms of observable economic entities. Various useful derivatives for options such as delta, vega, rho, and gamma are analytically obtainable, making hedging and option trading strategies easily achievable in an internally consistent manner. One can back out the structural parameters from cross-sectional option prices, much like practitioners have been building implied volatility matrices and implied binomial trees. Furthermore, the new option formula inherits the intuitive structure of its constant-volatility counterpart: the call price is the spot exchange rate multiplied by the option delta minus the discounted strike price multiplied by a risk-neutral probability (for the call option to expire in-the-money). This chapter has outlined a starting point for more realistic currency option formulas than the extant ones in the literature.

ACKNOWLEDGMENTS

We thank Narasimhan Jegadeesh and Bruce Tuckman for their comments on this project.

REFERENCES

Bakshi, G., C. Cao, and Z. Chen. (1997). "Empirical Performance of Alternative Option Pricing Models," *Journal of Finance, 52,* 1003–1049.

Bakshi, G., C. Cao, and Z. Chen. (1998). "Pricing and Hedging Long-Term Options," *Journal of Econometrics* (forthcoming).

Bakshi, G. and Z. Chen. (1997). "Equilibrium Valuation of Foreign Exchange Claims," *Journal of Finance, 52*(2), 799–826.

Barone-Adesi, G. and R. Whaley. (1987). "Efficient Analytic Approximation of American Option Values," *Journal of Finance, 42,* 301–320.

Bates, D. (1995). "Testing Option Pricing Models," in G.S. Maddala and C.R. Rao (Eds.), *Handbook of Statistics, Volume 15: Statistical Methods in Finance.* Amsterdam: North Holland, pp. 567–611.

Bates, D. (1996). "Jumps and Stochastic Volatility: Exchange Rate Processes Implicit in Deutschemark Options," *Review of Financial Studies, 9*(1), 69–108.

Chesney, M. and L. Scott. (1989). "Pricing European Currency Options: A Comparison of the Modified Black-Scholes Model and a Random Variance Model," *Journal of Financial and Quantitative Analysis, 24,* 267–284.

Garman, M. and S. Kohlhagan. (1983). "Foreign Currency Option Values," *Journal of International Money and Finance, 2,* 231–237.

Grabbe, O. (1983). "The Pricing of Call and Put Options on Foreign Exchange," *Journal of International Money and Finance, 2,* 239–253.

Heston, S. (1993). "A Closed-Form Solution for Options with Stochastic Volatility with Applications to Bond and Currency Options, *Review of Financial Studies, 6,* 327–343.

Hull, J. and A. White. (1987). "The Pricing of Options with Stochastic Volatilities," *Journal of Finance, 42,* 281–300.

Margrabe, W. (1978). "The Value of an Option to Exchange one Asset for Another," *Journal of Finance, 33,* 177–186.

Melino, A. and S. Turnbull. (1990). "Pricing Foreign Currency Options with Stochastic Volatility, *Journal of Econometrics, 45,* 239–265.

Neuberger, A. (1994). "The Log Contract," *The Journal of Portfolio Management Bell, 20,* 74–80.

PART IV

Numerical
Valuation
Techniques

When term structure models first began to be used, there was a large premium placed on being able to obtain closed-form solutions for quantities of interest, like zero-coupon bond prices. At the time, this approach made sense. Without empirical work supporting the choice of less tractable models, there was little reason not to choose a model that provided closed form solutions. Without much experience in pricing derivatives, closed form results were extremely useful for building intuition about how prices and hedge ratios behave as a function of model inputs.

Today, general properties of many derivatives are widely understood. So, for these products, there is more of a premium on selecting the best possible model and more of a willingness to do without closed form solutions. As a result, efficient numerical procedures for calculating prices and hedge ratios have become more and more important.

The chapters in this part discuss the two categories of numerical approaches. Chapter 12 works with techniques to solve the partial differential equations inherent in contingent claim pricing. Chapter 13 reviews Monte Carlo techniques.

12

Exploring the Relation between Discrete-Time Jump Processes and the Finite Difference Method

Steve Heston and *Guofu Zhou*

Interest rate derivatives can be valued by various models, such as those of Vasicek (1977) and Cox, Ingersoll, and Ross (1985). However, in many cases and in more realistic models, numerical solutions have to be computed as no analytical solutions are available. Nelson and Ramaswamy (1990), among others, provide discrete-time models that approximate the continuous-time process. The advantage of the discrete-time models is that many interesting insights on a continuous-time model, such as how contingent claims can be hedged or spanned by using available assets, can be understood by taking the limits of certain discrete-time models. An additional advantage is that numerical solutions of the continuous-time model may be approximated by using the discrete-time ones.

An alternative approach to discrete-time models is the finite difference method. Based on the continuous-time model, the finite difference method approximates the valuation partial differential equation by an equation in terms of finite differences. Since both the discrete-time models and the finite difference method provide numerical solutions to the same continuous-time problem, it seems natural to expect that there may be interesting relations between the two approaches. In the context of options on stocks, Brennan and Schwartz (1978) appear the first to provide a jump process interpretation of the finite difference method.

This chapter explores the relation between the discrete-time process approximations and the finite difference method in the context of interest rate derivatives valuation. Our analysis of interest rate contingent claims addresses complexities that are not encountered in the valuation of equity options. When interest rates change through time, it is not clear whether one should discount using the beginning-of-period or the end-of-period interest rate. Also, interest rate processes must remain nonnegative, and may have zero variance (singular behavior) near the origin. This requires special boundary conditions for the approximating jump processes. By interpreting the finite difference method as certain jump process approximations, we obtain useful sights on the convergence and properties of the finite difference method. On the other hand, insights from the finite difference method allow us to provide a unified treatment of the boundary conditions imposed by interest derivatives. In contrast, from only the perspective of discrete-time process approximations, it is not an easy matter to specify such boundary conditions. Earlier studies, such as those of Nelson and Ramaswamy (1990), are shown to be incorrect by Tian (1992) and further by Li (1993). But from the perspective of the finite difference method, the correct boundary conditions are almost straightforward to specify. In addition, the linkage between the discrete-time process approximations and the finite difference method allows us to propose a new jump process approximation of the underlying interest rate process. In contrast with existing procedures, this is highly accurate. Its accuracy is a function of $1/n^2$, where n is the number of time steps, whereas existing methods only achieve $1/n$ accuracy.

We first provide a simple binomial motivation of both the continuous models and finite difference approximations. This is to pave the way for many practitioners, such as MBA graduates, to follow and understand later discussions. We then outline the finite difference method for valuing interest rate derivatives, and provide its jump process interpretations. Then, we show further how to obtain highly accurate discrete-time approximations to the continuous-time solution. The next section demonstrates how the jump process interpretations offer insights to specify interest rate boundary conditions. The section on pp. 360–363 provides numerical comparisons of the proposed methods with some of the existing ones.

LATTICE MODELS

Recent financial innovations give rise to interest rate derivatives ranging from simple options on yields to complicated structures such as yield-curve swaps. For simplicity, let $V(r,t)$ be a value of such a contingent claim that depends only on the interest rate and time. Our task is to determine $V(r,t)$. We start the analysis with a simple binomial model on the movement of the short-term interest rate. Assume that over a time interval of length (Δ), the period interest rate $r(t)$ may go up to

$$r(t + \Delta) = r(t) + \sigma\Delta \tag{12.1}$$

or go down to

$$r(t + \Delta) = r(t) - \sigma\Delta$$

where σ is a constant representing the volatility of the interest rate. If the respective risk-neutral probabilities are p and $(1 - p)$, the price of the contingent claim is simply its expected (risk-neutral) discounted value,

$$V(r(t),t) = \frac{pV\big(r(t) + \sigma\Delta, t + \Delta\big) + (1 - p)V\big(r(t) - \sigma\Delta, t + \Delta\big)}{1 + r(t)\Delta} \tag{12.2}$$

For example, $V(r,t)$ is the price of a 5-year zero-coupon bond. It is known that the price of the bond in year 5 is its face value. By dividing the time from today to the fifth year into periods of length Δ (say, $\Delta = 1/60$ for monthly periods), we can determine the bond's price today by using Equation (12.2) recursively (i.e., by solving back from the usual binomial tree).

In comparison with stock option valuations, the above procedure works almost exactly in the same way except that we assume now the interest rate moves over time as a binomial tree instead of the stock price. With this in mind, it is not surprising that the binomial model implies that the interest rate is assumed as a log-normal random walk. In other words, as the time length shrinks, the interest rate converges to a diffusion, which can be represented mathematically as

$$dr(t) = \sigma dz \tag{12.3}$$

where z is a Wiener process. In contrast to the usual stock price process underlying the Black-Scholes formula, Equation (12.3) contains no drift terms, and is a special case of Vasicek's (1997) model in the absence of mean-reversion. Unfortunately, the interest rate can become significantly negative in this case. To prevent this possibility, one might specify that $r(t) = x(t)^2$, where $x(t)$ follows the early binomial process or the random walk. Then the binomial tree for $r(t)$ becomes

$$r(t + \Delta) = \left(\sqrt{r(t)} + \sigma\sqrt{\Delta}\right)^2 = r(t) + 2\sigma r(t)\sqrt{\Delta} + \sigma^2\Delta \tag{12.4}$$

and

$$r(t + \Delta) = \left(\sqrt{r(t)} - \sigma\sqrt{\Delta}\right)^2 = r(t) - 2\sigma r(t)\sqrt{\Delta} + \sigma^2\Delta$$

As the time interval Δ shrinks, $r(t)$ converges to a diffusion process with drift σ^2 and volatility $2\sigma\sqrt{r(t)}$,

$$dr(t) = \sigma^2 dt + 2\sigma\sqrt{r(t)}\, dz \tag{12.5}$$

This is a special case of the Cox, Ingersoll, and Ross (1985) model without mean-reversion.

By using lattice approximations of the interest rate process with comparable mean and variance, we obtain two diffusions which are the continuous limits of the discrete models. Proceeding in similar fashion, one can generate many different diffusion processes for the interest rate. But this procedure is somewhat backward in motivation. Instead of starting with an arbitrary binomial model, one should start with a desired (diffusion) description of the interest rate behavior. For example, one might incorporate non-negative interest rate with mean-reversion easily into a diffusion. Then one can use an approximation to this process, which might be binomial or trinomial. The rest of this chapter shows how to start with a general diffusion process and generate accurate binomial and trinomial approximations.

THE CLASSIC EXPLICIT METHOD

Suppose the interest rate follows a diffusion process (in the risk-neutral probabilities)

$$dr = \mu(r)dt + \sigma(r)dz \tag{12.6}$$

where r denotes the instantaneous interest rate and z is a Wiener process. Contingent claims will be functions of r, and the value of a contingent claim, $V(r,t)$, satisfies the partial differential equation

$$\frac{1}{2}\sigma^2(r)V_{rr}(r,t) + \mu(r)V_r(r,t) - rV(r,t) + V_t(r,t) = 0 \tag{12.7}$$

where subscripts on the function V denote partial derivatives. One can approximate the derivatives by finite differences as follows

$$V_{rr}(r,t) \approx \frac{V(r+h,t) - 2V(r,t) + V(r-h,t)}{h^2}$$

$$V_{rr}(r,t) \approx \frac{V(r+h,t) - V(r-h,t)}{2h} \tag{12.8}$$

$$V_t(r,t) \approx \frac{V(r,t) - V(r,t-\Delta)}{\Delta}$$

Substituting these finite difference approximations into the partial differential equation and evaluating V at $(r, t - \Delta)$ yields the following approximation

$$V(r, t - \Delta) \approx \frac{p_1 V(r + h, t) + p_2 V(r, t) + p_3 V(r - h, t)}{1 + r\Delta} \tag{12.9}$$

where

$$p_1 = \frac{\sigma(r)\Delta}{2h^2} + \frac{\mu(r)}{2h}, \quad p_2 = 1 - \frac{\sigma(r)\Delta}{h^2}, \quad p_3 = \frac{\sigma(r)\Delta}{2h^2} - \frac{\mu(r)}{2h} \tag{12.10}$$

Equation (12.9) is similar to the classic explicit finite difference solution to partial differential Equation (12.7). In general, certain boundary conditions have to be imposed on (12.7) to obtain unique solutions, and these boundary conditions must also be incorporated into the finite difference approximation (12.9).

Following Brennan and Schwartz (1978), we interpret the finite difference method as discrete jump models of the interest rate process. There are at least two advantages for doing so. First, knowing how the jump process approximates the continuous-time diffusion process provides economic insights as to why the discrete-time solution converge to the continuous-time one. Second, the linkage between finite difference method and the jump process also helps to yield a unified (and correct) treatment of the boundary conditions.

The jump process interpretation of Equation (12.9) is straightforward. Equation (12.9) says that the value of V at an early time step is approximately a weighted average of adjacent values, discounted at the simple interest rate r. The weights can be interpreted as probabilities in a jump model of interest rates since they are positive (for normal and suitable choice of grid sizes), and sum to unity

$$p_1 + p_2 + p_3 = 1$$

In other words, the interest rate r can be thought of a three-point jump process, from today's level r to $r + h$, r, and $r - h$ next period with probability p_1, p_2, and p_3, respectively. To see why the finite difference method approximates the continuous-time diffusion, it is seen that the resulted jump process matches both the first and second moments of the continuous-time process,

$$p_1 \times h + p_2 \times 0 + p_3 \times (-h) = \mu(r)\Delta$$

$$p_1 \times h^2 + p_2 \times 0 + p_3 \times (-h)^2 = \sigma(r)\Delta$$

HIGH-ORDER METHODS

Although the jump models provide an intuitive interpretation, the finite difference approach helps to derive high-order or more accurate numerical solutions to the valuation equation. For example, to obtain high-order solutions, it is not clear at all from the perspective of jump processes that whether one should discount V in Equation (12.9) at the beginning-of-period interest rate, or the end-of-period interest rate, or perhaps an average interest rate. In contrast, the finite difference method provides a way to obtain suitable weights so that the resulted solution is of high-order accuracy.

To illustrate, consider the following form of valuation equation

$$V_t(z,t) = -\frac{1}{2}V_{zz}(z,t) + r(z,t)V(z,t) \tag{12.12}$$

Many term structure models, such as those of Vasicek (1977), Dothan (1978), Cox, Ingersoll, and Ross (1985), Longstaff (1989), and Black and Karasinski (1991), have valuation equations of this form after suitable transformations. For example, for Vasicek's (1977) model which many practitioners use to fit the actual yield curve, the valuation equation is

$$\frac{1}{2}\sigma^2 U_{rr}(r,s) + \kappa(\theta - r)U_r(r,s) - rU(r,s) + U_s(r,s) = 0 \tag{12.13}$$

The transformation $U(r,s) = V(z,t)$, $z = \sigma^{-1}(r-\theta)e^{\kappa s}$, and $t = (e^{2\kappa s} - 1)/(2\kappa)$ reduces this equation to the form of (12.12),

$$V_t(z,t) = -\frac{1}{2}V_{zz}(z,t) + (1+2\kappa t)^{-1}[\theta + \sigma(1+2\kappa t)^{-1/2}z]V(z,t) \tag{12.14}$$

For other models, such as Cox, Ingersoll, and Ross (1985) and Black and Karasinski (1991), similar transformations may apply (see Appendix 12.1).

To obtain highly accurate numerical solutions, the idea of the finite difference method is to expand the analytical solution with higher order terms. By using a second order Taylor series expansion, we can relate the value of V at time $t - \Delta$ to those at t as

$$V(z, t - \Delta) = V(z,t) - \Delta V_t(z,t) + \frac{\Delta^2}{2} V_{tt}(z,t) + O(\Delta^3) \qquad (12.15)$$

Now we want to solve $V_{tt}(z,t)$ in terms of finite differences. To do so, we first differentiate Equation (12.12) with respect to t to obtain

$$V_{tt}(z,t) = -\frac{1}{2} V_{zzt}(z,t) + [r(z,t)V(z,t)]_t \qquad (12.16)$$

Then, differentiating Equation (12.12) twice with respect to z and substituting the result, $V_{zzt} = V_{tzz} = -V_{zzzz}/2 + (rV)_{zz}$, into Equation (12.16), we have a useful expression for V_{tt},

$$V_{tt} = \frac{1}{4} V_{zzzz}(z,t) - \frac{1}{2} [r(z,t)V(z,t)]_{zz} + [r(z,t)V(z,t)]_t \qquad (12.17)$$

Based on Equations (12.15) and (12.17), our remaining task is to replace the derivatives of (12.15) by finite difference approximations and then solve for $V(z,t - \Delta)$. To do this, we denote by $\psi(V)$ the left-hand side of the following important finite difference approximation,

$$\frac{V(z + \sqrt{3\Delta}, t) - 2V(z,t) + V(z - \sqrt{3\Delta}, t)}{3\Delta} = V_{zz}(z,t) + \frac{\Delta}{4} V_{zzt}(z,t)$$
$$+ O(\Delta^2) \qquad (12.18)$$

Making use of (12.15) and (12.17), and the finite difference operator ψ, we obtain from (12.15) a complete discrete approximation to the valuation function,

$$V(z,t-\Delta) = V(z,t) + \frac{\Delta^2}{2}\psi(V)$$

$$-\frac{\Delta^2}{4}\left[\psi(rV) + \frac{r(z,t)V(z,t) - r(z,t-\Delta)V(z,t-\Delta)}{\Delta}\right] \quad (12.19)$$

$$+O(\Delta^3)$$

Solving (12.19) for $V(z,t-\Delta)$, we obtain a trinomial model for the contingent claim,

$$V(z,t-\Delta) = q_1 V(z + \sqrt{3\Delta}, t) + q_2 V(z,t) + q_3 V(Z - \sqrt{3\Delta}, t) + O(\Delta^3) \quad (12.20)$$

where

$$q_1 = \frac{1}{6}\frac{\dfrac{1 - r(z + \sqrt{3\Delta}, t)\Delta}{2}}{\dfrac{1 + r(z, t-\Delta)\Delta}{2}}$$

$$q_2 = \frac{2}{3}\frac{\dfrac{1 - r(z, t)\Delta}{2}}{\dfrac{1 + r(z, t-\Delta)\Delta}{2}}$$

$$q_3 = \frac{1}{6}\frac{\dfrac{1 - r(z - \sqrt{3\Delta}, t)\Delta}{2}}{\dfrac{1 + r(z, t-\Delta)\Delta}{2}}$$

Equation (12.20) is a trinomial model for the valuation of derivatives. It is easy to verify both theoretically and numerically that this trinomial model is highly accurate. The numerical error is of order Δ^2. In contrast, usual methods are only of order Δ.

Motivated by the trinomial model, a three point jump process that approximates the underlying diffusion can be proposed and the discrete-time solution is

$$V(z,t-\Delta) = p_1 D_1 V(z + \sqrt{3\Delta}, t) + d_2 D_2 V(z,t)$$

$$+ p_3 D_3 V(z - \sqrt{3\Delta}, t) \quad (12.21)$$

where

$$p_1 = \frac{1}{6} \qquad p_2 = \frac{2}{3} \qquad p_3 = \frac{1}{6} \tag{12.22}$$

and

$$D_1 = e^{-\frac{\left(r(z+\sqrt{3\Delta},t)+r(z,t-\Delta)\right)\Delta}{2}} \qquad D_2 = e^{-\frac{\left(r(z,t)+r(z,t-\Delta)\right)\Delta}{2}} \qquad D_3 = e^{-\frac{\left(r(z-\sqrt{3\Delta},t)+r(z,t-\Delta)\right)\Delta}{2}}$$

Equation (12.21) states that the current value is equal to its expected value under the "risk neutral probabilities," p_1, p_2, and p_3, and discounted back to today by the discount factors D_1, D_2, and D_3. In other words, the value of the derivative is computed by taking the interest rate as a three point, $z+\sqrt{3\Delta}$, z, and $z+\sqrt{3\Delta}$, jump process with jump probabilities p_1, p_2, and p_3.

There are several interesting aspects of the above discrete-time approximation to the continuous limit. First, it is highly accurate. In fact, it has the same high-order accuracy as the finite difference solution (12.20), following from the fact that $p_i D_i$ approximates q_i. Second, the discount factors have the economic interpretation that, in order to obtain highly accurate results, the future value should be discounted at the average interest rate of the current and future node. In contrast, many lattice models discount the future value only at the current interest rate, resulting in less accurate numerical solutions. Third, from the perspective of jump process approximations, there is no obvious reason why the finite difference solution should converge faster than existing procedures, or converge at all. But from the linkage between the two methods, insights on the convergence of (12.21) should help to understand the convergence of (12.20). Indeed, it is straightforward to show that

$$p_1 + p_2 + p_3 = 1$$

$$p_1 \times \sqrt{3\Delta} + p_2 \times 0 + p_3 \times \left(-\sqrt{3\Delta}\right) = 0$$

$$p_1 \times 3\Delta + p_2 \times 0 + p_3 \times (-3\Delta) = \Delta$$

$$p_1 \times \left(\sqrt{3\Delta}\right)^3 + p_2 \times 0 + p_3 \times \left(-\sqrt{3\Delta}\right)^3 = 0 \tag{12.23}$$

$$p_1 \times \left(\sqrt{3\Delta}\right)^4 + p_2 \times 0 + p_3 \times \left(-\sqrt{3\Delta}\right)^4 = 3\Delta^2$$

In other words, the proposed jump process matches the first four moments (actually five) of the normal distribution for z. Hence, from the perspective of jump process approximations, (12.21) should converge, so should (12.20). However, it is the insights of the finite difference method that motivates the jump process, and that shows theoretically it has the high-order rate of convergence.

Existing binomial or trinomial methods for interest contingent claims usually have a rate no better than Δ. This is because, applying the classic explicit finite difference methods with $\Delta_x = \sqrt{\Delta}$ to (12.12), one has a trinomial model similar to (12.20)

$$V(z,t-\Delta) = \frac{1}{2}V\left(z+\sqrt{\Delta},t\right) - r(z,t)\Delta V(z,t)$$
$$+ \frac{1}{2}V\left(z-\sqrt{\Delta},t\right) + O(\Delta^2) \tag{12.24}$$

but the local error is $O(\Delta^2)$, rather than $O(\Delta^3)$. It is observed that replacing $r(z,t)\Delta V(z,t)$ by $r(z,t-\Delta)\Delta V(z,t-\Delta)$ will not change the order of the local error. As a result, one obtains a binomial model with the same theoretical accuracy,

$$V(z,t-\Delta) = \frac{\frac{1}{2}V\left(z+\sqrt{\Delta},t\right) + \frac{1}{2}V\left(z-\sqrt{\Delta},t\right)}{1+r(z,t-\Delta)\Delta} + O(\Delta^2) \tag{12.25}$$

This is Heston's (1995) binomial model. However, the trinomial model (12.24) is not the one often used. Motivated from analogues to the trinomial model for stock options, Hull and White (1990) suggest the use of spacing $\Delta_x = \sqrt{3\Delta}$ in term structure models. With this spacing, it is easy to show that the trinomial model (12.24) becomes

$$V(z,t-\Delta) \approx \frac{1}{6}V\left(z+\sqrt{3\Delta},t\right) + \left(\frac{2}{3}-r(z,t)\right)\Delta V(z,t) + \frac{1}{6}V\left(z-\sqrt{3\Delta},t\right) \tag{12.26}$$

This is the trinomial model used by Hull and White (1990) and others.

BOUNDARY CONDITIONS

The previous sections derived a finite difference method that applies to the interior of a lattice. The associated jump process also holds only in the interior of this lattice. As pointed out earlier, certain boundary conditions have to be imposed on (12.7) to obtain unique solutions. However, it may not be an easy matter to lay out the right conditions for both the discrete-time and the continuous-time processes. Nelson and Ramaswamy (1990) develop a general procedure for determining the boundary conditions. However, as pointed out by Tian (1992), corrections have to be made to make their procedure work. Li (1993) further analyzes the problem.

By linking the finite difference method to the jump process, many aspects of the boundary conditions become apparent. As a result, we can obtain a unified treatment of the boundary conditions. To illustrate, consider the square-root process of Cox, Ingersoll, and Ross (1985), where $\mu(r) = \kappa(\theta - r)$ and $\sigma(r) = \sigma\sqrt{r}$. Then, the valuation Equation (12.7) becomes

$$\frac{1}{2}\sigma^2 r V_{rr}(r,t) + \kappa(\theta - r)V_r(r,t) - rV(r,t) + V_t(r,t) = 0 \qquad (12.27)$$

This partial differential equation is numerically ill-posed because the second order derivative vanishes at the origin. To eliminate the problem, we make the transformation $V(r,t) = U(x,t)$ and $x = \sqrt{r}$, then Equation (12.27) can be written as

$$\frac{1}{2}\sigma^2 U_{xx}(x,t) + \left(\frac{\kappa\theta - \sigma^2}{2x} - \frac{\kappa x}{2} \right) U_x(x,t) - x^2 U(x,t) + U_t(x,t) = 0 \qquad (12.28)$$

As shown by Feller (1951), the process can reach zero only if $\kappa\theta < \sigma^2/4$. Otherwise the origin is inaccessible and the interest rate will never reach zero. In this case, it is not possible to impose boundary conditions on the partial differential equation. Whether or not the origin is accessible, the "natural" boundary condition that the derivatives of $V(r,t)$ remain bounded in Equation (12.27) is

$$\kappa\theta V_r(0,t) + V_t(0,t) = 0 \tag{12.29}$$

In terms of the transformed Equation (12.28), this condition is

$$U_x(0,t) = 0 \tag{12.30}$$

This is the condition for a reflecting boundary, where the (square root of the) interest rate "bounces" off the origin, ensuring that interest rates are almost always positive. From the perspective of the finite difference method, the reflecting condition (12.30) is easily implemented by letting

$$U(0,t) = U(h,t) \tag{12.31}$$

for some small enough h. In fact, this is equivalent to the reflecting condition proposed by Tian (1992), but motivated from discrete-time process approximations.

Alternatively, one can derive yet another boundary condition by using a finite difference approximation to the boundary condition (12.29). Substituting the finite difference derivative

$$V_r(0,t) \approx \frac{V(r+h,t) - V(0,t)}{h} \tag{12.32}$$

into (12.29) gives an approximation for the boundary value that is easy to program

$$V(0,t-\Delta) = \frac{\kappa\theta\Delta}{h} V(h,t) + \left(1 - \frac{\kappa\theta\Delta}{h}\right) V(0,t) \tag{12.33}$$

Intuitively, Equation (12.33) is the expected value for a discrete jump process with no discounting since the interest rate is zero. This jump process approximates the diffusion process (12.6) by making $r(t) - r(t-\Delta)$ have a mean $\kappa\theta\Delta$ over the time interval Δ, while $r(t) - r(t-\Delta)$ has a variance that is close to zero. Interestingly, this two-point process, motivated in a rather different perspective, performs the same task as the three point process of Li (1993) which exactly matches the mean and variance.

NUMERICAL RESULTS

Finally, it is of interest to show the numerical accuracy of the proposed jump process and compare it with existing methods, such as Heston's (1995) binomial model and Hull and White's (1990) trinomial one. We consider first the valuation of a zero-coupon bond in Vasicek's (1977) model, where the instantaneous interest rate, $r(z,t)$, follows a mean-reverting process

$$dr = \kappa(\theta - r)dt + \sigma dz \tag{12.34}$$

where κ, θ, and σ are parameters of the model, and dz is the standard Gaussian-Wiener process. Let $\kappa = 0.15$, $\theta = 0.054$, and $\sigma = 0.0418$. These are not unreasonable values for the parameters. Suppose the current rate is $r_0 = 6\%$. We compute the price of a zero-coupon bond with face value 1 and maturity 5 and 15 years, respectively.

The results are provided in Table 12.1. The first column is $n = T/\Delta$, the number of periods in the discrete-time models with T the time to maturity of the bond. There are three models. The first one is Heston's binomial model (12.25). The second is the trinomial finite difference model (12.26), and the third is the proposed jump process model (12.21). The second column of the table is the analytical price given by Vasicek, and the rest of the columns are the errors and error ratios of the three discrete-time models. Consider the 5-year bond first. The results are in the first panel of the table. For all of the three methods, the accuracy improves as the number of periods, n, increases. But it is clear that the jump process is by far the most accurate. For the periods considered, the first two approaches achieve only up to the fourth and fifth digit accuracy, whereas the jump process reaches the seventh digit accuracy. However, the accuracy itself is not a measure for the rate of convergence. Theoretically, if both the binomial and the trinomial models are of first-order accuracy (the numerical error is proportional to $1/n$), the ratios (of the errors of the successive solutions) should be close to two. Indeed, the ratios behave so nicely that they are almost exactly equal to 2 for all the n's. In the jump model case, it is also remarkable that the ratios are virtually four, confirming our earlier analysis that it has a second-order rate of convergence (the numerical error is proportional to $1/n^2$). Interestingly, the jump process obtains the fourth digit

TABLE 12.1. Vasicek Model

n	Exact	Binomial	Error Ratio	Trinomial	Error Ratio	New Jump Process	Error Ratio
5-Year Bond							
10	0.76370227	-0.01745277		-0.00193621		-0.00193621	
20	0.76370227	-0.00848389	2.05716694	0.00416542	2.14157443	-0.00049113	3.94238224
40	0.76370227	-0.00417507	2.03203546	0.00198883	2.09440690	-0.00012325	3.98477539
80	0.76370227	-0.00207019	2.01675282	0.00096802	2.05454370	-0.00003084	3.99609392
160	0.76370227	-0.00103070	2.00853888	0.00047701	2.02932204	-0.00000771	3.99920588
320	0.76370227	-0.00051424	2.00430919	0.00023671	2.01520789	-0.00000193	3.99924511
640	0.76370227	-0.00025684	2.00216256	0.00011790	2.00774044	-0.00000048	4.00051018
1280	0.76370227	-0.00012835	2.00108375	0.00005883	2.00390761	-0.00000012	3.99930617
15-Year Bond							
10	0.54962515	-0.28677911		-0.25970819		-0.25970819	
20	0.54962515	-0.18868225	1.51990511	0.03477173	1.95814830	-0.12419112	2.09119778
40	0.54962515	-0.10658437	1.77026198	0.01381484	2.51698463	-0.04763388	2.60720119
80	0.54962515	-0.05376976	1.98223632	0.00316221	4.36872511	-0.01511569	3.15128638
160	0.54962515	-0.02589147	2.07673613	-0.00064490	-4.90341992	-0.00419045	3.60717557
320	0.54962515	-0.01247378	2.07567110	-0.00125312	0.51463614	-0.00108442	3.86423048
640	0.54962515	-0.00609016	2.04818741	-0.00093576	1.33914200	-0.00027374	3.96153297
1280	0.54962515	-0.00300534	2.02644716	-0.00055765	1.67804311	-0.00006861	3.99001801

Note: This table provides the price of a zero-coupon bond with face value 1 and maturity 5 and 15 years, respectively. The first column is the number of periods of the discrete-time models. The second column is the exact price given by Vasicek's (1977) formula in which the instantaneous interest rate follows a mean-reverting process, $dr = \kappa(\theta - r)dt + \sigma dz$ where the parameters are $\kappa = 0.150$, $\theta = 0.054$, $\sigma = 0.0418$, and $r_0 = 6\%$. The remaining columns are the error and the ratio of the errors of the three discrete-time models: the binomial model, the trinomial model. and the new jump model.

TABLE 12.2. CIR Model

n	Exact	Binomial	Error Ratio	Trinomial	Error Ratio	New Jump Process	Error Ratio
5-Year Bond							
10	0.76340936	-0.00655702		-0.00044279		-0.00044279	
20	0.76340936	-0.00322681	2.03204151	0.00711609	2.01899450	-0.00011104	3.98747610
40	0.76340936	-0.00160006	2.01668273	0.00354038	2.00997877	-0.00002778	3.99688895
80	0.76340936	-0.00079665	2.00849207	0.00176570	2.00508514	-0.00000695	3.99898948
160	0.76340936	-0.00039747	2.00428460	0.00088172	2.00256331	-0.00000174	3.99938522
320	0.76340936	-0.00019852	2.00214819	0.00044058	2.00128572	-0.00000043	4.00033222
640	0.76340936	-0.00009921	2.00107961	0.00022022	2.00064465	-0.00000011	3.99828525
1280	0.76340936	-0.00004959	2.00053715	0.00011009	2.00032225	-0.00000003	3.99979350
15-Year Bond							
10	0.51104756	-0.06094798		-0.01845517		-0.01845517	
20	0.51104756	-0.03011104	2.02410761	0.04784980	1.99058635	-0.00517390	3.56697710
40	0.51104756	-0.01474157	2.04259313	0.02363224	2.02476766	-0.00134310	3.85219693
80	0.51104756	-0.00726640	2.02873077	0.01169814	2.02017036	-0.00033910	3.96077637
160	0.51104756	-0.00360452	2.01591528	0.00581528	2.01162020	-0.00008496	3.99111582
320	0.51104756	-0.00179482	2.00829089	0.00289879	2.00610693	-0.00002125	3.99827157
640	0.51104756	-0.00089552	2.00422143	0.00144714	2.00311489	-0.00000531	3.99999723
1280	0.51104756	-0.00044728	2.00212882	0.00072300	2.00157142	-0.00000133	4.00032966

Note: This table provides the price of a zero-coupon bond with face value 1 and maturity 5 and 15 years, respectively. The first column is the number of periods of the discrete-time models. The second column is the exact price given by the Cox, Ingersoll, and Ross (CIR, 1985) formula in which the instantaneous interest rate follows the square-root process, $dr = \kappa(\theta - r)dt + \sigma\sqrt{r}dz$ where the parameters are $\kappa = 0.150$, $\theta = 0.054$, $\sigma = 0.180$, and $r_0 = 6\%$. The remaining columns are the error and the ratio of the errors of the three discrete-time models: the binomial model, the trinomial model, and the new jump model.

accuracy with n as small as 20. In contrast, the same accuracy has to take $n = 320$ to achieve for the Heston's binomial model, and $n = 160$ for the classic trinomial model. For the 15-year bond, the same observations hold as seen from the results in the second panel of the table. However, as the maturity lengthens, it requires a larger n to obtain the same accuracy. In addition, the ratios for the trinomial model are not as stable as previously. But it is seen that they are closer to two as n approaches 1280. It is also easy to verify that they get even closer as n increases beyond 1280. In contrast, the ratios of both the binomial method and the jump process still behave very nicely, which are almost 2 and 4 as suggested by theory.

For comparison, we also consider the valuation of the same zero coupon bond in the Cox, Ingersoll, and Ross (1985) model, where the instantaneous interest rate, $r(z,t)$ follows the square-root process

$$dr = \kappa(\theta - r)dt + \sigma\sqrt{r}dz \qquad (12.35)$$

where κ, θ, and σ are parameters of the model, and dz is the standard Gaussian-Wiener process. Let $\kappa = 0.15$, $\theta = 0.054$, $\sigma = 0.18$, and $r_0 = 6\%$. The results are provided in Table 12.2. As the case in Vasicek's (1977) model, the methods converge to the continuous-time solution as n increases. Although the binomial and the trinomial models should converge at the same rate, the numerical results show that the binomial model performs better in the Cox, Ingersoll, and Ross model despite the fact that it uses less information than the trinomial model. In contrast, the trinomial model has higher numerical accuracy in the Vasicek model. However, either in the Vasicek model or the Cox, Ingersoll, and Ross model, the proposed jump process has the best numerical accuracy, consistent with its high-order rate of convergence. The higher rate of convergence is clearly confirmed by the ratios which are remarkably close to four. In contrast, the ratios of both the binomial and trinomial models are very close to two.

CONCLUSIONS

This chapter explores the relation between the discrete-time process approximations and the finite difference method in interest rate derivatives models. We interpret the finite difference method as a suitable interest rate jump process. Insights from the analysis of the relation and the interpretation allow easy treatment of boundary conditions encountered for valuing interest rate derivatives. In addition, they allow us to obtain highly accurate numerical solutions for the valuation equation of interest rate derivatives. Numerical examples are provided to demonstrate the procedures and their potential applications. However, our studies are focused mainly on the explicit finite difference method. One can extend these results to implicit finite difference methods and multiple dimensions.

APPENDIX 12.1

TRANSFORMATIONS TO THE
STANDARD VALUATION EQUATION

The high-order methods assume a standard valuation equation of the following form

$$V_t(z,t) = -\frac{1}{2}V_{zz}(z,t) + r(z,t)V(z,t) \tag{12.36}$$

It is shown that the valuation equation of the Vasicek's (1977) model can be transformed into this form. In this appendix, we show how to do such transformations for the valuation equations of Cox, Ingersoll, and Ross's (1985) and Black and Karasinski's (1991) models, a special case of the latter is Dothan's (1978).

For the following type of the Cox, Ingersoll, and Ross's (1985) square-root model,

$$dr = \left(\frac{1}{4}\sigma^2 - \beta r\right)dt + \sigma\sqrt{r}\,dz$$

the valuation equation is

$$\frac{1}{2}\sigma^2 r U_{rr} + \left(\frac{1}{4}\sigma^2 - \beta r\right)U_r - rU + U_s = 0$$

The transformation $U(r,s) = V(z,t)$, $z = 2\sigma^{-1}e^{\beta s/2}r^{1/2}$, $t = (e^{\beta s} - 1)/\beta$ reduces this equation to

$$V_z(z,t) = \frac{1}{2}V_{zz}(z,t) + \frac{1}{4}\sigma^2(1+\beta t)^{-2}z^2V(z,t)$$

which is a special case of Equation (12.36).

The constant version of Black and Karasinski's (1991) model has the following form,

$$dx = \kappa(\theta - x)dt + \sigma dz$$

with $r = e^x$. The associated valuation equation is

$$\frac{1}{2}\sigma^2 U_{xx} + \kappa(\theta - x)U_x - e^x U + U_s = 0$$

A transformation similar to Equation (12.14), $U(x,s) = V(z,t)$, $z = \sigma^{-1}(r - \theta)e^{\kappa s}$, $t = (e^{2\kappa s} - 1)/(2\kappa)$, gives rise to

$$V_t = -\frac{1}{2}V_{zz} + (1+2\kappa t)^{-1}e^{\theta + \sigma(1+2\kappa t)^{-1/2}z}V$$

When the parameters are time-dependent, a similar time-dependent transformation applies.

ACKNOWLEDGMENTS

We are grateful to the editors, Bruce Tuckman and Narasimhan Jegadeesh, for helpful discussions and comments.

REFERENCES

Black, F. and P. Karasinski. (1991). "Bond and Option Pricing When Short Rates Are Lognormal," *Financial Analysts Journal* (July–August), 52–59.

Brennan, M.J. and E.S. Schwartz. (1978). "Finite Difference Methods and Jump Processes Arising in the Pricing of Contingent Claims: A Synthesis," *Journal of Financial and Quantitative Analysis, 13,* 461–474.

Cox, J.C., J.E. Ingersoll, and S. Ross. (1985). "A Theory of the Term Structure of Interest Rates," *Econometrica, 53,* 385–407.

Dothan, M. (1978). "On the Term Structure of Interest Rates," *Journal of Financial Economics, 7,* 229–264.

Feller, W. (1951). "Two Singular Diffusion Problems," *Annals of Mathematics, 54,* 173–182.

Heston, S. (1995). "Discrete Versions of Continuous-Time Interest Rate Models," *Journal of Fixed Income, 5,* 86–88.

Hull, J. and A. White. (1990). "Valuing Derivative Securities Using the Explicit Finite Difference Method," *Journal of Financial and Quantitative Analysis, 25,* 87–99.

Li, A. (1993). "Binomial Approximations of Singular Diffusion Models," *Journal of Financial Engineering, 2,* 443–465.

Longstaff, F.A. (1989). "A Nonlinear General Equilibrium Model of the Term Structure of Interest Rates," *Journal of Financial Economics, 23,* 195–224.

Nelson, D.B. and K. Ramaswamy. (1990). "Simple Binomial Processes as Diffusion Approximations in Financial Models," *Review of Financial Studies, 3,* 393–430.

Tian, Y. (1992). "A Simplified Binomial Approach to the Pricing of Interest-Rate Contingent Claims," *Journal of Financial Engineering 1,* 14–37.

Vasicek, O. (1977). "An Equilibrium Characterization of the Term Structure," *Journal of Financial Economics, 5,* 177–188.

13

Monte Carlo Methods for the Valuation of Interest Rate Securities

Leif Andersen and *Phelim P. Boyle*

This chapter examines the application of the Monte Carlo method to the valuation of interest rate securities. The Monte Carlo method has proved to be a powerful and flexible computational tool for numerical problems in modern finance. It is often convenient to model the prices of the basic securities and the underlying state variables as continuous time stochastic processes. From the no-arbitrage assumption it is well known (see Duffie, 1996) that the price of a generic derivative security, suitably normalized, forms a martingale with respect to a particular probability measure known as *the equivalent martingale measure*. Thus, we can write the current price of the security in terms of an expectation. In many cases, the expectation is taken over several state variables and thus it can be expressed as a multidimensional integral. This formulation leads naturally to the use of the Monte Carlo method. The higher the dimension of the problem the more appealing the Monte Carlo method becomes as compared to other numerical methods.

The earliest application of the Monte Carlo method in finance is due to Boyle (1977). He used a Monte Carlo simulation approach to value options on dividend paying stocks. In recent years, Monte Carlo methods have gained significantly in popularity, their flexibility making them ideal to handle exotic securities and models with complicated dynamics. In particular, there is currently significant interest in the application of Monte Carlo methods to problems involving stochastic interest rates. This interest is driven partly by the path-dependent dynamics of many modern fixed-income models and partly by the introduction of highly structured fixed-income derivatives. For instance, the pricing of some mortgage-backed securities requires numerical evaluations of large-scale multidimensional integrals with dimensions as high as 360. Stochastic interest rate models are required to value these instruments.

One can distinguish between two different types of interest rate models. First, we have models based on the evolution of the short-term or instantaneous interest rate process. Models of this genre include the well-known Vasicek model and the one factor Cox, Ingersoll, and Ross model. The main advantage of these one-factor models lies in their tractability and we will use them to illustrate various aspects of the Monte Carlo method. Since simple closed-form solutions are available for many types of securities under these models we can often benchmark the accuracy of our answers. In practice we would not need to use the Monte Carlo method if we have the exact solution available but these simple models serve to illustrate many important concepts.

The second type of interest rate model is based on modeling the dynamic evolution of forward rates. The first model of this type was developed by Ho and Lee (1986) but the major advance is due to Heath, Jarrow, and Morton (HJM, 1992). The HJM approach models the entire forward rate curve as a multidimensional stochastic process. One of the advantages of this approach is that it naturally reproduces the initial yield curve at inception. Except for a few special cases (see, e.g., Jamshidian, 1991; Ritchken & Sankarasubramanian, 1995), the HJM model gives rise to non-Markovian evolution of the forward curve. As such, Monte Carlo simulation is frequently the method of choice for numerical evaluations in the HJM framework.

Monte Carlo implementations of the HJM model are described in, for example, Carverhill and Pang (1995), and Turnbull (1997). Recently, Miltersen, Sandmann, and Sondermann (1997); Jamshidian (1997); and Brace, Gatarek, and Musiela (1997) have suggested a useful modification of the HJM model, the so-called *market model*. In this framework, the instantaneous forward rates of the HJM model are replaced by discretely compounded (Libor) forward rates. Besides causing certain useful improvements in model stability, the market model conveniently price caps or swaptions according to market conventions. Glasserman and Zhao (1998) discuss the implementation of the market model.

In the present chapter, we restrict ourselves to one-factor short-rate models. Short-rate models require much less development of notation than forward-rate models, yet illustrate many of the problems encountered in implementing simulation schemes for such models. For expositional purposes, we will only consider the valuation of pure discount bonds. While this instrument might appear straightforward, it is in fact "path-dependent" in the sense that it requires evaluation of a path-integral of the short rate. To value discount bond prices in a short-rate model, we discretize time to maturity and devise schemes to perturb the short rate through time and approximate its distribution. There are two sources of numerical error in this approximation. There is a systematic bias due to the imperfect discretization of the short-rate process and a statistical error arising from the Monte Carlo simulations. We analyze the nature of these two errors and discuss methods to reduce their impact.

The next section describes how the price of a pure discount bond may be written as the expectation of the path integral of the short-term interest rate. This expectation can be evaluated using the Monte Carlo method and we provide a brief summary of the method. We then discuss the discretization of the short-rate process and the two different errors that arise when we use the Monte Carlo method to estimate prices of derivatives in this setting. These errors arise from the discretization procedure used and from the sampling error associated with simulation. Next we discuss the first-order discretization scheme, known as the Euler scheme, in the context of the Vasicek model and find an exact expression for the bias in the bond price that arises from the discretization in this case. We then examine the accurate discretization of the Vasicek model and demonstrate that the accuracy of the bond price estimate is improved when we employ the accurate discretization procedure. We follow with a discussion of the simulation of bond prices under the Cox, Ingersoll, and Ross model. Next we discuss discretization schemes of orders two and above, followed by a discussion of different methods that can be used to control the variance of the bond price estimator, including antithetic sampling, control variates, and moment matching. We then review some recent advances in the application of importance sampling, and conclude the chapter.

MODELS BASED ON THE SHORT-TERM INTEREST RATE

In this section, we describe how the Monte Carlo method can be used to value a pure discount bond. We will see that this involves the approximation of a path-dependent integral. The price at time t, of the pure discount bond which matures at time $(t + T)$, can be written as

$$B(t, t+T) = E_Q\left\{e^{-\int_t^{t+T} r(s)ds} \mid I_t\right\}$$ (13.1)

where r denotes the instantaneous short-term rate of interest (the short rate) and I_t is the information revealed up to time t. The expectation is taken under the Q-measure or the risk neutral measure. Often in the sequel we will simply use the expectation operator E instead of E_Q. To evaluate (13.1), it suffices, in principle, that the stochastic process for $r(t)$ (under Q) is known. A reasonable—and certainly parsimonious—starting point for an interest-rate model is to write down the process for $r(t)$ directly, typically as an Ito process or as the solution to a stochastic differential equation (SDE). Two of the most popular short-rate models are the Vasicek (1977) model and the one-factor Cox, Ingersoll, and Ross (CIR) (1985) model. Under the Vasicek model, the risk neutral[1] stochastic process for the short rate is

$$dr(t) = \kappa(\theta - r(t))dt + \sigma_v dW_t$$ (13.2)

---

[1] The risk neutral process for the interest rate is constructed from the real world process by removing the market price of interest-rate risk from the drift term. For a discussion of this issue see Cox, Ingersoll, and Ross (1985).

where κ, θ, and σ_v are constants and W is a standard Brownian motion. The interest rate can become negative in this model but in spite of this drawback, the Vasicek model is often used because it leads to simple closed-form solutions for the prices of many types of instruments. As shown by Hull and White (1990), the analytic tractability of the Vasicek model stays intact even if the parameters in (13.2) are allowed to be deterministic functions of time.

Under the one factor CIR model, the risk neutral stochastic process for the short rate is

$$dr(t) = \kappa(\theta - r(t))dt + \sigma\sqrt{r(t)}\,dW_t \tag{13.3}$$

where κ, θ, and σ are constants and W is a standard Brownian motion. We assume that $2\kappa\theta \geq \sigma^2$, since this condition ensures that the short rate cannot reach zero (see CIR, 1985, for details).

For both the Vasicek and the CIR models, the integral in Equation (13.1) for the bond price has a closed-form solution. For more general specifications of the interest-rate process, such closed-form solutions may not exist and one must rely on numerical methods. We shall use the pure discount bond contract as a generic example to illustrate the application of the Monte Carlo method. We apply the method to cases where we know the exact answer since the accurate answer provides a benchmark to assess the accuracy of the method. We first recall some features of the Monte Carlo method.[2]

Suppose we wish to evaluate a K-dimensional integral of the function f using the Monte Carlo approach. Assume the domain of integration has been normalized to be the unit hypercube $[0,1]^K$. The objective is to approximate the integral

$$\int_{[0,1]^K} f(u)\,du$$

We generate N independent and identical random numbers that are uniformly distributed throughout the unit hypercube $\{x_1, x_2, \ldots,$

---

[2] The survey paper by Boyle, Broadie, and Glasserman (1997) provides an overview of the Monte Carlo method and its application to problems in finance. While many of the examples in their paper assume the underlying assets are stocks, several of the concepts are also useful in dealing with interest-rate derivatives.

x_N}. In practice, these numbers are generated using a computer and are more accurately described as *pseudo random* numbers. The Monte Carlo estimate of the integral is given by

$$\hat{f} = \frac{1}{N} \sum_{1}^{N} f(x_n)$$

(13.4)

This estimate is a random variable but it will tend to the true value as N becomes large by the law of large numbers. From the central limit theorem, the distribution of the estimate tends to normality as N gets large and so we are able to generate confidence intervals. Indeed the error is proportional to $\frac{1}{\sqrt{N}}$ and this error bound is independent of the dimension, K, of the problem. The required regularity conditions on the function f are relatively mild. All that is needed is that the function be square integrable.

SIMULATING THE SHORT-RATE PROCESS USING THE EULER APPROXIMATION

In this section, we illustrate how to estimate the pure discount bond price by simulating the first-order discrete approximation to the interest-rate process. The key idea is to approximate the stochastic differential equation for the short-term interest rate by its first-order Taylor approximation. Suppose the stochastic differential equation for the short-term interest rate is

$$dr(t) = a(r(t),t)dt + b(r(t),t)dW_t$$

(13.5)

We divide the interval $[0,T]$ into K equal intervals of length h. The *Euler scheme* approximates the continuous time stochastic differential Equation (13.5) by the following set of equations

$$\hat{r}_{k+1} - \hat{r}_k = a(\hat{r}_k, t_k)h + b(\hat{r}_k, t_k)z_{k+1}\sqrt{h}$$

(13.6)

where

$$k = 0, 1, \cdots (K-1), \qquad t_0 = t, \cdots t_K = (t+T), \qquad \hat{r}_0 = r(t)$$

and the zs are independent standard normal variates.[3] Note that Equation (13.6) only provides an approximation for the distribution of $\hat{r}_{k+1}$. In a sense that will be quantified shortly, the approximation becomes more precise as h tends to zero.

To generate a single interest-rate path using this approximation, we draw K normal variates. From this path set, we can approximate the inner integral in Equation (13.1) using, for example, the trapezoidal rule (see Press, Flannery, Teukolsky, and Vetterling, 1986).[4] Let the values of the short rate along this path be

$$\{\hat{r}_0, \cdots, \hat{r}_K\}$$

The trapezoidal approximation to the bond price (13.1) based on the first path is

$$\exp\left[-\left(\frac{\hat{r}_0 + \hat{r}_K}{2} + \sum_{j=1}^{K-1} \hat{r}_j\right)h\right] \tag{13.7}$$

As is well-known, the trapezoidal rules converges quadratically in h (i.e., is $O(h^2)$). Using our trapezoid approximation for the bond price, suppose we now simulate a total of N K-dimensional short-rate paths. Let $f(h,n)$ denote the sample bond price of path n. The Monte Carlo estimate of the price of the pure discount bond will be denoted by $\hat{B}_{K,N}(t, t+T)$ where

$$\hat{B}_{K,N}(t, t+T) = \frac{\sum_{n=1}^{N} f(h,n)}{N} \tag{13.8}$$

The difference between this estimate and the true bond price

$$\hat{\varepsilon} = \hat{B}_{K,N}(t, t+T) - B(t, t+T) \tag{13.9}$$

---

[3] As in practice the generation of the zs is generally based on samples from uniform distributions on [0,1], notice how a short-rate path with K observation dates corresponds to a random point in the K-dimensional hypercube.

[4] As shown in Andersen (1995), another approach is to write down the SDE for the path-integral and work with a two-dimensional vector SDE.

represents the error in the Monte Carlo estimate. This error can be decomposed into two components, the *systematic error* and the *statistical error*. We write

$$\hat{\varepsilon} = \hat{B}_{K,N}(t, t+T) - B(t, t+T)$$

$$= E_Q[\hat{B}_{K,N}(t, t+T)] - B(t, t+T) + \hat{B}_{K,N}(t, t+T) - E_Q[\hat{B}_{K,N}(t, t+T)]$$

$$= \varepsilon_{sys} + \hat{\varepsilon}_{stat}$$

where

$$\varepsilon_{sys} = E_Q[\hat{B}_{K,N}(t, t+T)] - B(t, t+T)$$

and

$$\hat{\varepsilon}_{stat} = \hat{B}_{K,N}(t, t+T) - E_Q[\hat{B}_{K,N}(t, t+T)]$$

Holding K fixed, we know from the previous discussion that the variance of the statistical error $\hat{\varepsilon}_{stat}$ will approach zero (with convergence order $N^{-\frac{1}{2}}$) as N tends to infinity. The systematic error $\hat{\varepsilon}_{sys}$, however, is not a random number and is independent of N. Instead, it depends on the discretization scheme, the numerical integration rules, and the number of time steps in the simulation. As shown in Kloeden and Platen (1992), the error of the Euler scheme decreases linearly in h (i.e., the scheme is convergent with (weak) order 1). As the trapezoidal rule used to approximate the integral is of order 2 (that is, of higher order than the Euler scheme), we conclude the total systematic error of our scheme is of order 1. Hence

$$|\varepsilon_{sys}| \leq C_1 h$$

where C_1 is a constant and h is the size of the time step.

   If we are conducting a Monte Carlo simulation with K discretization points then ε_{sys} depends ultimately on K while for a given K, $\hat{\varepsilon}_{stat}$ depends on N. We would like to have these two errors of same order of magnitude. There is no point in making $\hat{\varepsilon}_{stat}$ very small if ε_{sys} is much larger (and vice versa). To make $\hat{\varepsilon}_{stat}$

smaller we can increase N or use variance reduction techniques. To make $\hat{\varepsilon}_{sys}$ smaller we can increase K or use a higher order discretization scheme. We will illustrate these points in our numerical examples.

It turns out that we can get useful insights into the behavior of the systematic error in the Vasicek framework since there is a closed form expression for the value of the pure discount bond in the Vasicek model under the Euler discretization. This permits us to compute ε_{sys} exactly for any value of K without the need to do any simulations.

THE VASICEK BOND PRICE UNDER THE EULER DISCRETIZATION

We now present the derivation of the formula for the price of a pure discount bond under the Vasicek model starting from the Euler discretization in the previous section of the stochastic differential equation for the short rate. We saw in the last section that using the trapezoidal numerical integration scheme gives rise to a bond price that can be expressed as the exponential of the (negative of the) sum of the realized short-rate values. As this sum has a normal distribution, the bond price expression reduces to the expectation of the exponential of a constant plus a normal distribution. This has a closed-form solution.

We assume that the short rate corresponds to the Vasicek model as given by Equation (13.1). Suppose we are interested in the evolution of the process during the interval $[t, t + T]$. We use the Euler discretization with K time steps (each of length h) so that $T = Kh$. The Euler discretization enables us to write down the $\hat{r}_k$ in terms of the earlier $\hat{r}$ values as follows

$$\hat{r}_1 = (1 - \kappa h)\hat{r}_0 + \kappa\theta h + z_1\sigma_v\sqrt{h}$$

$$\hat{r}_2 = (1 - \kappa h)\hat{r}_1 + \kappa\theta h + z_2\sigma_v\sqrt{h}$$

$$\hat{r}_3 = (1 - \kappa h)\hat{r}_2 + \kappa\theta h + z_3\sigma_v\sqrt{h}$$

$$\cdots = \cdots$$

$$\hat{r}_k = [1 - \kappa h]\hat{r}_{k-1} + \kappa\theta h + + z_k\sigma_v\sqrt{h}$$

By substituting in the earlier equations, we can show that

$$\hat{r}_k = [1 - \kappa h]^k r(t) + \kappa \theta h \left[1 + (1 - \kappa h) + (1 - \kappa h)^2 + \cdots (1 - \kappa h)^{k-1} \right]$$
$$+ \sigma_v \sqrt{h} \left[(1 - \kappa h)^{k-1} z_1 + \cdots (1 - \kappa h) z_{k-1} + z_k \right]$$

Since $\hat{r}_k$ equals a constant plus a sum of normal variates, $\hat{r}_k$ is itself normal. We now take the expected value of $\hat{r}_k$ and notice that since the normal variates all have mean zero, the contribution from all the stochastic terms is zero. The coefficient of $\kappa \theta h$ is a geometric progression which has a compact expression for its sum. Hence the expected value of $\hat{r}_k$ is

$$[1 - \kappa h]^k r(t) + \frac{1 - (1 - \kappa h)^k}{\kappa h} \kappa h \theta = [1 - \kappa h]^k r(t) + [1 - (1 - \kappa h)^k] \theta \qquad (13.10)$$

The variance of $\hat{r}_k$ is

$$\sigma_v^2 h \sum_{j=0}^{k-1} (1 - \kappa h)^{2j} = \sigma_v^2 h \frac{\left(1 - (1 - \kappa h)^{2k} \right)}{\left(1 - (1 - \kappa h)^2 \right)} \qquad (13.11)$$

Under this discretization the pure discount bond price can be obtained by taking the expectation of Equation (13.7) to give

$$E\left[\hat{B}_K(t, t+T) \right] = E\left(\exp\left[-\frac{(\hat{r}_0 + \hat{r}_K)}{2} h - \sum_1^{K-1} \hat{r}_k h \right] \right) \qquad (13.12)$$

The term in the exponent is a sum of normal variates and is therefore itself a normal variable. We will therefore be able to obtain a closed-form expression for the value of the pure discount bond price since it has a lognormal distribution and we can compute the mean of the lognormal distribution.

The exponent we are interested in, apart from the minus sign and the factor h, is

$$\frac{(\hat{r}_0 + \hat{r}_K)}{2} + \sum_1^{K-1} \hat{r}_k$$

Using the Euler discretization equations, this expression can be written in terms of the parameters of the problem and k normal variates as follows

$$\frac{(\hat{r}_0 + \hat{r})_K}{2} + \sum_{1}^{K-1} \hat{r}_k = \hat{r}_0 \left[\frac{1}{2} + (1-\kappa h) + \cdots + (1-\kappa h)^{K-1} + \frac{1}{2}(1-\kappa h)^K \right]$$

$$+ \kappa \theta h \left[1 + \{1 + (1-\kappa h)\} + \cdots + \left\{ 1 + (1-\kappa h) + \cdots + (1-\kappa h)^{K-2} \right\} \right.$$

$$\left. + \frac{1}{2} \left\{ 1 + (1-\kappa h) + \cdots + (1-\kappa h)^{K-1} \right\} \right]$$

$$+ \sigma_v \sqrt{h} \sum_{1}^{k} b_k z_k$$

where the b_k are constants and are as follows

$$b_1 = 1 + (1-\kappa h) + (1-\kappa h)^2 + \cdots + (1-\kappa h)^{K-2} + \frac{1}{2}(1-\kappa h)^{K-1}$$

$$b_2 = 1 + (1-\kappa h) + (1-\kappa h)^2 + \cdots + (1-\kappa h)^{K-3} + \frac{1}{2}(1-\kappa h)^{K-2}$$

$$\cdots = \cdots$$

$$b_{K-1} = 1 + \frac{1}{2}(1-\kappa h)$$

$$b_K = \frac{1}{2}$$

We can rewrite the exponent as follows

$$\frac{(\hat{r}_0 + \hat{r}_K)}{2} + \sum_{1}^{K-1} \hat{r}_k = \hat{r}_0 \left[\frac{1}{2} + (1-\kappa h)\frac{\left(1-(1-\kappa h)^{K-1}\right)}{\kappa h} + \frac{1}{2}(1-\kappa h)^K \right]$$

$$+ \theta \left[(K-1) + \frac{1}{2}\left(1-(1-\kappa h)^K\right) - (1-\kappa h)\frac{1-(1-\kappa h)^{K-1}}{\kappa h} \right]$$

$$+ \sigma_v \sqrt{h} \sum_{1}^{k} b_k z_k$$

We can now obtain an explicit expression for the pure discount bond price in the Vasicek model under the Euler discretization. We insert the last expression into the expression for the pure discount bond price in Equation (13.12) and use the result that

$$E(\exp[X]) = \exp\left[E(X) + \frac{1}{2}Var(X)\right]$$

when X is normal with mean $E(X)$ and variance $Var(X)$. Applying this result, we can derive the explicit expression for the pure discount bond price in the Vasicek model (under the Euler discretization) as follows

$$
\begin{aligned}
E\left[\hat{B}_K(t,t+T)\right] = \exp\Bigg\{ &-\hat{r}_0 h\left[\frac{1}{2} + (1-\kappa h)\frac{\left(1-(1-\kappa h)^{K-1}\right)}{\kappa h} + \frac{1}{2}(1-\kappa h)^K\right] \\
&-\theta h\left[(K-1) + \frac{1}{2}\left(1-(1-\kappa h)^K\right) - (1-\kappa h)\frac{1-(1-\kappa h)^{K-1}}{\kappa h}\right] \\
&+\frac{1}{2}\sigma_v^2 h^3 \sum_1^K b_k^2 \Bigg\}
\end{aligned}
$$

We complete the derivation by obtaining the explicit expression for the sum of the b_k^2. Note that

$$b_1 = \frac{1-(1-\kappa h)^{K-1}}{\kappa h} + \frac{1}{2}(1-\kappa h)^{K-1}$$

$$b_2 = \frac{1-(1-\kappa h)^{K-2}}{\kappa h} + \frac{1}{2}(1-\kappa h)^{K-2}$$

$$\cdots = \cdots$$

$$b_K = \frac{1-(1-\kappa h)^0}{\kappa h} + \frac{1}{2}(1-\kappa h)^0 = \frac{1}{2}$$

Hence this gives us

$$\sum_1^K b_k^2 = \sum_{j=0}^{K-1} \left[\frac{\left(1-(1-\kappa h)^j\right)}{\kappa h} + \frac{1}{2}(1-\kappa h)^j \right]^2$$

$$= \sum_{j=0}^{K-1} \left[\frac{1}{\kappa h}(1-(1-\kappa h)^j)\left(1-\frac{\kappa h}{2}\right) \right]^2$$

$$= \sum_{j=0}^{K-1} \frac{1}{(\kappa h)^2} \left[1-2(1-\kappa h)^j\left(1-\frac{\kappa h}{2}\right) + (1-\kappa h)^{2j}\left(1-\frac{\kappa h}{2}\right)^2 \right]$$

$$= \frac{1}{(\kappa h)^2} \left[K - 2\left(1-\frac{\kappa h}{2}\right)\frac{\left(1-(1-\kappa h)^K\right)}{\kappa h} + \left(1-\frac{\kappa h}{2}\right)^2 \frac{\left(1-(1-\kappa h)^{2K}\right)}{\left(1-(1-\kappa h)^2\right)} \right]$$

With this substitution, we can obtain an explicit expression for the pure discount bond price in the Vasicek model under the Euler discretization. The result is given in Proposition 1.

Proposition 1

Using a combination of a K-step Euler discretization of the short rate and a trapezoidal approximation for the bond price path integral, the approximated price of the T-maturity discount bond in the Vasicek model is, with $T = Kh$

$$E\left[\hat{B}_K(t,t+T)\right] = E\left(\exp\left[-\frac{(\hat{r}_0+\hat{r}_K)}{2}h - \sum_1^{K-1}\hat{r}_K h\right]\right)$$

$$= \exp\left[-\hat{r}_0 h\left\{\frac{1}{2} + (1-\kappa h)\frac{\left(1-(1-\kappa h)^{K-1}\right)}{\kappa h} + \frac{1}{2}(1-\kappa h)^K\right\}\right.$$

$$- \theta h\left\{(K-1) + \frac{1}{2}\left(1-(1-\kappa h)^K\right) - (1-\kappa h)\frac{1-(1-\kappa h)^{K-1}}{\kappa h}\right\}$$

$$+ \frac{\sigma_v^2 h}{2\kappa^2}\left\{K - 2\left(1-\frac{\kappa h}{2}\right)\frac{\left(1-(1-\kappa h)^K\right)}{\kappa h}\right.$$

$$\left.\left. + \left(1-\frac{\kappa h}{2}\right)^2 \frac{\left(1-(1-\kappa h)^{2K}\right)}{\left(1-(1-\kappa h)^2\right)}\right\}\right]$$

If we let h tend to zero and K tend to infinity in such a way that $Kh = T$ then the bond price given in Proposition 1 tends to the (continuous time) Vasicek bond price as given in the original paper by Vasicek (1977) or Jamshidian (1989). The (continuous time) Vasicek bond price is

$$B(t,t+T) = \exp\left[-T\theta - (r(t)-\theta)\frac{1-e^{-\kappa T}}{\kappa} + \frac{\sigma_v^2}{4\kappa^3}g(\kappa,T) \right] \qquad (13.13)$$

where $g(\kappa,T) = 4e^{-\kappa T} - e^{-2\kappa T} + 2\kappa T - 3$.

If we discretize the short-term rate (in the Vasicek model) under the Euler scheme then the bond price under this discretization is given by Proposition 1. So if we estimate the bond price based on the Euler discretization and use a simulation approach the asymptotic bond price (as the number of simulations becomes large) is given by Proposition 1. The systematic discretization error, ε_{sys}, can be computed exactly in this case. It is given by the difference between the bond prices in Proposition 1 and the bond price given by Equation (13.13).

Table 13.1 shows how the systematic error, ε_{sys}, behaves as a function of K. We note that as the number of time steps K becomes large, the Euler approximation tends to the accurate value. Consistent with the predicted first-order convergence of our Euler scheme, we note that the systematic error is linear in h: when we double the number of time steps, the systematic error is roughly halved. For example, with eight time steps the systematic error is .189 while for 16 time steps it is .092. We recall that under Monte Carlo simulation the variance of statistical error (or standard error) is halved when we increase the number of simulations by a factor of four. This suggests that if we are estimating a security price using simulation based on the Euler scheme, then as we double the number of time steps we should increase the number of simulations by a factor of four if we want the two types of error to remain in balance.

In Monte Carlo simulation, we are concerned with the tradeoff between these two errors. In other words, we are concerned with the tradeoff between the number of time steps, K and the number of simulations N. Duffie and Glynn (1995) show that, under fairly general conditions, the optimal tradeoff in the case of the Euler

TABLE 13.1. The Systematic Bias of a Five-Year Bond in the Euler-Discretized Vasicek Model

K	Continuous Time Price	Euler Discretization	ε_{sys}
2	76.143	77.073	0.931 (−24.3)
4	76.143	76.542	0.400 (−10.5)
8	76.143	76.332	0.189 (−5.0)
16	76.143	76.235	0.092 (−2.4)
32	76.143	76.188	0.046 (−1.2)
64	76.143	76.165	0.023 (−.6)
128	76.143	76.154	0.011 (−.3)
256	76.143	76.148	0.006 (−.1)
512	76.143	76.146	0.003 (−.1)
1024	76.143	76.144	0.001 (.0)

Note: The first column lists the number of time steps K. The second column lists the true continuous time bond price of the Vasicek model as given by Equation (13.13). The third column lists the bond price under the Euler discretization scheme, as given in Proposition 1. The fourth column contains the systematic bias in prices and, in parentheses, rates (basis points). Parameters $r_0 = .06$, $\kappa = 0.4$, $\theta = 0.054$, and $\sigma_v = 0.04183$.

discretization scheme is to increase the number of simulations by a factor of four when the number of time intervals K is doubled. Our numerical results for the Vasicek model are consistent with this general result. These results also show the nature of the discretization error and how it contributes to the bias in the bond price.

THE VASICEK BOND PRICE UNDER THE EXACT DISCRETIZATION

As discussed, the systematic error of our Euler scheme can be split into two parts: the discretization error in the distribution of r and the error associated with the trapezoidal approximation of the bond price path integral. For the Vasicek model, it is possible to eliminate the first error source completely, leaving only the integration error. In particular, it is possible to obtain the exact solution of the SDE for

r and derive the estimated discount bond price based on this solution. As one would expect, the systematic error under this discretization is lower than that of the Euler discretization.

The linear Vasicek SDE (13.1) is known to have an explicit solution under which the distribution of $r(s)$ at time $s \geq t$, given the value of $r(t)$ at time t, is normally distributed. The mean and variance of $r(s)$ are as follows at time t is normal. The mean of $r(s)$ is

$$E[r(s) \mid r(t)] = r(t)e^{-\kappa(s-t)} + \theta\left(1 - e^{-\kappa(s-t)}\right)$$

(13.14)

and the variance is

$$Var[r(s) \mid r(t)] = \sigma_v^2 \frac{1 - e^{-2\kappa(s-t)}}{2\kappa}$$

(13.15)

This exact distribution enables us to obtain the accurate discrete time process that corresponds to the continuous time process for the evolution of the short rate as follows

$$\hat{r}_k = e^{-\kappa h}\hat{r}_{k-1} + (1 - e^{-\kappa h})\theta + z_\kappa \sigma_v \sqrt{\frac{1 - e^{-2\kappa h}}{2\kappa}}$$

(13.16)

Notice that as h becomes small the last equation tends to

$$\hat{r}_k = (1 - \kappa h)\hat{r}_{k-1} + \kappa\theta h + z_\kappa \sigma_v \sqrt{h}$$

(13.17)

the Euler discretization. We can derive the expression for the price of the pure discount bond based on the discretization given by Equation (13.16). The procedure is exactly the same as in the last section with the only difference that (13.16) is used in place of the Euler discretization. The explicit result is given in Proposition 2.

Proposition 2

Using a combination of a K-step *exact* discretization of the short rate and a trapezoid approximation for the bond price path integral, the price of the T-maturity discount bond in the Vasicek model is, with $T = Kh$,

$$
E\left[\exp\left[-\frac{(\hat{r}_0 + \hat{r}_K)}{2}h - \sum_{1}^{K-1}\hat{r}_K h\right]\right] = \exp\left[-\hat{r}_0 h\left\{\frac{1}{2} + e^{-\kappa h}\frac{1 - e^{-\kappa h(K-1)}}{1 - e^{-\kappa h}} + \frac{1}{2}e^{-\kappa h K}\right\}\right.
$$

$$
- \theta h\left\{(K-1) + \frac{1}{2}\left(1 - e^{-\kappa h K}\right) - e^{-\kappa h}\frac{1 - e^{-\kappa h(K-1)}}{1 - e^{-\kappa h}}\right\}
$$

$$
+ \frac{\sigma_1^2 h^2}{2[1 - e^{-\kappa h}]^2}\left\{K - \left(1 + e^{-\kappa h}\right)\frac{1 - e^{-\kappa h K}}{1 - e^{-\kappa h}}\right.
$$

$$
\left.\left. + \frac{1}{4}\left(1 + e^{-\kappa h}\right)^2\frac{1 - e^{-2\kappa h K}}{1 - e^{-2\kappa h}}\right\}\right]
$$

where $\sigma_1^2 = \sigma_v^2\frac{(1 - e^{-2\kappa h})}{2\kappa}$

We can illustrate the impact of the different discretization assumption using the same numerical parameters as in Table 13.1. The results are given in Table 13.2.

TABLE 13.2. Prices of Five-Year Pure Discount Bond under Vasicek Model Based on Different Discretization Schemes

K	Bond Price under Exact Discretization	Bond Price under Euler Discretization	ε_{sys} Exact Discretization	ε_{sys} Euler Discretization
2	76.012	77.073	−0.130 (3.4)	0.931 (−24.3)
4	76.111	76.542	−0.031 (.8)	0.400 (−10.5)
8	76.135	76.332	−0.008 (.2)	0.189 (−5.0)
16	76.141	76.235	−0.002 (.0)	0.092 (−2.4)
32	76.142	76.188	0.000 (.0)	0.046 (−1.2)

Note: The first column gives the value of K, the number of time steps. The second column gives the bond price under the exact discretization scheme. The third column gives the bond price under the Euler discretization. The fourth column gives the systematic error under the exact discretization in prices and, in parentheses, rates (basis points). The fifth column gives the systematic error under the Euler discretization in prices and rates. The continuous time price is 76.1427. Parameters $r_0 = .06$, $\kappa = 0.4$, $\theta = 0.054$, and $\sigma_v = 0.04183$.

It is obvious from the results in Table 13.2 that the exact discretization of the Vasicek process for r results in much faster convergence than the Euler discretization (see Table 13.1). To be more precise, one would expect the convergence of the results for the exact discretization in Table 13.2 to be of the same order as the trapezoid integration method, namely $O(h^2)$. This is easily verified to be the case: whenever K is doubled in Table 13.2, the systematic error is reduced by (roughly) a factor of 4. What is going on here is that our discretization rule for r is perfect (of order infinity) whereas our trapezoidal integration rule is just of order two. The estimate of the bond price in these circumstances is therefore of order two. We could increase the order of the estimate by using a higher order integration rule.

While the discretization scheme used to generate Table 13.2 was specific to the Vasicek model and hinged very strongly on the existence of an exact solution to the SDE for r, our results suggest that there may be efficiency gains in general by using more accurate discretization schemes than the Euler approximation. It turns out that the general methods to construct such schemes exist, even for SDEs that cannot be solved explicitly. A popular example of such a scheme, the Milstein approximation, is presented later as are other possible generalizations.

EULER SCHEME SIMULATION OF THE CIR MODEL

In this section, we use the Monte Carlo method to estimate the prices of pure discount bonds under the CIR model. As was done earlier, we use the Euler discretization scheme combined with trapezoid path integration. We confirm that the results obtained in the Vasicek model also hold for the CIR model.

We now use Monte Carlo simulation to estimate the price of a five-year pure discount bond under the one factor CIR model. We assume that at current time t the short-rate dynamics are given by Equation (13.3). The closed-form solution for the bond price is (see Cox, Ingersoll, & Ross, 1985)

$$B(t,t + T) = a(T)e^{-b(T)r(t)} \tag{13.18}$$

where

$$a(u) = \left\{ \frac{2\gamma e^{\frac{u}{2}(\gamma+\kappa)}}{(\gamma+\kappa)(e^{\gamma u}-1)+2\gamma} \right\}^{\frac{2\kappa\theta}{\sigma^2}}$$

$$b(u) = \frac{2(e^{\gamma u}-1)}{(\gamma+\kappa)(e^{\gamma u}-1)+2\gamma}$$

$$\gamma = \sqrt{\kappa^2 + 2\sigma^2}$$

The price given by Equation (13.18) is the analytical solution of the integral in Equation (13.1) for the one-factor CIR model.

For our numerical calculations we consider a five-year pure discount bond with a face value of 100 and we use the following parameters: $\kappa = .4$, $\theta = .054$, and $\sigma = .18$. We assume that the initial value of the short-term interest is .06. The accurate bond price for these parameters from formula (13.18) is 76.1423.

In Table 13.3 we fix the value of K at 6 and increase the number of simulations trials N. Notice that for $N = 10$ the standard deviation

TABLE 13.3. Analysis of the Statistical Error of Simulated Five-Year Bond Price under the CIR Model as N Varies

K	N	Sample Error	Approximate ε_{sys}
6	10	3.412	0.300
6	100	1.160	0.300
6	1,000	0.369	0.300
6	10,000	0.117	0.300
6	100,000	0.037	0.300
6	1,000,000	0.012	0.300
6	10,000,000	0.004	0.300

Note: The first column gives K, the number of time steps. The second column gives N, the number of simulation trials. The third column gives the sample standard deviation of the Monte Carlo estimator (the sample error). The fourth column gives the systematic error, ε_{sys}. The simulation estimate uses the Euler approximation, Equation (13.6). Parameters $r_0 = .06$, $\kappa = 0.4$, $\theta = 0.054$, and $\sigma = 0.18$.

is large (3.412) but as N increases, the standard deviation decreases. When $N = 10,000,000$, the standard deviation on the estimated bond price is only 0.004, hence we may take the corresponding estimate of the bond price, 76.442, as an accurate estimate of $E[\hat{B}_{6,N}(t, t+5)]$. From the earlier discussion, we conclude that the systematic error for our six-step Euler scheme must be close to 0.300. As no improvement in the bias can be obtained by raising N, it is clear that it would be more efficient to increase the number of time steps K rather than keep increasing the number of simulation trials and holding K constant.

To investigate the behavior of the systematic error as a function of K, Table 13.4 lists the estimated systematic bias (from 10,000,000 paths) as K is increased from 6 to 96. The table also lists the sample standard deviation obtained by using $N = K^2$ simulations (recall our discussion of balancing systematic and statistical errors).

In Table 13.4, the systematic bias and the standard deviation of the statistical error decrease at the same rate when we increase K and N as shown. If we double K and increase N by a factor of four we see that both errors are halved. This is consistent with our discussions on the Vasicek model and also is consistent with the results of

TABLE 13.4. Comparison of Statistical Bias and Systematic Bias for Simulated Five-Year Bond Price as Both K and N Vary under the CIR Model

K	N	Sample Error	Approximate ε_{sys}
6	36	1.920	0.300
12	144	0.909	0.137
24	576	0.440	0.065
48	2,304	0.220	0.031
96	9,216	0.110	0.016

Note: The first column gives K, the number of time steps. The second column gives N, the number of simulation trials. The third column gives the sample standard deviation of the Monte Carlo estimator *(the sample error).* The fourth column gives the systematic error ε_{sys}. The accurate bond price based on Equation (13.18) is 76.1423. The simulation estimate uses the Euler approximation, Equation (13.6). Parameters $r_0 = .06$, $\kappa = 0.4$, $\theta = 0.054$, and $\sigma = 0.18$.

Duffie and Glynn. In particular, notice that the Euler scheme, as expected, converges linearly in h.

THE MILSTEIN APPROXIMATION

The Euler scheme discussed can be interpreted as a first-order (stochastic) Taylor approximation to the true increments of the short rate. Not surprisingly, one can devise schemes with faster convergence in h by including more terms in such Taylor approximations. For instance retaining terms up to order h^2 gives rise to the so-called *Milstein scheme*. Due to differences in ordinary and stochastic calculus, the Milstein scheme is considerably more complicated than second-order schemes used for ordinary differential equations. (For an introduction to stochastic Ito-Taylor expansions, see Kloeden and Platen, 1992.) The Milstein scheme for the general short rate SDE (13.5) can be found in Andersen (1995). For brevity, we will discuss only the autonomous case, where the coefficients a and b in (13.5) are not dependent on time (as is the case for the Vasicek and CIR models). In (13.5), suppose that $a(x,t) = a(x)$ and $b(x,t) = b(x)$ and all t. The "K"-step Milstein approximation of (13.5) is now

$$\hat{r}_{k+1} - \hat{r}_k = h\left[a(\hat{r}_k) - \frac{1}{2}b(\hat{r}_k)b'(\hat{r}_k) \right] + \sqrt{h}\,[b(\hat{r}_k)z_{k+1}]$$

$$- \frac{h}{2}\left[b(\hat{r}_k)b'(\hat{r}_k)(x_{k+1})^2 \right] + h^{\frac{3}{2}}\left[f(\hat{r}_k)z_{k+1} \right] + h^2[g(\hat{r}_k)]$$

where

$$f(x) = \frac{1}{2}a(x)\,b'(x) + \frac{1}{2}a'(x)b(x) + \frac{1}{4}(b(x))^2 b''(x)$$

$$g(x) = \frac{1}{2}a(x)\,a'(x) + \frac{1}{4}(b(x))^2 a''(x)$$

The Milstein approximation can be shown to converge with (weak) order 2 in the time-step h. Assuming that we retain the trapezoid integration rule discussed earlier (also order 2 in h), the systematic error of the resulting bond price simulation scheme will be of order 2

$$| \varepsilon_{sys} | \le C_2 h^2$$

Using the CIR model as a test example, Table 13.5 compares the systematic errors of the Euler and Milstein schemes for various values of K. (For an explicit representation of the Milstein scheme for the CIR process, see Andersen, 1995.) As in Table 13.4, the systematic error has been estimated by using $N = 10,000,000$ simulation paths.

The table confirms the second-order convergence of the Milstein scheme. Note that the Milstein scheme has much smaller systematic errors than the Euler scheme. For second-order schemes, such as the Milstein scheme, Duffie and Glynn (1995) show, as one would expect, that the number of simulations N should be of the order K^4. Thus, as we double the number of time steps in the Milstein scheme, we should increase the number of simulations by a factor of 16 so that the optimal rate of error reduction is achieved. The fast convergence of the Milstein scheme strongly suggests the application of variance reduction techniques to prevent the variance of the statistical error from dominating the systematic error.

TABLE 13.5. Analysis of the Systematic Bias under the Euler and Milstein Schemes in Simulating Five-Year Bond Price under the CIR Model

K	Approximate ε_{sys} (Euler)	Approximate ε_{sys} (Milstein)
6	.300 (–7.9)	–0.045 (1.2)
12	.137 (–3.6)	–0.012 (.3)
24	.065 (–1.7)	–0.004 (.1)
48	.031 (–0.8)	–0.001 (.0)

Notes: The accurate bond price based on Equation (13.8) is 76.1423. The first column gives the number of time steps K. The second column gives the systematic error in the Euler scheme in prices and, in parentheses, rates (basis points). The third column gives the systematic error in the Milstein scheme in prices and rates. Parameters $r_0 = .06$, $\kappa = 0.4$, $\theta = 0.054$, and $\sigma = 0.18$.

OTHER HIGHER ORDER SIMULATION SCHEMES

By including more terms, the stochastic Taylor-expansion technique underlying the Milstein scheme can be used to generate simulation schemes of a higher order than two. Unfortunately such schemes tend to get very complicated and require the evaluation of a large number of derivatives. A much simpler way to generate high-order simulation schemes is through *Romberg-Richardson extrapolation*, a method first suggested and analyzed by Talay and Tubaro (1990). As in the deterministic case, the basic idea of Romberg-Richardson extrapolation is to combine bond price estimates obtained at different step-lengths in such a way that leading order error terms cancel. To illustrate the method, assume for instance that we have simulated N short-rate paths in a K-step Milstein scheme and obtained the bond price estimate $\hat{B}_{N,K}^{Milstein}(t,t+T)$. Suppose we now double the size of the time-step (i.e., we halve the number of steps, and generate $\hat{B}_{N,\frac{K}{2}}^{Milstein}(t,t+T)$. Now, under mild regularity conditions it can be shown that the linear combination

$$\hat{B}_{N,K}^{3rd}(t,t+T) = \frac{1}{3}\left[4\hat{B}_{N,K}^{Milstein}(t,t+T) - \hat{B}_{N,\frac{K}{2}}^{Milstein}(t,t+T)\right]$$

converges with *weak order 3*. We point out that for this, and any method with convergence order higher than 2, to work properly, it is necessary to replace the trapezoid integration rule used so far to compute the short-rate path integral by a higher order integration method (for instance a fourth-order Simpson scheme). Analysis and tests of the third-order extrapolation scheme for the CIR process can be found in Andersen (1995).

Romberg-Richardson methods can also be used to combine Euler schemes to generate second-order schemes. This is particularly attractive when the coefficients of the short-rate SDE (13.5) are time-dependent or are difficult to differentiate, in which case the Milstein scheme becomes less useful. We do point out, however, that schemes based on explicit derivatives, should they exist, generally outperform schemes based on extrapolation. In particular, sometimes one finds that the error cancellation effect in the extrapolation schemes are not achieved in practice for the step size and number of simulation paths used.

Another derivative-free alternative to the Milstein scheme is based on replacing the derivatives in the Milstein scheme by finite differences. Schemes of this type are analyzed thoroughly in Kloeden and Platen (1992).

VARIANCE REDUCTION METHODS

Recall from the earlier discussion that the total error in the Monte Carlo estimate of bond prices can be divided into a systematic and a random component. Having spent the last few sections on methods to reduce the systematic error, we now turn to the *classical* Monte Carlo problem of reducing the variance of the random error. Many of these techniques are reviewed in the paper by Boyle, Broadie, and Glasserman (1997). We have already noted that such schemes are likely to be more productive in conjunction with a Milstein scheme (than the Euler scheme) if one is using a small number of time steps. In this section, we discuss some of the variance reduction techniques that are useful for estimating the prices of path dependent securities. The techniques discussed here are antithetic variates, control variates, moment matching methods, and importance sampling.

Antithetic Variates

The basic idea here is to use symmetry to improve the efficiency of the simulation estimate. Let us suppose that we are using K discrete time steps to generate the short-rate path. We generate the first interest-rate path using K normal variates

$$\{z_1, z_2, \ldots, z_K\}$$

Suppose that the estimate of the bond price based on this path is P_1. Note that if z has a standard normal distribution so has $-z$. The variates z and $-z$ are known as antithetic variates. If we use the path generated by

$$\{-z_1, -z_2, \ldots, -z_K\}$$

we obtain another estimate of the bond price which we denote by P_{-1}. We can see that if P_1 overestimates the true price that P_{-1} will generally underestimate the true price. This provides us with two interest-rate paths. If we generate another batch of K independently and identically distributed normal variates, this provides us with two more interest-rate paths and we can compute P_2 and P_{-2}. With N batches of K normal variates we obtain $2N$ paths. The antithetic variate estimate of the bond price is

$$\hat{P} = \frac{1}{N} \sum_{1}^{N} \frac{P_i + P_{-i}}{2} \qquad (13.19)$$

The antithetic variate approach increases efficiency for securities that depend monotonically on the inputs. This is the case for a bond since its value decreases as the interest rates rise. To compute the standard error when using antithetic variates we should consider the N pairs

$$\frac{P_i + P_{-i}}{2}$$

as the N inputs to the computation since they are independent. Note that P_i and P_{-i} are not independent but are negatively correlated.

In Table 13.6, we provide some sample numerical calculations using antithetic variates to compute the pure discount bond price in the Vasicek model. We see that the use of antithetic variates produces a significant increase in efficiency. The bond price provides a good candidate for the application of the antithetic variate method since the term in the exponent in the integral is a *linear function* of the input random variates. This approach will also work for derivatives such as bond options but the improvement will not always be as dramatic. It is a very simple technique to apply and it is easy to test if it yields any improvement in efficiency.

Control Variates

The control variate approach is useful when there is a related problem for which we have an accurate solution. This solution can be

TABLE 13.6. Comparison of Standard Monte Carlo and Monte Carlo Using Antithetic Variates for Simulated Five-Year Bond Price as Both K and N Vary under the Vasicek Model

K	N	Sample Error Basic Monte Carlo	Sample Error Using Antithetic Variates	Ratio of Sample Errors
4	16	2.969	0.315	9.45
8	64	1.448	0.153	9.50
16	256	0.710	0.074	9.61
32	1,024	0.350	0.036	9.70
64	4,096	0.174	0.018	9.74
128	16,384	0.086	0.009	9.84

Note: The first column gives K, the number of time steps. The second column gives N, the number of simulation trials. The third gives the sample error under the standard Monte Carlo method and the fourth column gives the sample error using antithetic variates. The fifth column gives the ratio of these two sample errors. Parameters $r_0 = .06$, $\kappa = 0.4$, $\theta = 0.054$, and $\sigma = 0.04183$. The simulation estimate uses the Euler approximation, Equation (13.6).

used to help improve the accuracy of the simulation estimate. Both the related problem and the problem of interest are solved by simulation using the *same random numbers* as inputs. Since we know the accurate answer for the related problem, we can estimate the bias in the estimate for the problem of interest. The earliest application of the control variate approach in finance is by Boyle (1977). For a more complete discussion of the control variate approach see Boyle, Broadie, and Glasserman (1997).

Suppose we have a financial security that we wish to evaluate using Monte Carlo simulation. For European securities, we can represent this value as an integral. Suppose that its accurate value is $P = P(t)$, an unknown quantity that we wish to estimate using Monte Carlo simulation. We also assume that there is a related security whose accurate price is known. The accurate value of the related security is $H = H(t)$. We write $P = E[\hat{P}]$ and $H = E[\hat{H}]$ where $\hat{P}$ and $\hat{H}$ are the simulated values of the two instruments based on the same set of input random numbers. The control variate estimate for this simulation path is given by

$$\hat{P}^{CV} = \hat{P} + [H - \hat{H}]$$

Notice that

$$E[\hat{P}^{CV}] = E[\hat{P}] + H - E[\hat{H}] = P$$

hence $\hat{P}^{CV}$ is an unbiased estimator for P.

We estimate the average value of $\hat{P}^{CV}$ over N paths to obtain the control variate estimate of the security. If $\hat{H}$ and $\hat{P}$ are positively correlated, the term $H - \hat{H}$ will tend to be negative for paths where $\hat{P}$ is too high (and vice versa), effectively reducing the deviations of $\hat{P}$ from its true mean (and hence its variance). If one suspects that the payoffs in the two problems are not perfectly correlated further improvements are possible. In general, Boyle, Broadie, and Glasserman (1997) show further improvement on this estimate can be obtained by letting

$$\hat{P}^{CV} = \hat{P} + \beta[H - \hat{H}]$$

and solving for the optimal β via a regression procedure. With the optimal choice of β, one can show that the variance of $\hat{P}^{CV}$ is

$$Var\left(\hat{P}^{CV}\right) = Var(\hat{P})(1 - \rho^2) \leq Var\left(\hat{P}\right)$$

where ρ is the correlation between $\hat{H}$ and $\hat{P}$. Notice how introducing the parameter β allows us to take advantage of situations where $\hat{H}$ and $\hat{P}$ are negatively correlated.

The trick is to be able to find a good control variate and sometimes this is difficult. In the case of interest-rate models, we can use the exact solutions for the one-factor case. These include both the Vasicek model and the CIR model. We can use one of these as the control in simulating short-rate models. For example, we can use the Vasicek solution as the control variate in estimating the CIR bond price by simulation. The exact bond price under the Euler discretization of the Vasicek model is given in Proposition 1. To make the CIR and Vasicek bond prices compatible, the moments of the approximating Vasicek process should be set to be close to those of the CIR process. For instance, if $r(0)$ is not too far from the reversion level θ, one could set the volatility of the Vasicek model as follows

$$\sigma_v = \sigma\sqrt{\theta}$$

Andersen (1995) analyses the impact of using the Vasicek solution as the control variate in simulating the prices of different pure discount bonds. (See Andersen, 1995, for a different procedure to align the volatility of the Vasicek model with the CIR model.) He finds that while the control variate does reduce the standard error the antithetic variate approach is more efficient. The reason is that the pure discount bond calculation is extremely amenable to the use of antithetic variates. This will not necessarily be the case for other types of interest rate securities such as options on bonds. Andersen also finds that the antithetic variate approach dominates the combined control variate/antithetic approach in the simulation of pure discount bonds.[5] This illustrates the point that one should not combine different variance reduction methods in an uncritical fashion.

Moment Matching Methods

The basic idea here is to adjust the inputs to the simulation so that they better capture the properties of the distribution we are simulating. If a simulation path is based on K independent standardized normals, then the sample moments of these inputs will not match those of a standard normal. In particular, the sample mean, in general, will not be zero and the sample standard deviation will not be unity. The idea of moment matching is to transform the input normal variates so that the first few sample moments match those of the underlying population. Suppose we have generated a sample of K i.i.d normal variates: $z_1, z_2, \ldots, z_K$. The sample mean m and sample standard deviation s of z based on these draws are given by

$$m = \frac{1}{K}\sum_1^K z_i$$

$$s^2 = \frac{\sum_1^K z_i^2 - Km^2}{K-1}$$

---

[5] The antithetic variate approach works best when the payoff is a linear (and therefore) monotonic function of the random variables. This will not be the case for some interest rate derivatives and the method will not perform as well in these circumstances.

We can match the first two moments with those of the population by the transformation

$$y_i = \frac{z_i - m}{s} \tag{13.20}$$

This approach is appropriate if we are simulating a terminal stock price using Monte Carlo simulation. For the details, see Boyle, Broadie, and Glasserman (1997).

In the case of the stochastic interest rate model when we are simulating the price of an interest rate security, we need to be more careful. Indeed if the approach outlined above is used to simulate the Vasicek bond price the resulting estimates turn out to be biased and *worse than if we just used plain Monte Carlo.* We can gain insight as to why this occurs and see how to properly implement the moment matching approach by considering the nature of the dependence of the bond price on the input normal variables. The discrete approximation to the pure discount bond price is

$$E\left(\exp\left[-\sum_0^{K-1} \frac{\hat{r}_k + \hat{r}_{k+1}}{2} h\right]\right) = E\left(\exp[-\hat{r}_0 h a_1 - \theta h a_2] - \sigma_v h^{\frac{3}{2}} \sum_1^K b_k z_k\right) \tag{13.21}$$

where a_1 and a_2 are deterministic constants depending on κ, h and K. We see that the linear combination of normal variates

$$y = \sum_1^K b_k z_k$$

is also a normal variate with expected value zero and variance $\sum b_k^2$. If we are computing the bond price by simulation it is the moments of the normal variate y that are of concern rather than those of the individual zs. Hence if we wish to apply the moment matching method in this case we should transform the ys so that the expected value of the sample of ys is zero and the variance of the sample of ys is $\sum b_k^2$. This transformation significantly improves the efficiency of the method over the standard Monte Carlo method. Indeed, we saw that the antithetic variable approach that corresponds to matching the first moment already improves the efficiency considerably.

Some numerical results are provided in Table 13.7. For example, when $K = 4$ and we use $N = 16$ simulations, the statistical error of crude Monte Carlo is 2.969. However, when we match the first two moments as suggested above, we find that the sample error is reduced to 0.027. We see that the sample errors when we match the first two moments are about 110 times smaller than if we just use plain Monte Carlo. This means that to achieve the same accuracy using standard Monte Carlo we would need to increase the number of simulations by a factor of 11,100. These dramatic gains have been achieved with the Vasicek model and it may not be as straightforward to apply the method to non-linear SDEs such as the CIR process.

IMPORTANCE SAMPLING

The basic idea of the importance sampling method is to redistribute the probability in such a way that the draws of a Monte Carlo simulation have a higher chance of ending up in regions of interest. For instance, if we are simulating a knock-in option, only paths that cross the barrier contribute to the value of the option. This particular application is discussed in more detail in Boyle, Broadie, and

TABLE 13.7. Comparison of Standard Monte Carlo and Monte Carlo Using Moment Matching for Simulated Five-Year Bond Price as Both K and N Vary under the Vasicek Model

K	N	Sample Error Basic Monte Carlo	Sample Error Using Moment Matching	Ratio of Sample Errors
4	16	2.969	0.027	110
8	64	1.448	0.012	116
16	256	0.720	0.006	111
32	1,024	0.350	0.003	115

Note: The first column gives K, the number of time steps. The second column gives N, the number of simulation trials. The third gives the sample error under the standard Monte Carlo method. The fourth column gives the sample error under moment matching. The fifth column gives the ratio of these two sample errors. Parameters $r_0 = .06$, $\kappa = 0.4$, $\theta = 0.054$, and $\sigma = 0.04183$.

Glasserman (1997). Through a shift of probability measure, we can adjust the sampling distribution to increase the probability of hitting the barrier, hopefully causing a reduction in variance. Clearly, the shift of probability measure introduces a bias which must be corrected for through the so-called likelihood ratio, to be defined shortly.

To formally define the method of importance sampling, we follow Glasserman et al. (1998) and consider the specific problem of estimating the quantity

$$\theta = E[G(Z)1_D]$$

where G is a function, 1_D is the indicator function[6] of the set D in R^n, and Z is an n-dimensional normal random variable with multivariate normal density g. Assume that f is another density function with the property that when $g > 0$ then $f > 0$. We can transform the expectation in g to an expectation in f as follows

$$E[G(Z)1_D] = \int_D G(z)g(z)dz$$

$$= \int_D G(z)\frac{g(z)}{f(z)}f(z)dz$$

$$= E_f\left[G(z)\frac{g(Z)}{f(Z)}1_D\right]$$

where E_f denotes the expectation with respect to f. The ratio g/f is the likelihood ratio (or Radon-Nikodym derivative) which serves to correct the bias introduced when integrating over f rather than g. If we draw random variables Z from f, then the *importance sampling estimate*

$$G(z)\frac{g(z)}{f(z)}1_D$$

---

[6] The indicator function is useful for option-type securities.

is an unbiased estimate of θ. The variance of the estimator is

$$\int_D \left[G(z) \frac{g(z)}{f(z)} - \theta \right]^2 dz$$

We see that if we could chose

$$f(z) = 1_D \frac{G(z)g(z)}{\theta}$$

then the variance of the estimator would be 0. Unfortunately, as θ is unknown, this choice of density is not available to us. As a general rule, however, the form of the perfect importance sampling density suggests that a good importance sampling scheme should weight points in proportion to the product of their probability and their payoff.

Andersen (1995) shows how one can sometimes use information from a simple model to come up with a good guess for the optimal choice of importance sampling density. In particular, Andersen illustrates how results from the Vasicek model can be used to develop a good measure transformation for simulation of more complicated models, including the CIR model. The approach is shown to yield results that outperform most other variance reduction techniques. By limiting themselves to measure transformations that involve deterministic changes of drift only, Glasserman et al. (1998) are able to develop a more general approach, which we will briefly discuss here.

Suppose that the mean of the n-dimensional normal density g is zero and the covariance matrix is I, the n by n identity matrix. We induce a change of drift of the multivariate normal density as follows. For any μ belonging to R^n, let $f = f_\mu$ be the multivariate normal density with mean μ and covariance matrix I_n. We use this density f to obtain the importance sampling estimate. From the properties of the normal density

$$\theta = E\left[G(Z)1_D \right] = E_f\left[G(Z)e^{-\mu' + \frac{1}{2}\mu'\mu} 1_D \right] \tag{13.22}$$

The distribution of Z under f is the same as the distribution of Z + μ under g, the original density. Hence

$$\theta = E_f\left[G(Z)e^{-\mu'+\frac{1}{2}\mu'\mu}1_D\right] = E\left[G(Z+\mu)e^{-\mu'+\frac{1}{2}\mu'\mu}1_{D(Z+\mu)}\right]$$

The problem remaining is how to select μ. We can write down the expression for the variance of the estimator in terms of μ, and select μ to minimize the variance of the estimator. In this case the optimal μ minimizes

$$E\left[G(Z)^2 e^{-\mu'Z+\frac{1}{2}\mu'\mu}1_D\right]$$

Glasserman et al. show that in the multivariate normal case the optimal μ minimizes the expression

$$\log[G(z)] - \frac{1}{2}z'z \qquad (13.23)$$

This choice of importance sampling effectively eliminates the variance from the linear part of the log payoff. While Glasserman et al. show that (13.23) is optimal in an asymptotic sense, it will normally not provide a zero-variance estimator. Its effectiveness depends on the degree to which it resembles the optimal density choice discussed earlier.

$$1_D \frac{G(z)g(z)}{\theta}$$

In the case of the CIR model, Glasserman et al. show that one can solve for the optimal drift μ, using numerical methods. They apply the method to evaluate bond prices and option prices in the CIR model and find that the method produces dramatic increases in efficiency. In the case of the Vasicek model, the method works perfectly in simulating bond prices since the log of the payoff is linear in the underlying random variables. We start with Equation (13.21) which provides the expression for the bond price under the Vasicek model in terms of the normal random variables.

In this case the optimal solution to Equation (13.23) can readily be obtained from the first-order conditions. The k'th coordinate of the optimal drift is readily found as

$$\mu_k = -\sigma_v h^{\frac{3}{2}} b_k \qquad (13.24)$$

We now compute the importance sampling estimate using this value of μ and expression (13.21). We find that with this choice of μ we eliminate all the stochastic terms and simply end up with the accurate value of the bond price under this discretization as given in Proposition 1.

The method can be applied to more complicated path-dependent options. Glasserman et al. apply this method to the valuation of bonds and caplets under the CIR model. They find efficiency gains of the order of 100 in the case of a one-year bond when they incorporate both importance sampling and stratification. For the case of caplets, the efficiency gains are of the order of 25. This is attributable to the nonlinearity in the cap payoffs.

CONCLUDING REMARKS

This chapter has surveyed Monte Carlo methods for the valuation of fixed-income securities. Our main focus was on one-factor short-rate models and the computation of path integrals for zero-coupon bond pricing. In this framework, two sources of numerical error must be dealt with:

- The systematic bias caused by imperfect discretization of the short-rate SDE; and
- The random Monte Carlo error caused by the stochastic nature of the bond price estimator.

We discussed methods to control both sources of errors. In the first part of the chapter, we analyzed the systematic discretization bias and described methods to reduce it. Numerical examples based on the Vasicek and CIR models were provided. For the Vasicek model, it was shown that many of the common discretization schemes lead to analytically tractable discretization errors. In the second part of the chapter, we focused on methods to reduce the variance of the random Monte Carlo error. The linear form of the bond-price estimator was shown to favor the method of antithetic sampling and, in particular, moment matching methods. We also discussed some recent applications of importance sampling to the valuation of interest rate securities.

ACKNOWLEDGEMENTS

The authors thank Ken Seng Tan, Ken Vetzal, and Baoyon Ding for helpful comments and PPB acknowledges research support from the Social Sciences and Humanities Research Council of Canada and the editorial assistance of Marta Poterski.

REFERENCES

Andersen, L. (1995). "Efficient Techniques for Simulation of Interest Rate Models Involving Non-Linear Stochastic Differential Equations," working paper General Re Financial Products, New York.

Boyle, P.P. (1997). "Options: A Monte Carlo Approach," *Journal of Financial Economics*, 4, 323–338.

Boyle, P.P., M. Broadie, and P. Glasserman. (1997). "Monte Carlo Methods for Security Pricing," *Journal of Economics, Dynamics and Control*, 21, 1267–1321.

Brace, A., D. Gatarek, and M. Musiela. (1997). "The Market Model of Interest Rate Dynamics," *Mathematical Finance*, 7, 127–155.

Carverhill, A. and K. Pang. (1995). "Efficient and Flexible Bond Option Valuation in the Heath, Jarrow, and Morton Framework," *Journal of Fixed Income*, 5, 70–77.

Duffie, D. (1996). *Dynamic Asset Pricing Theory* (2nd ed.), Princeton, NJ: Princeton University Press.

Duffie, D. and P. Glynn. (1995). "Efficient Monte Carlo Simulation of Security Prices," *Annals of Applied Probability*, 5, 897–905.

Glasserman, P., P. Heidelberger, and P. Shahabudding. (1998). "Asymptotically Optimal Importance Sampling and Stratification for

Pricing Path-Dependent Options," working paper, Graduate School of Business, Columbia University, New York.

Glasserman, P. and X. Zhao. (1998). "Arbitrage-Free Discretization of Lognormal Forward LIBOR and Swap Rate Models," working paper, Graduate School of Business, Columbia University, New York.

Heath, D., R. Jarrow, and A. Morton. (1992). "Bond Pricing and the Term Structure of Interest Rates: A New Methodology for Contingent Claims Valuation," *Econometrica, 60,* 77–105.

Ho, T.S.Y. and S-X. Lee. (1986). "Term Structure Movements and Pricing Interest Rate Contingent Claims," *Journal of Finance, 41,* 1011–1029.

Hull, J. and A. White. (1990). "Pricing Interest-Rate Derivative Securities," *Review of Financial Studies, 3,* 573–592.

Jamshidian, F. (1989). "An Exact Bond Option Pricing Formula," *Journal of Finance, 44,* 205–209.

Jamshidian, F. (1991). "Bond and Option Evaluation in the Gaussian Interest Rate Model," *Research in Finance, 9,* 131–170.

Jamshidian, F. (1997). "Libor and Swap Market Models and Measures," *Finance and Stochastics, 1,* 293–330.

Kloeden, P. and E. Platen. (1992). *Numerical Solutions of Stochasitc Differential Equations.* New York: Springer.

Miltersen, K., K. Sandmann, and D. Sonderman. (1997). "Closed-Form Solutions for Term Structure Derivatives with Lognormal Interest Rates," *Journal of Finance, 52,* 409–430.

Press, W.H., B.P. Flannery, S.A. Teukolsky, and W.T. Vetterling. (1988). *Numerical Recipes; The Art of Scientific Computing,* Cambridge: Cambridge University Press.

Ritchken, P. and L. Sankarasubramanian. (1995). "Volatility Structures of Forward Rates and the Dynamics of the Term Structure," *Mathematical Finance, 5,* 55–72.

Tulay, D. and L. Tubaro. (1990). "Expansions of the Global Error for Numerical Schemes for Solving Stochastic Differential Equations," *Stochastic Analysis and Applications, 8(4),* 483–509.

Turnbull, S. (1997). "Monte Carlo Simulatuion of the Jarrow, Morton Interest Rate Model," working paper, School of Business, Queen's University, Kingston, Ontario, Canada.

Vasicek, O.A. (1977). "An Equilibrium Characterization of the Term Structure," *Journal of Financial Economics, 5,* 177–188.

Index